A HISTORY OF
LATER GREEK LITERATURE

A HISTORY OF
LATER GREEK LITERATURE

FROM THE DEATH OF ALEXANDER IN
323 B.C. TO THE DEATH OF JUSTINIAN
IN 565 A.D.

BY

F. A. WRIGHT, M.A.

PROFESSOR OF CLASSICS IN THE UNIVERSITY OF LONDON

NEW YORK
THE MACMILLAN COMPANY
1932

PRINTED IN GREAT BRITAIN BY THE EDINBURGH PRESS, EDINBURGH

To

A. D. KNOX

' I would as soon read Dio as Xenophon, Aristides
as Demosthenes, Ælian as Aristotle.'

CONTENTS

vii

CONTENTS

CONTENTS

PART III—BYZANTIUM, A.D. 313–565

PREFACE

The insistence of classical scholars in concentrating their attention on two remote periods of Greek and Latin literature has led the ignorant to call both languages ' dead.' The word is not true of either, and even if Latin now is sleeping, it is still the language of the Church. As for Greek, it has an unbroken history of some thirty centuries, which may be divided into three periods. The first of these extends from Homer to Aristotle, the third from the sixth century A.D., until our own days. Of the second period, which includes the nine centuries from the death of Alexander in 323 B.C., to the death of Justinian in A.D. 565, when the Greeks were acting as teachers to the civilized world, this book attempts to give an account. I believe that there is no continuous history of this kind in English, but my task has been lightened by the recent labours of many scholars. I desire to express my special obligations to the *New Chapters in Greek Literature* by J. A. Powell and E. A. Barber, to the translation of Lucian by H. W. and F. G. Fowler, to Sir R. W. Livingstone's *Mission of Greece*, and above all to the invaluable Loeb Library, which has rendered so many ancient authors easily accessible for the first time to the English public. To its editors and to the Syndics of the Clarendon Press I tender here my thanks.

xi

History of Later Greek Literature

INTRODUCTION

THE Greeks of the great age have left us a body
of literature which is of unique value and stands
in a class by itself as a model of excellence for all future
ages. In tragedy and comedy, in epic, lyric, and elegiac,
in history, philosophy, and rhetoric, they not only
created the forms of expression which were proved by
later experience to be most suitable, but they also in
the use of those forms reached a standard of individual
perfection which has never been surpassed. Beauty,
simplicity, and truth, the cardinal qualities of their
sculpture and architecture, are also the cardinal
qualities of their writing; and with them literature
is never divorced from life. For a century and a half
at Athens the human mind, helped by favourable
circumstances, was working at full power, and when
we consider the years that saw the birth of Pindar,
Æschylus, Herodotus, Sophocles, Euripides, Aristophanes, Thucydides, Plato, and Demosthenes, all other
periods are apt to seem flat and colourless.

But though we do well to recognize the unique
quality of classical Greek literature, it is a mistake to
imagine that the Hellenic genius suffered a sudden and
complete eclipse when the free city states were overthrown by Philip of Macedon on the field of Chæronea
338 B.C. The first flush of creative vigour vanished,
but enough of the original inspiration survived in the
centuries that followed to produce one of the remaining
five world-literatures which no one can with impunity

neglect. Classical Latin, Medieval Latin, French, and English are the only serious rivals to Later Greek, and it may be doubted whether any one of these four can justly challenge its claim to the first place. To take but half a dozen names from its long list : Theocritus is still the most universally attractive of all poets ; Euclid wrote the one text-book which could hold its own for over twenty centuries ; Polybius is a perfect example of what we mean by a scientific historian ; Plutarch is unmatched in any language ; Lucian in his blend of wit and sagacity is only equalled by Voltaire ; and Epictetus has had more influence on human conduct than any lay teacher save Thomas à Kempis. Lastly, there appear in this volume the three men of ancient times whose inmost thoughts we know best : St Paul, Marcus Aurelius, and the Emperor Julian.

It is sometimes said that the later Greeks were altogether lacking in originality and that they merely followed along the paths which their great ancestors had made. It would be more correct to say that the men of the fifth and fourth centuries B.C. were the pioneers who constructed the main roads through a new country, and that the later Greeks were the settlers who completed their work by thoroughly surveying the whole land. In any case there is scarcely one of the subsidiary forms of literature which we do not owe to them. The sermon, in the hands both of pagan and christian teachers, is their creation. So is the letter, real or fictitious, the encyclopædia, the essay, and all the various kinds of art and literary criticism. So also is biography, whether it be used, as by Plutarch, to tell the lives of historical characters, or, as by Philostratus, to draw a picture of a person who is largely imaginary. And so, finally, is the form which in our times tends to overshadow all others, the novel of adventure and the novel of love.

INTRODUCTION

In classical Greek the natural love of man and woman occupies the very smallest place in literature : in later Greek, from Menander to Musæus, it is constantly emerging as a main theme both for verse and prose. The plays of Menander, it is true, usually deal with the more sordid aspects of love and have little of tenderness in them ; but in Alexandria, where women played a much more prominent part than they had done at Athens, romance at last entered into its own. The elegiac couplet, after the time of Philetas and Callimachus, became both for Greeks and Romans the recognized medium of love poetry ; and the fifth book of the Palatine Anthology, which consists entirely of pieces in this style is one of the most charming collections of amatory verse which we possess. The love theme, moreover, was not confined in Alexandria to the epigram. Theocritus employs it frequently in his Idylls, and Apollonius in the Argonautica uses the wider canvas of the epic to paint a masterly picture of the dawn of passion in a young girl's heart. Then comes an interval, while prose was gradually being adapted for imaginative literature, and it is among the Greeks of the Empire that the prose romance, as we know it, appears at length in the pages of Longus and Heliodorus.

The centuries when the literature with which this volume is concerned was being written fall into three periods of about equal length. The first period, the Hellenistic, extends from the death of Alexander in 323 B.C. to the battle of Actium in 31 B.C., and may itself be subdivided into three sections. In the earliest of these, from the death of Alexander to the battle of Ipsus in 302, years when Alexander's successors were filling the world with the din of battle, Athens, under the benevolent rule of Demetrius of Phalerum, enjoyed comparative peace and prosperity, and with Theophrastus, Menander, and Epicurus all living within her walls still remained the chief centre of literary activity. The second section coincides roughly with the third century B.C., when Greek civilization spread to all the cities of the eastern Mediterranean. Authors now wrote not for one small community but for the whole world, and on the basis of Attic a common speech was developed which took the place of the varying dialects of the past. Alexandria became the world centre and there under the early Ptolemies an immense amount of first-class creative work was done : we know of over a thousand authors, but owing to a curious chain of reasons very few of them ever reached the copying rooms of Byzantium. Compared with this section the third is somewhat barren of genius ; for the Hellenic world in the second and first centuries before Christ was caught between the Oriental reaction and the power of Rome. We have, it is true, the great name of Polybius, and some remnants of late Alexandrian poetry : otherwise the most attractive work is done by the group of Syrian poets which includes Antipater of Sidon, Philodemus, and Meleager of Gadara.

The second period, of something over three centuries, opens a new era ; Rome abandons the rôle of oppressor for that of protector ; Hellenistic civilization ends and Græco-Roman civilization begins. In the first century, from Augustus to Domitian, when the world enjoyed such advantages as spring from almost universal peace, the greatest writings, if we except the New Testament, are in Latin, and among the Greeks we only find such minor authors as Diodorus, Dionysius of Halicarnassus, and Josephus. Strabo the geographer is perhaps the most useful of them, and poetry is scantily represented by a few epigrammatists like Crinagoras and Antipater of Thessalonica. Early in the second century, however, the Greek spirit revived once more, and turning to practical philosophy produced a series of works which are still widely read and are of inestimable value. Epictetus, Plutarch, and Dion come first, and it is a significant fact that when the emperor Marcus Aurelius soon after their time wrote his *Meditations*, he chose Greek for his medium in preference to Latin. By his day indeed Greek had regained the primacy in letters, and the second century A.D. is among the most brilliant periods in her literature. Historians like Arrian and Appian, scientists like Galen and Ptolemy, travellers like Pausanias, and men of letters like Lucian and Alciphron, form in themselves a sufficient galaxy of genius : but in addition this was the age of the great sophists, from Polemon onwards, who made rhetoric for a while the most popular of all the arts and enjoyed in their own lifetime such world-wide fame as is now only won by a cinema star.

The pursuit of art for art's sake which the sophists inculcated lingered on till the end of our second period, and when the third period begins in the opening years of the fourth century, Græco-Roman civilization was showing plain signs of exhaustion. Diocletian tried to stem the tide by reverting to an Oriental despotism ; but his attempt failed, and soon afterwards Constantine took the two steps that were radically to change the course of European history. In 313 he recognized Christianity as a state religion, and a few years later he moved the seat of government eastwards to Byzantium. These changes had a profound affect on literature, and in this period a triple division may again be made. In the first section come the Christian writers, beginning with Eusebius and Athanasius, and passing from Basil, Gregory of Nazianzus and John Chrysostom to Nonnus and Synesius, both of whom began life as pagans and ended in the Christian fold. The second section contains the last efforts of dying

5

INTRODUCTION

paganism, the discourses of Themistius, Libanius, and Julian, the poetry of Quintus Smyrnæus and Palladas, and the final products of Neo-Platonism in Proclus and his school. Finally we come to the reign of Justinian and to the brilliant circle of writers who gathered at his court ; and with the death of Justinian in A.D. 565 this record ends.

PART I

ALEXANDRIA
(323–31 B.C.)

CHAPTER I

THE OLD AGE AND THE NEW

(323–302 B.C.)

THE death of Alexander the Great in 323 B.C. forms a fit beginning for this narrative. Not only was it an event of world-wide importance, but it has also a significance in the history of literature, for within eighteen months from the time when the great conqueror passed away at Babylon, Demosthenes and Aristotle, the last survivors of the classical age, followed him to the tomb. In 323 Theophrastus succeeded Aristotle as head of the Peripatetic school, in 321 Menander produced his first play, *Temper*, and with Theophrastus and Menander the later literature of Greece begins. They lived, it is true, in the transition period ; but they themselves still clung to the parochialism of the past, and thus form a link between the old age and the new.

But before we consider these men's work it may be well to describe briefly the conditions of social life in their day. Athens had seen her first dream of empire vanish at Ægospotami in 404, and realized then that the other Greek cities would never accept the place which Pericles had assigned them of being willing instruments subservient to a higher culture. Her second dream of a confederation of free Greek states united against a foreign power had been shattered by the battle of Chæronea in 338, which destroyed the life work of Isocrates and Demosthenes alike. Then came the ten stirring years of Alexander's reign,

9

followed by his sudden death in 323, an event so unexpected that no precautions had been taken against it. When the news reached Athens the orator Demades cried—'Impossible : if it were true, the whole world would be stinking of his carcase': but the impossible had happened, and the Greeks under Leosthenes made one more desperate effort to secure their independence. Leosthenes, however, was killed, and at the public funeral given to him in the Ceramicus Hypereides delivered an oration, the *Epitaphios*, which is the last great effort of Athenian eloquence :

'First, as is just, I shall speak about our general. Leosthenes seeing all Hellas cowering in abasement and brought to ruin by those who received bribes from Philip and Alexander against their fatherland, seeing too that our city needed a man and Hellas needed a city to stand forth as champion, devoted himself to our city and our city to the Hellenes in the cause of freedom. . . .

'As for those citizens who were slain in this war, who would not justly praise them? They gave their lives to set Hellas free, and considered that the plainest proof of their desire to give her freedom was to die on her behalf. No men ever fought in a nobler cause, against heavier odds, or with fewer resources. They judged valour to be strength, and manliness, not numbers, to be greatness. Are they not then to be thought fortunate because of this exhibition of courage rather than unfortunate because of their departure from life? Men of mortal body they have gained immortal fame, and by their individual bravery have won common freedom for all. Those who lie here, taking upon themselves the burdens of others, have by the peril of one day removed for all time the fears of their fellow citizens, and have given their own lives that the rest might live well.'

Words, however, were of little avail against Antipater, and the result of the battle of Crannon in 322 left all Greece at the mercy of Macedonia. Permanent garrisons were established at Demetrias, Chalcis, and Corinth, and the last vestiges of freedom disappeared.

Still, the loss of liberty did not mean for Athens the

loss of prosperity. In 318 Demetrius of Phalerum was appointed governor under the Macedonians, and for the next ten years the city trod a primrose path. Demetrius himself was one of the most typical figures of his time. He was a philosopher of some distinction, and one of the first to spread the belief that Fortune was the divinity who ruled the world. He was an eloquent orator and is credited with the invention of a new type of speech recommending a state to the protection of some powerful patron. He was an encyclopædic scholar interested alike in art and literature and science ; and he was also so adroit a ruler that three hundred and sixty statues of him were set up in Athens in one year. But in character he was a medley of contradictions.

Though he was an earnest student of philosophy, he also put rouge upon his cheeks and kept half a dozen mistresses ; though he was a careful administrator, he also lavished the resources of the state on cooks, minions, and parasites. It is not surprising then that under his rule Athens became the arbiter of elegance for the whole world : no courtesan was truly famous unless she had walked her streets, no philosopher could command a really high fee unless he had studied in her schools. But amid this material well-being the ancient vigour of her people disappeared, and acquiescence in a comfortable tyranny quickly brought with it an indifference to most of the higher motives of conduct. Religion, family life, chastity, and economy went out of fashion ; men's one desire in life was to escape from boredom ; and with the loss of their political interests this proved to the Athenians a very difficult task. Literature was the only noble thing left them, and the writings of Theophrastus and Menander, pictures though they be of a decadent society, are the most valuable products of their time.

11

Theophrastus of Eresus (372-287)

Theophrastus, whose real name was Tyrtamus, was born in Lesbos, the son of a fuller, and owing probably to political disturbances in the island migrated to Athens about 350. He was at first a pupil of Plato, but before Plato's death in 347 he left him for Aristotle, with whom he lived for a time at Stageira and in whose company he returned to Athens in 335. When Aristotle retired to Chalcis in 323 Theophrastus succeeded him as head of the Peripatetic School, and soon afterwards received as bequests from his old master the autographs of all his books and also the garden in the Lyceum. There he taught, as many as two thousand pupils attending his lectures, and there he peacefully pursued his botanical studies until 307. In that year his patron Demetrius of Phalerum was expelled from Athens by that romantic figure Demetrius, 'Taker of Cities,' and philosophers for a time fell into popular disrepute. A certain Sophocles seized the opportunity to propose that their schools should be suppressed, and when the decree was passed Theophrastus went into exile. In the next year, however, there was a reversion of feeling, and it was discovered that the decree contravened a law of Solon which recognized schools of philosophy as religious associations devoted to the service of the Muses. Accordingly, Sophocles in his turn was prosecuted and had to stand his trial. The orator Demochares, nephew of Demosthenes, hired in his defence, argued that philosophers were notoriously bad citizens : 'Aristotle betrayed his native town : Plato's pupils were all rascals, men of ill-gotten wealth and disreputable character. Look at Chæron of Pellene, who drove out all the honest citizens, gave their property to slaves, and established a community of wives compelling women to give their favours promiscuously. By its fruits the Academy stands condemned ; and the state will benefit if we drive out Plato's brood and at the same time destroy the Peripatetic nest of traitors.' In spite of this choice harangue, however, the jury, who perhaps now realized that the schools were one of their city's chief attractions, gave a verdict against Sophocles. The decree was annulled, and the philosophers returned in triumph.

For the rest of his life Theophrastus lived in Athens, and when he died in 287 his funeral was attended by the whole city. His will, a fairly long document, has been preserved, one provision running as follows : ' My garden and the walk and the houses adjoining I bequeath to such of my friends hereinafter named as may wish to study literature and philosophy there in common.' The names of these foundation fellows are then given and so the first college, in our sense of the word, was established.

Diogenes Laertius gives us the titles of over four hundred volumes attributed to Theophrastus. Many of these must have been quite short pamphlets, but the list shows that Theophrastus dealt not only with natural science but also with rhetoric, politics, psychology, ethics, love, indeed with most of the topics that are of interest to men. The vast majority, however, are now lost ; and with one important exception all of his works which we now possess are of a scientific nature. We have, for example, a treatise on weather signs, which was one of the authorities used by Aratus in his poem. Another is on odours, a subject of particular interest to Demetrius, who was in the habit of dyeing his hair and lavishly scenting his person. Fragments also survive from treatises on sense perception, stones, winds, dizziness, and sweat ; but these are very incomplete and his reputation as a scientist depends now on his two great botanical works the

13

Causes of Plants in six books and the *Enquiry into Plants* in nine. This is how the *Enquiry* begins :

> 'In dealing with the distinctive features of plants and their nature generally, one need only consider their parts, their qualities, their births, and their lives ; for plants, unlike animals, have neither characters nor activities. Their differences in birth, quality, and life are comparatively simple and easy to observe ; those shown in their parts offer more variety. Indeed no satisfactory definition has been given as to what are parts and what are not ; the point still remains doubtful.'

Theophrastus, who was a great believer in system and said that he would as soon trust a horse without a bridle as a book without classification, then proceeds to distinguish the chief parts as root, stem, branch, twig, leaf, flower, and fruit, and next makes a classification of all plants under the headings of tree, bush, shrub, and herb. Trees, their growth and propagation and their wild and cultivated varieties, occupy the first three books. The fourth contains a mass of valuable information, gathered possibly by Theophrastus' pupils, concerning trees and plants peculiar to different parts of the world ; the fifth deals with timber and the various uses to which it can be put. Then come three books on shrubs, herbs, and cereals, and in the ninth book the medicinal qualities of plants are discussed. Of dittany, for example, Theophrastus tells us :

> 'Dittany, which is peculiar to Crete, is a plant of marvellous virtue, and is useful in many ways but especially so for women in childbirth. Its leaf is like pennyroyal and it has some resemblance to it also in taste but the twigs are more slender. They use the leaves not the twigs nor the fruit. It is useful for many purposes, but especially, as was said, for difficult labour in women. People say that either it makes labour easy or at least confessedly stops the pains. It is given as a draught in water. It is a scarce plant : the district which produces it is small and the goats bite it down because they like its taste. The story of the arrows is also said to be true— that if goats eat it when they have been shot it expels the arrow.'

This extract is a fair specimen of the style in which the *Enquiry* is written, and it will be seen that Theophrastus takes little account of literary elegance : his sentences are short and abrupt, and he does not avoid repetition ; in fact we get the impression here, as so often with Aristotle, that we are reading the notes of a lecture rather than a finished work.

But Theophrastus besides being a philosopher and a great scientific investigator was also a man of the world and, as his portrait bust in the Villa Albani shows, a humorist. Many of his shrewd sayings have reached us : ' Time is the most valuable thing a man can spend ' ; ' Marriage is excellent, if you are perfect yourself and can find a perfect woman ' ; ' We men are just beginning to live when we die ' ; ' For the ignorant silence is wise, for the educated folly.' We may imagine that with such remarks as these he enlivened the public lectures of which Hermippus [1] gives us an account :

> ' At the exact hour Theophrastus used to make his appearance in the Garden, spruce and ornate, and when he had taken his seat would deliver his lecture, indulging, as he went along in every kind of movement and gesture. For example, on one occasion he portrayed an epicure, by putting out his tongue and licking his lips.'

We need not then be surprised that the book by which Theophrastus is best known, the *Ethical Characters*, is a masterpiece of vivid portraiture and humorous observation. The *Characters* is a small book but it is full of flavour. Meleager said of the poems of Sappho that though they were few each one was a rose : we might as truly say of the *Characters* that though they are few each one is an onion. Whether Theophrastus derived the idea from Aristotle's description of the Magnanimous Man in the Ethics is

---

[1] Quoted in Athenæus, I. 21.

immaterial. In his hands the *Characters* becomes a new literary form, a minor but distinct branch of prose as the sonnet is in poetry ; and none of his many modern followers—Hall, Overbury, Earle, Butler, La Bruyère, Vauvenargues—have approached him either in clearness of vision or in precision of statement.

The book consists of thirty characters, all of them short and none much exceeding a page. They are written on one model : the particular foible is defined— ' Officiousness is a presumptuous benevolence in word and deed '—and then comes a list of the officious man's typical mistakes : he offers to show a short cut and loses his way ; he separates strangers who are fighting ; he comes and tells his father that his mother has already gone to bed, etc. The subtlety of the book is shown especially in the differentiation of types. The garrulous man, for example, to whom one topic immediately suggests another, is distinguished from the loquacious man who is a mere chatterer, so that his very children say ' Papa, start talking, and then we shall fall asleep.' In the same way meanness, penuriousness and avarice are separated ; unpleasantness, offensiveness and boorishness ; recklessness, buffoonery, and shamelessness. There is always, of course, a difficulty in finding exact equivalents in English for the Greek, and what Theophrastus meant by shamelessness can be best seen by quotation :

> ' Shamelessness may be defined as disregard for one's reputation, due to a desire for base gain.
> ' The shameless man is the sort of person who starts the day by going to someone whom he is already keeping out of money and borrowing some more from him. Then, after sacrificing to the gods, he will put the meat into the salt tub and go out to dine with a friend. There he will call up his page-boy and give him bread and meat from the table, saying in the hearing of all, " Enjoy yourself with that, my honourable friend." When he goes marketing he will remind the butcher of any services he may have rendered him, and,

standing by the scales, will throw in, for preference, a piece of meat, or if not that, a bone for the soup. If he gets it, he is happy : if he does not, he snatches up a piece of tripe from the counter and goes off with a laugh. Moreover, he will buy seats at the theatre for foreign guests, and then go himself without paying his contribution ; and on the next day bring his children as well and their attendant. When anyone gets a thing cheap, he will ask to have a share. He will go to another man's house and borrow barley or bran, and then will force the lenders to deliver it. He is apt, too, to go up to the cauldrons in the bath-house, and, dipping in the bucket, to souse the water over himself, in spite of the bath-man's cries ; then he will say, " I have had my bath," and, as he goes away, " No thanks to you." '

The *Characters* abounds in pictures of Athenian life. We see the boaster standing on the quay at Piræus and talking of his campaigns with Alexander. We see the late-learner practising the steps of a dance when women are near and whistling his own accompaniment. We see the reckless man gathering a crowd round him and abusing interrupters in a loud cracked voice. We see the gross man telling everyone that he means to get drunk and spitting over the table at the butler. Each sketch is a miniature play, but perhaps no character approaches more closely to the spirit of comedy than that of the flatterer.

' One may hold flattery to be a sort of association which, though degrading, is profitable to him who practises it.

' The flatterer is the sort of person who as he walks by your side will say : " Do you realize how people turn their eyes towards you ? This happens to no one in Athens except you. They were singing your praises yesterday in the Arcade. There were more than thirty of us sitting there, when the question was started : Who is our most worthy citizen ? Everyone began with you, Sir, and ended, Sir, by coming back to your name." While he is talking like this, he will pick a morsel of fluff from his companion's cloak ; and if the wind has blown a piece of chaff on to the other's hair, he will remove it, adding with a smile : " Do you see ? Just because I have not met you for two days, your beard is full of white hairs ; although no one has darker hair for his age than you." While his patron is speaking he will bid the company be silent, and will praise him in his hearing, and when he pauses, act as fugleman with a " Bravo ! " If he makes a frigid joke, he will burst out laughing, and stuff his cloak into his mouth, as though otherwise unable to restrain his mirth. To people whom he meets he will call out : " Halt, until the great man has passed by." He will buy apples and pears for the children and bring them to the house and give them in the father's presence, saying, with a kiss, " Chicks of a noble sire." When he goes with his patron to the shoe-market to buy a pair of slippers, he will declare that the foot is more graceful than the shoe ; and if he is visiting a friend he will hurry ahead and say, " He is coming to see you," and then, turning back, " I have announced your approach." He is quite capable of running full tilt to the women's market and doing commissions there. At a dinner-party he is the first to praise the wine, and from his place next to the host will say, " What delicious fare ! " and, taking something from the table, " Really, how excellent this is ! " He will then ask the host if he is not cold, and whether he would not like a wrap, and while he is speaking will put one carefully round him. Moreover, he will lean close to his ear and whisper, and while he is talking to other people will keep his eyes fixed on him. At the theatre he will take the cushions from the slave and put them in place with his own hands. He will say that his patron's house is the perfection of architecture, that his farm is a model of cultivation, and that his portrait is an exact likeness.'

Dicæarchus (fl. 310 B.C.)

Theophrastus is the most distinguished of Aristotle's pupils, but there are three other members of his school, Eudemus, Dicæarchus, and Aristoxenus, who must be mentioned here. Eudemus is at least partly responsible for the *Eudemian Ethics* and also wrote a most valuable *History of Geometry* and a *History of Astronomy*, both of which unhappily are lost. Dicæarchus for his part is the author of an even more interesting book, the *Life of Greece*, which seems to have been a general account of Greek civilization : but this again, although it is frequently cited by other authors, has now perished. A mangled version, however, generally known as the

18

Pseudo-Dicæarchus, a sort of popular guide-book, was published towards the end of the second century B.C., and of this considerable fragments remain, some of which may represent the original work. In any case the descriptions of Athens, Oropus, Tanagra, and especially Thebes, are the work of a very lively pen :

> ' In spite of its antiquity the streets of Thebes are new, because, as the histories tell us, the city has been thrice razed to the ground on account of the morose and overbearing character of the inhabitants. They are rash and insolent, ready to come to blows with any man, be he citizen or stranger : as for justice they set their faces against it. Business disputes are settled not by reason but by fisticuffs, and murders are perpetrated on the most trifling pretexts. . . Such are the men as a whole, though some respectable persons are to be found among them. The women are the tallest, prettiest, and most graceful in all Greece. Their faces are so muffled up that only the eyes are seen. All of them dress in white and wear low purple shoes laced so as to show the bare feet. Their yellow hair is tied up in a knot at the top of the head. In society their manners are Sicyonian rather than Boeotian. They have pleasing voices, while the voices of the men are harsh and deep.'

Aristoxenus of Tarentum (fl. 310 B.C.)

Dicæarchus must remain a shadowy character, but of Aristoxenus, author of the *Harmonics*, it is possible to give a fuller account. Aristoxenus *the* Musician was born at Tarentum some time in the fourth century B.C. His youth was spent in Mantinea, and after studying for a time under the Pythagorean, Xenophilus of Chalcis, he became a pupil of Aristotle. He is described as being very austere and dignified in behaviour, with a pronounced antipathy to laughter. But he was a disagreeable man, a backbiter and slanderer. When Theophrastus was chosen to succeed Aristotle as head of the Peripatetic school, a position which Aristoxenus had expected for himself, the musician took his revenge by propagating unseemly stories—for he was also a

19

writer of biographies and general essayist—concerning his own teacher Aristotle, Aristotle's teacher Plato, Plato's teacher Socrates, and even Socrates' wife. His personal character, however, does not affect the merits of his scientific work, and the three books of his Harmonics—which are excellently translated by Dr. Macran—are by far the best guide to Greek musical theory. Suidas assigns to Aristoxenus the authorship of 453 works but of these none now remain except *The Harmonics*, portions of a treatise on rhythm, and some fragments recently found in Egypt.

The Harmonics, a book of about seventy pages, begins in the true Aristotelian manner with a definition of the subject.

> ' The branch of study which bears the name Harmonic is to be regarded as one of the several divisions, or special sciences, embraced by the general science that concerns itself with melody. Among these special sciences Harmonic occupies a primary and fundamental position. Its subject matter consists of the fundamental principles— all that relates to the theory of scales and keys. . . . In advancing to the profounder speculations which confront us, when scales and keys are enlisted in the service of poetry, we pass from the study under consideration to the all-embracing science of Music.'

The first step, he argues, to a scientific investigation of music is to adjust our different notions of change of voice, *i.e.* change in position of voice. This will lead us on to musical intervals, to melody and to scales. Then will come notes, and finally, as every scale is located in a certain ' region of the voice,' we must treat of these regions in general and detail. A discussion of voice precedes an account of the chromatic scale, and Book I ends with an investigation of continuous melody. The Second Book starts with a personal experience. Plato's pupils, says Aristoxenus, used to come to his lectures on ' The Good,' expecting to get some practical advice on Riches, Health, or Strength. When they found that his real subject was 'The Good' as a predicate to 'The Finite,' or perhaps some sort of Geometry or Astronomy, they were proportionately disgusted. It is therefore necessary to realize what Harmonic is : it is not a sublime science and it has no moral value ; but on the other hand it is a necessary part of a musician's equipment, and appeals in the last resort to the two faculties of hearing and intellect. A recapitulation of the seven divisions of the science follows. The method pursued is admirable, and many a shrewd blow is dealt both to the Pythagorean theorists and the professional musician. Of the first Aristoxenus says : 'To make the amateur a judge in science is the mark of ignorance, profound and invincible'; of the second, 'No instrument will supply a foundation for the principles of harmony : harmony is permanent and immutable, and it is sheer folly to find it in the finger-holes of the aulos or the strings of the cithara.' The third book is shorter and less interesting. It consists of twenty-six musical problems and axioms, stated in the manner of Euclid : e.g. 'It is required to prove that from the highest note of a " Pycnum " there is but one progression in either direction'; and so the 'Harmonics' ends. This brief summary gives a very inadequate idea of the enormous importance of Aristoxenus in musical history. His method—a combination of scientific experiment and common sense—revolutionized the treatment of theory; and his method, as so often happens with the Greeks, is more important than the actual facts he gives us.

Menander (342–291 B.C.)

It is possible that the *Characters* of Theophrastus was originally composed to be read at the monthly dinners of the Peripatetic society ; and in that case Menander, who was a pupil of Theophrastus, may well have been among the audience. In any case there was a close connection between the two men, and to Menander we may now turn. Menander, born in Athens 342 B.C., was the son of a wealthy citizen, Diopeithes, his uncle being Alexis, one of the best-known writers of the Middle Comedy. Of his life we know little, but he was the friend of Theophrastus and Epicurus, and a popular member of the circle who gathered round Demetrius of Phalerum. The Latin poet Phædrus describes his appearance at one of the governor's banquets :

'unguento delibutus, vestitu adfluens
veniebat gressu delicato et languido'

'he came perfumed in flowing robe
with languid step and slow.'

After the expulsion of Demetrius he was attacked in the law courts by professional accusers ; but the charges against him were not pressed and he lived peacefully in Athens until his death, which is said to have been due to a fit of cramp while swimming in the Piræus. Suidas tells us that he squinted, but if the portrait busts at Copenhagen and Boston are authentic he was a man of remarkable beauty. Like Theophrastus he never married but lived in free union with the courtesan Glycera, remaining faithful to her and to Athens in spite of the pressing invitations made to him by Ptolemy Soter to take up his home in Alexandria. The imaginary letters assigned to him and Glycera by Alciphron, who wrote in the second century A.D., seem to be based on real knowledge, and in default of more exact information one passage from them may be quoted :

'By the Eleusinian goddesses, Glycera, I want no further glory and I never mean to leave you. What pleasure could I have without you ? What greater glory than your affection ? Your loving care

22

and your loving ways will make old age seem youth to me. . . . I want to be crowned always with Athenian ivy, to sing my song to Dionysus every year by my own hearth, to take part in the mystic rites, and to bring out a new play each annual performance. I want to be happy, to laugh, and to fear, and to enter for the competition, and to win.'

From the end of the sixth century of our era down to the middle of the nineteenth all that western Europe possessed of Menander was a number of short quotations by later writers and a collection of single line ' sentiments,' two of them world-famous—' Evil communications corrupt good manners,' and ' Those whom the gods love die young.' As for the dramatic quality of his plays, that had to be inferred from the Latin adaptations of Plautus, who based his *Bacchides*, *Pœnulus*, and *Stichus* on three of Menander's comedies, and a little more definitely from Terence, who took the ' *Heauton timorumenos* ' from Menander's play of the same name and ' contaminated ' Menander's *Andria* and *Perinthia* to make his *Andria* and also Menander's *Kolax* and *Eunouchos* to make his *Eunuchus*. In 1844, however, Tischendorf found in a monastery on Mount Sinai three papyrus fragments containing 52 lines from *Phasma*, ' The ghost,' and 41 lines from *Epitrepontes*, ' The arbitrants,' which were edited by Jernicke in 1891. Then Nicole in 1897 published from a papyrus at Geneva 87 lines of *Georgos* ' The farmer,' and Grenfell and Hunt in 1903 51 lines of *Perikeiromene*, ' The girl with clipped hair.' Finally, G. Lefebvre in 1905 had the greatest good fortune of all and unearthed near Cairo in the little village which represents the ancient Aphroditopolis a papyrus containing 83 lines of the *Hero*, 341 lines of the *Girl from Samos*, 324 lines of the *Girl with clipped hair*, and 659 lines of the *Arbitrants*. Of these six plays therefore it is possible now to form some idea, although it must be remembered that the *Arbitrants* is the only one of which we possess even half.

The plot of the *Georgos* is as follows. Cleainetus, an old farmer, injures himself with a mattock, is tended by his young workman Gorgias, and in gratitude determines to marry Gorgias' sister. But the girl is probably his own unacknowledged daughter and moreover already has had an affair with the son of a rich neighbour. How the play developed we do not know, but it possibly ended with a recognition scene and a triple marriage. Of the *Ghost* Donatus on Terence's *Eunuchus* gives a summary. A young man has a stepmother who before marriage has had a daughter by a neighbour. The girl is brought up secretly next door, and the wall between the two houses is pierced, the opening being disguised by an altar so that mother and daughter can pay each other visits. The young man sees the girl and at first thinks she is a ghost ; but later he recognizes his mistake, falls in love with the maiden, and all ends happily with their marriage. One of the characters is the household god who speaks the prologue.

A household god, the ' Hero,' is also a character in the play that bears his name ; and of this we have both a metrical argument and a list of characters. Eighteen years before the action begins Myrrhina, seduced by Laches, had given birth to twins, a boy and a girl, who were exposed by her nurse. Subsequently she married Laches, and the children, whose parentage was unknown, came as servants to her house. The girl Plangon has an affair with a rich youth, and Davus, another of the house slaves, who is in love with her and eager to save her from disgrace pretends that he is responsible for her condition. His generous falsehood, however, is discovered by Myrrhina, and the girl eventually marries her seducer.

Of the *Girl from Samos* we have over three hundred

lines, and as the parts preserved form almost an unbroken whole we get for the first time a fairly close idea of Menander's method in continuous scenes, and also in the two persons of Chrysis and Demeas an example of his skill in character drawing. Demeas, a wealthy bachelor, is living with Chrysis, the girl from Samos, as his mistress, and during his prolonged absence abroad Chrysis gives birth to a child by him which dies. Meanwhile his adopted son Moschion has seduced Plangon, the daughter of his neighbour Niceratus, and Chrysis takes the resulting infant under her care. Demeas on his return thinks that the baby is the fruit of an amour between Moschion and Chrysis, turns the latter out of his house, and arranges a marriage between his son and Plangon. The ensuing scene, which we possess entire, is wildly comical and gives a better idea of Menander's humour than the fragments ever suggested. Demeas has found out the truth about the child, and Niceratus has guessed that his daughter is its mother. Anxious to discover the facts he rushes into the house ; but Chrysis, who has persuaded Plangon to deny everything, seizes the baby and makes her escape. Niceratus in hot pursuit is stopped by Demeas, who assures him that the marriage will take place, and suggests that they consider together seriously the question of the child's paternity. He reminds his friend how Zeus got through the roof of a house to visit Danae, and as Niceratus admits that his roof is very leaky, they soon agree that Zeus must be the father. With that the scene ends, and although in the last act Moschion is still indignant with his father because of his unjust suspicions it would seem that the play ended happily with two marriages.

The fifth piece, *The girl with the clipped hair*, was one of Menander's most famous plays, so that eight centuries later the Byzantine poet Agathias can assume it as being known to all his readers. Here also there is a divine personage, Agnoia 'Misapprehension,' who speaks a belated prologue at the beginning of Act II. The plot runs thus. Some twenty years before the play begins Patæcus had exposed his two children. An old woman found them who handed over the boy, Moschion, to a rich woman, Myrrhina, and on her death-bed, after telling the girl Glycera of Moschion's position, consigned her to the protection of a bluff soldier named Polemon. One day the brother and sister meet and Moschion in youthful folly kisses the pretty girl. Glycera, who knows that he is her brother, returns the kiss; and at that moment Polemon appears on the scene. In a fit of jealous fury he cuts off Glycera's hair and she in indignation takes refuge with Myrrhina. Glycera is one of the most attractive of Menander's heroines, and the rest of the play is concerned with the steps whereby her righteous anger is appeased, until at the end, recognized by Pataecus as his daughter, she is again united to the repentant Polemon.

Lastly we have the *Arbitrants*, a play which, read in Wilamowitz's edition, gives us Menander in something like the shape in which the Athenians knew him. Of Act I we have only fragments, for the Cairo papyrus begins with the incident in the second act from which the play takes its name. Two slaves come in quarrelling over some trinkets found with an exposed baby—a scene borrowed and enlivened by Plautus on the Rudens—and submit their difference to an old gentleman, Smicrines. His son-in-law's slave, Onesimus, notices that one of these trinkets is a ring that formerly belonged to his master, Charisius, and takes it to the harp-girl, Habrotonon, with whom Charisius is wasting his substance, having discovered to his horror that his young wife, Pamphila, had given birth to a child in his absence five months after their marriage. Habrotonon at once suspects the truth, namely, that Charisius himself was the man who violated Pamphila at a nocturnal festival where the harp-girl was present and that he is the father of the child. She therefore determines to help the unhappy wife, and getting possession of the baby, confronts her in what is Menander's most effective scene :

'PAMPHILA (*coming from her house*). My eyes are sore with weeping.

HABROTONON (*standing unnoticed with the baby*). How he cries and cries. He has been strangely ailing for hours.

PAM. Ah me ! Will no god have pity.

HAB. (*to the baby*). You sweet little thing ! You shall soon see your mother. Here she is just right.

PAM. Well, I must go.

HAB. (*stepping forward*). Wait one moment, madam.

PAM. Were you speaking to me ?

HAB. Yes. Look at me and see if you recognize me—(*to herself*) She is the girl I saw—Oh, my dear, I am so glad.

PAM. Who are you ?

HAB. Give me your hand. Tell me, my sweet ; didn't you come to the Tauropolia last year and spoil a pretty dress there ?

PAM. (*catching sight of the baby*). Woman, where did you get that child ?

HAB. Darling, do you see something that you know among these trinkets ? Oh, madam, don't be frightened of me.

PAM. Is it not your own baby ?

HAB. I only pretended that it was. I did not mean to wrong the mother. I intended to find her when I had time. And now I have found—you. You are the girl I saw that night.

PAM. But who is the father ?

HAB. Charisius.

PAM. Are you sure of that, dear ?

HAB. Yes, yes, indeed. And you are his wife living here, are you not ?

PAM. Yes.

HAB. O woman blest, some god *has* taken pity on you.'

Pathos and realism, such as we see here, were the qualities which the ancients most admired in Menander, and few writers after the third century B.C. enjoyed a higher reputation. Aristophanes of Byzantium, the great Alexandrian critic, ranked him as second after Homer among poets, and cried : ' Menander ! Life ! I wonder which of you copied which ? ' In Roman times Ovid wrote of him :

> ' So long as fathers bully, servants lie,
> And women smile, Menander cannot die.'

> (*Amores*, 1, XV, 17.)

and Quintilian considered that a careful study of Menander alone would produce the perfect orator, ' so complete is his picture of life, so fertile his imagination and command of language, so perfect his adaptation to every circumstance, character, and emotion ' (Ins. Or. X. 1. 69). Plutarch, Dion Lucian, and Ælian were all his warm admirers, and an anonymous poet in the Anthology says : ' The bees themselves culling the varied flowers of the Muses brought the honey to thy lips ; the Graces themselves bestowed their gift upon thee, Menander, and endowed thy dramas with the happiest eloquence. Thou livest for ever, and Athens from thee has a glory that reaches to the clouds of heaven.'

Modern critics have been less enthusiastic, and it must be confessed that to-day Menander is not for everyone. The grandeur of Æschylus, the beauty of Sophocles, the pathos of Euripides make a universal appeal : Menander is for the few. His genius lies not in his plots but in the subtlety of his character drawing and the actuality of his dialogue—two points in which he resembles Theophrastus—and these are apt to be disregarded. A modern reader puts plot first, and he finds Menander's plots monotonous, sordid, and artificial ; but he does not remember that an original plot in our sense of the word was scarcely required from a Greek dramatist. The tragedians by a binding convention were compelled to take their stories from the

ancient saga ; the Old Comedy was a burlesque-revue
of everyday life ; the Middle Comedy seems to have
chiefly consisted of parodies of the old myths. Menander
and his contemporaries took a bold step forward when
they invented plots of their own, and any excessive
novelty might well have been dangerous. Indeed it is
obvious from their prologues that their audiences
expected to be informed beforehand of what was going
to happen in the play.

The questions may still be asked, Why is it that
Menander favoured one subject above all others ? Why
is it that his hero or his heroine is nearly always a
foundling ? Why is it that seduction is so common ? and
Why do most of his plays end with a recognition scene
followed by a marriage ? The answer to some of these
points is to be found in the conventions of Attic
comedy and in the secluded life of Athenian free-born
women ; but the question of the foundling motive
requires more detailed examination. The foundling,
although he has been a rare figure in our literature
since the days when Fielding wrote *Tom Jones*, offers
one of the most obvious opportunities for Recognition,
and Reversal of Fortune, the two things that Aristotle
considered to be the essence of drama. With us happily
foundlings are infrequent, but in Greece and in Rome
the exposure of new-born children was sanctioned both
by law and custom, and many an infant thus found was
foisted off by a childless wife upon an unsuspecting
husband. So the rich man's daughter might fall into
the hands of a brothel-keeper, the poor man's son
might become the heir of a noble house. As Juvenal
says, Satire, VI, 595 :

> ' Suppositititious children—what a theme
> For satire is there here ! But yet I deem
> 'Tis better not to tell how we, poor fools,
> Find prayers and hopes deceived at those foul pools

Whence come the foundlings, who some day shall wear
The Salian dress, the name of Scaurus bear.
There wanton Fortune stands and in the gloom
Smiles on her naked babes and makes them room
Upon her breast, and then, her whims to please,
Fills our great families with brats like these.'

In the foundling, then, Menander found a plot ready-made to his hand and familiar to his audience. But it may not be fantastic to suggest that there was another and deeper reason which led him to cling so persistently to this motive. To the men of his age it must have seemed that the gods of Greece had forsaken their people. In Menander's childhood Thebes had been razed to the ground by the Macedonians and all her inhabitants sold into slavery. In his early manhood half the citizens of Athens had been forcibly deported by Antipater and sent into exile. The whole world was in an uproar of strife and no one could say with certainty what the morrow would bring forth. Menander tried to draw a picture of life as he saw it ; and to him men were not God's children but God's foundlings, and the unseen power who swayed their fortunes was Chance.

The New Comedy was so essentially Athenian that all attempts to transplant it failed, and the death of its last great writer, Philemon, in 262 coincides with the loss by Athens of all political importance. We have the names of sixty-three comedians besides Menander, but only four of them, Philemon, Diphilus, Poseidippus and Apollodorus, are much more than names. Philemon in his lifetime was more popular than Menander, against whom he used his paid supporters so successfully that his rival was wont to say, ' Do you not blush, Philemon, when you gain a victory over me ? ' He is represented by fragments and by three plays of Plautus, the *Mercator*, *Trinummus*, and *Mostellaria* ; and as far as we can judge, when he was not broadly comic he was apt to be tedious. Poseidippus and Apollodorus were of much the same type, the latter, from whom Terence took the *Hecyra* and *Phormio*, being more sentimental than impassioned, more mournful than pathetic, and producing on the whole an effect of monotony. Diphilus, on the other hand, seems to have depended chiefly on coarse humour : from him Plautus adapted the *Casina* and *Rudens*, and the following fragment from the *Parasite* is probably a fair example of his style :

' Where can you find a more unlucky wight than Master Belly ?
We put our cakes in baskets but we don't use them for jelly ;
A bag is right for bread but soup would very soon run through it,
And bottles won't hold lobsters ; that's a fact and well we know it.
But when it comes to belly's turn poor belly has no say ;
He has to take all sorts of things and put the lot away.'

Epicurus and the new philosophies

Menander in his dialogue and stagecraft suggests the influence of Theophrastus, but in the thought that lies behind his plays, and especially in his tolerant sympathy with human weakness, he is nearer to Epicurus, his contemporary and friend. Epicurus (341–271), son of the Athenian Neocles, was born at Samos in 341, and at the age of eighteen came to study and perform his military service in Athens. In 322 the Athenian settlers in Samos were expelled by Perdiccas ; and Epicurus then joined his father, who was a schoolmaster, at Colophon and for a time acted as his assistant. But from his fourteenth year philosophy had been his first love, and in 306, when the law against philosophic schools at Athens was repealed, he left Lampsacus, where he was living, bought a piece of land at Athens for three hundred pounds, and established there the

31

School of the Garden. Round him gathered a circle of friends, men and women like Metrodorus and Leontion, united by a common set of principles and by a common affection for a master whom they almost worshipped ; and here he laboured for thirty-six years, impressing his personality so deeply on his disciples that for the next six centuries no change in his doctrines was ever made. In 270 he succumbed to the strangury and dysentery which had long tormented him ; but on his death-bed he wrote to one of his disciples : 'On this blissful day, which is also the last day of my life, I am writing to you. . . . All my sufferings are outweighed by the joy I feel when I remember our past discussions. Let your care for Metrodorus' children match the attachment which from boyhood you have shown to me and to philosophy.'

To Plato philosophy had been a star guiding men in their search for wisdom. To Aristotle it had been a sign-post pointing out the way to knowledge. Neither to Plato nor to Aristotle did the individual man seem of any great importance : he was a member of a community, and ' good living ' for him consisted in performing adequately his proper functions in that community. If the community prospered, the individual prospered with it ; and it was better to be a poor man in a great city than a rich man in a small one.

The conquests of Alexander changed all this : for the city state was substituted the inhabited world, for a feeling of security the sight of universal change, for duty to one's fellow-citizens a vague sense of brotherhood with all mankind. As for philosophy, she turned from theory to practice, from the intellectual to the moral sphere, and instead of spurring men on to knowledge she tried to show them what is the true end of life and to find them in the turmoil of the world some sure abiding place and rock of refuge.

Theophrastus is the last of the old philosophers, Epicurus is the first of the new.

To discuss the tenets of these new systems, Stoic, Sceptic, Cynic, and Epicurean belongs to the history of philosophy rather than to the history of literature : and in any case the fragments which we have left of the writings of Zeno, Pyrrho, and Crates are so scanty that a judgment of their literary quality is almost impossible. The case of Epicurus is different, for the pious care of Diogenes Laertius has preserved us forty of the Master's maxims, *Kuriai Doxai*, which all good Epicureans learned by heart, as well as three long epistles explaining the principles of physics, natural science, and morals as he would have them taught, which enable us to get a clear idea of his style and manner of thought. Here are some of the maxims :

'A blessed and eternal being has no trouble himself and brings no trouble upon any other being ; hence he is exempt from movements of anger and partiality, for every such movement implies weakness.'

'Death is nothing to us ; for the body, when it has been resolved into its elements, has no feeling, and that which has no feeling is nothing to us.'

'The magnitude of pleasure reaches its limit in the removal of all pain. When pleasure is present, so long as it is uninterrupted, there is no pain either of body or of mind or of both together.'

'It is impossible to live a pleasant life without living wisely and well and justly, and it is impossible to live wisely and well and justly without living pleasantly.'

'No pleasure is in itself evil, but the things which produce certain pleasures entail annoyances many times greater than the pleasures themselves.'

'Of all the means which are procured by wisdom to ensure happiness throughout the whole of life, by far the most important is the acquisition of friends.'

'Of our desires some are natural and necessary ; others are natural but not necessary ; others again are neither natural nor necessary but are due to illusory opinion.'

C

33

The letters on physics and meteorology are too long for quotation, although Epicurus recommends his disciples to learn them by heart ; but some passages from his letter on the conduct of life may be given :

'Epicurus to Menœceus, greeting. Let no one be slow to seek wisdom when he is young nor weary in the search thereof when he is grown old. For no age is too early or too late for the health of the soul. And to say that the season for studying philosophy has not yet come, or that it is past and gone, is like saying that the season for happiness is not yet, or that it is now no more. Therefore both old and young ought to seek wisdom, the former in order that, as age comes over him, he may be young in good things because of the grace of what has been, and the latter in order that while he is young he may at the same time be old, because he has no fear of the things which are to come. So we must exercise ourselves in the things which bring happiness, since if that be present we have everything, and if that be absent all our actions are directed towards attaining it.

'Those things which without ceasing I have declared unto thee, these do, and exercise thyself therein, holding them to be the elements of right life. First believe that God is a living being immortal and blessed, according to the notion of a god indicated by the common sense of mankind ; and so believing, thou shalt not affirm of him ought that is foreign to his immortality or that agrees not with blessedness, but shall believe about him whatever may uphold both his blessedness and his immortality. For verily there are gods, and the knowledge of them is manifest ; but they are not such as the multitude believe, seeing that men do not steadfastly maintain the notions they form respecting them. . . . When we say that pleasure is the aim and end, we do not mean the pleasures of the prodigal or the pleasures of sensuality, as we are understood by some to do through ignorance, prejudice, or wilful misrepresentation. By pleasure we mean the absence of pain in the body and of trouble in the soul. It is not an unbroken succession of drinking-bouts and of revelry, not sexual love, not the enjoyment of the fish and other delicacies of a luxurious table which produce a pleasant life ; it is sober reasoning, searching out the grounds of every choice and avoidance, and banishing those beliefs through which the greatest tumults take possession of the soul. Of all this the beginning and the greatest good is prudence. Wherefore prudence is a more precious thing even than philosophy ; from it spring all the other virtues, for it teaches that we cannot lead a life of pleasure which

34

is not also a life of prudence, honour, and justice ; nor lead a life of prudence, honour, and justice, which is not also a life of pleasure. For the virtues have grown into one with a pleasant life, and a pleasant life is inseparable from them. . . .

' Exercise thyself in these and kindred precepts day and night, both by thyself and with him who is like unto thee ; then never, either in waking or in dream, wilt thou be disturbed, but will live as a god among men. For man loses all semblance of mortality by living in the midst of immortal blessings.' [1]

As it happens, we have no account from Epicurus himself of his famous doctrine of the Swerve, by which the origin of the world was attributed to a fortuitous concourse of atoms. Probably this theory, like the rest of his system, was a deduction from experience. We know that there is a Universe ; therefore the atoms, must have clashed. We know also that we have freewill ; this quality, like all others, has its cause in the atoms, and therefore at uncertain times and places they must swerve. Epicureanism has its weak sides ; but its efficacy is proved by its long existence, and a recent writer has well said [2] : ' It is easy enough to criticize Epicurus. He is shrewd but superficial, amiable but indolent ; his quietism suggests the charge of " sour grapes " or lack of vitality, and his exaggerated dread of pain is a mark of decadence. . . . But from an age of Science rather than of Faith, and a society which, like his own, has seen its foundations shaken, Epicurus may win better understanding and greater sympathy. The individual who keeps his own door-step clean and shows himself neighbour to other individuals is perhaps a more real benefactor than many eager publicists and big movements.'

As regards the other philosophers who were contemporary with Epicurus, brief details must suffice. The founder of the Stoic system was Zeno (333–261),

[1] Diogenes Laertius, Bk. x., tr. R. D. Hicks, Loeb Library.
[2] C. F. Angus in Cambridge Ancient History, vii, 248.

a Greek from Citium in Cyprus and perhaps of Semitic descent, who came to Athens on business about 315, and after attending the lectures of Crates opened his own school in the Stoa Poikile 302. Swarthy and lean, he loved to lie in the sun and eat ripe figs ; but he was also a good business man, and the youths of Athens who in 302 had been released from military service found the Painted Porch in the centre of the city more attractive than the Lyceum and the Garden which were on the outskirts. The fragments left of his writings have been carefully collected,[1] but they are too scanty for literary valuation, and it is from the anecdotes in Diogenes Laertius that we get the best idea of the methods by which he led his pupils to follow the path of duty and to avoid the path of sin, duty and sin being words which he is said to have first brought into common use. On his death in 261 his place as head of the school was taken by Cleanthes of Assos, whose hymns give him a definite place in literary history. The most famous of them, quoted by St Paul, was considered by so good a judge as Bishop Lightfoot to be the noblest expression of devotional feeling which Greek literature has left us, and its beginning and end are here given in James Adam's translation :

> ' O God most glorious, called by many a name,
>   Nature's great King, through endless years the same ;
>   Omnipotence, who by thy just decree
>   Controllest all ; hail, Zeus, for unto thee
>   Behoves thy children in all lands to call.
>   We are thy children, we alone, of all
>   On earth's broad ways that wander to and fro
>   Bearing thine image wheresoe'er we go ;
>   Wherefore with songs of praise thy praise I will forth shew. . . .

> ' Zeus, the all-bountiful, whom darkness shrouds,
>   Whose lightning lightens in the thunder clouds,

[1] The Fragments of Zeno and Cleanthes. A. C. Pearson. Cambridge, 1891.

Thy children save from error's deadly sway.
Turn thou the darkness from their souls away.
Vouchsafe that unto knowledge they attain ;
For thou by knowledge art made strong to reign
O'er all, and all things rulest righteously.
So by thee honoured we will honour thee
Praising thy works continually with songs
As mortals should ; nor higher meed belongs
E'en to the gods than justly to adore
The universal law for evermore.'

The sceptics, founded by Pyrrho (360–270), who denied all real existence and said that there was no such thing as just and unjust, made restfulness, *ataraxia*, their ideal in life. They combated the doctrines of the other schools, but enunciated none of their own, and as Pyrrho never put anything in writing he may here be passed over. On the other hand, the cynics, whose leader at this time was Crates of Thebes (fl. 320), were responsible for much satirical verse, and Crates himself was a writer of considerable skill. His best-known poem was Pera, a parody of Homer, in which he sung the praises of Wallet-town, the cynics' paradise, ' rich in thyme and garlic, figs and bread, but other-wise possessed of nothing.' Another of his pieces is addressed to lovers : ' The best cure for love is hunger, the next best is time. If both these fail, there is the halter.' A third epigram gives a rich man's expenditure :

' Fifty pounds for the cook ; for the doctor a shilling ;
A thousand for Tom who with praise is so willing ;
Two hundred and fifty for Moll at the least ;
For my counsellor nix ; and five pence for the priest.'

Crates had been left a fortune, but after his con-version by Diogenes he sold all his property, gave it to the poor, and adopted the life of a mendicant preacher. One day a girl of good family, named Hipparchia, heard him discoursing, and from that

37

moment, as we are told[1] : 'To her Crates was everything. She threatened her parents that she would
kill herself if she were not given in marriage to him.
They therefore begged him to dissuade her, and he
did all he could. At last being unsuccessful he got up,
took off his clothes before her face and said : " This
is the bridegroom, here are his possessions ; make your
choice ; you will be no partner for me unless you share
my pursuits."' The girl chose, and adopting the cynics'
dress became the first woman philosopher, com-
memorated by Antipater of Sidon.[2]

> ' Gowns that with jewels shine,
>   And slippers fine,
> The scented gear that women wear,
>   Shall never more be mine.
> I take instead the ground for bed,
> The cynic's wallet and the stick,
> The double blanket coarse and thick,
>   And girdled robes resign.
> As Atalanta in the race
>   Did once for glory strive,
> So I a greater fame embrace
>   And will for wisdom live.'

For the rest of their days Crates and Hipparchia
were outstanding examples of what the cynics meant
by ' autarkeia,' ' self-sufficiency.' It is true that they
sometimes appeared at the banquets of kings, but
usually they lived the simple life, and they crowned
their modernity by being the first parents to give their
daughter in companionate marriage.

The women poets

Hipparchia is one type of the new woman who in
this period was beginning to emerge. Another sign of

---

[1] Diogenes Laertius, vi, 7.
[2] Anth. Pal., vii, 413.

feminine activity is to be seen in the women poets of this age, Erinna, Anyte, Mœro, and Nossis. It is true that Suidas, writing in the tenth century A.D., makes Erinna a contemporary of Sappho : but Suidas is a goose, even if his *Lexicon* has furnished us with many golden eggs. It is practically certain that Erinna lived, like the other three women, about the end of the fourth century ; and her *Distaff*, a hexameter poem of three hundred lines seemed to the Alexandrians a perfect model for verse ; it was short, a blend of romance and realism, and simple in its elegance. Unfortunately only five lines survive, so that we are unable to form our own judgment.

Anyte of Tegea, however, is a more definite figure, for twenty of her epigrams—the red lilies of Anyte— are included in the Anthology. Her verse has all the qualities which it is usual to call masculine : simple, vigorous, restrained, she knows exactly what she wants to say, and says it with the utmost economy of effort. She for the first time brings into literature the conception of the countryside as a place of rest ; for the typical Athenian regarded the country as rather terrifying than attractive, a place where you felt lonely. To him the country gods, Pan and the Nymphs, were mysterious powers who visited strangers with panic fear and sudden madness, and it was only within the walls of his own city that a man was really safe. Anyte, who lived in Arcadia, knew better, and her poems are a series of rustic pictures. Here is one for a statue of Hermes :—

> ' Here by the windswept orchard,
>   Here where the three roads meet,
> I watch the grey cliffs rising
>   And wayworn travellers greet.
> My fountain murmurs cool and clear—
> " Draw near and rest, O weary feet, draw near." '

On all country things she writes with equal charm, on the cock killed by the fox with stealthy bite, on the dolphin cast upon the beach by the waves, and on the haughty he-goat standing alone :

> ' Look at the hornèd goat, how proud he seems
> With shaggy beard, how bright his red eye gleams.
> A rosy Naiad once upon some hill
> Caressed those cheeks, and he remembers still.'

Mœro of Byzantium has been less kindly treated by fortune, and only two short poems of hers now remain in the sixth book of the Anthology. They are beautifully written, with a touch of Eastern splendour :

> ' Here in Aphrodite's bower
>   Where the golden panels shine,
> Thou thy Bacchic juice dost pour,
>   Cluster of the vine.
>
> Never more above thy head
>   Shall thy mother tendrils cast
> Nor her leaves nectareous spread :
>   Lo, thy day is past.'

From Byzantium we cross the sea to Southern Italy where Nossis, ' whose tablets' wax was melted by Love's flame,' wrote love poems which she herself, at least, claimed to rival those of Sappho. Meleager seems to have included these ' fair flowers of the iris with their perfumed breath ' in his *Garland*, but the prudery of monks has robbed us of these more passionate verses, and the best specimen of Nossis left is her epitaph for the comic dramatist Rhinthon :

> ' Pass by and wish me well,
>   Smile and be not afraid,
> Within this narrow cell
>   Rhinthon is laid.
> A humble bird of song,
>   A mimic playwright gay ;
> But yet the crown I won
>   Abides alway.'

The historians

Lastly we come to the three historians, Ephorus, Theopompus, and Timæus, who taken together bridge the period between Athenian and Alexandrian literature. The exact date of Ephorus' birth is unknown : Suidas makes him exactly contemporary with Theopompus ; but this is wrong, and he was certainly somewhat his senior. There is a well-known anecdote that Isocrates (436–338) said of these two, who were his pupils, that Ephorus needed the spur and Theopompus the bridle. Another story tells us that Ephorus was sent to Isocrates to be made an orator, and proving a failure was persuaded by his master to turn to history. Neither of these tales, however, has much authenticity, and all that we really know of Ephorus is that he was born at Cyme and wrote a universal history of the Greek peoples in twenty-nine books, from the return of the Heracleidæ to 356 B.C., the year of his own death, one more book being then added by his son. Of this work, which for many years was the vulgate of Greek history, we now possess very little, for it was incorporated by Diodorus Siculus, and as usual the epitome killed the original. Nor need we much regret its loss ; for Ephorus seems to have been a second-class mind and even his best fragments, such as the following, quoted by Strabo,[1] give an impression of confused thinking :—

' The Lacedæmonians were at war with the Messenians, who had killed King Teleclus when he went to Messene to offer sacrifice, and they took an oath not to return home until they had either destroyed Messene or were all killed. When they set out they left only the youngest and the oldest of the citizens to guard the city, and when the war had lasted ten years the Lacedæmonian women met together and sent certain of their number to their husbands to reproach them. " You are fighting the Messenians," they said,

[1] Strabo, VI, iii, 3.

41

" on unequal terms. They are staying at home and begetting children, you have left your wives as widows and are campaigning in an enemy's country, so that there is a risk of our fatherland soon being short of men." Thereupon the Lacedæmonians, both keeping their oath and at the same time bearing in mind their wives' argument, sent back their most vigorous and at the same time their youngest men, knowing that they had not taken part in the oaths, since they were still boys when they went out with the men of military age. Furthermore they ordered them to cohabit with the maidens, every man with every maiden, thinking that thus there would be more children : and when this was done the children were called Partheniæ " Maidens' Sons." '

Theopompus of Chios (378–c. 300) is more interesting, both as a man and as a writer, than Ephorus. He possessed a large private fortune, and won considerable fame by going from town to town making display speeches in their honour. About 333 he returned to his native island, and in spite of the hostility evoked by his egregious vanity and censorious disposition, he held his own there with Macedonian support until some years after Alexander's death. He was then expelled as a disturber of the public peace, and spent the rest of his life finishing his two long histories, the *Hellenica*, a continuation of Thucydides in twelve books, and the *Philippica*, a history of his own times in fifty-eight. These now only exist in small fragments, but for many years they were very popular, and even in the ninth century A.D. fifty-three books of the *Philippica* were extant. But here again our loss is not great, for Theopompus even more than Ephorus appears to have followed Isocrates in trying to make history both amusing and also a vehicle for moral lessons. He interrupts his narrative to indulge in philosophic disquisitions ; he invents long rhetorical speeches which he puts into the mouth of generals at the moment before a battle ; he relates an elaborate tale of an imaginary land, Merope, where the golden age

42

still exists ; and he endeavours to give spice to history by repeating slanders of great men's private life. One extract,[1] relating to Philip of Macedon, will give an idea of his method :

> ' When Philip became master of great wealth he did not spend it quickly. No ! he flung it away and threw it into the street. He was the worst manager in all the world, both himself and his associates. In a word, not one of them had the least knowledge of right living or the prudent management of an estate. For this he himself was responsible, being both insatiable and extravagant, and doing everything offhand, whether he was getting or giving. He was always busy with his soldiering and had no time to reckon up income and expenditure. Moreover, his companions were men who had come pouring in from many places ; some were from his home country, others from Thessaly, others from all the rest of Greece, and they were not selected on grounds of merit. No ! pretty well every lecher and daredevil and buffoon in the Greek and barbarian world flocked to Macedonia and got the title of " Philip's companion." Even if a man was not a ruffian on his arrival, he soon became one under the influence of the Macedonian life and habits. It was partly their wars and campaigns, partly their extravagances that turned them into daredevils, living not in an orderly fashion but prodigally like highwaymen.'

Timæus (340–256), a native of Tauromenium, the modern Taormina, lived through a period of vast political changes. Born in 340, two years before the battle of Chæronea, he died in 256, four years after the beginning of the First Punic War. On being exiled from Sicily by Agathocles in 317 he took up his home in Athens, although he also travelled widely in Spain and Gaul collecting information for his *History of Sicily and Italy*. This work, in which for the first time he introduced dating by Olympiads, originally ended at 320 B.C. ; but it was subsequently enlarged to include a record of the rule of Agathocles and the campaigns of Pyrrhus. As a collector of local legends Timæus

---

[1] Quoted by Athenæus, IV, 167.

was highly esteemed by the Alexandrians, and one such tale [1] will illustrate his style :

> 'There is a house in Agrigentum which is called the " galley," and for this reason. Some young fellows were drinking there, and getting overheated with liquor became so wild that they imagined they were on board a galley and were being tossed by a storm at sea. Indeed they so completely lost their senses that they started flinging the furniture and bedding into the street, being convinced that the pilot was bidding them lighten the ship because of the storm. A crowd collected and began to carry off the jetsam, but even so the youngsters did not stop their mad prank. The next day the military authorities came to the house, and the young men, still half-seas over, were brought into court. In answer to the magistrates they said that under stress of bad weather they had been forced to throw their superfluous cargo into the sea ; and when the authorities expressed surprise at their alarm one of the young men, albeit he seemed the eldest of the company, declared—" Good Triton sirs, I was so frightened that I threw myself under the rowing benches at the very bottom of the hold and stayed there." The magistrates, therefore, taking their delirium into account, discharged them from court, only sentencing them never to drink too much again.'

Timæus was not a pleasant person. He was both pedantic and quarrelsome—hence his nickname Epitimæus, the Fault-finder—and his writing is one of the earliest examples of the florid rhetoric known as the Asianic style. In his history he was guilty of many errors of fact, and he was fully repaid for his criticisms of Ephorus by Polybius, who among the other qualities which have endeared him to scholars possessed a power of vituperation that enabled him to devote one whole book of his history to an exposure of Timæus' mistakes.

The 'Oxyrhynchus historian' still remains for consideration. In 1907 Grenfell and Hunt published, from a papyrus they had found in Egypt, a long extract from a history of Greece dealing with the events of the years 396 and 395 B.C., and also giving a clear account of the Bœotian constitution. Wilamowitz and Meyer

[2] Quoted by Athenæus, II, 37.

consider the author to be Theopompus, E. M. Walker is in favour of Ephorus, J. B. Bury and Blass incline to Cratippus, a younger contemporary of Thucydides. It would be presumptuous to decide between these opinions, and it is sufficient here to say that although the style of the fragment is lucid and simple it is also very dull.

CHAPTER II

ALEXANDRIA UNDER THE PTOLEMIES

(302–180 B.C.)

The first period (302–283 B.C.)

THE history of Alexandrian literature begins with two events, the battle of Ipsus in 302 B.C., and the arrival of Demetrius of Phalerum in Egypt some few years later. Until the battle of Ipsus Ptolemy I Soter, the most capable of Alexander's generals, who had taken Egypt as his share of the conqueror's inheritance, had been compelled to make military strength the first aim of his policy. But when the air was cleared by that battle, in which he took no part, and some sort of definite policy established between the kingdoms of Macedonia, Syria, and Egypt, he was enabled to turn his attention to the peaceful development of his country. As for Demetrius, after his expulsion from Athens in 307 and the overthrow of all his statues save one by an ungrateful people, he had gone into retirement in Bœotia to write the history of his ten years' government. But he was too active a spirit to be content long with idleness, and in the early years of the third century he determined, like many Greeks after him, to try his fortune in Egypt. During the period of his rule at Athens he had realized the advantages which accrue to a city from the organization of learning, and had seen the attraction exercised by Athens on strangers owing to the permanent establishment of her philosophic schools. Soon after his appearance at Alexandria therefore, he suggested to Ptolemy the foundation of a Library and a Museum, the latter to be a state-endowed college serving as a centre for organized science and literature ; and, as the proposal came at a favourable time, it was quickly put into effect. Whether the actual establishment was due to Ptolemy I Soter, or to Ptolemy II Philadelphus, is immaterial : it is fairly certain that Demetrius was the father of the idea and that it was in the early years of the third century that both institutions came into being.

The Museum and Library

There are three stages in Alexandrian literature ; a period of rapid growth under Ptolemy I 305–283 ; a period of full fruition under Ptolemy II and Ptolemy III 285–221 ; a period of decline under Ptolemy IV and Ptolemy V 221–180. But in all three stages the Museum and the Library play such an important part that an account of the two institutions is necessary here.

The Museum, ' the temple of the Muses,' is described by Strabo, who visited Alexandria in 24 B.C., as forming part of the royal quarter of the city. It contained a covered walk and an arcade furnished with recesses and seats, as well as a large building in which was the common hall, where the scholars who were members of the Museum met for their meals. The association had a common fund, and its president, nominated by the king, was called ' the priest of the Muses' shrine.' The members of the Museum probably received a yearly stipend, but it is not clear what branches of knowledge were represented on the foundation. Strabo speaks of the members simply as ' scholars,' and says nothing of lecture rooms or laboratories ; but we know that lectures were delivered and that definite schools of medicine and mathematics were formed at Alexandria. It is probable indeed that the Museum was the centre of organized research in science, and we may get some idea of its nature if we imagine a composite of the Royal Society, a college at Oxford and Cambridge, and one of the new National Laboratories.

Of the Library—or rather of the libraries, for there were two—we have fuller details. The larger building was in the Brucheion, the N.E. quarter of the city, near the Museum ; the smaller was in the Rhakotis, the S.W. quarter, near the temple of Serapis. As to the number of MSS. which they contained accounts differ. It is said that Demetrius in 285 B.C. told Ptolemy that they already had 200,000, and that the number would soon be increased to 500,000. With this agrees the statement of the Byzantine scholar Tzetzes who says that the larger library contained 400,000 ' mixed ' and 90,000 ' unmixed ' volumes, the smaller 42,800 ' unmixed,' these latter probably being papyrus-rolls containing a single work of small dimensions. The classification of these MSS., their cataloguing and study, was essentially a literary task ; and perhaps the Library organization corresponded to the Arts Faculties in a modern university, while the Museum took the place of Science. However that may be, the list of head librarians shows us that the chief post was usually given to a literary man who also acted as tutor to the royal household. Zenodotus, a pupil of Philetas, was followed by Eratosthenes the polymath, Apollonius Rhodius the poet, Aristophanes the Homeric scholar, Apollonius the Eidograph, and Aristarchus the literary critic ; while Callimachus was responsible for the *Pinakes*, a descriptive catalogue of the whole collection.

The Samian Poets

It would seem that the organization of the Museum was completed about 290 B.C.; the cage was ready, but at present there were no birds, and it was to Athens and the islands of the Ægean that Demetrius turned for its first inmates. From Athens he got only refusals, but at Samos and Cos, where songsters were then as numerous as they had been at Lesbos and Teos in the seventh century, he was more successful. In Samos literature already enjoyed the advantage of State patronage of a rather special kind. The type of ruler who encourages art for political reasons, a Pisistratus or Augustus, was always fairly common in ancient times, but in Douris, who became tyrant of Samos in 301 B.C., writers found not only a patron but a fellow craftsman. Like Demetrius himself Douris began life as a student of literature, and then, by one of those turns of fortune so common in that age of transition, found himself upon the throne of his native land. His historical studies, which had included a life of Agathocles, were doubtless of some assistance to him in his new position, and his brother Lynceus, who was both a writer of comedies and also a great authority on gastronomy, maintained the family tradition of *belles lettres*. Other authors were soon attracted. Aethlius compiled the local records of Samos, Poseidippus came from Cnidos, Hedylus with his mother Hedyle from Athens. Nicaenetus left Abdera in Thrace and devoted himself to the task of commemorating in verse the chief episodes in the history of his new country. Aeschrion the iambic poet, Philaenis authoress of 'The Pleasures of Love,' and Phalaecus, who gave his name to the hendecasyllabic metre in which Catullus, and Martial afterwards, found their best medium for intimate verse, were all members

D 49

of the circle, and the leader of the whole company was Asclepiades.

All these writers, whether their medium was prose or verse, had one characteristic in common, which they passed on to Alexandrian literature. They were realists ; in history preferring the personal anecdote to political theory, in philosophy dealing with rules of conduct rather than with metaphysical speculations, in poetry avoiding any flight of imagination and describing familiar incidents of every-day life. With two of their number, Hedylus and Poseidippus, Asclepiades was clearly on terms of close intimacy. The three poets are linked together by Meleager in one couplet of his Proem—' the wild field flowers of Hedylus and Posei-dippus, together with the wind blossoms of Sikelidas '— Sikelidas being the name by which for some unknown reason Asclepiades is often called. It is highly probable that the ' Soros ' or ' Garner,' of which a scholiast on Homer speaks, was a selection of their verse written in collaboration and published jointly by the three, such a volume as the ' Lyrical Ballads ' or the ' Poems by three brothers ' in our own literature. Doubtless it was from the *Garner* that Meleager took those pieces which in the MS. of the Anthology are attributed to Asclepiades or Hedylus or Poseidippus, and it is possible still to get some indication of the book's contents and the authors' methods of composition.

Of the three poets Hedylus, who was, as his name shows, a son born out of lawful wedlock, seems to have been distinguished for a certain vigour of satire. ' The Daughter of limb-relaxing Bacchus and of limb-relaxing Aphrodite,' he writes, ' is limb-relaxing Gout.' This and four other short pieces are all that now remain of his in the Anthology, and the three most characteristic specimens of his style are preserved for us by Athenæus. One is an epigram on a greedy lady, the other two are convivial songs addressed to one Socles—'A more sturdy fellow even than Sikelidas himself.'

> ' From eve till break of day
> From morning until night
> Let pleasure still hold sway
> And drink and love and write.
> Drink, boys, and drink amain ;
> While fast the wine-cups fly
> Some new sweet subtle strain
> Shall grace our revelry.
> Drench me with wine.   Life is but vain,
> Unless I drink and drink again.'

Poseidippus [1] is a more graceful writer, with a much wider range, and both in style and feeling closely resembles Asclepiades.   Counting pieces of doubtful authorship we have just over twenty epigrams by him remaining in the Anthology, together with a few more preserved by Athenæus.   By Poseidippus probably is the charming madrigal to Irene—' the flower of beauty, from head to foot carved of white marble, laden with virgin graces.'   To Poseidippus also it is best to attribute the delightful piece of sportive verse, ' The Bather,' with its fantastic conceit of fire and water :

> ' Along the beach where Love was born
> Cleander strolled one summer morn
> And saw his Nico swimming there
> Breasting the waves with bosom bare.
> He saw and burned : for strange to say
> Water gave birth to fire that day,
> And from the briny drops she threw
> A parching fire within him grew.
> She tossed the waves with dimpled arm
> And shoreward turned nor knew of harm ;
> But he who on the dry land stayed
> Most lamentable shipwreck made.

This Poseidippus must be distinguished from the comedian of the same name.   Some think that Poseidippus ' of Pella ' and Poseidippus ' of Cnidus ' are different persons : here their identity is presumed.

Yet all proved well. An equal love
Venus has sent them from above.
The boon he asked has granted been,
And now he thanks our sea-born queen.'

A.P. v, 209.

But of the three poets Asclepiades, as we have said,
is by far the most important.   In dedication and in
epitaph he follows a long-established tradition ; but
in the other sections of his work, the colloquial and the
amatory poems, he strikes out a new path which his
successors, Greek and Latin, were destined to follow
with such brilliant success.   Unfortunately of his light,
humorous pieces only two survive.   The first, ' The
Rakes' Progress,' with its Latin slang and quick tripping
sentences, is the perfection of impromptu, as the young
gallant rails against his steward :

' Five wreathes ! When will he come, I say !
What's that I hear you grunt—" Assez ? "
" You've got no change," deuce take you then ;
Servants forsooth, you're highwaymen.
" You've done no wrong," well, we will see :
Here, Jenny, bring his book to me.
" Five shillings wine." You dirty dog !
I'll truss you up, you Lapith hog !
And what's this—" Sausage, half a crown,
" Fish, eggs and pastry," all put down,
" And honey "—Stop. I've had enough.
To-morrow I'll go through the stuff.
Now off to Truefitt's, and be quick
Unless you want to feel my stick.
Five silver vials I must have
One for each kiss my darling gave.
Our bed was witness to my vow,
And I must pay the price, I trow.'

A. P. v. 181.

This is the realistic side of love, in the world of
spendthrifts and parasites, flute girls and courtesans,
wherein Asclepiades lived, the side that stirred Lucretius

52

to his outbursts of indignation ; where money ceases
to be sacred and is lavished wantonly to gratify an idle
fancy. True love, in our sense of the word, was
obviously impossible when the object of a lover's
affections was herself usually a slave, a piece of property
earning money for her master, and only able to indulge
her own inclinations in so far as they did not run
counter to her owner's will. Asclepiades himself
expressed the cruel irony of such a position in ' The
Girdle ' :

> ' It fell that once upon a day
> I with Hermione would play ;
> And round her waist did then behold
> A girdle bright with words in gold :
> It said " Come take me if you will,
> " Nor grieve if I'm another's still." '

A. P. v. 158.

But such romance as could be extracted from these
mercenary amours Asclepiades gets into his verse. Often
he is curiously modern in tone, in the French rather
than the English style, another Chénier or de Musset,
as in the despairing cry of the rejected lover :

> ' Long are the hours, the storm winds blow,
> Night passes ere the Pleiads set ;
> But still before her door I go
> With driving rain all wet.
>
> This is not love, this torturing smart,
> These arrows forged in flaming fire ;
> I know her false, but yet my heart
> Still burns with mad desire.'

A. P. v. 189.

How far these emotions are genuine, how far they
merely serve as an occasion for verse are questions,
with Asclepiades, that admit of no very definite
answer. He is certainly an artist before all, and it is
the vivid grace of his love poems rather than their

emotional force that gives them their charm. But in clearness of presentment he is unrivalled, and in a few lines can draw a picture that it is hard to forget. Here, for example, is his portrait of Dorcion, the 'young gazelle,' who long before our days delighted to appear in a semi-male disguise :

> ' She seems a soft-cheeked boy
>   As with the men she goes
> And from her eyes in joy
>   A glance voluptuous throws.
>
> Her cap and cloak loose hung
>   Float lightly in the air
> And from her shoulder flung
>   Leave all her white thigh bare.'

A. P. xii. 161.

This dramatic quality appears equally plainly in the little vignette of the girl waiting for her lover :

> ' Oft would she gaze from out the lattice high,
> Her cheeks with longing wet, and lonely cry
>   Till he came to her door.
> But Cleophon's blue eyes with their bright fire
> Have dried her tears and filled her heart's desire ;
>   And now she weeps no more.'

A. P. v. 153.

These attempts at translation give only the faintest idea of the grace and charm of the Greek originals : but perhaps even from them it may be possible to realize the exquisite truth of Meleager's criticism when he chose the anemone as the flower best corresponding to Asclepiades. The Samian poet's verse has all the bright colour and the delicate shape of the wind-blossom, but it has also its fragility and its absence of scent. His poems are beautiful, but as compared with Sappho and Meleager, they are as the anemone to the rose and violet : they are flowers, but they lack the essential quality of flowers—perfume.

The circle of Cos

Most of these Samian writers gravitated eventually to Alexandria ; but they do not seem to have shared very largely there in the royal bounty. More susceptible to patronage was the coterie who came from Cos ; Philetas, Hermesianax, Phanocles and Alexander the Ætolian ; Philetas was appointed by Ptolemy joint tutor to Philadelphus, his son by Berenice, together with Strato the great physicist ; Alexander received a commission to classify the tragic poets in the Library collection. Philetas was a scholar and antiquarian, so thin and emaciated that it is said his sandal soles were made of lead to prevent him being blown away by the wind. His reputation, however, as a love poet was very great and is attested both by his contemporaries and such later writers as the Roman Propertius :

'Callimachi manes et Coi sacra Philetæ.'

But of the verses addressed to his mistress Bittis we have only the scantiest remnants, and from them it is hard to estimate his poetical qualities. We know also the names of two of his longer poems, the *Demeter* and the *Hermes*, the latter apparently dealing with the love affairs of Odysseus at the court of King Æolus ; but here again judgment is impossible.

The other three elder writers of the Coan school are in much the same case with Philetas as far as their extant poems are concerned. Alexander in his lifetime was renowned as a writer of tragedies and is one of the seven Alexandrians known as the 'Tragic Pleiad.' But his plays, perhaps fortunately, have perished, and the one considerable fragment of his verse, a piece of thirty-four lines from a poem called *Apollo*, is a very dull bit of work. Hermesianax also is an author whose remains hardly inspire a reader with a great desire for more. We have one long quotation in Athenæus from the poem he called by the name of his mistress *Leontium*, but its length is its most striking feature, for it is merely a tedious catalogue of the great lovers of the past. Its sentiment is frigid, its learning pedantic, its theme ridiculously treated; and although its style and language are highly elaborate it possesses very little real grace. As for Phanocles, the last of the four, he seems slightly more attractive, if we can base a tentative opinion upon the fragment of twenty-eight lines on the death of Orpheus, preserved for us by Stobæus. In this there is a certain melancholy charm, and Virgil may well have read it before he wrote the Orpheus episode in the Fourth Georgic.

Simias and Phœnix

The younger members of the Coan circle belong to the reign of Ptolemy Philadelphus, and to them we shall return. But before we come to the prose writers under Ptolemy Soter there are still two poets to be mentioned, Simias of Rhodes and Phœnix of Colophon (fl. 285 B.C.). Simias was the inventor of the curious freak poems, usually included with the Bucolic Poets, in which the lines are arranged to make the shape of some object. The original idea seems to have been that a dedicatory epigram might correspond in form to the thing dedicated, and Simias' first essay was a poem engraved upon an axe, in which the lines follow the shape of the axe itself. This seemed so ingenious that Simias followed it with another in the shape of a pair of wings, and with a third arranged like an egg, while others took a shepherd's pipe and an altar as their models.

To these *Technopægnia* the verses of Phœnix form a complete contrast, for they have a very close connection with life. Five quotations in Athenæus and twenty-two lines in the Heidelberg papyrus published by Gerhard in 1909 give us a very fair idea of his style. The papyrus fragment is a diatribe against profiteers :

> ' How their riches they should spend
> They know not. An they gain their dearest end,
> Houses they buy with millions, houses bright
> With colonnades and floor of malachite.
> But for the food whereon their souls should feed,
> They mix it with the scourings of their greed.'

The best specimen of Phœnix, however, is the *Chough-Song* quoted by Athenæus, a begging ditty sung by men who on certain occasions went round from house to house with a chough. The last of its twenty-one lines run thus : [1]

> ' I, as I wander over dale and hill
> Keep my eyes fixed upon the Muses still ;
> And, be ye churl or lavish, at your wicket
> More blithely will I sing than any cricket.
> Kind sirs, set forth what cupboard has in store ;
> Kind master give, kind mistress give me more.
> So give the chough a fistful as is fit.
> So sing I. Give. You'll ne'er repent of it.'

Isyllus of Epidaurus (fl. 300 B.C.)

Before we leave the early Alexandrian poets we must mention the writers of hymns and pæans, chief among them Isyllus, whose *Pæan to Asclepius* was found inscribed on a stone in the temple hospital at Epidaurus. Isyllus was a person of importance, and he caused an ordinance to be passed that the noblest men in the city should walk in procession ' with hair flowing down ' to the temple, and there sing his hymn ; which is, however, in spite of good intentions a very wooden and uninspiring production. More vigorous is the

---

[1] Translations by A. D. Knox. Loeb Library.

Hymn to the Idæan Dactyls, found on a stone, unfortunately much broken, in Eretria, containing an account of these minor gods of metal craft and their father Eurystheus. Even better than this is the *Hymn to the Kouretes*, found in Crete 1903, a marching song of thirty-six lines written in the early third century, and ending with four jumps :

> ' Leap for our cities, leap for our sea-borne ships,
> Leap for our young citizens, leap for our goodly laws.'

Prose Writers : Callisthenes (fl. 300 B.C.)

So much then for the poets. When we turn to the prose writers of this period it is only fair to mention Ptolemy himself first, for his history of Alexander the Great, together with that of Aristobulus, was among the chief sources used by Arrian. Both were sober records of facts and were far surpassed in popularity by the work of Callisthenes of Olynthus, nephew of Aristotle, *The Deeds of Alexander*, a work abruptly terminated by the execution of the author at his hero's order. This was *the* Life of Alexander, and in its later forms, enlarged by a mass of fabulous anecdotes and much inferior verse, it became one of the most widely read of all ancient books.

Hecatæus and Euhemerus (fl. 300 B.C.)

Two other semi-historians who approximate to Callisthenes, are Euhemerus of Messana and Hecatæus of Abdera. Hecatæus, who was a friend of Ptolemy Soter and accompanied him on his Syrian campaign, wrote two books of historical fantasia, one *Ægyptiaca*, in which the Egyptians are described as the originators of civilization from whom all the Greek philosophers, from Orpheus to Plato, borrowed ; the other *Con-*

cerning the Hyperboreans, an imaginary people represented as living in the bliss of innocence on an island
off north-west Europe. This, of course, is as pure
fancy as Swift's *Gulliver's Travels*, and Euhemerus was
only using the same licence of imagination when he
wrote his famous book *The Golden List*. In it he told
how sailing into the Indian Ocean he came to the three
islands of Panchæa and their capital city Panara.
There on a golden pillar in the shrine of Zeus Triphylios
he found an inscription recording the deeds of Ouranos,
Kronos, and Zeus, all three once kings of Panara.
Thus far his book was fiction ; but he then proceeded
seriously to propose a similar origin for the other
Greek gods and goddesses, who on his theory were all
deified mortals like Heracles and Dionysus ; Aphrodite,
for example, having been in her time on earth a
notorious courtesan of Cyprus who for the first time
instructed women in the prostitute's art. Euhemerus
is perhaps more important in the history of religion
than in the history of literature. His book was popular
with the vulgar, but both Callimachus and Eratosthenes
were severe in their criticisms. The Romans, however,
received it with enthusiasm. Ennius made himself the
preacher of this new gospel, and it is from his writings,
as quoted by Lactantius and the other Latin Fathers,
that we get most of our knowledge of Euhemerism.

Manetho and Berosus

The conquests of Alexander opened out fresh
horizons to the Greeks and in the early third century
there was a copious output of literature, partly historical
partly geographical, describing the new countries which
had now come to men's knowledge. Pytheas of Mar-
seilles (fl. 290) took the extreme West as his subject,
and travelling beyond Gades into the Atlantic as far

north as Britain gave the result of his explorations in a book called *The Ocean*. Megasthenes about the same time went to the extreme East, as an ambassador to the Indian king Sandracotta from Seleucus Nicator, and on his return wrote the *Indica*, giving an account not only of the geography of the great peninsula but also of the history, the legends and the customs of the Indian people. To the early years of the third century also are attributed the histories of Chaldea and ancient Egypt which pass under the names of Berosus and Manetho. Berosus is said to have been a priest of Baal in the time of Alexander, Manetho a priest at Sebennytis during the reign of Ptolemy I. Their works are now only known to us by the copious quotations made from them by later writers such as Josephus, Tatian, Clement of Alexandria, and Eusebius, and although these extracts are of considerable historical value, it is very doubtful whether the books from which they are taken were written at the date and by the authors alleged. Indeed, the French scholar, Ernest Havet, who made a special study of the subject, came to the conclusion that both histories are due to forgers of the late second century B.C.

Philochorus (fl. 300 B.C.)

As a contrast to these pictures of remote countries we have the Greek local histories, equally popular at Alexandria, of which the *Atthides*, chronicles of Athens, are the best example. We know the names of six writers on this subject, Philochorus being the most famous of them. Philochorus was a soothsayer by trade, and the longest fragment of his history, pre-served by Dionysius, is reminiscent of his calling. In his eighth book he had described the capture of Athens by Demetrius Poliorcetes in 308 and the consequent banishment of Demetrius of Phalerum and his party ; and in the next book he proceeds as follows :

'When this year had passed and another year was just beginning a portent in the Acropolis happened. A bitch entered the temple of Athenê Polias, made her way into the Pandroseion, and climbing to the altar of Zeus Herkeios under the sacred olive-tree lay down upon it. Now it is an ancestral custom at Athens that no dog may go up to the Acropolis. About the same period in the heavens at day time when the sun was out and the air quite clear a bright star appeared. When I was asked about the portent and the appearance of the star as to what they meant, I replied that they foreshadowed the return of the exiles, and that this would happen not after a change of government, but under the existing constitution. And as it happened, my interpretation proved correct.'

Euclid (fl. 290 B.C.)

Thus far the third century authors we have mentioned have been comparatively unfamiliar. But there was one man living in Alexandria during the reign of Ptolemy I whose name is known to all, and whose works—or rather one of his works—have been as widely read as any book in the world save the Bible. The teaching of mathematics to-day has been somewhat altered, but the present writer can remember the time when Euclid and Geometry were nearly synonymous words, and a geometry lesson at school meant simply the writing out of two or three of Euclid's propositions. Euclid—or to give the Greek form of his name, Eucleides—flourished in Alexandria about 290 B.C., and established there a school at which Apollonius of Perga in the next generation was a pupil. Of his life and personality we know scarcely anything, although there are two stories about him which reveal the true scientific spirit. One is that Ptolemy asked him if he could not make his subject easier and he replied ' Sir, there is no royal road to geometry.' The other tells us that when a pupil after a proposition asked him 'What shall I get by learning all this?' Euclid called up a slave and said 'Give this fellow three pence, since he must needs make money by what he learns.' So famous was he in later times that he is usually quoted not by his own name but as Stoicheiotes 'The Elements Man,' while the Arabs invented an etymology from their own language and said that Eucleides is derived from *ucli* a key and *dis* a measure.

Of the *Elements* as literature it is unnecessary here to speak, but those who wish to read Euclid in his original Greek may now conveniently do so in Sir Thomas Heath's excellent little edition of Book I. From the first it was accepted as the authoritative treatise on its subject and quickly superseded all other books, Euclid being especially praised for his definitions, postulates, and axioms, and for his choice of fundamental propositions. Commentaries on it were written by Pappus and Heron in Alexandrian times, and at a much later age by Porphyry and Proclus, while Theon of Alexandria in the fourth century A.D. produced a new edition of the text with some alterations and additions. Boëthius is said to have translated it into Latin and in the eighth century A.D. it passed into Arabia. From the Arabic were made the first medieval translations, those of Athelhard of Bath and Gherard of Cremona in the twelfth century, as also the first printed version, that of Campano issued at Venice in 1482. The Greek text was not printed until 1533, when it appeared under the auspices of Erasmus at Basle.

The *Elements*, although they are the best known, are by no means Euclid's only work. We still possess the *Data*, a collection of propositions meant to be of service in problems of construction; the *Optics*, an elementary treatise on perspective; the *Phænomena*, propositions in spherical astronomy; and the *Sectio*

Canonis, a treatise on music, which, if not by Euclid himself, is based directly on his work. Other books which now are lost include the *Fallacies*, the *Conics*, which were probably superseded by Apollonius, the *Surface-Loci* dealing also with problems of conics, and the *Porisms* of which we have a long account in Pappus. Finally, the book *On Divisions* exists in Arabic but is lost in Greek.

The golden age (285–221 B.C.)

In 285 Ptolemy Soter retired from the throne and contrary to the advice of Demetrius handed over the royal power to his son Ptolemy II Philadelphus. The new ruler naturally looked with no great favour on Demetrius ; indeed he put him under arrest until he could decide what to do with him, and the unfortunate adviser soon afterwards was stung by an asp and conveniently died. But although Demetrius disappeared from the scene, the policy which he had initiated was continued, and even extended, by Ptolemy II and by his successor Ptolemy III Euergetes. For the sixty years of their reigns Alexandria was the world centre of literature and science, Callimachus being recognized as the chief living man of letters, Eratosthenes as the chief scientist. Writers and scientists alike were in close relations with the royal court, and the deification of the Ptolemies, Soter and his wife Berenice, Philadelphus and his wife Arsinoë, gave both poets and astronomers opportunities to display their skill. Conon, for example, discovered in the heavens a group of stars near Ursa Major and declared that they were the lock of hair which Berenice, wife of Euergetes, had cut off on her husband's safe return from Syria. Callimachus, not to be undone, promptly wrote a poem on the subject, adorned with much superfluous learning, in which he makes the lock express its grief in leaving the queen's head even for a place in heaven. Such well-disposed persons as Conon and Callimachus found a considerable benefit in royal patronage ; but writers of a more independent type who ventured on any criticism discovered that an autocrat can be ruthless as well as benevolent. Ptolemy Philadelphus was a man of very indifferent moral character, and when he divorced his first wife to marry Arsinoë, his full sister, who had already been the wife of his half-brother Ptolemy Keraunos, this action offended Greek ideas of decency as much as it does ours. But, as far as we know, only one writer Sotades made any public protest, and he was immediately clapped into prison. He managed to escape but was caught, and then was placed alive in a leaden chest and thrown into the sea. Such was the manner in which Ptolemy discerned between his friends and his enemies.

Lycophron of Chalcis (fl. 280 B.C.)

One of the results of Demetrius' fall was the arrival at Alexandria of Lycophron, whose ancestral enemy Demetrius had been. Lycophron was a pupil of the genial philosopher Menedemus of Eretria, in whose honour he wrote a satyr-play, *Menedemus*, and probably came to Alexandria from the court of Antigonus Gonatas, king of Macedonia. He was given a commission by Ptolemy to arrange the comic poets in the Library, and after doing this wrote his treatise *On Comedy*. He also wrote a number of tragedies, now lost, on the less familiar themes of ancient legend, and finally indulged his taste for the recondite in what is one of the most curious of all poems, the *Alexandra*.

Alexandra is another name for Cassandra, daughter of Priam of Troy, just as Alexander is another name for her brother Paris. The poem in some fifteen hundred iambic lines recounts to Priam by the mouth of a slave Cassandra's prophecies : ' Dawn was just soaring over the steep crag of Phegion on swift Pegasean wings, leaving Tithonus, thy brother by another mother, in his bed by Cerne, and the sailors loosed the calm cables from the grooved rock and cut the land-ward ropes. The centipede fair-faced stork-hued daughters of Phalacra smote maiden-slaying Thetis with their blades, over Calydnæ showing their stern posts like white wings, with sails outspread by the northern blasts of the fiery gale, when Alexandra opened her inspired Bacchic lips on the high Hill of Doom that was founded by the wandering cow.' So the *Alexandra* begins and though an English translation gives but a faint idea of the obscurity of the Greek, it may be obvious that Lycophron is about as difficult to understand as Mallarmé was in his more esoteric moods. The poem was probably written some time after 273, when Ptolemy received an embassy from the Romans who had just defeated Pyrrhus, and the two most interesting prophecies refer to Rome : ' The fame of my ancestors' race shall hereafter be exalted to the highest by their descendants, who shall with their spears win the foremost crown of glory, obtaining the sceptre and monarchy of earth and sea ' (1226), and— ' With the wolf leader of Galadra ' (*i.e.* Pyrrhus) ' my kinsman, ace among wrestlers, after six generations shall join battle by land and sea before he reduce him to terms : and when he has taken the spear-won first fruits of the spoil, his friends ' (*i.e.* Ptolemy) ' shall call him most excellent.'

The Macedonian circle

About the same time that Lycophron came south to Egypt it would seem that some of the Greeks who had been living in Alexandria during the reign of Ptolemy I went northwards again and joined the circle which Antigonus Gonatas (283–239) gathered round him at Pella. Among these returning voyagers were Poseidippus and Alexander, who at Pella met Aratus and Antagoras, former pupils of Menedemus, Timon of Phlius, Hieronymus of Cardia, Bion the Borysthenite, and probably Leonidas of Tarentum. Of these six Antagoras is the author of some beautiful epigrams in the Anthology, and Hieronymus is regarded by some good judges as an historian worthy to rank with Thucydides and Polybius. Unfortunately his *History of Alexander's Successors*, which recounted events wherein he himself played a great part, has now completely perished, and we can only judge of its value by the use that Diodorus and Plutarch made of its material. It is certain, however, that Hieronymus was the greatest, if not the only real, historian in this period.

The two philosophers, Timon of Phlius and Bion of Olbia, roamed from country to country; but Pella seems to have been their headquarters. Timon (320–230 B.C.) was a sceptic, a pupil of Pyrrho, who began life as a professional dancer and after embracing philosophy devoted his spare time to poetry. He wrote epics, tragedies, comedies, an elegiac poem ' *Conceits* ' and three books of *Silloi*, lampoons. This last was his most famous work and in it all the philosophies of the past are put on the rack. The two later books are in the form of a dialogue between Bion and Xenophanes who have very little good to say of anyone except Pyrrho. Epicurus is ' MacUsher, the most uneducated of men ' : Zeno ' a greedy Phœnician old woman with no more sense than a banjo ' : Menedemus ' a puffing, supercilious purveyor of humbug ' : Socrates ' an inventor of subtle arguments, a prater about laws, the enchanter of Greece.' In spite of all this Timon

66

himself seems to have been an attractive man : he was fond of gardening, frequently forgot to have his dinner, and always minded his own business. His well-known lines on the Alexandrians, translated by Sandys, reveal his independent spirit

> ' In the thronging land of Egypt
> There are many that are feeding,
> Many scribblers on papyrus,
> Ever ceaselessly contending
> In the bird-coop of the Muses.'

Bion the Borysthenite was a stronger character and a close friend of Antigonus. When he first appeared at Pella the king asked him in Homer's words : ' Who and whence are you ? What your parents and your city ? ' and received this answer : ' My father was a freed slave who wiped his nose on his sleeve. He had no face ; it was obliterated by the writing which his master's cruelty had put upon it. As for my mother, she was such a woman as such a man would marry : she came from a brothel.' Bion is a figure of great importance in the history of thought, and Eratosthenes said of him that he was the first man to dress Philosophy in a gay frock. But unfortunately his *Diatribes*, conversational lectures, are lost, although we have Horace's testimony to their influence on his own verse :

' Bionæis sermonibus et sale nigro.' (Ep. 2. 260). Two of his sayings may be quoted : ' Renown is the mother of virtue, wealth the sinews of success.' ' A miser has not got money ; money has got him,' and it is thought that Teles, a writer of this period quoted much later by Stobæus, reproduces the substance, at least, of some of his discourses. In one fragment of Teles *On Self-sufficiency* Bion is mentioned by name :

' Wherefore, as Bion says, if things could find a voice and were able to argue with us, would not Poverty say to her detractors : " Why do you quarrel with me ? Do I rob you of any good thing ?

Of temperance ? Of justice ? Of manly courage ? Do you lack anything which is really necessary ? Are not the roads full of herbs and the springs of water ? Do I not give you the whole earth for a bed and leaves for a mattress ? Can you not be merry in my company ? Have you not seen old women singing blithely as they munched their barley bread ? Do I not provide you with hunger as a cheap and inexpensive sauce ? Does not the hungry man enjoy his food more and need a sauce less than anyone ? Is any one hungry for cake or thirsty for Chian wine ? Do not men only crave for such things in wantonness ? Do I not offer you lodgings free of charge, the public baths in winter and the temples in summer ? " '

Leonidas of Tarentum (fl. 280 B.C.)

Timon and Bion were both vagrants : Leonidas is an even better example of a type not uncommon in the third century, the man without a country and without a home. He was born at Tarentum about 325 B.C., and his youth coincided with the first awakening of the Greek cities in Italy to the danger which threatened them from Rome and their first attempts to seek protection from the warlike kings of Epirus. To one of these kings, Neoptolemus, Leonidas himself went, and for him wrote what is probably the earliest of his hundred epigrams now preserved in the Anthology.

> ' Ye caves and thou most sacred hill
>   Where nymphs with white limbs gleam,
> Ye rocks that front the babbling rill
>   And pine trees by the stream.
>
> Thou, too, great Hermes, Maia's child,
>   Four-squared our flocks to guard,
> And Pan who from the cliff peaks wild
>   The pasturing goats dost ward.
>
> Accept ye all these gifts of mine
> This barley cake, this cup of wine.'

Anthologia Palatina vi. 334.

Neoptolemus was not destined to render much assistance to his harassed countryman, for in 295 B.C. he was murdered by a more energetic ruler, that genial ruffian, his cousin, Pyrrhus. But the new king took up with enthusiasm the rôle of champion of the Greeks against the barbarians, and Leonidas returned to Italy to stimulate the wavering courage of the Tarentines and to prepare the way for open hostilities against Rome. We still possess the two dedications he wrote to celebrate the capture of arms from the Lucanians, arms which were offered as a trophy in the temple of Pallas Athene, and in 281 he was doubtless one of the leaders of the democratic war party who took the decisive step of inviting Pyrrhus to bring his army overseas.

As it happened, neither the martial spirit of Pyrrhus nor the poetical fervour of Leonidas availed to check the progress of the Roman broadsword, and when Pyrrhus withdrew from Italy in despair, Leonidas returned with him to North Greece to celebrate in verse a minor triumph which the Epirot won over the Galatian mercenaries of King Antigonus in 274 B.C. Tarentum meanwhile had been occupied by a Roman garrison, and two years later a street brawl in Argos and a tile thrown from the roof by a woman's hand put an end to the ambitions of Pyrrhus, so that Leonidas was left without a country and without a protector. From that time onward he seems to have lived as a vagrant, roaming up and down the Greek lands of the Eastern Mediterranean, from island to island and from shore to shore. Like Homer before him, he was poor and a wanderer, a sort of scholar gipsy, and it was probably because he had forfeited his Tarentine citizenship that Crete gave him her own franchise. In Crete he evidently lived for some time ; many Cretans gave him employment, and he is one of the few Greek poets who write of that peculiar race in anything save uncomplimentary terms.

In his wanderings Leonidas probably went to Pella and he was certainly at Cos about 280 B.C. By a lucky chance we have even a picture of him in the seventh idyll of Theocritus :

> ' We had not yet reached the midpoint of the way, nor was the tomb of Brasilas yet risen upon our sight, when—thanks be to the Muses—we met a certain wayfarer, the best of men, a Cydonian. Lycidas was his name, a goatherd was he, nor could any that saw him have taken him for other than he was, for all about him bespoke the goatherd. Stripped from the roughest of he-goats was the tawny skin he wore on his shoulders, the smell of rennet was clinging to it still, and about his breast an old cloak was buckled with a plaited belt, and in his right hand he carried a crooked staff of wild olive ; and quietly he accosted me, with a smile, a twinkling eye, and a laugh still on his lips—" Simichidas, whither, pray, through the noon dost thou trail thy feet, when even the very lizard on the rough stone wall is sleeping, and the crested larks no longer fare afield ? Art thou hastening to a feast, a bidden guest, or art thou for treading a townsman's winepress ? For such is thy speed that every stone upon the way spins singing from thy boots ! " '

> (Theocritus VII. 10–26. Lang's translation.)

This Lycidas is obviously no figure of imagination. He is a real man drawn from life and every detail reminds us of Leonidas as he reveals himself to us in his poems. The old cloak, the crooked stick, the twinkling eye—in such guise we may be sure Leonidas trudged the country roads and gained that intimate acquaintance with the actual life of working folk that gives his epigrams their peculiar savour. Nowhere in Greek literature—except perhaps in the ' Fishermen Idyll ' of Theocritus, a poem which itself is very possibly by Leonidas—do we get such a clear picture of the existence of the humble sailors and fishermen who then, as now, formed the majority of the coast-land people. The poems are profoundly real : there is no straining after sentiment, no exaggeration of misery. The life they describe is one of constant manual work, but it is work performed contentedly and with some amount of pleasure, work for oneself and not for a master, in which machinery has no part. In the background there is always the sea and the fresh countryside, and with the country those divine presences on whose favour prosperity depends, Pan the hidden helper in the hunt, the trusty guardian of the flocks, the Nymphs who give water and shade to a thirsty land, and above all kindly Hermes the luck bringer.

> ' Some gather herbs upon the hillside steep,
>   And some their goats, great Hermes, here do keep
>   On fennel and on rue.
>   To gatherer and to goatherd be thou kind,
>   And then in pail and basket thou shalt find
>   The share that is thy due.

A. P. ix. 318.

As the Athenian vase painter stands to Polygnotus and Apelles, so stands Leonidas to poets of the study like Philetas and Callimachus. He works close to life and is a craftsman first and foremost, with words for tools, his trade being to write epitaphs and dedications for country folk. Sometimes those who employ him are women. Bitto, Antianira and Bitie bring a piece of tapestry to Artemis and he commemorates the gift. The four industrious daughters of Lycomedes present their weaving gear to Athena and he draws up the catalogue. A mother vows her son's picture, ' poorly painted indeed,' to Bacchus. Melo and Satyra, the flute girls, ' now advanced in years,' dedicate flute and pipe to the Muses. Ambrosia and Atthis, in gratitude for safe delivery, offer to Aphrodite their hairbands and robes, their smocks and tasselled zones. Calliclea, equally fortunate, pays as her vow a silver image of

Eros, her anklet and bronze mirror, her purple hair-ribbon and blue bosom-band, and ' the broad boxwood comb that gathered in her locks.' Occasionally even the commission is to record a gift of children's toys such as little Philocles makes :

> ' This noiseless ball and top so round,
> This rattle with its lively sound,
> These bones with which he loved to play,
> Companions of his childhood's day,
> To Hermes, if the god they please,
> An offering from Philocles.'

A. P. vi. 309.

Leonidas wrote for poor people and earned only a bare subsistence from his art. In one grimly humorous poem he addresses the mice that haunt his meal tub, and warns them that he has only one lump of salt and two barley cakes for his own needs. In another piece he inveighs fiercely against gluttony and greed, and in a third describes a wardrobe which might well be his own : a wallet, a rough goatskin, a dirty oil flask, a purse without a copper in it, a felt hat, and a walking stick. His existence seems to have been as simple as that of Whitman and Thoreau, and like our own Mr. W. H. Davies, he can describe the life of the vagrant from intimate experience:

> ' I tramp the roads and wander far,
> Yet know not want and know not care.
> Flat stones for kneading trough I take,
> And make myself an oaten cake.
> Some mint or thyme serves me for meat,
> Or lump of rock-salt bitter-sweet ;
> And o'er my head a well-thatched barn
> With fire of sticks to keep me warm.'

A. P. vii. 736.

Yet even if he lived in poverty he was not unhappy ; and in one of his finest poems, beautifully translated by Mr. Edwyn Bevan, he expresses his Stoic philosophy :

' Measureless time or ever, thy years, O man, were reckon'd ;
   Measureless time shall run over thee, low in the ground ;
And thy life between is—what ?   The flick of a flying second,
   A flash, a point—or less, if a lesser thing can be found.

Poor little life !—not even, so fugitive, fill'd with pleasure !
   Hateful is death, but life hath a bitterer taste of tears.
Behold the groundwork of bones !   Exactly drawn to that measure,
   Do ye exalt your brows, O men, to the cloudy spheres ?

Nay, my friend, what use ?   The tissue wherewith thou art clothèd,
   See at its end the worm, in the rag of the weftage undone,
Like a slough'd skin, like a skeleton leaf, more loathèd
   Far than some dusty web which an old dead spider spun.

Study, morning by morning, O man, how much thy strength is ;
   So find rest : be a life plain, without pride, thy law :
All thy days upon earth, how long soever their length is,
   Ponder of what thou art made, that thou art but a man of straw.'

A. P. vii. 472.

Aratus of Soli (315–c. 235 B.C.)

Of all the Macedonian writers Aratus was the most
highly honoured in his lifetime and the most widely
read after his death : he is also of them all the dullest
and the least attractive.   Aratus was born at Soli in
Cilicia and studied at Athens under Zeno and at
Eretria under Menedemus.   Zeno probably recommended him to Antigonus Gonatas, and in 276 when
Antigonus had defeated the Gauls and was celebrating
his marriage with Phila, daughter of Seleucus Nicator,
Aratus went to Pella and established himself as court
laureate by writing two hymns, one an epithalamium,
the other addressed to Pan as having inspired the Gauls
with the panic fear which gave Antigonus his victory.
Apparently it was in the next year at the instigation
of Antigonus that he wrote the *Phænomena*, the poem
which made him famous and is the only one of his
works surviving.   In 274 the circle at Pella was broken

up by the invasion of Pyrrhus, and Aratus, who was a man of peace, took refuge in Asia with Antiochus I. At his court he completed an edition of the Odyssey, and probably visited Alexandria before he returned to Pella, where he died some years before his royal patron.

The *Phænomena* is a hexameter poem of 1154 lines, the first 732 being a popular exposition of astronomy based upon the prose work of Eudoxus (390–337 B.C.) ; the last 422, sometimes separately quoted as *Diosemeia*, an equally popular account of the signs of the weather. Both as poetry and as science it is negligible, but as a practical handbook easily committed to memory it was in its day of considerable value : sailors found the information in its first part useful, farmers were catered for in the second. It was its practical character perhaps that so commended it to the Romans, and led both Varro and Cicero to translate it into Latin. Virgil also, of course, followed Aratus closely in some parts of the Georgics, and it is interesting to compare such a passage as Georgics I, 356–382 with the corresponding lines in the *Phænomena*, 909–941, and to notice how Virgil transfigures his original.

As a didactic poem the *Phænomena* canot compare with the *Georgics* or the *De Rerum Natura* ; but it is only right to say that it has qualities which are rare in Alexandrian poetry. It is neither pedantic nor obscure, and it is written not to display its author's learning, but to vindicate the Stoic doctrine that God is ever mindful of His children. Its exordium, based on Cleanthes and quoted by St Paul, puts this clearly :

'From Zeus let us begin ; him we mortals never leave unnamed. Full of Zeus are all the streets and all the markets of men ; full is the sea and its havens ; at every season we all have need of Zeus. His offspring also are we ; and in kindness he gives favourable signs to men and rouses folk to work, reminding them of livelihood. He tells us when the soil is best for oxen and for mattock, he tells us when the seasons are favourable for the planting of trees and the sowing of seeds. With his own hand he set the signs in heaven, and marked out the constellations, and in the year devised which stars especially should give to men sure signs of the seasons, that all things might grow and fail not.'

Alexandrian prose

In Alexandria during the third century B.C., prose literature was produced in abundance, although very little of it has survived. It was prose of a utilitarian sort, and moreover much of it was vitiated by two defects. One was the Peripatetic idea that a book need be nothing but a compilation of facts put baldly down ; the other, going to the opposite extreme, considered that narrative was only an excuse for the introduction of tasteless and elaborate rhetoric. It was right that it should be allowed to perish, and if we except the scientists and the Greek Apocrypha, only three prose authors, Satyrus, Phylarchus, and Hegesias require mention here.

Satyrus and the biographers

Autobiography in this period is rare, the *Memoirs* of Aratus of Sicyon, now lost but used by Plutarch, being perhaps the only example. Biography on the other hand was very popular and we know the names of a long line of writers, Aristoxenus, Chamæleon, Hegesander, Hermippus, Sotion and many others. Their books were meant to be light reading and they have shared the fate of most ephemeral literature ; but, as chance would have it, one specimen of the class has come to us in the *Life of Euripides* by Satyrus, discovered in 1911 and first published by Dr Hunt in Oxyrhynchus Papyri, vol. ix. The Life, strangely enough, is in the form of a dialogue, and of the three speakers one certainly, and another possibly, is a woman ; the third character is a man, who answers the questions put by his companions and calls them to order when they show signs of wandering from the subject. The scene of the dialogue is apparently the *salon* of Eucleia, one of the ladies, the language is easy and correct Greek, and the whole tone of the conversation is graceful and in good taste. It is unfortunate that the papyrus is sadly mutilated in many places.

Antigonus of Carystus (fl. 250 B.C.)

Satyrus wrote mainly to amuse his readers : Antigonus was a man of much greater talent and the loss of his *History of Art* and *Lives of Philosophers* is greatly to be regretted. Born at Carystus in Eubœa about 290 B.C., Antigonus was in his youth a pupil of Menedemus of Eretria, but abandoned philosophy to study and to practise the sculptor's art at Athens. When Attalus I of Pergamum, after his victory over the Gauls in 239, began to make his capital a rival to Alexandria as a centre of art and literature, Antigonus was one of the men whom he invited, and it is quite possible that some of the well-known groups of Pergamene sculpture are by Antigonus' hand. In any case, his *History of Art* was the work of a professional with expert knowledge, and it is most unfortunate that the only traces of it which remain are the scraps of miscellaneous information extracted from it by Pliny the Elder in his *Natural History*. Equally lamentable is the disappearance of the *Lives of Philosophers* which supplied Diogenes Laertius with most of the more lively passages in his book. Fortunately, however, Athenæus gives us one quotation from it which enables us partly to realize the vividness of its style.[1] Antigonus is describing the simple manner of Menedemus' life :

[1] Athenæus. Deipnosophists. 419 E.

' He used to share a light meal at home with one or two friends : the rest of the company had had their dinner before they arrived, for with Menedemus lunch took the place of dinner. Later on they called in the guests, some of whom, it appears, coming before time, would do sentry duty outside the front door and ask the slaves as they came out what course was on and how much longer they had to wait before the meal was over. If they were told it was vegetables or dried fish, they would go back ; but when they heard it was a bit of meat, they would enter the room which had been arranged for the occasion. In summer a mat was provided for each couch, in winter a sheepskin ; but each guest had to bring his own cushion. The loving-cup that went round held no more than half a pint, the dessert was usually a lupine or a bean, though sometimes a seasonable fruit was brought in—in summer a pear or a pomegranate, in spring dried peas, in winter-time dried figs.'

Of the *Collection of Marvels* attributed to Antigonus it suffices to say that it is by another and very inferior author of the same name.

Phylarchus of Naucratis (fl. 230 B.C.)

History did not flourish to the same extent as biography, and as we have already dealt with Timæus, whose long life extended into this period, Phylarchus is the only other historian who remains to be considered. His history in twenty-eight books embraced the period from the accession of Pyrrhus in 290 to the death of Ptolemy III in 221, and although he is accused of partiality by Polybius, his vivid account of Agis and Cleomenes of Sparta was of great use to Plutarch. Like all his contemporaries he was very fond of anecdote, and Thucydides would have frowned at some of his tales. Here is one :

' There was once a female elephant called Nicæa ; and to her the wife of the King of India, when dying, entrusted her child then just a month old. After her death the affection for the child displayed by the animal was most wonderful : it could not endure the baby to be out of its sight, and whenever it was away it was out of spirits. Therefore, when the nurse gave the child its milk, she placed it in

77

its cradle between the beast's feet; and if she did not do so the elephant refused its food. When the child was sleeping it would keep off the flies with a bundle of grass; and if it cried it would rock the cradle with its trunk and lull it to rest.'

Of somewhat greater historical value is his account of the people of Sybaris : how they exempted from all taxes the makers of purple dye and the sellers and catchers of eels ; how cooks who invented a new dish had the sole rights to sell it for a year ; how their men were not allowed to wear robes more ornate than the usual unless they meant to confess to profligate living, and their women might not walk abroad in the evening unless they were going to commit adultery. Somewhat similar to this is his description of the Byzantines, ' who are so exceedingly fond of wine that they live for choice in the wine shops, and let out their own houses and their wives also to strangers, and they cannot endure to hear the sound of a trumpet even in their sleep.'

From Phylarchus too comes the well-known story of Ptolemy Philadelphus :

' Ptolemy, king of Egypt, the most admirable of all princes, and the most learned and accomplished of men, was so besotted by his immoderate luxury that he fancied he would live for ever and declared that he had discovered how to become immortal. But once, when he had been suffering for many days with the gout and was a little better, he saw some Egyptians lying at their ease in the sand by the river and lunching on whatever it might be they had ; and then he cried " O wretched man that I am ! Why am I not one of those ? " '

Hegesias of Magnesia (fl. 250 B.C.)

The corrupting influence of the Asianic style of rhetoric has been mentioned, and the culprit to whom the origin of this style is usually attributed is Hegesias, an orator, an historian, and a teacher of rhetoric who lived about the middle of the third century. The term ' Asianic,' however, as commonly used covers two quite different perversions, and it is only for one of these that Hegesias is responsible. The most popular kind of Asianism was the bombastic and flamboyant oratory which Cicero found cultivated everywhere in Asia Minor, and of which we have an example in the curious inscription of Antiochus of Commagene written in the first century B.C. This was not the manner that Hegesias and his followers used, but one of a more subtle and epigrammatic sort. Abandoning the long periods of Demosthenes as involving too great a strain on his audience, Hegesias substituted short sentences, simple in their structure and depending for their effect on antithesis, metaphor, and play on words. He stands to Demosthenes as Seneca stands to Livy, and Macaulay to Gibbon, and ancient critics strongly disapproved his staccato style. Cicero says of him ' saltat incidens particulas' ' he cuts his stuff up into short jumpy phrases,' and Dionysius is never tired of reviling him for such inversions of natural order as ' After a good feast a good one we celebrate and another one,' ' From Magnesia am I the glorious a man of Sipylus.' ' No small amount into thy water of Thebes did Dionysus spit : it is indeed sweet but it makes men mad.' One passage from Hegesias' *Life of Alexander,* describing an attempt to murder him by a man called Bætis, is quoted by Dionysius at length,[1] and a translation of some sentences may give a faint idea of his manner :

' As for Bætis himself, Leonatus and Philotas brought him up still alive. And Alexander seeing that he was very fleshy and big and most grim (for he was black even in colour) detested both the deed which he had planned and also his looks, and ordered his men to pass a bronze ring through his feet and drag him round naked. In pain, pounded by the many roughnesses of the ground, he began to scream. And it was just what I am now saying that brought

[1] Dionysius. De compositione verborum, Ch. xviii.

people together. His agony racked him and he kept on uttering outlandish cries, asking " master " for mercy. And the solecism made them laugh. His fat and the bulge of his flesh suggested another sort of animal, a huge Babylonian beast. So the crowd mocked him, insulting with military insolence an enemy repulsive in feature and uncouth in his ways.'

The scientists

Most of the Alexandrian prose which has survived deals with science in its various branches. In medicine we have Herophilus the anatomist and Erasistratus the physiologist, who both came to Egypt from Asia Minor about 260. Their works are lost, but frequent references are made to them by Galen and Celsus. In astronomy there is Conon (fl. 240) a native of S. Italy, who dedicated his seven books on the science to Ptolemy Euergetes, and a greater than Conon in Aristarchus of Samos (fl. 250). The extant treatise of Aristarchus *On the sizes and distances of the sun and moon* is written from the geocentric standpoint, but we know that he also anticipated Copernicus by suggesting that the earth as well as the planets revolves round the sun, and that he thereby incurred from Cleanthes the charge of impiety, inasmuch as he put the Hearth of the Universe in motion. To mathematics we can assign Apollonius of Perga (fl. 235), author of the *Conics*, now surviving in four books in Greek and three in an Arabic translation, and with him one of the most original of all thinkers, Archimedes.

Archimedes of Syracuse (287–212 B.C.)

Archimedes was born at Syracuse and was killed there, when his native town was taken in 212, by a Roman soldier whom he brusquely told to stand away from his diagrams. The use of pulleys in drawing weights, the employment of the screw in pumping water, and the various mechanical devices which he invented during the siege of Syracuse are proofs of his practical capacity ; and it was he who said ' Give me a place to stand on and I will move the earth.' But his real interest was in pure mathematics, and he regarded as his greatest triumph the discovery of the ratio 3 : 2 which the cylinder bears to the sphere. His complete works seem to have been extant in the fourth century A.D., but we now only have *On Plane Equilibriums, On the Sphere and Cylinder, Spirals, Conoids, Floating Bodies, Measurement of a Circle, Quadrature of the Parabola*, the *Sand Reckoner*, and the *Method*.

Eratosthenes of Cyrene (276–195 B.C.)

To Eratosthenes the *Method* was dedicated, and to Eratosthenes, perhaps the most typical of all the Alexandrians, we may now turn. His published works embrace poetry, philosophy, philology, chronology, geography, astronomy, and mathematics ; and accordingly he was known to the specialists of the Museum as ' Beta,' next after the first in all subjects. The nickname was possibly due to professional jealousy but it has some justification. Eratosthenes in poetry was second to Callimachus, in philosophy second to Chrysippus, in astronomy second to Aristarchus, in mathematics second to Archimedes, and in scholarship second to Zenodotus. On the other hand, in chronology and in geography he holds indisputably the first place.

We know the names of three of his poems, the *Anterinys* telling the tale of Hesiod's murder, the *Erigone* which is concerned with the origin of the vine, and the *Hermes* in which comes the story of the Milky Way. From the *Hermes* comes our longest fragment, seventeen hexameters on the five Zones. This passage is followed closely by Virgil in Georgics, I, 233 sq., but

F
81

Virgil turns it into poetry by the addition of two lines :

> ' has inter mediamque, duæ mortalibus ægris
> Munere concessæ divom.'

In scholarship Eratosthenes' chief book was a treatise *On the Old Comedy*, and he wrote a number of philosophic dialogues. But, as we have said, it is on his work in chronology and geography that his real fame depends.

The *Chronographicae*, in nine books, started with the capture of Troy, which is dated 1184 B.C., and went down to the death of Alexander in 323 B.C. Eratosthenes considered that history proper begins in 776 with the first Olympiad, and that all events before that time belong to the age of myth. For the earlier periods of history he followed the lists of the Spartan kings, for the later he used the system, introduced by Timæus, of reckoning by Olympiads ; and he had also examined the Egyptian records. His book is only known to us now by very small fragments, but even in them we see traces of a definitely critical method : *i.e.* he infers that Homer is earlier than Hesiod from the difference in their geographical outlook, and he points out that Homer, who knows nothing of the Panionia, must have preceded the Ionian migrations.

Even more important than his Chronology was his work in geography, and especially in geography regarded as a science. His two chief books were the treatise *On the Mensuration of the Earth* in which he calculated the earth's circumference as about 28,000 miles, and the *Geographica*, arranged in three parts. In the first part he reviewed the systems of his predecessors, and as regards Homer's geography remarked : ' To find the route followed by Odysseus you must first find the cobbler who sewed up the bag of the winds for Æolus.' In the second part he explained his views on the size of the earth and its shape, which he considered to be spherical, and also on the nature and extent of the ocean. Finally, in the third part he gave a geographical description of the world of his day, with a map in which the inhabited globe was divided into north and south by a line running from the south of Spain to the middle of Asia.

The greatness of Eratosthenes as a scholar and man of science is undoubted : his greatness as a writer is much more open to question. We have the negative evidence that none of his prose works were thought worth transcribing by the Byzantine copyists. There is the further fact that although his opinions are freely quoted by Strabo, Pliny, and Arrian, little attempt is made to give his actual words. Thirdly—and this is more important—the one long piece of his writing which we possess is a rather disconcerting medley and hardly makes us wish for more. It is in the form of a letter to Ptolemy Euergetes, preserved for us by Eutokios, describing the mathematical instrument called a mesolabe, and begins thus :

> ' They tell us that one of the old tragedians introduced Minos as preparing a tomb for Glaucus ; and when he heard that the tomb was one of four sides, each a hundred feet long, he said :
>
> > " Small is your measure for a royal tomb.
> > Let it be twice the size, but do not fail
> > To keep the due proportion when each side
> > Has twice the length which now it doth extend." '

Eratosthenes then points out the tragedian's mistake and gives a long account of his instrument, bursting into poetry once more at the end with a frigid panegyric on his royal patron.

The Septuagint and the Apocrypha

Before we pass from the prose writers to the poets a brief account must be given of a body of literature which was written in Greek, or at least translated into that language, during the third century and therefore belongs to this chapter. The Jews from the time of Alexander had always enjoyed special privileges in Egypt ; the Ptolemies recognized their financial ability, and they received many marks of royal favour. Among others, if the tradition be true, Ptolemy Philadelphus, wishing to draw still closer the ties between Greek and Hebrew, sent to Eleazar, high priest at Jerusalem, and asked him to despatch some competent scholars to translate the Old Testament into Greek. Eleazar chose seventy-two men, six from each of the twelve tribes, who, arriving in Alexandria, completed their task in seventy-two days : hence the name Septuagint. Such is the account given in the letter of Aristeas, a document of some fifty printed pages, ostensibly written by a Greek in Ptolemy's service to his brother, which may be read in Swete's *Introduction to the Old Testament in Greek*. The details must be taken with several grains of salt, but the fact remains that a translation of the Pentateuch into Greek was certainly made at Alexandria in the early third century and the other books of the Old Testament followed later.

The Septuagint for the most part is a translation, but it also contains some books not in our canon which were originally written in Greek. One of them is the *Wisdom of Solomon*, warning Hellenistic Jews against the influence of idolatry, a book than which, as Bishop Westcott says, 'no existing work represents more completely the style of composition which would be produced by the sophistic school of rhetoric' as it existed in Alexandria. Another Greek book is Maccabees in its second, third, and fourth sections, the second very uneven and broken in style, the third loaded with rhetorical ornament, the fourth a really fine piece of descriptive writing. These two books certainly never existed in Hebrew : more doubtful is the *Song of the Three Children*, an addition to Daniel, with its invocation to nature : ' O all ye winds, ye dews and storms of snow, ye seas and rivers, ye whales that move in the water, ye holy and humble men of heart ; bless ye the Lord, praise and exalt him above all for ever.'

Alexandrian poetry

Alexandrian poetry is in a very different position from Alexandrian prose. Its four chief exponents, Aratus, Callimachus, Apollonius and Theocritus, are well represented by surviving works, and moreover they exercised an influence on Roman poetry which it is difficult to overestimate. They themselves perceived that Athenian literature was so essentially the product of a particular time and place that imitation was useless, and they turned for their models to the early Ionians, Homer, Hesiod, Mimnermus, and Hipponax. But they did not follow slavishly, and created two new forms which were destined to have a very long life. One was the epigram, developed from an inscription piece into a short poem expressing one simple emotion, especially the emotion of love. The other was the extension of the elegiac couplet from mournful themes to the purpose of narrative of any kind.

Callimachus of Cyrene (fl. 270 B.C.)

Literary comparisons whether they be of persons or of periods, are proverbially dangerous, and often seem to obscure rather than illumine the truth. But because they are dangerous they are attractive, and it is tempting to set side by side the chief figures of the Alexandrian and the Elizabethan periods. Shakespeare, of course, must be taken out of the account ; for to the Alexandrians he would have seemed frankly incredible. It will be convenient also to include among the Alexandrians those Syrians, Meleager and his contemporaries, who passed on their traditions to Rome, and to extend the Elizabethan age over the reigns of the early Stuarts until the time when the Puritan and the Whig Revolutions between them brought an end to merry England. Then it will be found that similar conditions produced in Egypt and our own country a series of poets who may without too much straining be put in parallel columns.

Under the Ptolemies as under Elizabeth there was a surprising activity in theatrical production, and the Alexandrian ' Pleiad,' the seven brightest stars in a galaxy of dramatic authors, enjoyed a prodigious vogue. The tragedies of Philiscus, Homerus, Alexander, Lycophron, Sositheus, Aeantides, and Euphronius have now, fortunately or unfortunately, perished ; but if we can trust their contemporary reputation they were probably of much the same degree of merit as Kyd and Greene and Heywood and Peele and Webster and Tourneur and Ford. In other words, if their works had been preserved they would have a certain archæological interest ; but looking at it from the standpoint of pure literature their loss is no very grievous misfortune. The same fact holds with the lighter forms of drama as practised among the Greeks by Sotades, Rhinthon, and Herodes, and among our people by Dekker, Marston, and Nash : they all have certain qualities of gross humour, but when compared with a truly comic genius such as Aristophanes they are negligible.

To turn now to other forms of literature. The epic poem that Rhianus composed on the early Messenian Wars can be matched by Daniel's *Civil Wars* and Drayton's *Polyolbion*. Timon of Phlius, the satirist of the *Silloi*, finds his analogy in Bishop Hall the author of *Virgidemiarum* and Samuel Butler the author of

86

Hudibras. Aratus, whose weakness it was to try and combine poetry with exact science, is not unlike George Chapman. Lycophron the obscure is nearly equalled by Abraham Cowley, and as for Philodemus, most of his witty and wanton pieces might well have been written by any of the Restoration poets, Suckling, Lovelace, Sedley, or Rochester.

Among the greater names, Theocritus, that superb dilettante who turned the epic into an idyll and invented the pastoral poem, has at least a worthy follower in the Edmund Spenser of *The Shepherd's Calendar* and the *Faery Queen*. The ill-fortune of Apollonius of Rhodes, a romantic born out of due season, is repeated again in the unhappy life of Kit Marlowe. Herrick, the old pagan priest, might be a reincarnation of Meleager, and both alike can say :

> ' I sing of books, of blossoms, buds, and bowers,
>   Of April, May, of June, and July flowers :
>   I sing of may-poles, hock-carts, wassails, wakes,
>   Of bridegrooms, brides, and of their bridal cakes.
>   I write of Youth, of Love.'

Lastly, dominating their whole periods by force of personality, it appears, rather than by actual achievement, but both possessed of a rare combination of critical and creative talent, come Callimachus and Ben Jonson.

Jonson was a bricklayer's son and worked with his father before he won success as a dramatist and became court poet to James I. Callimachus followed an equally humble and an equally useful trade, until by a lucky chance he attracted the notice of Ptolemy Philadelphus and rose to a high position on the staff of the Alexandrian Library. Both men in their later life held a place of undisputed supremacy in literature, but neither of them could forget their early struggles, and, as happens so often with people who have risen in this fashion, even prosperity did not make them genial. In most of their work there is a flavour of bitterness, a frown of conscious arrogance, a harsh note of intolerant criticism : they are not happy men ; for they have lost, if they ever possessed, the faculty of careless enjoyment. But though they were not happy, they were both essentially men of society, the centre of gatherings that combined conviviality with literature. Callimachus in the great library at Alexandria was surrounded by poets proud to call themselves his pupils, to whom he dispensed the doubtful blessings of Ptolemy's munificence. Jonson held a position less official but equally commanding, and at the Mermaid and the Apollo presided royally over the gatherings of his ' sons, sealed of the Tribe of Ben.' And being despots each was faced by at least one rebellion. Jonson had the playwrights' quarrel of 1599–1602 with Dekker and Marston as his opponents, Callimachus had the revolt of the romantics under Apollonius.

The bare facts of Callimachus' life are given us by Suidas :

'Callimachus, son of Battus and Mesatma, of Cyrene, grammarian, pupil of Hermocrates of Iasos, the grammarian, married the daughter of Euphrates of Syracuse. His sister's son was Callimachus the younger, who wrote an epic " On Islands." So diligent was he that he wrote poems in every metre and also wrote a great number of works in prose. The books written by him amount in all to more than eight hundred. He lived in the times of Ptolemy Philadelphus. Before his introduction to that king he taught grammar in Eleusis, a hamlet of Alexandria. He survived to the time of Ptolemy, surnamed Euergetes.'

To this a few dates may be added. He was born about 310 B.C., studied under Praxiphanes the Peripatetic philosopher 287–281, opened his school at Alexandria 280, gained the notice of Ptolemy Philadelphus 276, died in the reign of Ptolemy Euergetes 235 B.C.

It has generally been inferred from the notice in Suidas that Callimachus was a member of the old and opulent family, the Battiadae, descendants of the famous stammerer who was guided by the oracle of Delphi to the silphium fields of Cyrene. According to one of the poet's own epigrams (A.P. vii. 525) his grandfather Callimachus held high office in Cyrene as general of the city forces : and at first sight there seems no more to be said. But against this presumption of Callimachus' distinguished origin there is one rather strong piece of negative evidence. As Suidas tells us, and as we know from other sources, Callimachus during the early years of his manhood kept an elementary school in a suburb of Alexandria, and the profession of schoolmaster, noble as it is, seems one that is seldom followed by men of rank and wealth. It is possible of course that his father Battus was banished from Cyrene in some faction quarrel and lost his ancestral fortune, so that the son had to make his own way in the world. But it is possible also that his father was a man of no importance and that the name ' Battiades ' by which the poet is so often known, with its suggestions of the heroic past, is itself only a reminiscence of the school-room, a glorified nickname invented by Callimachus for himself as he invented the name Simichidas for Theocritus, Astacides and Lycidas for Leonidas, Sicelidas for Asclepiades, and Tityrus for Alexander of Ætolia.

Some twelve hundred years after his death it seems that there still existed a collection of Callimachus' poems consisting of the six *Hymns*, the *Aitia*, the *Ibis*, and a poem on Athene. Of these until lately we only possessed the *Hymns* ; but since 1893 Egypt has given us substantial portions of the *Aitia*, the *Hecale*, and the *Iambi*, so that we are in a much better position than we were once to judge the range of Callimachus' achievement. The most important of the new fragments belong to the four books of the *Aitia* 'Causes,' a poem dealing with the local legends of Greece in which for the first time Callimachus used the elegiac metre for the purpose of narrative. One of these fragments contains the conclusion of what was perhaps the most famous single incident in the *Aitia*, the story of Acontius and Cydippe, known to us hitherto only in the prose paraphrase of Aristænetus. It gives us an invaluable clue to Callimachus' method, for from it we see that the story for him was not a love romance but merely a curious local tale. Another fragment of some thirty lines is a vivid description of a feast at the house of Pollis, an Athenian living in Alexandria, 'where talk is put into the cups to relieve the tedium of drinking.' A third, first published in 1927, refers to the quarrel with Apollonius, that heretic and his followers being contemptuously called 'Telchines,' the name given to the barbarians who in early times inhabited Rhodes.

The *Hecale*, it is said, was written in answer to those detractors who declared that Callimachus could not write a long hexameter poem. It was considered one of the best examples of his skill as a story teller, and relates how Theseus on his way to kill the bull of Marathon was entertained by the poor old woman from whom the piece takes its title. Of this we now have forty lines, published by Gomperz in 1893, ending thus :

> 'Not long did they sleep, for soon there came a neighbour all white with hoar frost : " Up, no longer do thieves' hands seek their prey ; by this time the lamps of morn are shining. The water drawer, I ween, is singing the Song of the Pump, and the creaking waggon axle wakes the dweller by the high road, and many a deafened smithy slave torments the ear with his din." '

In the *Iambi*, written in choliambi, we see Calli-machus as the most ingenious of all the followers of Hipponax. The Ionian is brought up from Hades and in one fragment he tells the story of the cup which Bathycles bequeathed to the best of the Seven Sages. Another fragment of one hundred lines relates the contest between the Laurel and the Olive, the following being part of the Olive's speech :

> ' Who made the Laurel ? The earth and sun, like any other tree. Who made the olive ? Pallas, when she contended for Acte against the seaweed dweller, and the snake-legged ancient judged between them. That is one fall for the laurel. What is the laurel's fruit ? For what shall I use it ? Eat it not, nor drink it, nor anoint thyself therewith. But the olive's has many uses. . . . A second fall I score against the laurel. Whose is the leafage that suppliants extend ? The olive's. For the third time the laurel is down.'

Of the six *Hymns* the first four, nominally addressed to Zeus, Apollo, Artemis, and Delos, are rather frigid specimens of court poetry, where the figure of the royal patron is continually reappearing amid the mass of legends, historical allusions, and geographical facts with which the poems are encumbered. The sixth, *The Hymn to Demeter*, written like the other four in hexa-meters but in the Dorian dialect, is more vigorous, but the most entertaining by far of the collection is the one elegiac poem *The Bath of Pallas*. Here Callimachus gives us a really lively and vigorous piece of narrative as even a rough translation of the first lines may show :

> ' Come forth, come forth, ye virgin crowd,
>   You who as helpers Pallas hath :
> I hear the noise of panting loud,
>   Our queen is ready for the bath.
> But ere she lave each dusty steed
> Her own stout arms she will not heed.

> Though all her gear was spotted o'er
>   She of her horses first did think
> Nor recked at all the Giants' gore,
>   But standing on far Ocean's brink
> Cleansed the sweat drops that on them lay
> And washed the clotted foam away.
>
> Come forth ! ye maids of Greece appear
>   Nor wait for myrrh and alabaster ;
> The noise of whirring wheels I hear,
>   Faster they come and ever faster.
> Bring her no jars of perfume blent ;
> Athene loves nor myrrh nor scent.

But it is in the sixty epigrams preserved in the Palatine Anthology that Callimachus reveals himself best. There are the lines to Heraclitus, author of *Nightingales*, well known in Cory's translation :

> ' They told me, Heraclitus, they told me you were dead,
> They brought me bitter news to hear and bitter tears to shed.
> I wept as I remembered how often you and I
> Had tired the sun with talking and sent him down the sky.
>
> And now that thou art lying, my dear old Carian guest,
> A handful of gray ashes, long, long ago at rest,
> Still are thy pleasant voices, thy nightingales, awake ;
> For Death, he taketh all away, but them he cannot take.'

There is the couplet for the grave of Saon of Acanthus :

> ' Say not the good are dead :
>   It is a mystic sleep
>   That now they keep :
> The grave is but their bed.'

And there is the epitaph for a twelve-year-old boy :

> ' The cheerful hopes that Philip once possessed
> Lie here : for here Nicoteles doth rest.'

The love poems addressed to ephebes are academic exercises, it is true, but for all that they are beautiful.

The epigram to Archinus, for example, initated so frequently by Roman poets :

> ' If I did come of set intent,
>   Then be thy blame my punishment.
>   But if by love a captive made,
>   Forgive my hasty serenade.
>   Wine drew me on, Love thrust behind,
>   I was not master of my mind.
>   And when I came I did not cry
>   My name aloud, my ancestry ;
>   Only my lips thy lintel pressed :
>   If this be crime, the crime's confessed.'

Another, to Menexenus, is equally charming :

> ' Nay, tempt me not, take those soft arms away,
>   There lurks a spark beneath these ashes gray
>   Still pregnant with desire.
>   By Pan I swear and Bacchus, lord divine,
>   Still do I tremble lest this heart of mine
>   Should wake its ancient fire.
>
>   E'en as a river by some crumbling wall
>   With silent tooth beguiles the stones to fall
>   Where soft the waters glide ;
>   So do I fear lest passion's tranquil stream
>   Lull all my soul in Love's enchanted dream
>   And drown me 'neath the tide.'

A third, in form a love poem to Lysanias, is really a profession of Callimachus' literary faith :

> ' The songs that other men have sung,
>   Familiar now to every tongue,
>   I loathe their old refrain.
>   The spring wherefrom the vulgar sip
>   Shall never pass within my lip,
>   I spit it forth again.
>
>   And as I hate the trodden road,
>   So do I hate the too much wooed,
>   Though he may lovely be.
>   " Above all others fair," I cried ;
>   But mocking Echo swift replied
>   With " Others' fare is he." '

93

This pawky humour is one of Callimachus' distinguishing traits, and with two illustrations of it we must conclude. One is on the choice of a wife :

> ' Little boys will cry at play—
> " Whip-top, fly in your own way."
> And if you would take a wife
> Let this be your rule of life.
> Do not choose a maiden grand :
> Whip a top that suits your hand.'

The other is ostensibly for a salt cellar dedicated to the gods of Samothrace :

> ' Plain bread and salt Eudemus ate,
> No other relish on his plate ;
> Until from out the waves of debt
> He managed thus at last to get.
> Now to the gods who rule the sea
> He brings the jar that set him free,
> And says, " I thank you, Lords divine,
> For I have safety found in brine." '

The sixty epigrams in the *Anthology* are written with the utmost skill. In refinement of technique they are unsurpassed, and modern critics have deduced from them long lists of rules and restrictions which Callimachus was the first to bring into the elegiac couplet. But neither the epigrams, nor the hymns, nor the new fragments quite explain the problem of Callimachus' predominant reputation. To modern readers Theocritus and Apollonius make a far stronger appeal : they seem to be true poets while he appears little more than a very skilful versifier. But in ancient times the two younger men were overshadowed by their master, and to the Greek and Roman world for nearly three centuries Callimachus was definitely the strongest influence in literature. Catullus translated the *Coma Berenices*, Propertius, the ' Roman Callimachus,' imitated his archæological verse, and his hand lies heavy on Ovid's *Metamorphoses* and *Fasti*.

Apollonius of Rhodes (fl. c. 260)

Whether Apollonius succeeded Eratosthenes as head of the Library is a matter of doubt. A papyrus found in Egypt gives him as preceding Eratosthenes in that post ; but if he ever was chief librarian, which some deny, it would seem that he came after Eratosthenes rather than before him. Although he is usually called the Rhodian he was born in Egypt about the beginning of the third century B.C., and probably died towards the end of the century. The chief events of his life are so closely connected with his quarrel with Callimachus that an account of that famous controversy is necessary here. Callimachus was by nature incapable of enthusiasm : he was an artist as meticulous as Horace in the choice of his words and the structure of his verse : but for romance, for the open spaces, for heroic adventures, he had no use and no inclination. Apollonius, as we see him in his writings, was the exact opposite, and it is not surprising, when we consider the effects of an academic atmosphere upon a poet's nerves that between these two men there raged a long and bitter and irreconcilable feud. The quarrel began in a difference of literary opinion. Apollonius, who was slightly the younger, was a fervent admirer of Homer. Callimachus admired with reservations and was definitely of opinion that the long epic was out of date—'A big book,' he said, 'is a big nuisance.' Apollonius refused to accept this dictum and about 270 brought out the first draft of the *Argonautica*, to which Callimachus perhaps replied with the first draft of the *Aitia*, a poem of the new style dealing in separate episodes with the more obscure Greek tales. The battle was now engaged, and as both combatants were scholars as well as poets, it soon took the form of violent and mutual abuse. Callimachus remarked—in verse—

that he himself was a blithe cicada, his opponents were loud-braying asses : in another piece he explained how he disliked those who tried to write in the Homeric style and followed on a road that was already too well trodden ; in a third, varying his metaphor, he said ' Great is the stream of the Assyrian river, but much filth of earth and much refuse it carries on its waters.' The word ' filth ' roused Apollonius to retaliate and he wrote an epigram (A.P. xi. 275) :

> ' " Blockhead," " Old Bogey," " Housewives' Slush " ;
> That's what I call Callimachus.
> His " Causes " lie upon my shelf ;
> Cause of my cursing he himself.'

This really annoyed Callimachus, and girding up his loins, he composed a poem on Apollonius, the *Ibis*, known to us in Ovid's adaptation. The title is explained by a passage in Strabo (xvii. 823) : ' Every crossing in Alexandria is full of these birds, in some respects usefully, in others not usefully. Usefully, because they pick up the offal from the butchers and fish-shops. But they are detrimental, because they are omnivorous and unclean.' Some think that the *Ibis* settled matters, inasmuch as it went to the extreme limit of vituperation and left nothing more to be said. At any rate Apollonius accepted defeat, and shaking the dust of Alexandria from his shoes retired to Rhodes. Here he spent some years re-writing the *Argonautica* and putting in at least one passage for Callimachus : ' What a pitiful seer is this, who has not the wit to perceive even what children know. . . . Begone, sorry prophet, foolish one : on thee neither Cypris nor the gentle Loves breathe in kindness.' The Rhodians seem to have received the poem with enthusiasm, and at last, perhaps after Callimachus' death in 235, Apollonius, then an elderly man, returned to Alexandria and was made Head of the Library. At Alexandria he died, and his body was placed in a state tomb next to that of his old enemy.

Apollonius, unlike most of the Alexandrians, is a man of one book : the *Argonautica* is the only thing he wrote, and that we possess entire. It is a hexameter poem written in the Homeric style, divided into four books, and about equal in length to half the *Odyssey*. Its subject is the voyage of the Argonauts to Colchis in quest of the golden fleece and their return to Greece. The first two books deal with the voyage out, the fourth book with the return journey : the third, for modern readers far the most interesting, is concerned with the loves of Medea and Jason.

The story, after a brief invocation to Phœbus, begins with a catalogue of the Argonauts, which fills two hundred rather tedious lines. Then follow the farewell speeches of Jason and his mother Alcimede, the final banquet, and the launching of Argo. The song of Orpheus sends the heroes on their way to Lemnos, where they waste some time sporting with the women until Heracles reminds them of their quest. From Lemnos they sail to the Propontis and then to Mysia : here Hylas is captured by an amorous naiad, and on the advice of Glaucus Heracles is left behind to discover his fate. The second book opens in the land of the Bembrycians with a fight between their king Amycus and Pollux—an episode which, like that of Hylas, is also treated by Theocritus. The next stopping-place is at the house of Phineus, whose persecutors, the Harpies, are driven away by Zetes and Calais, the winged sons of the North Wind. By the help of Athene the Argo then gets safely through the Clashing Rocks and passes on to the country of the Mariandyni, where her steersman, Tiphys, dies. The voyage is resumed to the island Aretias where the sons of Phrixus have been shipwrecked on their way to Greece, and then at length Colchis is reached.

The third book introduces us to the domestic life of the gods. Hera and Athena pay a visit to Aphrodite whom they find at her toilet, and ask her to bid her son inspire Medea with love for Jason. The little Eros is discovered by the ladies playing dice with Ganymede, and by the bribe of a magic ball is induced to give his help. The scene then shifts to the palace of Æetes, Medea's father, where Eros fulfils his promise and Jason undertakes to yoke the brazen bulls; and nearly all the rest of the book is a highly elaborate account of the growth of love for the stranger in Medea's heart. From her first sight of Jason, when ' her soul was filled with shy speechlessness and she could only dart at him bright looks, while her heart panted within her and the colour of her soft cheeks came and went,' we see all the long process of delicious agony and innocent shame. A second time, herself unseen, she gazes at him and ' her thoughts went winging after him like a dream; surely, she thinks, there can be no other man alive like him; terribly was she afraid for the youth, and in her grief and pity a tear ran slowly down her cheek.' So fear and desire fight their battle within her: she steals from her room to seek comfort with her sister, and three times turns back again, falling face downward on her bed, and ' all her body was on fire, and each fine nerve deep down beneath the nape of the neck where the pain of love enters keenest.' Her sister finds her and by an ingenious turn of the story aids unconsciously in bringing the lovers together. Medea with her twelve maids goes to meet the prince, and when at last she sees him face to face, ' her heart fell from out her bosom, her eyes were covered in sheer darkness, a hot blush mantled her cheeks. She had no strength to lift her knees backwards and forwards, her feet were rooted to the ground.' For a time the pair stand 'without a word, without a sound, like oaks or lofty pines which stay quietly side by side on the mountains when the wind is still.' Then the attendant maidens draw aside, the two talk together, and at the end love's victory is won : ' she cast down her eyes with a smile divinely sweet ; and her soul was all confused within her, uplifted by his praise, nor did she know what word to utter first, but was eager to pour out everything at once. Her heart grew hot and melted all away, even as the dew melts round roses when it is warmed by the morning's light.'

By the help of the charm which Medea gives him Jason yokes the fire-breathing bulls, sows the dragon's teeth, and compels the giants who spring up from the ground to slay one another. His task accomplished, Medea flies from the palace to join him, and with her aid Jason carries off the golden fleece. The Argonauts then start on their homeward voyage, and the Fourth Book is an ingenious but rather tiresome attempt to reconcile the various routes given in ancient legends for their return. Pursued by the Colchians they land in Paphlagonia and on the advice of Argus sail up the Ister and thence by a branch stream into the Adriatic. The Colchians, led by Medea's brother Apsyrtus, again intercept them and there is talk of giving Medea up. To this, however, she will not agree ; Apsyrtus is trapped by his sister and murdered by Jason ; and they then sail to Italy to be purified by Circe. In the land of the Phæacians they are hastily married, and being driven by a storm to Africa carry Argo to the Tritonian Lake. Triton himself then guides them to the sea, and so they get back at last to Pagasae, whence they had started.

With regard to the merits and defects of the

Argonautica there is an unusual consensus of opinion. Every one agrees that the poem is overloaded with irrelevant details, that many of the episodes are only of antiquarian interest, that the divine machinery lacks grandeur and creaks at times very clumsily, and that Jason is a weak and insignificant hero. Everyone also allows that the central episode, the love of Medea for Jason, used by Virgil as his model in the Fourth Æneid, is the first truly romantic thing in Greek, and that the picture of the birth of passion in a young girl's heart is unsurpassed in ancient literature. Balancing merits, then, against defects, the verdict commonly given is that the *Argonautica* is a magnificent failure.

Theocritus of Syracuse (fl. 260 B.C.)

Contemporary with Callimachus and Apollonius, and more attractive than either is Theocritus, the father of pastoral poetry. Theocritus was born about 310 B.C. at Syracuse, 'the greatest of Greek cities,' as Cicero calls it, ' and the fairest of all cities ; where the sun shines every day and there is never a morning so stormy but the sunlight conquers at length and breaks through the clouds.' His parents may have migrated to Sicily from Cos in the time of Timoleon, and to Cos in early manhood Theocritus went, studying medicine with his comrade Nicias under the great Erasistratus and literature under Philetas. To literature he finally turned and, like Herodes, was a younger member of the Coan school, acquainted not only with the elder Coan poets but with such visitors as Asclepiades and Leonidas, who under the names of Sicelidas and Lycidas are characters in his seventh idyll, the *Harvest Home*.

From Cos about 280 Theocritus seems to have returned for a time to Sicily seeking a wealthy patron, and there he wrote the *Graces*, an encomium addressed to Hiero who, after the departure of Pyrrhus in 278, had been elected general to resist the Carthaginian menace. Apparently he was unsuccessful in winning Hiero's favour, and about 274 set out for Alexandria. With Ptolemy Philadelphus, to whom he wrote a similar panegyric, he was more fortunate, and until 270 he remained at Alexandria in friendly relations with Callimachus and the rest of the court circle. Then it would seem that he wearied of the garish splendour of the great city and retired once more to Cos, staying there for a time before going on to Miletus, where Nicias, the friend of his youth, was then living. To this, the last period of his life of which we have any knowledge, the three Æolic poems probably belong ; but when and where he died is quite uncertain.

There are some pieces usually printed with the poems of Theocritus which are not his ; chief among them the *Oaristys*, a charming dialogue in alternate lines between a shepherd and a country maiden ; the *Fishermen*, a realistic but very graceful picture of humble life in a fisherman's cottage ; and the miniature *Heracleid*, relating the adventures of Hercules in the stables of Augeas, and the slaying of the Nemean lion. The genuine works fall under six heads, for Theocritus is one of the most versatile of artists. Firstly we have the ten pastoral poems : *Thyrsis, Harvest Home, Comus,* the *Shepherds, The Goatherd's Song,* the *Reapers,* the *Cyclops,* and the three *Bucolics,* in two of which Daphnis and Menalcas are interlocutors, in the third Daphnis and Damœtas.

The second section consists of the four ' epyllia,' epic idylls, short poems in the epic style on subjects taken from the ancient legend, *Hylas, Helen,* the *Infant Heracles,* and the *Dioscuri.* To the third section belong the two court poems already mentioned, the panegyrics on Hiero and on Ptolemy ; and to the fourth the three Æolic poems, one the *Spindle* addressed to Theugenis, wife of Nicias, the other two on boy lovers, a theme also treated in the *Aites*. The fifth section contains the twenty short epigrams included in the Palatine Anthology, and the sixth the three dramatic sketches, the *Incantation*, the *Cynisca*, and the *Syracusan Women*.

The pastoral poems are the most original part of Theocritus' work and also the best known. With him the pastoral is not a mere bucolic masquerade ; his characters are usually real shepherds singing such songs as he himself had heard, and the scenery is that of the Sicily which in his boyhood he knew so well. His own poems are a genuine imitation of life : Virgil and his other followers imitate an imitation, and are therefore three steps removed from truth. In the first idyll Thyrsis meets a goatherd and challenges him to a contest of song. The goatherd describes the carvings on his wooden bowl, a fisherman with his cast net and a boy scaring foxes from the vineyard. Thyrsis replies by the dirge for Daphnis with its refrain ' Begin, ye Muses dear, begin the pastoral song,' the first of the long line of pastoral laments. In the next a goatherd leaving his flock approaches the cave where Amaryllis hides behind a veil of ferns and ivy, and tries to win her by song. She does not answer, and at last he cries : ' My head aches but thou carest not. I will sing no more, but dead will I lie where I fall, and let the wolves devour me. Sweet as honey in the mouth may my death be to thee.' The scene of the third and fourth is laid in South Italy and both are frankly realistic, full of rustic banter and country gossip. Equally lifelike is the *Reapers* where Battus defends his love : ' Gracious Bombyca, thy feet are fashioned like carven ivory, thy voice is drowsy sweet, and thy ways, I cannot tell of them '—while Milon answers with the Lityerses song, a string of homely couplets such as reapers sing in the fields.

The three Bucolics in which Daphnis appears strike, as is proper, a more romantic note, and the scene is among the mountain pastures of Sicily. In one, Daphnis and Menalcas sing the praise of love and friendship and nature, and in another the same two contrast the joys of the neatherd's and the shepherd's life. The third has for its theme the love of Polyphemus for the Nereid Galatea, and to this Theocritus returns in the *Cyclops* idyll addressed to Nicias, where he makes the Cyclops sing : ' Leave the grey sea to roll against the beach : more sweetly in my cavern shalt thou fleet the night with me. Here laurels grow, and slender cypresses, and dark ivy, and sweet clustered grapes ; and here is cool water, which wooded Etna sends down for me from her white snow, a draught divine.' Only in the seventh idyll, *Harvest Home*, does literature obtrude, and here the shepherds' names are but a playful disguise for Theocritus' friends, while any unreality is amply atoned for by the description of the summer scene :

> ' High above our heads waved many a poplar, many an elm, and close by the sacred water from the nymphs' own cave welled forth with murmurs musical. On shadowy boughs the burnt cicalas kept their chattering toil, the little owl cried in the thick thorn, the larks and finches sang, the ring-dove moaned, the yellow bees were flitting round the springs. All breathed the scent of the opulent summer, of the season of fruits.'

The four epic idylls are not so interesting as the pastorals ; but like everything that Theocritus wrote they contain many beautiful passages. The *Helen* is an epithalamium for the marriage of Menelaus and Helen sung by a chorus of Spartan girls, and is supposed to have been suggested by a poem of Stesichorus on the same subject. The *Hylas* tells the fate of the beautiful youth beloved by Heracles, who was drawn down to death by the water nymphs : the same theme is treated in Latin by Propertius, and here it may possibly be thought that the copy surpasses the original. The *Dioscuri* is a battle piece, and its two hundred lines give us two fierce fights, the sword duel between Castor and Lynceus and the boxing match between Pollux and Amycus imitated by Virgil in the Fifth Æneid. The *Infant Heracles*, which describes the slaying by the baby hero of the serpents sent against him by Hera, is of a milder type, and opens with a delightful family scene : ' On a time when Heracles was but ten months old, Alcmena took him and his brother Iphicles, and gave them both their bath and their fill of milk, and laid them down in the buckler of bronze, and stroked their heads, and said " Sleep, my little ones, a light delicious sleep." So speaking, she rocked the huge shield, and in a moment sleep laid hold on them.'

The next three sections need only brief mention : the court poems have the artificiality which is inseparable from panegyrics written to order ; the epigrams are no better than many others written by poets of far less renown ; the Æolic pieces are merely very graceful examples of occasional verse. But when we come to the dramatic sketches we find Theocritus again at his best. Of the three one is tragic, one is comic, and one though comic might well have a tragic ending. The tragedy is the *Incantation*, a romantic and highly idealized treatment of a theme which the mime actors probably often presented to their audience. Simætha, deserted by her lover Delphis, tries to draw him back by magic charms— ' Bring back to me, my wheel, the man I love.' Then she tells the story of her passion—' Bethink thee of my love and whence it came, O Lady Moon '—and the piece ends with four lines of wistful beauty : ' Do thou farewell, and turn thy steeds to Ocean, Lady ; and my pain I will bear, as even till now I have endured it. Farewell, Selene bright and fair, farewell ye stars that follow the wheels of quiet Night.'

The scene of the *Cynisca* is a drinking party at a farm in Cos, the characters a man from Argos, a Thessalian horse dealer, a soldier of fortune, and the host Æschines who tells the tale to his friend Thyonicus. His mistress Cynisca has become infatuated with a youth named ' Wolf,' and a chance remark at the party revealed her secret and led to blows. Æschines is torn between resentment and desire ' like a mouse that has tasted pitch,' and Thyonicus advises him to pack up his kit and take service in Egypt under Ptolemy, ' the freeman's best paymaster, the Muses' darling, the top of good company, who knows his friends, and still better knows his enemies.' The *Cynisca* is realistic enough : even more so is the *Syracusan Women*, and as our quotations from Theocritus have been brief it may be permissible to give two of the three scenes into which the little play can be divided. The stage directions, it should be said, are not in the Greek.

SCENE I

A room in Praxinoë's villa. In the centre stands a spinning-wheel, at which the lady of the house is working : her maid Eunoë is carding wool for her to spin : her little boy Zopyrion is playing on the floor.

GORGO [*entering*]. Praxinoë in ?

PRAXINOË [*starting up*]. Yes, indeed. Oh, my dear,
What a pleasant surprise ! So you really are here !
[*To Eunoë*]. A chair and a cushion. Now, Gorgo, sit down.

GORGO [*settling herself comfortably*]. That's nice. It's as well I've a mind of my own,
Or else I should never have got here alive.
What a crowd ! And the cars ! And the way that they drive !
The soldiers in uniform look very smart ;
But the distance ! We really live too far apart.

PRAXINOË [*beginning a favourite subject*]. That madman of mine is the cause of it all.
He *would* take this hovel—for no one can call
It a house—at the end of the earth, so that we
Might never a glimpse of each other's face see.

The mean jealous wretch, he loves nothing but strife,
And he's been just the same all the days of his life !

GORGO [*pointing to the little boy*]. Don't run down your husband,
my dear, or get wild
When the little one's here. Have a care for the child.
How frightened he's looking. [*To Zopyrion.*] Now, don't be
afraid,
'Twas not meant for papa what your mother just said.

PRAXINOË [*indifferently*]. Good lord, he takes notice.

GORGO. Nice pa !

PRAXINOË [*with more vigour*]. Yesterday—
Or so we will call it—to get him away
I sent him to buy me some rouge and saltpetre ;
And he came back with—*salt*, the great big silly creature.

GORGO [*warming to the topic*]. Well, mine is the same, a real terror
with cash !
Seven shillings apiece for the merest old trash.
Five fleeces, forsooth ! Nasty, dirty dog skins !
It's trouble on trouble when once he begins.

[*Interrupting herself.*]

But come, let's be off. At the Palace to-day
It's the feast of Adonis. The queen, people say,
Does things grandly. So put on your shawl and your cloak.

PRAXINOË [*spitefully*]. Fine feathers, of course, always go with
fine folk.

GORGO [*in a soothing voice*]. What a tale to the stay-at-homes you'll
have to tell !
Come along.

PRAXINOË [*still grumbling*]. Ah, for idlers that's very well ;
They never are busy ; but I've work to do.
[*To Eunoë.*] Gather up all my wool : put it in the bureau.
Stir yourself, lazybones. You cats love to lie still
Asleep on a cushion. I'll teach you, I will.
Quick now with some water ; I must have a wash.
I did not say soap ! Pour it out and don't splash.
You're wetting my clothes. Oh, good lord, what a mess !
Well, that's over. Now fetch me the key of the press.

[*Goes to the clothes-press and brings out a new bodice.*]

GORGO [*exclaiming*]. What a sweet pretty bodice ! How awfully
nice !
And what beautiful fabric ! Pray, tell me the price.

PRAXINOË [*gloomily*]. Don't talk of it. Eight pounds I paid for the stuff
As it came from the weaver's loom quite in the rough,
And the work on it brought me almost to death's door.

GORGO [*consoling*]. Well, it is *most* successful. No one could wish more.

PRAXINOË [*slightly mollified*]. Many thanks. [*To Eunoë.*] Now my shawl ; and then put on my hat
In the way it should go. [*To Zopyrion.*] No, I shan't take you, brat.
Biting horse, big black bogey ! It's no use to cry.
Would you like to have both your legs broken and die !
[*To the nurse.*] Take care of the child, Nan, and help him to play :
Call the dog in—and lock the door while I'm away.

> [*With these parting injunctions the two ladies, each attended
> by her maid, at last manage to leave the house.*]

SCENE II

*The streets of Alexandria : filled with a motley throng of Greeks and
Egyptians, Syrians and Jews. The soldiers of Ptolemy's body-
guard, in their jack-boots and full cloaks, jostle pale scholars from
the Museum, who, in their turn, rub shoulders with flute-girls and
respectable matrons. The whole crowd is moving slowly towards
the Palace.*

PRAXINOË. Ye gods, what a throng ! Shall we ever get through ?
They're like ants beyond counting, this jostling crew.
But thanks to our monarch, so gracious and kind,
Rogues now don't come creeping up to you behind
In the old Egypt fashion, and try some sly game,
Like they once used to play at without any shame.
Since his father went up to high heaven to rest,
Of his many good deeds this is surely the best.

> [*These patriotic sentiments occupy the time while the ladies
> are pushing their way to the Palace. They have just
> arrived at the royal square when a troop of cavalry
> approach.*]

PRAXINOË. Ah, here come the horses ! Oh, what shall we do ?
My good sir, be careful ; don't tread on me. Oh !
Look how that bay's rearing. Get out of his way,

You foolhardy girl. [*To Eunoë.*] I am sure that this day
He'll be doing some mischief. It's lucky for me
That my brat stayed at home, or how scared I should be.

GORGO [*taking Praxinoë's hand*]. We're safe : they've gone past
to their place on parade.

PRAXINOË [*slightly recovering from her agitation*]. Of horses and
snakes I've been always afraid
Ever since my young days. Ah, I feel better now.
Quick, or we'll be swamped in this huge overflow.

[*As they move slowly towards the Palace they meet an old
lady coming in the opposite direction.*]

GORGO. Have you come from the Palace ?

THE OLD LADY. Yes, pretty one, yes.

PRAXINOË. And can we get in without too much distress ?

THE OLD LADY. By trying the Greeks got to Troy in the end.
If you try hard enough, you'll succeed, little friend.

[*She passes on.*]

GORGO. The oracle's spoken—and now she has gone.

PRAXINOË. Ah, women know everything, how it is done :
Yes, even how Zeus married Hera.

[*By this time they have arrived at the Palace.*]

GORGO. Oh dear,
There's a terrible crowd round the Palace, I fear.

PRAXINOË [*taking charge of her party*]. It's wonderful. Gorgo,
cling close to my arm :
If we keep all together we shan't come to harm.
You, Eunoë, hold on to Eutychis tight.
Don't separate, then we shall get in all right.

[*They are now in the thick of the crowd trying to pass through
the Palace gate.*]

Oh dear, how unlucky ! My skirt's torn in two.
Take care of my shawl, sir, whatever you do,
And may the gods love you !

A GOOD-NATURED MAN. I'm trying my best ;
But I scarcely can help it, so closely we're pressed.

PRAXINOË. What a jostling crowd, packed like pigs all around !

GOOD-NATURED MAN. Don't be scared, little lady, we're quite safe
and sound.

[*He gives what assistance he can to the ladies.*]

PRAXINOË [*fervently*]. And may you live safe, sir, for ever and aye !

108

[*To Gorgo.*] What a nice thoughtful man, and most kind, I
    must say !
Look at Eunoë there getting squeezed. Come along ;
You must push your own way, silly girl, in this throng.
Now close up together.
                        [*With one final effort they enter.*]
            We're right now inside—
As the bridegroom remarked when locked in with the bride.

Herodes (fl. 250)

To the three dramatic idylls of Theocritus we have
an interesting parallel and contrast in the eight mimes
of Herodes, first published in 1891 by Sir F. Kenyon
from a papyrus in the British Museum. Herodes—
the forms Herondas and Herodas are wrong spellings—
was perhaps an Athenian by birth, but he seems to
have spent most of his life at Cos and Ephesus, doubtless
making frequent visits to Alexandria. Of his career
we know almost nothing, and although he was certainly
a contemporary of Theocritus, it cannot be said
definitely which was the earlier of the two. Both
followed in the lines of Sophron, the great Sicilian
mime writer of the fifth century, but which of them
introduced Sophron's style into Alexandrian literature
is a matter of doubt. Some think that Herodes wrote
first ; others believe that the success gained by Theocritus in his dramatic sketches of domestic life led
Herodes in imitation to advance still further along the
path of realism. In any case there can be no question
as to which is the greater artist : the idylls of Theocritus
are pictures, the mimes of Herodes photographs.

It is usual to say that Herodes is a realist of the most
unflinching kind ; and he is indeed a realist in his
choice of subjects and in his treatment of them, as a
brief analysis will show. The first mime is a dialogue
between Gyllis an old bawd and Metriche a young

grass widow whose husband Mandris has been for ten months away in Egypt, that land, as Gyllis says, ‘ which is Aphrodite's own home where everything that is or ever was can be found.’ Gyllis has come on a delicate errand ; for while Mandris has been drinking from new cups in Egypt, Gryllos, a famous athlete, has fallen desperately in love with his deserted wife, and Gyllis has been sent to see if Metriche will not commit one little *faux pas.* Metriche rejects the proposal but is not excessively shocked, and the piece closes with the two women enjoying a bottle of wine together.

The scene of the second mime is laid in the law court of Cos where Battaros, a brothel keeper, is laying an action for assault against one of his patrons. His speech is a sardonic replica of the harangues commonly made to an Athenian jury, and anyone unacquainted with the Attic orators might think it an extravagant parody. But as a matter of fact it is not far removed from reality, and Battaros is not much more disreputable and shameless than the crippled client for whom Lysias wrote his extant speech. To Battaros, however, we will return.

The third mime gives us a school with the master and boys at their lessons. Enter Metrotimê, an angry mother, dragging in her truant son Kottalos for punishment. The boy will not go to school or even play quietly with knuckle-bones ; he prefers to gamble in low haunts with porters and runaway slaves. He scowls at his writing tablet as though it were Hades, and though his old father tries to help him with his reading he does not know the first letter of the alphabet. When he is scolded, he either runs off to his grand-mother or else climbs on the roof like a monkey and breaks the tiles. For all this a sound flogging from the master is indicated : ‘ Fetch me my stinging strap,’ he cries, ‘ the bull's pizzle wherewith I flay the unruly ’ ;

and the scene ends with poor Kottalos bellowing under the lash.

In the fourth mime, which may be compared with the *Syracusan Women* of Theocritus, we are introduced to the temple of Æsculapius at Cos. Two poor women, Coccale and Cynno, have brought a cock as votive offering to the god, and before entering the inner shrine look round at the statues and sculptures outside the temple. Then the verger admits them and they inspect the paintings inside the building ; among them a picture by Apelles, which allows Herodes to put into their mouths his own views on realism in art : ' True are the hands of Apelles. No one can say of him " This man looked on one thing and gave no thought to another." May any man who sees his works without justly admiring them be hung up by the foot in the fuller's house.'

The fifth mime is set in a house at Ephesus and there are three characters, Bitinna the mistress ; Gastron her slave and unfaithful paramour ; and Cydilla her confidential maid. Bitinna suspects that Gastron has been spending his vigour on other women and orders him to be sent off to the flogging house, where he is to have a thousand stripes on his back and a thousand on his belly, before he is branded with the hot iron. Cydilla, however, intercedes for the unfortunate wretch, and his punishment is remitted or at least deferred.

In the sixth and seventh mimes the two chief characters are the same, Metro a lady of Ephesus and Cerdon a maker of shoes—and of other things. In the sixth mime Metro comes to a friend's house to inquire about a certain article of women's intimate use, an article which in Greek is called a baubo and in French a godmiche. She is told that the maker of this delectable article is Cerdon and hastens off to find him.

III

In the seventh mime we are in Cerdon's shop. Metro
has become an honoured patron and brings her friends
to buy shoes—'Sicyonians, little Ambracians, Nossians,
Chians, parrots, hemps, Baucises, slippers, Ionian
buttoned hop o' nights, ankle-tops, crabs, Argive
sandals, scarlets, lads, stairs '—Cerdon has them all in
stock. The prices are high but Cerdon is an eloquent
salesman, and at last all the ladies are fitted.

The eighth mime, which was first made readable by
Walter Headlam, is a literary fantasy and quite different
from the others. Herodes himself is the speaker, and
we see him on a winter's morning at his farm waking
his servants and then telling them how in a dream he
had offered a goat to Dionysus which was then divided
among the herdsmen and a certain hook-nosed old man.
His interpretation ends the piece : ' As I offered the
fair goat to Dionysus, so from Dionysus I shall gain
a fair reward. As the herdsmen rent the goat asunder,
so will poetasters rend my writings. I shared with old
hook-nosed, and so by the Muses I shall either win
fame by my iambics or else my second intent will urge
me on after the manner of Hipponax to sing halting
measures to my Xuthos-born kin.'

Herodes may be regarded as a realist in respect to
his subject matter, but he is far from being a realist
in his language. It was once thought that in him we
had an example of the common speech of the people,
but this is almost the exact opposite of the truth. As
his latest editor [1] says : ' Herodes' whole process is one
of distortion. The vocabulary is taken from the Attic
drama. The structure of the sentence is Attic. Over
this is laid a thick coating of Ionic forms taken perhaps
largely from corrupt manuscripts of Hipponax. His
metre is the more or less loose metre of Attic tragedy,
not of old Ionic : with variations and licences intro-

[1] A. D. Knox in the Loeb Library.

duced arbitrarily. Even with all these loosenesses, his metrical ability is at fault : and he is compelled constantly to distort sentences in such a manner that all illusion of real conversation is lost—still more all illusion of the plain simple tongue of vulgar folk.' The preciosity of his style has a parallel in our John Lyly, and Mr Knox in his translation makes a gallant attempt to reproduce the effect of the medley by using a kind of modern Elizabethan prose, as will be seen by the following quotation from the second mime. Battaros has been recounting to the jury the injuries he has received at the hands of Thales, a wandering merchant, and to clinch his case he exhibits one of his protégées to them, as Hypereides is said to have done with Phryne :

'Come hither, Myrtale ; shew thyself to all : be shamefast toward none : think, in this jury thou seest, that thou beholdest fathers and brethren. See, sirs, round about her smoothness, how smooth was this pluckt by this mucky man, when he raunched and shent her.—Eld, let him render thankoffering to thee : els had he spat forth his blood, as did once Philip the Locust in Samos. Dost laugh ? I am a Boye, I denay not—and my grandsire was Patchouli hight, and my sire Patchouletto, and panders were they all : but for prowes wolde I chivy a lion, were I as Thales. You lust after Myrtale perchance ; small matter that ; and I, after loaven ; give one and thou shalt get the other. Or els 'a god's name, an thou be inly warmed, stuff the price into Boye Battaros his hand, and take thine own and drub thine own to thy desire. One thing, sirs—for this has been said unto him—do ye sirs, since witnes is there none, rule your sentence by æquitie. And, an he will merely assay the bodys of slaves and call unto torture, lo ! I offer mine own self freely : take me, Thales, and torture me : only let the price be in the midst : no better ruling could Minos himself have made were he judge here with his balaunce. For the rest, sirs, deme not that ye give vote for Battaros the pandar but for all the straungers within your gates. Now shall ye prove Cos and Merops their puissance, and Thessalus and Hercules their glorie, and with what intencioun Æsculapius came hither from Tricca, and wherefore 'twas here that Phœbe bare Leto. Think on all these thynges and steer justice by æquity, sin now this Phrygian ye will find better for his beating, an out of ages past yon saw spit sooth.'

Herodes cannot be called a pleasant author ; but he has the one quality essential, he is interesting. His mimes may be artificial in their diction, obscure in their phrasing, coarse in some places and trivial in others : but they give an impression of reality. He is usually sordid and occasionally obscene ; that is, he is very like our James Joyce : but perhaps both writers might say that they are very like life.

Cercidas of Megalopolis (fl. 250)

In Alexandria Homer, Hesiod, and Hipponax were the most widely read of the ancient poets ; and Cercidas, like Herodes, shows plainly the influence of the last of the three. Cercidas was an ardent devotee of poetry, and being a person of some importance in his native city he insisted on the children of Megalopolis learning by heart Homer's *Catalogue of Ships*. His own enthusiasm for literature was shewn in the composition of an Anthology of moral verse which became a familiar school book and drove out the authors from whom Cercidas made his selections. It was a great favourite with Gregory of Nazianzus in the fourth century A.D., and he quotes from the existing preface, written in choliambic verse, as being by Cercidas. This, however, is very doubtful, for though the sentiments may be those of Cercidas, the versification is quite unworthy of his skill. We have a specimen of the real Cercidas in the six meliambi first published by A. S. Hunt in the Oxyrhynchus series from a papyrus now in the British Museum. These are a clever and vigorous combination of hexameters and iambics, each metre managed in the most graceful fashion, and one example may be given :

> ' Thou, O Damonomus, art
>   Not ill instructed :
> " Twain are the blasts," we are told
>   That Aphrodite's
> Offspring doth breathe from his cheeks,
>   The azure-wingéd.
> Unto whomsoe'er of men
>   With gentle mildness
> Kindlily-out-of-the-right
>   His jaw hath breathéd,
> Tranquil the sea is of love
>   Whereon that mortal
> Ruddered by discipline calm
>   His ship directeth.
> But 'gainst whomsoe'er the boy,
>   His left jaw loosing,
> Rouseth the storms and the fierce
>   Typhoons of passion,
> These have their voyages fraught
>   With waves unceasing."
> Nobly said, Euripides !
>   Since twain the choice is,
> Better far is it for us
>   To choose out the wind in our favour.' [1]

The Papyri Letters

In the various collections of Egyptian papyri, and especially in the seventeen volumes of the Oxyrhynchus series edited by Grenfell and Hunt, 1893–1927, there is a mass of documents, some literary, some non-literary, and some upon the verge of literature. To the non-literary class the many hundreds of letters in the Oxyrhynchus Papyri belong, but even in a literary history room must be found for the schoolboy's letter to his father :

> ' Theon to Theon his father, greeting. That was a fine trick, not taking me to the city with you ! If you don't take me to Alexandria with you, I won't write to you ! I won't speak to you ! I won't wish you good-morning ! If you do go to Alexandria, I won't hold

[1] Translation by A. D. Knox, Loeb Library.

your hand or have anything more to say to you. That's what will happen if you don't take me ! Mother said to Archelaus, "Take him out of my way, he upsets me." That was a fine thing you did, to send me that fine present of beans ! They kept me in the dark at home on the 12th, when you sailed. Please send for me. If you don't I won't eat or drink. Goodbye.'

Of greater literary and historical value are the Zenon papyri, edited by C. C. Edgar, a collection of business letters, interesting in themselves, important for the light they throw on social life in Egypt, and exceptionally good specimens of the ordinary Greek of the Alexandrian age. Zenon was a Carian who came to Egypt in the reign of Ptolemy II and entered the service of Apollonius, the king's finance minister. In his retinue Zenon journeyed up and down the Nile, and in the spring of 256 was sent to manage the great estate near the town of Philadelphia which Ptolemy had given to his master. The letters passing on both sides give innumerable details of farming, irrigation, and village life in the Fayum ; and as the years pass by we see that Zenon, faithful steward as he was, began to accumulate a fortune of his own. Apollonius disappears from the correspondence soon after the accession of Ptolemy III, but Zenon remained as a private resident at Philadelphia, and beneath the ruins of his house the letters lay buried for over twenty centuries until the fellahin, digging for manure, brought them once again to light.

The Zenon papyri are documents of the first importance in economic history, but, as Mr Edgar says,[1] they also give us a panorama of everyday life in Ptolemaic Egypt : 'Men and women of the most diverse races pass across the stage—Greeks from east and west, Ethiopians, Troglodytes, Cilicians and Cappadocians, Arabs and Jews. . . . Apollonius is asked to provide

[1] New Chapters in Greek Literature, 2nd series, p. 129.

myrrh for the burial of the sacred cow in whom the goddess Hathor was periodically incarnated; the Egypto-Phœnician priests of Astarte demand sesame oil and castor oil at the reduced price at which they were furnished to other temples; and libations are poured to the Samothracian Cabiri in their shrine at Philadelphia. We catch a glimpse of Apollonius himself starting by lantern light on a winter morning to visit the great Serapeum beyond Memphis. When Dromon suffers from ophthalmia, he consults, not the physician for whose maintenance he no doubt paid the fee, but the god himself, who straightway orders him to smear his eyes with Attic honey. Government offices are closed during the great festival of Isis; but if the Greek clerks get a holiday, the baker and his female slaves work till late at night grinding corn and baking cakes. . . . Zenon's travelling wardrobe is described in full; Cleon begs him to send a couple of soft breast-bands for his wife; and Paramonus orders a dozen strigils of Sicyonian make " which can be got cheap at Memphis." We have an estimate from a painter for the decoration of a new house, and, what at this period is more curious, a design for a mosaic floor in the women's bathroom.'

The decline (221–180)

With the death of Ptolemy III in 221 the flowering time of Alexandrian literature comes to an end. Ptolemy IV Philopator was an artist, a king of the same type as Otto of Bavaria, and preferred writing tragedies to the duller tasks of government. But though he built a temple to Homer and tried to establish the worship of Dionysus as a state religion, the day of Homer and Dionysus in Egypt was almost over. The battle of Raphia in 217, when an Egyptian phalanx fighting for

Ptolemy IV defeated the Greek soldiers of Antiochus, brought about a sudden revival of the national spirit, the priests regained a large part of their former influence, and by them the later Ptolemies were invested with all the titles and attributes of the Pharaohs. Literature felt the change; and even if scholarship flourished vigorously for half a century longer, the only other authors of any importance are two descriptive writers and three very minor poets, of whom only two are Alexandrians in the full sense of the word.

Aristophanes of Byzantium (257–180 B.C.)

The tradition of verbal scholarship established by Zenodotus at Alexandria reached its highest point in this period with Aristophanes and Aristarchus. They are the first Librarians who were not poets as well as scholars; but in scholarship they stand supreme. To Aristophanes we owe a definite system of accentuation and punctuation in Greek, for he invented the three accents and the three stops, as well as the asterisk and the marks of long and short quantity. His editions of ancient authors were invaluable, and included Homer, Hesiod, Pindar, the Attic tragedians, and Plato. Besides these he wrote a treatise on lexicography, and another on grammar, developing the idea of Analogy, or grammatical regularity, in contrast with Anomaly, or grammatical irregularity. Finally, he drew up a collection of proverbs, a descriptive account of the masks used in comedy, and a classified list of the ancient poets foremost in the various styles.

Aristarchus of Samothrace (220–145)

Aristophanes was an untiring worker, but Aristarchus, his successor at the Library, surpassed even Aristophanes in the abundance of his production. His commentaries on ancient authors filled eight hundred rolls, and they are only a small part of his work. As a grammarian he was one of the earliest to recognize eight different parts of speech ; Noun, Verb, Participle, Pronoun, Article, Adverb, Preposition, Conjunction ; and he did much to clarify the Stoic conception of grammar, and to put the study on a sound basis. His edition of Homer also is of cardinal importance and marks a great advance on that of Zenodotus. As a textual critic he is both sober and judicious, relying entirely on manuscript authority and refraining from all conjecture. His comments too on the language and subject-matter reveal a most acute intelligence, and it is with truth that he has been called the father of scientific scholarship and criticism.

Callixenus of Rhodes (fl. 210 B.C.)

The works of the two prose writers we have next to mention were possibly more entertaining than those of the great scholars ; but that is all which can be said for them. Callixenus was by trade an art critic, but he also wrote a *Description of Alexandria* from which Athenæus gives two long extracts in his fifth book. The first is an account of the two ships which Ptolemy Philopator had constructed, one of them a huge and very useless war galley with two prows and two sterns, manned by four thousand oarsmen and three thousand marines, the other a more serviceable house-boat, 600 feet long and 45 feet broad, with banqueting halls in its centre constructed of cedar and cypress and adorned with gold and ivory. Both the ships are described with an abundance of detail, but even more elaborate is the description of the show given to the people of Alexandria by Ptolemy Philadelphus. First comes the banqueting tent with its golden—probably gilded—furniture and its floor strewn deep with lilies and roses. Then the various processions which began with Lucifer in the early morning and ended with Hesperus in the evening. Nothing is spared us—the crowds of gaily dressed performers, the troops of wild animals, the fully caparisoned soldiers in their tens of thousands, and the enormous floats representing such scenes as the Triumph of Bacchus, the Cave of the Nymphs, the Bedchamber of Semele, and the Satyrs at the Vintage—and even if the description becomes monotonous, it gives a good idea of the Oriental extravagance in which the Ptolemies occasionally indulged.

Polemon of Ilium (fl. 185 B.C.)

What Callixenus did for Alexandria Polemon did for innumerable cities in the Greek world. Polemon, nicknamed ' Stelocopas ' ' Brass-rubber,' was an antiquarian by taste and a writer of guide books by profession. He was apparently born at Ilium, but even Homer's birthplace did not lead to more controversy than his, and it would seem that he became an honorary citizen of all the towns whose attractions he successfully celebrated. He travelled extensively, and the titles of some of his books are *The Acropolis of Athens, The treasures of Delphi, The sights of Ilium, The rivers of Sicily,* and *The Peplus of Carthage.* All his works abounded in archæological information, and three of the many citations made by Athenæus will reveal their main features.

One story is reminiscent of the Pygmalion legend : ' At Delphi in the hall of the pictures there are marble statues of two boys. Of one of these statues a visitor became so enamoured that he shut himself in alone with it, made love to it, and presented it with a garland.

When he was detected, the Delphians consulted the oracle as to what they should do to him ; but the god replied : " Let him go free ; he has given me a handsome offering." ' A second tale tells the death of the famous courtesan Lais, who was beaten to death with wooden stools by jealous women in the temple of Aphrodite. A third gives a curious piece of natural history information respecting the porphyrion, the bird which Buffon calls ' poule sultane.' ' The porphyrion, if it is kept in a house, always watches married women closely ; and if the wife takes a lover the bird gives information at once to its master by hanging itself.'

Rhianus of Crete (fl. 210 B.C.)

Of the three poets Rhianus in his versatility is a typical Alexandrian. Born in Crete he came to Alexandria towards the end of the third century and gained some reputation as a scholar by his edition of Homer. He then came forward himself as an epic poet and produced a *Heracleid* and four long poems treating of the legends of Achæa, Elis, Thessaly, and Messenia. The last of these is the only one of which we have definite information, for the traveller Pausanias in his chapter on Messenia tells us that one of his authorities is Rhianus. The hero of the poem was Aristomenes, whose marvellous adventures form one of the most romantic episodes in early Greek history, and there was also a love story in the plot. The prose narrative of Pausanias probably follows Rhianus closely, but the only fragment we possess of the poem itself is a passage of moral reflections on the cowardice of the poor, and the arrogance of the rich. We have also ten epigrams by Rhianus in the *Anthology*, but more than half of them are in Strato's collection, the *Musa Puerilis*, and are distasteful to modern ideas.

Euphorion of Chalcis (276–187 B.C.)

Euphorion was born in Eubœa 276, and after studying at Athens was appointed by Antiochus the Great head of the Library at Antioch, a post which he held until his death in 187. Euphorion's chief poems, it would seem, were short epics, the *Dionysus*, the *Hyacinthus*, the *Hippomedon*, written in the obscure and allusive style favoured by Lycophron and Callimachus. They only existed in brief quotations until recently, when two fragments were found in Egypt. One of these is a laboured description of Cerberus brought up from Hades by Heracles ; the other is a list of recondite curses upon someone who has stolen a cup ; may he have the fate of inquisitive Herse, or of the victims of Sciron, or may he roll the stone of Ascalaphus in Hades. Neither piece makes us regret the loss of Euphorion's complete works.

Alcæus of Messene (fl. 190 B.C.)

Alcæus is somewhat more interesting then Euphorion as a man ; for so far from being a flatterer of kings he dared openly to challenge Philip V of Macedon. The story is told in five epigrams in the *Anthology*, three by Alcæus, two by Philip. The first was written by Alcæus after the battle of Cynoscephalæ (197 B.C.) ' whence Philip fled nimbler than a fleet-footed deer.'

> ' Tombless, unwept we lie, O thou who passest by,
>   Full thirty thousand men on this mound in Thessaly.'
>
> *A. P.* vii. 247.

To this Philip retorted thus :

> ' Leafless, unbarked it stands, O thou who passest by,
>   The cross upon the hill, where Alcæus shall hang high.'
>
> *A. P.* xvi. 26.

Alcæus replied with a bitter satire on the defeated monarch, bidding the gods shut their gates, since Philip had conquered earth and sea and had only heaven left to master. In an even fiercer outburst he wishes that he could drink Philip's brains ' Philip who tastes his friends' blood at the feast, pouring poison into the wine.'

Philip's answer was an epitaph : ' This is the tomb of Alcæus who was killed by a radish, broad-leaved daughter of earth, the punisher of adulterers.'

Popular literature

One of the chief differences between Athenian and Alexandrian writers is that the Alexandrians were professional men of letters writing with a definite purpose either to instruct or to amuse. The Athenians, although endowed with greater talent, were amateurs, and their writings are part of their public, not of their private life. They do not try to amuse ; indeed they rather hold their readers aloof and seldom take them into their confidence. At Alexandria literature moved in a wider, and also in a lower sphere : it lost in depth but it gained in diffusion, and authors like Herodes and Satyrus, even if they had no very high idea of their functions, undoubtedly reached an audience who could never have appreciated Thucydides and Æschylus. Many books were written simply to please ; and with the help of Athenæus and the papyri we can now form some idea of this popular literature, and classify it in its various forms.

Firstly we have the intimate biographies full of personal detail, such as those written by Hermippus and Antigonus, and the imaginary letters attributed to the illustrious dead ; then melodramatic histories like that of Alexander by Cleitarchus ; then the informative collections of marvels and strange happenings known as *Paradoxa*; and closely connected with them the tales of foreign travel of which we have an example in the Munchausen adventures of Iambulus quoted by Diodorus Siculus. Slightly more instructive than all these were the *Diatribes*, discourses often delivered in the street by itinerant philosophers, which frequently contained scenes drawn from everyday life put into dramatic form, with characters arguing one against the other. Of a lighter sort were the *Chriæ*, collections of witty sayings such as those of Simonides, 'Everything grows old save love of gain,' and of Demades, who, when a friend sympathized with him on a bad reception, remarked 'The public has its bad days.'

The best-known book of *Chriæ* was the one composed in iambic verse by the comic poet Machon, who lived in Alexandria at the beginning of the second century B.C., and from the long quotations in Athenæus we can estimate the quality of Greek wit. From Machon comes the tale of the drinker who wished for a throat five feet long, and of the sick man who, when dying from a surfeit of cuttle fish, begged for at least one more helping. Many of his jokes are repartees, not in themselves very funny, made to their lovers by the famous courtesans who played such a prominent part in the life of this age, Lais of Corinth, Phryne of Athens, Thais the mistress of Ptolemy I, and Lamia, Leæna, and Mania, who were all favoured by Demetrius Poliorcetes. But his chief source is that curious figure Stratonicus, a professional humorist who sailed from city to city in his own yacht making a handsome livelihood by his witty speeches. One example of Stratonicus' humour possibly will suffice. He was originally a music teacher and having only two pupils set the statues of the nine muses and Apollo in his classroom : then, if he was asked how many pupils he had, he would say, 'With the help of the gods I have twelve.'

Machon writes in verse, but he is very prosaic and poetry is better represented in the popular lyric. There is the soldier's song book, a papyrus found in a grave at Elephantine in Egypt, containing six rollicking ballads. There are the Locrian Songs, of which Athenæus says Phœnicia was full, and of which we have an example in the *Marisæum Melos* written about 150 B.C., a dialogue between a man and a woman ending thus :

> ' " Well, I must go." " Do as you please."
> " I'll leave the coast all clear."
> " Don't make a noise ; the walls are thin ;
> " The neighbours must not hear." '

Of much higher quality than these ditties is the well-known *Erotic Fragment*, discovered by Grenfell and published in the first volume of the Oxyrhynchus Papyri. Of its sixty lines forty are intact, and the lament of the girl deserted by her lover has something even of Sappho's passion :

> ' O grief when I remember
> How once the traitor kissed me
> Who was so soon to leave me !
> How he who gave me love
> Has brought me now unrest ! . . .
> Dear stars and Lady Night, my fellow lover,
> Guide me now to him whom Cypris
> Has made my lord and master,
> To whom strong Eros hales me :
> And with me on my way the fierce fire will go
> Burning within my breast.'

Songs such as this, highly dramatic in form, were sung, as we know, by the strolling actors—Hilarodoi, Lysiodoi, Simodoi, and Magodoi—who supplied the Alexandrians with their favourite entertainment. The account given by Athenæus [1] of their various kinds of performance is confused, but he makes it plain that the hilarodoi drew their subjects from tragedy, the magodoi from comedy ; and it is possible that we have an example of each sort in two pieces first published in Oxyrhynchus Papyri vol. 3. One of them is a realistic adaptation of a comedy plot on the lines of melodrama with the 'archimima,' the actress manager, who plays the part of a faithless wife, taking all the fat. The plot is this : the lady failing to force one of her men slaves to do her husband's duty orders him and his female friend to be killed, and then finding another instrument of her pleasure plots to poison her legal partner. All three of her victims, however, escape, and the play ends with her well-deserved punishment. The other piece is a farcical parody of Euripides' 'Iphigenia in Tauris,' the characters being Charition, a Greek maiden taken captive by an Indian king, her brother, her slave, and a number of Indians. There are three scenes, the second in two versions, the first, which is very fragmentary, consisting largely of rude noises made by the buffoon slave. In the second scene the three captives are preparing to escape, and we have some lines of dialogue intact :

SLAVE. Lady Charition, if you can, be ready to snaffle some of the temple offerings.

CHARITION. Hush, hush. Those who crave safety should not make their prayer to heaven with sacrilegious hands. How can the gods hearken, if you forfeit pity by doing wrong ? We must leave the goddess what is hers.

SLAVE. You need have no hand in it. I will take them.

CHARITION. Enough fooling. If the Indians appear, ply them with strong wine.

SLAVE. But suppose they won't drink it ?

THE BROTHER. You fool, wine is not on sale in these parts. If they get a drop of the real stuff, they won't know and will drink it neat.'

[1] Athenæus. Deipnosophists. Bk. xiv.

CHAPTER III

GREECE IN DECAY

(180–31 B.C.)

ALEXANDRIAN literature in spite of its splendid achievements was but of short duration, and by the second decade of the second century B.C. its day was over. It was an artificial product in so far as it was definitely supported by the state ; and for literature at least state support is not an unmixed benefit. It may encourage a young plant to a swift and luxuriant growth, but that plant when its blooming is done will not produce offspring of any strength. The first four Ptolemies were all men of practical ability and literary taste, but it is a rare thing to find an unbroken line of even four hereditary autocrats able both to govern and to cultivate the arts. Their successors were men of feeble character and little knowledge, and it became plain that the Greek civilization which the Ptolemies had introduced into Egypt was not destined to take firm root in the country as a whole. Alexandria therefore as the chief Greek literary centre ceased almost as quickly as it had begun. Its trade and political importance remained for a time, but during the second and first centuries it is at Athens, Pergamum, Rhodes, or finally at Rome that we shall find the chief Greek writers settled.

In this chapter then we may begin with a return to Athens and a survey of its philosophic schools, for moral philosophy was the one branch of literature which even in the third century was never greatly practised in Alexandria. Of the Peripatetics little need be said ; after the death of Theophrastus they abandoned pure philosophy for the collection of historical and scientific facts, and by the middle of the third century their work was over. The Cynics, too, devoted themselves mainly to the popular satire with which we have already dealt. As for the Epicureans, they were quite content to absorb their master's writings, without indulging in literary comment, while Philodemus, their only representative in this period, is more interesting as a poet than as a philosopher. But the other two great schools, the Academy and the Porch, both produced writers who deserve mention here.

The Academy in Polemon (fl. 300) and Crantor (fl. 290) had two philosophers of distinction, and in Arcesilaus (318–242) an original thinker who gave the school a new direction by his doctrine of suspension of judgment. Diogenes Laertius quotes his will and some verse epigrams, but we get a better idea of the man from his pithy sayings, such as ' Poverty is burdensome but it educates a man for virtue,' and ' Where there are most laws, there are most transgressions of Law.' On one occasion, when he was requested to explain his doctrines at a banquet, he said :—' The peculiar province of philosophy is just this, to know that there is a time for all things.' At another time, when asked why pupils from the other schools went over to Epicurus, but converts were never made from his followers, he replied : ' Because men may become eunuchs, but a eunuch never becomes a man.' After his death his followers drew nearer and nearer to scepticism, and when we come to Carneades (215–129) we find little difference between the two schools. Carneades indeed carried the doctrine of suspension of judgment so far that we are told his pupils could never discover what their master thought on any subject. As for his lectures, he refused to write them down, and they were published for him by his successor Clitomachus. He was a native of Cyrene, but went in early life to Athens, where he developed his eristic system at the expense of his teachers in logic. ' If my reasoning is right,' he would say, ' well and good : if it is wrong, give me back my fee.' In spite of some peculiarities—he let his hair and nails grow to an immoderate length and had to be fed at table—he was held in high esteem by the Athenians, and was sent with two other philosophers to Rome in 155 to deprecate the fine of 500 talents imposed on Athens for the destruction of Oropus. The deputation came before the senate, and on the first day Carneades proved that justice was the highest of virtues ; on the second day with equal eloquence he showed that it was a mere social compact ; on the third day Cato had the three Greeks sent home as a danger to public morals.

So much for the Academy, which in this period is easily outstripped by the Porch with its three great representatives, Chrysippus, Panætius, and Poseidonius. Chrysippus of Soli (282–206) is in fact the real founder of Stoicism as the Romans knew it, and as it exists to-day. After his time we hear no more of Zeno's social reforms, his community of wives, his uniformity of dress or undress for both sexes, his abolition of money as a means of exchange. All this was thrust out of sight by Chrysippus, and in its place the ethical system of Stoicism was so expanded and codified that nothing was left for his successors to do. He was regarded by all later writers as the fountain-head of doctrine, and the popular belief crystallized into the line of verse— ' If there had been no Chrysippus, then there would have been no Porch.' He was a most prolific author, and the list of his 750 ' volumes ' fills ten long pages in Diogenes Laertius ; but, perhaps fortunately, they

have now almost entirely disappeared. Ancient critics
are unanimous in complaining of his careless and impure
language, his dry and obscure style, his lengthy citations
and endless repetitions ; and Dionysius of Halicarnassus
cites him as a perfect example of how not to write.

After Chrysippus we know of two distinguished
Stoics, Diogenes of Babylon and Crates of Mallos. The
latter of these flourished about 170 B.C. and was head
of the school of Pergamum during the reign of Eumenes
II. His work was chiefly in grammar, where he supported the view of 'anomaly' in language against
Aristarchus' doctrine of analogy. But he was also
probably responsible for drawing up the classified lists
of authors in the Pergamene Library, and had a certain
influence on literary studies in Rome. He accompanied
Attalus of Pergamum on his embassy to Italy in 168,
and while roaming about the Palatine happened to
break his leg. He was thus compelled to stay some
time at Rome, and used the opportunity to give public
lectures on Greek literature, probably the first that
were ever delivered to a Roman audience.

Crates is more important as a scholar than as a
writer, and the next great name is that of Panætius
(c. 175–115). Panætius, unlike Chrysippus, was a
philosopher of some skill with his pen, and although
most of his work left to us is too fragmentary for
quotation, yet Aulus Gellius has preserved one fair
specimen, from the treatise *On Duty*, translated into
Latin :[1]

'The life of men who pass their time in the midst of affairs, and
who wish to be helpful to themselves and to others, is exposed to
constant and almost daily troubles and sudden dangers. To guard
against and avoid these one needs a mind that is always ready and
alert, such as those athletes have who are called " pancratiasts."
For just as they, when they are called to the contest, take their stand

[1] Aulus Gellius. Attic Nights, xiii, xxviii.

with uplifted arms and protect their head and face by opposing their hands as a rampart ; and as all their limbs, before the battle has begun, are ready to avoid or to deal a blow—so the spirit and mind of the wise man, on the watch in every place and at every time against violence and wanton injuries, ought to be alert and on tiptoe, firmly fortified, ready in time of trouble, never blinking, never wheeling in the battle line, opposing judgement and forethought, in the place of arms and hands, to the strokes of fortune and the snares of the wicked, lest in any way a hostile and sudden attack be made upon us when we are unprepared and unprotected.'

The treatise from which this quotation comes is familiar to many readers, for Cicero used it as the basis of his *De Officiis*, and in the first two books of that exemplary work he seems to have followed his model very closely. Panætius was also well known to other Romans besides Cicero. Though he was born at Rhodes he lived for a long period in Rome and was a member of the Scipionic circle. With Scipio Æmilianus he went on the embassy to the Kings of Egypt and Syria in 144, and finally died at Athens in 115. For many years he was a housemate of Polybius, when they were acting as joint tutors to the sons of Æmilius Paulus ; and, if it were possible, it would be interesting to trace the influence of the philosopher upon the great historian to whom we next proceed.

Polybius (c. 208–126 B.C.)

Polybius was born about 208 B.C. at Megalopolis in Arcadia. His father Lycortas was one of the most prominent statesmen of the Achæan League, being Strategus in 184 and on three occasions going to Rome and Egypt as its ambassador ; and from his youth Polybius was initiated into public affairs. He seems to have served with the Romans in their campaign against the Gauls of Asia Minor in 189 ; he carried the urn of Philopœmen at his state funeral in 181 ; and he was Hipparchus of the League in 169. In that year probably Lycortas died, and the prudent policy of acceptance of Roman supremacy, which he consistently advocated, was for the time abandoned by the more hot-headed of his countrymen. The Roman senate, who had always regarded the Greeks with suspicion, seized the opportunity afforded them by the crushing victory of Pydna in 168, and transported a thousand Achæans, among them Polybius, to Italy to stand their trial for their alleged opposition to Rome. For sixteen years, quartered in country towns, they waited for the judgment which never came, and it was not until only three hundred of them were left that the Senate at last took their case into consideration. Even then there was a conflict of opinion, and the debate dragged on until Cato cried—'Are we to sit here all day discussing whether some old Greek dotards are to be buried by Italian or Achæan undertakers?' His opinion carried the day, and it was resolved to let the poor remnant go home; but when Polybius wished to raise the question of the restitution of their property, Cato gave him this significant warning—'Remember Ulysses who wanted to go back to the Cyclops' cave for his cap and belt.'

In this unhappy company Polybius was comparatively favoured by fortune. He had made the acquaintance of Æmilius Paulus, the victor of Pydna, in Macedonia, and was taken into his house at Rome to act as tutor to his two sons, the younger of these boys being afterwards adopted by Scipio and becoming the Publius Scipio Æmilianus Africanus Minor with whom Polybius was to remain in close friendship for the rest of his life. With Æmilius Paulus Polybius stayed for sixteen years, and during that time used his ample opportunities to study every detail of Roman life and character, the framework of the Roman constitution, and the structure of Roman society. It was in this period that he conceived the idea of telling the story of Rome's conquest of the world, and before he returned to Greece he had written at least fifteen books of the forty which finally composed the whole work. In 151 he at last left Italy, but two years later he was summoned back to take part in the negotiations that preceded the Third Punic War, and in 147 he went with Scipio Æmilianus to Africa. He was present at the burning of Carthage in 146, and came back to Greece soon after the sack of Corinth by Mummius in the same year. When the Roman commissioners withdrew from Greece Polybius was appointed to settle the administration of the cities in the Peloponnese, and so well did he perform the task that in many places statues were erected in his honour, one of them bearing this inscription : 'Greece would not have been ruined if she had listened to the warnings of Polybius.'

Of the last twenty years of his life we have less detailed knowledge. He probably went with Scipio to Spain in 134, and at Numantia saw the beginning of demoralization in the Roman army. In the next year Tiberius Gracchus started the social revolution, in 129 Scipio was assassinated, and the Roman constitution, which had seemed to Polybius the type of stability, began to break up before his eyes. The *History*, which to the end of his life he was constantly revising, bears plain marks in inserted paragraphs of the impression made upon him by these untoward events ; and it was perhaps fortunate for him that an accidental fall from his horse in his eighty-second year brought his days to a close three years before the death of Caius Gracchus.

Besides the *History* Polybius wrote a *Life of Philopæmen*, a *Treatise on Tactics*, and a *History of the Numantine War*. These latter three are now lost and of the *History* itself only the first five of its forty books

133

have come down to us complete, forming in bulk an amount just about equal to the extracts made by the Byzantines from the other thirty-five.

Of these five the first two serve as an introduction to the whole work, continuing the history of Timæus which ended at 264 and sketching the earlier relations of Rome and Carthage in the First Punic War and the previous history of the Achæan League. Early in the third book Polybius outlines his main subject, which originally was to have been a history of the period from 220 to 168, that is, from the beginning of the Second Punic War to the destruction of the Macedonian monarchy—' a space of fifty-three years which included a greater number of grave and momentous events than any period of equal length in the past.' But, as he says, this original plan was extended so as to take in the troubled time that ensued after Pydna—' owing to the importance of the actions and the unexpected character of the events, especially as I was not only a spectator of most of them but in some cases took part and even directed their course.' Therefore, in its augmented form the *History* went down to 146, the year when Corinth was sacked and Carthage razed to the ground, and there are even some allusions in the narrative to events that happened after the year 133 B.C.

How far the forty books were composed on a symmetrical plan is a matter of doubt. Nissen and Susemihl are both inclined to think that it was divided into seven parts, each part consisting of six books, except the sixth part which contained four. The first part, on this theory, contained the introduction; the second the culminating years of the contest between Rome and Hannibal; the third, beginning with the war in Africa, ends with the overthrow of the Macedonian monarchy; the fourth deals with the process by which Rome became the controlling power in the Mediterranean world, and the fifth describes how the other nations were gradually reduced to the position of subject states ; the sixth takes the transition period and leads to the last rising against Rome, which forms the subject of the seventh part. The three books which are in the nature of digressions, Book VI on Roman Institutions, Book XII on the history of Timæus, and Book XXXIV on geography, come each at the end of one of these parts ; and it is supposed that Book XL, which contained a summary of the whole work, was added to round off the last part.

This suggestion has a certain plausibility, but it is not entirely convincing ; and Polybius himself, who is most careful to explain everything to his readers, says nothing about it. His own account of his plan runs as follows :[1]

'First I shall indicate the causes of the war between Rome and Carthage known as the Hannibalic War, and tell how the Carthaginians invaded Italy, broke up the dominion of Rome, and cast the Romans into great fear for their safety and even for their native soil, while great was their own hope, such as they had never dared to entertain, of capturing Rome itself. Next I will attempt to describe how at the same period Philip of Macedon, after finishing his war with the Ætolians and settling the affairs of Greece, conceived the project of an alliance with Carthage ; how Antiochus and Ptolemy Philopator first quarrelled and at length went to war with each other for the possession of Cœle-Syria, and how the Rhodians and Prusias, declaring war on the Byzantines, compelled them to stop levying toll on ships bound for the Euxine. Interrupting my narrative at this point, I shall draw up my account of the Roman Constitution, as a sequel to which I shall point out how the peculiar qualities of the Constitution conduced very largely not only to their subjection of the Italians and Sicilians, and subsequently of the Spaniards and Celts, but finally to their victory over Carthage and their conceiving the project of universal empire. Simultaneously in a digression I shall narrate how the dominion of Hiero of Syracuse fell, and after this I shall deal with the troubles in Egypt and tell

[1] Tr. W. R. Paton, Loeb Library.

how, on the death of Ptolemy, Antiochus and Philip, conspiring to partition the dominions of his son, a helpless infant, began to be guilty of acts of unjust aggression, Philip laying hands on the islands of the Ægean and on Caria and Samos, while Antiochus seized on Cœle-Syria and Phœnicia.

'Next, after summing up the doings of the Romans and Carthaginians in Spain, Africa, and Sicily I shall shift the scene of my story definitely, as the scene of action shifted, to Greece and its neighbourhood. I shall describe the sea-battles in which Attalus and the Rhodians met Philip, and after this deal with the war between the Romans and Philip, its course, its reason, and its result. Following on this I shall make mention of the angry spirit of the Ætolians, yielding to which they invited Antiochus over and thus set ablaze the war from Asia against the Achæans and Romans. After narrating the causes of this war, and how Antiochus crossed to Europe, I shall describe in the first place how he fled from Greece ; secondly, how on his defeat after this he abandoned all Asia up to the Taurus ; and thirdly, how the Romans, suppressing the insolence of the Galatian Gauls, established their undisputed supremacy in Asia and freed its inhabitants on this side of the Taurus from the fear of barbarians and the lawless violence of these Gauls. Next I shall bring before the reader's eyes the misfortune that befell the Ætolians and Cephallenians, and then make mention of the war of Eumenes with Prusias and the Gauls and of that between Ariarthes and Pharnaces. Subsequently, after some notice of the unification and pacification of the Peloponnese and of the growth of the Rhodian State, I shall bring the whole narrative of events to a conclusion, narrating finally the expedition of Antiochus Epiphanes against Egypt, the war with Perseus, and the abolition of the Macedonian monarchy. All the above events will enable us to perceive how the Romans dealt with each contingency, and thus subjected the whole world to their rule.'

It will be seen that Polybius has a great and inspiriting subject, and we may now consider some of the qualities in his work which make him the great historian that he is. First and foremost, comes his love of truth and his determination to shrink from no trouble in discovering facts and putting them clearly before his readers. If we compare, for instance, his description of Hannibal's journey over the Alps with that of Livy, it will be obvious that the Greek had visited the actual pass by which Hannibal came down into Italy, and that the Roman had not. Generally Livy has a great advantage in literary style, but in this passage the account given by Polybius from personal knowledge is far more vivid and interesting than that which Livy wrote, relying on the information of others in the comfort of his study.

In the second place, Polybius is impartial, the most impartial perhaps of all the ancient historians. He is large-minded in his judgments and scrupulously fair, while his profound study of human nature inclines him to take an indulgent view of all human action. 'A good man,' he remarks, ' should be fond of his friends and his country ; but when he undertakes to write history he must forget all personal feelings, and, if facts require it, give praise to his enemies and censure to his friends.' In treating of Grecian affairs he is possibly somewhat inclined to be unjust to the Ætolians, but in his estimate of the Roman governing classes his impartiality is absolute, and though he fully recognizes their merits he is by no means blind to their faults.

Finally, Polybius realizes with especial clearness the philosophic basis of history. He is essentially didactic, and is never tired of calling attention to the fact that the true object of the historian is not to amuse but to instruct. The historian, he considers, must not be satisfied merely with narrating events, but must investigate and explain their causes and connections. His own idea of causality, it may be noticed, changed in the course of writing. At first he believed in Fortune, ' which has caused the whole world and its history to tend to one single purpose—the empire of Rome.' But in later life he changed his opinion, and could say : ' It was not by fortune, as some of the Greeks think, nor causelessly that the Romans succeeded ; their success was natural ; it was due to their training and discipline.'

As an historian Polybius can stand comparison with the greatest ; it is as a literary artist that he falls short. It would be worth while to learn Greek merely in order to read Thucydides in the original, but Polybius loses very little in translation. It is not that he writes badly, and his narrative is pleasantly free from the tricks of rhetoric which were fashionable in his day. But his style has no magic in it, and even in his best descriptions, such as that of the ' Truceless War ' between the Carthaginians and their mercenaries, with which this account may close, we feel that a master of words would have produced a more striking effect.

' There was a certain Campanian, a runaway Roman slave, called Spendius, a man of great physical strength and remarkable courage in war. He was afraid of his master coming to claim him, when, if given up, he would by Roman law be tortured and put to death. He therefore hesitated at nothing in his endeavour both by speech and action to break off the negotiations with the Carthaginians. He was supported by a Libyan named Matho, who was indeed a freeman and a member of the force, but had taken a leading part in the late disturbances. Consequently he stood in great fear of being singled out to bear the whole penalty, and therefore was of one mind with Spendius. Taking the Libyans aside, he pointed out to them that when the other nations departed to their own countries after being paid off, they would be left to bear the whole weight of the wrath of the Carthaginians, whose object it would be by the punishment they inflicted upon them to terrorize all their Libyan subjects. The men were soon stirred by such arguments, and availing themselves of the slender pretext that Gesco, while discharging their pay, postponed the compensation for the horses and corn, they at once held a meeting. When Spendius and Matho began to traduce and accuse Gesco and the Carthaginians, they were all ears and listened with great attention, but if anyone else came forward to offer an opinion, they did not even wait to find out if he were going to speak in favour of Spendius or against him, but at once stoned him to death. Numbers both of the officers and privates perished thus in the different meetings, and in fact this phrase, " Stone him," was the only one that became intelligible to all the different nations, owing to the frequency of the act. They used to behave thus mostly when they held meetings after their morning meal in a drunken condition, so that the moment anyone called out " Stone him " the stones flew from all sides and so quickly that it was impossible for anyone who once came forward to address them to escape.'[1]

Nicander, Moschus, and Bion (fl. 130 B.C.)

About the same time that Polybius was revising his *History*, Nicander was at work on his didactic poems, *Snake-bites* and *Antidotes to poisons*, and Moschus and Bion were composing the last specimens of the Alexandrian pastoral. Nicander of Colophon was a client of Attalus III, the bloodthirsty tyrant of Pergamum, whose chief interest was the cultivation of poisonous plants ; and it was probably at his patron's order that Nicander's two poems were written. Together they extend to nearly two thousand lines, and by malign chance they have been preserved entire. But they are dreary productions, and their chief claim to notice is that they are the last Greek poems of any length that we shall meet for three centuries. From Nicander it is a relief to turn to the two pastoral poets. Moschus of Sicily has left us two fairly long idylls, the *Megara* and the *Europa*, together with some epigrams. The *Megara* is in the form of a dialogue between Megara the wife and Alcmena the mother of the wandering Heracles. Megara in a long speech tells how her husband slew their children in a fit of madness and is now toil-worn with labours which keep him ever far from home. Alcmena in her turn relates an ominous dream in which she has seen Heracles compassed about with fire and Iphicles vainly trying to come to his aid. The *Europa* is a brighter effort and in the elaboration of its pictorial descriptions supplied a model for Catullus in his *Peleus and Thetis*. Europa after a strange dream goes into the meadows to gather flowers with her maidens. The devices on her basket and the flowers

---

[1] Tr. W. R. Paton, Loeb Library.

she picks are all enumerated ; and then suddenly the bull appears—' his body was a bright chestnut colour, a silver circle shone between his brows, and his eyes gleamed softly with the lightnings of desire.' Europa gets upon his back, is carried out to sea, and we have a picture of the Tritons and Nereids gambolling in the bull's wake before the piece ends with the maiden's lament and the god's answering speech of comfort.

A, third poem, the *Lament for Bion*, was formerly attributed to Moschus, but is now usually given to a later poet, who was a pupil of Bion. Whoever its author may be, the *Lament* is one of a great line and may fairly be put side by side with *Lycidas* and *In Memoriam*. It consists of one hundred and twenty-six hexameters, with a refrain thirteen times repeated. ' Begin, Sicilian Muses, begin the dirge,' and although perhaps it is somewhat overloaded with literary allusions, there is real feeling behind the literature. Its effect is largely one of beautiful sound, and translation here is particularly inadequate ; for it is impossible to reproduce in our rough Anglo-Saxon the melody of its broad Doric vowels and diphthongs. Still, here at least is the sense of some lines :

> ' Ah me ! when mallows in the garden die,
> Or curling anise and the parsley green,
> Not for all ages do they fallen lie ;
> They spring again to grace the vernal scene.
> But we, the wise and strong, we men of might,
> When death comes to us, in earth's hollowed deep
> Condemned to silence keep in dreary night
> A long, an endless, an unwaking sleep.'

Bion of Smyrna was probably some years younger than Moschus, and of his work we have one complete poem and a number of fragments. The first fragment, a dialogue between two shepherds, contains a plain reference to Theocritus. ' Sing me a love song,' says

Myrson, 'such as the Cyclops Polyphemus sang on the sea banks to Galatea'; and in answer we have some twenty lines from Lycidas on the amours of Achilles and Deidameia. Another fragment is a debate on the seasons, the palm being given to spring, 'when all is fruitful and all sweet things blossom.' Three others enlarge upon the Alexandrian idea of Love as a mischievous child, and there are some beautiful lines on the Evening Star. But all these are unimportant as compared with the *Lament for Adonis*, the opening of which is here given in J. A. Symonds' translation.

'Wail, wail, Ah for Adonis! He is lost to us, lovely Adonis!
Lost is lovely Adonis! The Loves respond with lamenting.

Nay, no longer in robes of purple recline, Aphrodite:
Wake from thy sleep, sad queen, black-stoled, rain blows on thy
    bosom;
Cry to the listening world " He is lost to us, lovely Adonis! "
Wail, wail, Ah for Adonis! The Loves respond with lamenting.

Lovely Adonis is lying, sore hurt in his thigh, on the mountains,
Hurt in his thigh with the tusk, while grief consumes Aphrodite:
Slowly he drops toward death, and the black blood drips from his
    fair flesh,
Down from his snow-white skin; his eyes wax dull 'neath his
    eyelids,
Yea, and the rose hath failed his lips, and around them the kisses
Die and wither, the kisses that Kupris will not relinquish:
Still, though he lives no longer, a kiss consoles Aphrodite;
But he knows not, Adonis, she kissed him while he was dying.
Wail, wail, Ah for Adonis! The Loves respond with lamenting.'

Limenius and the Delphic Hymns

Until recently our knowledge of Greek music was derived chiefly from theorists like Aristoxenus and Aristides Quintilianus. But in 1893 the French excavators at Delphi discovered fragments of two hymns which had a musical notation, and one of these not only can be dated with some certainty but is of known authorship. The date is fixed as 128 B.C. by an inscription praying for the welfare of Rome, the writer's name is Limenius, a professional musician, and the hymn itself was performed by professionals. It is in the Lydian mode and has an instrumental score, and some of its descriptive passages are quite pretty verse. The second Delphic hymn is of unknown authorship and cannot be exactly dated, but it probably was written about the same time as the first. The music here is vocal, written in the Phrygian mode, and the author writes with fluency and freedom, giving a vivid picture of the sacrifice on the altar, the cloud of incense spreading up to the sky, and the music of flute and harp blending with the singers' voices.

The scientists : Hipparchus, Heron, Dionysius Thrax, Didymus

As Bion and Moschus brought into the second century the last traces of Alexandrian poetry, so the writers we have now to mention were the last survivors of Alexandrian science. Hipparchus of Bithynia (fl. 140 B.C.), who lived most of his life in Rhodes, is represented now only by an early work, the *Commentary on the Phœnomena of Eudoxus and Aratus*. This fills over a hundred pages in the nineteenth volume of Migne's *Patrologia Grœca*, and consists chiefly of a vigorous refutation of errors. But Hipparchus was also an original thinker and his chief contributions to knowledge may be briefly catalogued. From his observation of the bright star Spica he discovered the precession of the Equinoxes ; he determined more exactly the sizes and distances of the sun and moon ; he calculated more accurately the length of the tropical year ; he accounted for the motions of the sun and moon by the simple epicycle and eccentric hypotheses; and he made a list of the fixed stars to the number of 850 or more. Hipparchus indeed is the last and greatest of ancient astronomers; as Pliny says, he left the heavens as a sort of heritage to all and sundry, and his system was not practically improved upon until the days of Copernicus, Galileo, and Kepler.

Heron of Alexandria is of rather uncertain date but probably he flourished about the same time as Hipparchus. Like Archimedes he was a mathematician who applied his knowledge to practical ends, and the most interesting of his surviving works, which fill four volumes in the Teubner series, is the *Pneumatica*, which describes various ingenious inventions, such as Heron's fountain, a water organ, a fire engine, and penny-in-the-slot machines. His other mechanical works include treatises on automatic devices and on artillery, together with a general history of mechanics which now exists only in Arabic. In geometry we have seven books, of which the most important is the *Metrica*, dealing with problems of mensuration, which was discovered in 1896 in a manuscript at Constantinople. Lastly, there is the *Dioptra*, a treatise on land surveying.

The other famous names in this period were mostly grammarians, and belong to the history of scholarship rather than to the history of literature. Demetrius of Skepsis (fl. 150) wrote thirty books on the list of the Trojan forces in the second book of the *Iliad*. Apollodorus of Athens (fl. 145) commented at equal length on the Homeric Catalogue of ships, and also wrote a handbook of chronology in verse. More interesting than these two is Dionysius the Thracian (fl. 110) the author of the first Greek Grammar. His *Grammatical Handbook* only fills fifteen printed pages in the second volume of Bekker's *Anecdota Græca*, but it is the acorn from which a great forest sprung and remained the standard work for over thirteen centuries. He begins by defining grammar as ' the practical knowledge of the usual language of poets and prose writers,' and then divides his subject into six parts and twenty-five sections of varying length. Section 7, a long one, is on the alphabet ; sections 8–11 on quantity ; section 14, in four pages, on the Noun, a term which includes adjectives and some pronouns ; sections 15–18 deal with the verb, ' tupto ' being taken as example ; section 24 is concerned with adverbs, and section 25 with conjunctions.

Lastly we come to that paragon of industry, Didymus, surnamed Chalcenterus, ' the man with the entrails of brass,' who was teaching in Rome about 45 B.C. Didymus is said to have written over three thousand ' volumes,' and is described by Macrobius as ' grammaticorum facile eruditissimus, omniumque quique sint quique fuerint instructissimus.' His works included two long books on the language of comedy and tragedy, from which Hesychius borrows largely ; a recension of Homer ; commentaries on the earlier lyric poets and the Attic tragedians ; and an edition of Thucydides with a life of the historian. Only fragments of all this now remain in its original form, but much of Didymus is embedded in the later scholiasts to whom he passed on his laboriously gained stores of knowledge.

Poseidonius of Apamea (135–50 B.C.)

The authors with whom we have just dealt were specialists : Poseidonius, the greatest name among Greek writers of the first century, was a man of encyclopædic knowledge, the most learned, as Strabo says, of all philosophers in his time. He began life as

a long-distance runner, whence his name ' the athlete,'
but in early manhood he migrated to Athens, and
there imbibed the principles of the Stoic philosophy
from Panætius. His studies at Athens finished, he set
out on a series of travels in Western Europe, visiting
Spain, Gaul, Italy, Dalmatia and Illyricum, and noting
on his way every point of social, geographical, and
historical interest which he thought worth recording.
He then returned to the eastern Mediterranean and
took up his home at Rhodes, where he became head of
the Stoic school and drew to the island pupils from every
part of the world. In political affairs he also played
a prominent part and was sent by the Rhodians as
their ambassador to Rome in 86. In 51, we are told,
he left Rhodes, intending henceforth to reside per-
manently at Rome, and in Rome the next year he died.

Poseidonius, as we have said, was one of the most
many sided of men. He was an astronomer who inferred
that the sun was many times larger than the earth,
and proved by personal observation at Cadiz that it
does not make a hissing noise when it descends into
the western ocean, constructing also a revolving sphere
to show the motions of the planets. He was a meteorolo-
gist and made an important contribution to the study
of tides in relation to the phases of the moon. He was
a mathematician who tried to evade the difficulty in
Euclid's theory of parallels by a different definition
based on equidistance. He was a moral philosopher
whose consolatory treatises were known and read by
St Jerome, and whose books on divination and the
nature of the gods form the basis of Cicero's *De
Divinatione* and *De Natura Deorum*. He was a student
of natural science and a geographer from whose book,
On the Ocean, Strabo drew much of his most interesting
information. And, lastly, he was an historian who
wrote a history of the Roman world from 144 B.C.,

where Polybius ends, down to 82 B.C. : a history which is our main source of knowledge for those years, the source from which Timagenes, Livy, Nicolaus of Damascus, Diodorus, Josephus, Plutarch, and Appian derive.

To most of the great Romans of his time Poseidonius was a familiar figure. Marius knew him well, and in the next generation Pompey attended his lectures at Rhodes just before his campaign against the pirates, hoping, perhaps, for the military information which he did not get. Cicero also was one of his pupils, and had such a high opinion of his literary skill that he asked him to write a monograph on the events of that *annus mirabilis*, the year of Cicero's consulship ; a task which Poseidinius apparently was prudent enough to evade. That we have now only fragments of his work, mostly preserved by Strabo and Athenæus, is a really serious loss to literature ; for it is plain, even from them, that he had an imaginative vision and a command of picturesque language which would have made him one of the most attractive of ancient writers. The few extracts that follow will perhaps give some idea of the variety of his information, while the long passage in Athenæus may serve as a specimen of his historical style.

Poseidonius is not averse to marvels and his strange tales are many. Once at Lipara after an eruption he saw the sea raised to an enormous height, with flaming mud upon its surface which killed the fish and drove men mad by its stench. On another occasion, as Tryphon's army was marching along the coast of Palestine, a huge wave appeared, which, dashing on the shore, engulfed all the men and drowned them beneath its waters, leaving a huge pile of fish among the dead bodies. Equally amazing are his stories of the sorcerers of the Dead Sea, who use a mixture of asphalt and urine in their incantations, and of the dragon that fell to earth near Lake Genessareth, a dragon 100 feet long, so bulky that horsemen could not see over it, with jaws large enough to admit a man on horseback and scales each one bigger than a shield. He seems also to have been something of a feminist, and frequently enlarges upon the virtues of the female sex. In his account of the Mysians, for example, who abstain from eating any live thing and subsist on honey, milk, and cheese, he controverts the idea that the especial sanctity of these people is due to the absence of female society. 'Women,' he says, 'are notoriously more religious than men. It is they who urge their husbands to pay the gods devout reverence and to take part in festivals and supplications. A man who lives by himself gives little attention to these things.' He thinks also that women, at least among the Celts, have more fortitude than men. 'Women till the soil, and when they have given birth to a child, they put their husbands to bed instead of going there themselves. Often they will be working in the fields when their babies are born, and they merely turn aside to a brook, wash themselves, and swaddle the infant in anything they can find.'

These stories are all in Strabo, and the best specimen of his historical style is the long extract in Athenæus,[1] which fills eight pages, and gives an account of one episode in the Mithradatic Wars, when the Athenians were persuaded by an adventurer named Athenion to join the King of Pontus. After relating Athenion's early history his entry into Athens is described :

'But lo ! here he comes. Pretty well half the population poured out to welcome him, and many others ran also to see the spectacle, marvelling at the paradox of fortune, this upstart Athenion conveyed back to Athens in a silver litter on purple rugs—he who in his ragged days had never even set eyes on purple ; and that too when no Roman

[1] Athenæus, v. 211–215.

had ever vaunted over Attica with such display. Up they ran to see the sight, men, women, and children, expecting something wonderful from Mithradates when the pauper Athenion, who once passed the hat round at his lectures, by the king's favour rides farting through country and town. The artists of Dionysus, too, advanced to meet him, inviting this messenger of the new Dionysus to a public feast with prayers and libations. He who once had gone out from a hired lodging was conducted to the house of Dieuches, the Delian millionaire, which was all decorated with banqueting couches and paintings and statues and display of silver beakers. Thence he emerged trailing a gorgeous white riding cloak and wearing a ring engraved with the portrait of Mithradates, while crowds of servants marched before him and behind in procession.'

Then follows the speech of Athenion, vaunting the success of Mithradates, a speech which resulted in his getting control of the city and establishing there a reign of terror; and the narrative ends with the collapse of the whole sorry business on the arrival of Roman troops.

The Syrian poets : (i) Antipater of Sidon

We have said that Poseidonius was a Syrian : his compatriots, Antipater, Philodemus, and Meleager play the same part in the Greek poetry of their age as he did in Greek prose. Antipater of Sidon (fl. 110 B.C.), as we know from Cicero, was living in Italy during the second half of the second century B.C., and was perhaps the first Greek teacher who took up his home there of his own free will. He became a well-known personage in Roman society, especially famous for his powers of improvisation in hexameter and lyric verse, and he seems to have been admitted as a friend to the inner circles of the Roman nobility. There he doubtless introduced the writings of the Alexandrian poets with which he himself was so familiar. Catulus, the conqueror of the Cimbri, was one of his pupils, and we still possess the first fruits of his teaching in the two

rather clumsy Latin epigrams which by the partiality
of Aulus Gellius are placed on a level with Anacreon.
Antipater probably returned to Syria about 105 B.C.,
and his place at Rome was taken by his young com-
patriot, Archias of Antioch, who arrived in Italy
102 B.C., the year when Marius and Catulus were
consuls. Of Archias we have a full length portrait in
Cicero's famous speech, and he also exercised for many
years a strong literary influence at Rome. But if we
may trust the specimens of his skill preserved in the
Palatine Anthology he was in himself a follower rather
than a leader, and it is to Antipater's verse that we
must look if we wish to find the link between Callimachus and Catullus.

In the Anthology Antipater is very fully represented,
coming third in number of epigrams after Palladas and
Meleager. The majority are either on works of art or
else belong to the sepulchral section ; for Antipater's
strength lies in description rather than imagination, in
literary and artistic criticism rather than the expression
of the emotions. Some of the epigrams are really
meant for tombs, and one particular form seems to be
his own invention : where the details of the monu-
mental sculpture are described and from these details
the name and station of the dead man or woman are
inferred. But most are merely literary tributes to the
illustrious writers of the past. To this class belong the
epigrams on Homer, Sappho, and Stesichorus ; the
acute criticism of Antimachus ; the eulogy on Pindar,
one of the rare tributes paid by ancient poets to perhaps
the greatest of their tribe ; and these lines on the
woman poet Erinna :

> ' Few were her words and all too short her songs,
> Yet to the Muses each brief strain belongs.
> Therefore she fails not of remembrance yet
> And night's dark wings are ne'er about her set.

But we, the singers of a later day,
Cast in great heaps sink swiftly to decay.
Even as jackdaws 'mid the clouds of spring
Caw loud unheeded if some swan shall sing.'

But in addition to the epigrams attributed to Antipater in the Anthology, there is another collection in which he may reasonably be supposed to have a considerable share. The body of poems called *Anacreontics* has come down to us in its present shape by the care of Constantinus Cephalas, who, when he refashioned the Anthology in the tenth century A.D., published also a *Sylloge* of these little pieces, fifty-nine in all. It is plain from his title page that Cephalas himself did not consider many of these to be written by the Teian poet of the sixth century B.C., and the fragments of the true Anacreon bear little resemblance to them in language, metre, or style. The collection is of very varying merit, and while some pieces were probably written in the reign of Hadrian, others are certainly Byzantine. But the best of them, such as those in which the baby Cupid appears, are so similar to Meleager's treatment of similar themes that it is tempting to assign them to Meleager's master. The *Midnight Visitor*, for example, is exactly in the Syrian manner :

' Once at the midnight hour,
    When the bright stars were wheeling
About the heavenly floor
    And sleep men's eyes was sealing,
A knocking at my gate
    Sent all my dreams a-flying,
And in the darkness late
    I heard young Cupid crying.

" O let me in "—he said,
    " 'Tis cold and wet and weary ;
No need to be afraid,
    For I am faint and weary."

'In pity swift I came
   And saw the urchin shiver,
Lit by my lantern's flame,
   With wings and bow and quiver.

" Come to my hearth "—I cried :
   And chafed his frozen fingers
And the dank moisture dried
   That in his tresses lingers :
Until at last now warmed
   He said—" 'Tis time for testing :
Are my dear shafts unharmed
   Within their quiver resting ? " '

He took one at his will
   And deftly aimed the arrow ;
And lo ! a sudden thrill
   Pierced to my very marrow.
He laughed in wanton glee
   And cried—" My bow is sound.
Stranger, rejoice with me :
   You soon will feel the wound." '

(ii) Philodemus the Epicurean (fl. 55 B.C.)

Of all the minor figures of Greek literature there is no one more interesting, no one who has been more favoured by the accidents of place and time than Philodemus of Gadara. To be mentioned by name and to be quoted twice by Horace in the Satires is in itself a piece of signal good fortune ; for although Roman poets depended so largely on the Greeks for ideas they are curiously chary of acknowledging their obligations. But Cicero goes further. In the *De Natura Deorum* he borrows largely from Philodemus, and in the *De Finibus* he couples him with Siro, Virgil's beloved master, as ' the best and most learned of men.' Finally in the speech against Piso he gives us a portrait of the Greek philosopher—known from other sources to be Philodemus—who was then attached to the household of the Roman noble.

151

'This Greek is a man of wit and learning—I know him well myself—and when he is away from Piso he is of the most refined taste. Not merely is he well versed in philosophy, but he possesses those other literary accomplishments which the Epicureans are said usually to despise. The verses he writes are so humorous, so graceful, so elegant that nothing more effective can be imagined. You may censure his morals, if you please, but a mild censure is sufficient. He may be a Greekling, a flatterer, a poet; but he is not an obscene and reckless scoundrel. Well, this Greek stranger came across Piso, or rather he fell into his trap, deceived by that grave severity which has misled so many of our wise men. When once he was in the toils he could not recover himself, and moreover he feared the charge of fickleness. At Piso's earnest request—a request that was practically compulsion—he has written a long poem about his patron, and has drawn in wanton verse a picture of his amours and debaucheries, his illicit intrigues, his banquets and entertainments. The piece might serve, indeed, as a mirror of Piso's life. Much of it is already common property, and I would read it to you now, gentlemen, if I were not afraid that topics of this kind were out of harmony with the character of this court. Moreover, I do not wish to damage the writer's reputation. If he had been more fortunate in his disciple he might perhaps himself have been more sober and sedate.'

Philodemus, as Cicero says, wrote both in prose and verse, and by a curious chance much of his prose has been preserved. When the great eruption of Vesuvius took place in A.D. 79, the villa of the Pisos at Herculaneum contained in its library eight hundred rolls, mostly treatises on the Epicurean system composed by Philodemus a century earlier. Consequently, of the twenty-two volumes of *Herculanensia* a very large proportion consists of fragments of Philodemus. Many of them have been edited, some by a brilliant scholar, the late Professor Gomperz of Vienna. But it would be idle to pretend that they are in themselves of any great value. The lightness and grace which distinguish Philodemus as a poet desert him altogether in these treatises, and their style is tediously dull and common-place. They seem to be based largely on notes taken at the lectures of the Epicurean Zeno, and their subjects bring them into a competition with master-pieces which they are quite unable to sustain. The treatise on music cannot be compared for a moment with Aristoxenus, nor the treatises on poetry, rhetoric and logic with Aristotle. The moral essays 'On Piety,' 'On Anger,' 'On Gratitude,' etc.—parts apparently of a larger work, *On Vices and their corresponding Virtues*—are a little more successful, but are much inferior to Cicero and Seneca. There are fragments of a life of Epicurus, and a catalogue with brief biographies of the chief teachers of the academic school ; but in so far as we can judge them they are not so good as Diogenes Laertius. Perhaps the most interesting of the series is the treatise ' Concerning the Life of the Gods ' ; for most of the questions that Philodemus raises and attempts, not very convincingly, to answer, are still disturbing spiritualists to-day. ' Do the gods sleep ? ' for example. Answer : ' No ; or perhaps they have a sort of repose *analogous* to sleep.' ' Do the gods need furniture ? ' Answer : ' Doubtful ; probably no.' ' Do the gods speak ? ' Answer : ' Yes ; they talk Greek, or something like it.'

If the Herculaneum papyri were all that we possessed of the writings of Philodemus, we should form a very imperfect idea of the man. From them we should picture him as a mere learned bookworm, spending his days in a library and chewing up again the *crambe repetita* of Epicurean doctrine for the benefit of a Roman audience. Fortunately, however, we have thirty-five epigrams attributed to him in the Greek Anthology, and although eight of these are almost certainly not by his hand, the remaining twenty-seven are probably authentic and cast a very different light upon his character. They show us plainly that a Greek philosopher of the first century before Christ was no more certain to be staid and serious than a French abbé of the eighteenth century after Christ was certain to be moral and devout, or an English chaplain of the same time to be sober and religious. ' Molle et facetum ' —the epithets that Horace applies to Virgil—exactly suit Philodemus and the difference between his prose and verse is due to the quality which the Greeks admired and called *eutrapelia*—' happy versatility ' ; while to the Romans it seemed *levitas*—' irresponsible frivolity.'

This faculty of turning at will from grave to gay, of making a mock on occasion of the serious facts of life, of escaping from the bonds of practical morality into the realm of tricksy imagination is displayed in full measure by Aristophanes, Plato, and Euripides to the confusion of sober commentators. It is not a quality that Englishmen commonly either possess or admire, but we shall never truly understand the ancient Greek or the modern French mind unless we allow for its existence. Not allowing for it we are apt to be harsh in our judgments, and from the moral standpoint Philodemus has often been criticized rather more severely than perhaps he deserves. Here are three specimens of his style. The first is in the form of a dialogue between a man and a girl :

' " Good evening, miss." " Good evening, sir, to you."
" And what's your name ? " " What's yours I'd like to know ? "
" You're rather curious, miss." " You're curious, too."

" Are you engaged ? " " To any one I please."
" Then sup with me. How much ? " " No advance fees.
To-morrow you shall settle at your ease."

" Fair terms. Where do you live ? When will you come ? "
" Just when you like." " At once ? " " Well, you are *some* !
I'll tell you where I live and you shall take me home." '

A. P., v. 46.

The English very inadequately expresses the exquisite lightness of the original, which is one of the most skilful pieces of versification in the whole Anthology. In the Greek the first line consists of fourteen words, eleven of them the lightest of monosyllables, and in the one line the speakers change five times—a, b, a, b, a ; and yet there is not the slightest confusion or sense of effort. The hexameter has shown itself capable of almost any modification, but nowhere is it used with a more novel effect than by Philodemus in this little poem of four elegiac couplets.

In another piece of the same light kind Philodemus tries to excuse his vagrant fancies by the example of the divine amorists :

' Fie upon you (people cry),
    Luring girls with wanton eye
Like some hunter in the street
    Skilled to snare each maid you meet.

So they say and yet we know
    Zeus and Pluto, king below,
And Poseidon, ocean's lord,
    All obeyed fierce Passion's word.

If the gods must yield to Love,
    Why should I more stubborn prove ?
Gods for men should models be ;
    Right for them is right for me.'

                    A. P., v. 99.

But in the four poems written to the mistress, whom he calls now Xanthippe and now Xantho, there is a note of deeper feeling ; and with one of these we may end :

' White waxen cheeks, soft scented breast,
    Deep eyes wherein the Muses nest ;
Sweet lips that perfect pleasure bring,
    Sing me your song : pale Xantho sing—

" Close shut within a bed of stone,
    Soon shall I rest in sleep alone,
And there for ever sleeping lie,
    For ever and eternity."

155

Too soon the music ends. Again,
   Again repeat the sad sweet strain.
With perfumed fingers touch the string ;
   O Love's delight, pale Xantho sing.'
A. P., ix. 570.

(iii) Meleager of Gadara (fl. 55 B.C.)

Even more attractive than Philodemus is his contemporary Meleager, son of Eucles, born towards the
end of the second century B.C., in the Syrian town of
Gadara. Meleager began literary work with a volume
of satirical prose dialogues in the manner of Menippus.
Its title, *The Graces*, and the names of two dialogues,
'The Symposium' and 'The Case of the Buttered
Pancake *versus* the Lentil Porridge,' are preserved by
Athenæus. The book itself, although famous in its day,
is now lost, eclipsed by the superior charm of Lucian's
essays in the same style. But while he was still a student
at Gadara and before the publication of *The Graces*,
Meleager had probably written the first draft of *The
Poems of Youthful Love*, celebrating the beauty of his
university comrades. A second volume, published at
Tyre and consisting of poems addressed to his various
mistresses, notably to Zenophila and Heliodora, records
the love adventures of his manhood. Towards late
middle age he left Tyre for the island of Cos, and formed
there an attachment to a young girl, Phanion. His
closing years were occupied by the compilation of the
Garland, and he died at an advanced old age.

Such in brief outline are all the facts we know of the
circumstances of Meleager's career, although we can
form an idea of the conditions amid which he lived.
We are apt to think of Gadara as a small Eastern
village, dirty and malodorous, with herds of pigs
roaming amid the houses ; but in Meleager's time it
was very far from being a village. To-day its site, a
rocky plateau, commanding the valley of the Yarmouk,

156

with the lake of Tiberias in the far distance, is a bare stretch of desert ; but the ruins of two theatres and a row of sculptured columns, which apparently bordered one of its main streets, still bear witness to a happier past. In the second century B.C., the land was filled with busy towns, and Gadara was but one of the group of ten Greek cities, scattered up and down the Jordan valley. It was a meeting-place where Greeks and Jews contended for mastery, arguing continually and occasionally coming to blows, famous for its trade and still more for its reputation as a literary and scholastic centre.

Like most Greek university towns, it owed its position originally to one great man. What Socrates was to Athens, that Menippus had been to Gadara in the third century B.C. The great cynic was one of the most remarkable figures of his age and attracted eager disciples from Egypt and Syria, from the islands of the Ægean, and even from Greece itself ; philosopher, teacher, and writer, a humourist and a scientist like Theophrastus before him, and the inventor of a new literary form, the Menippean Satire. We have no details of the teaching foundation which carried on the Master's traditions, but that such a foundation was established is a probable inference confirmed by the series of distinguished writers coming from Gadara after Menippus' death—Meleager, Philodemus, Theodorus, Œnomaus, and Apsines. Meleager himself speaks of his birthplace as the Syrian Athens, and we should perhaps be not far from the truth if we pictured Gadara in his day as a smaller provincial model of the great Greek university town, drawing its pupils, not like Athens from the whole world, but from the cities of Syria and the adjacent islands. Here the young Syrian received the usual training in rhetoric and literature, and formed those passionate attachments which he celebrates in his early poems. And then the

time came for him to say good-bye to his native fields
and seek his fortune at Tyre.

> ' Farewell ye vales, where once I loved to roam,
> Farewell the pleasures of my mountain home.
> No longer with the flocks, like goat-foot Pan,
> Shall I remain 'mid fields untouched by man.
> What joy to live now on these lonely hills ?
> What solace there to find for all my ills ?
> Daphnis is gone, who set my heart on fire :
> Daphnis is gone—and quenched my heart's desire.
> Let others hunt : the chase I now abhor,
> What once was dear is dear to me no more.
> From country clean and hillside I come down
> To live a sojourner in the crowded town ! '

The change from Gadara to Tyre was as though one
were to leave Oxford for Liverpool. Tyre was then
an independent city maintaining a shadow of freedom
amid the decaying anarchy of the Seleucid empire, a
market for Greeks and Romans, Phœnicians and
Syrians, as great a centre of commerce and pleasure as
ancient Corinth itself. Its inner streets were dirty
with the fumes of dye works, for Tyre was the chief
centre of the dye industry, producing from the crushed
shells of the murex the crimson and purple colours which
were for the ancients the very symbols of luxury and
magnificence. But the great temple of Melkarth and
Astoreth, with its holy fish and sacred courtesans, where
the worship of the Syrian Heracles was combined with
that of the Syrian Aphrodite, gave the pleasures of the
town something of religious mystery. The outer
suburbs, under the last slopes of Lebanon, were among
the most beautiful spots in all the world.

Of the poems he wrote at Tyre some fifty now
remain, and they form a series unique in Greek literature. His mistresses were many—too many a northerner
would think for one man truly to love. But with
Meleager the most short-lived of passions will inspire

a couplet that remains immortal. There is Demo, the pale Jewess, who even in Tyre yearned for the glories of the Temple at Jerusalem ; Asclepias, whose smiling face like the summer sea allured all men to brave with her the perils of Love's ocean ; Timarion, whose lips are a limed lure and in whose bright eyes Eros himself as he winged his way through heaven was taken prisoner. And there is Zenophila :

> ' Asleep, my Zeno ! With what wanton grace
> The damask blooms upon that smiling face.
> A wingless dream might I those eyelids close,
> And near inhale the fragrance of that rose.
> Not e'en the sleep that charms the gods above
> Should come between us then to mar our love.
> But in enfolding arms securely pressed,
> Alone I'd lull my darling to her rest.'

But Heliodora—rose of roses—was his grand passion, and to Heliodora he remained faithful to the end. ' Open my heart,' he cries, ' and you will find my Heliodora's name,' and the elegy that he wrote long after her death still reminds us of the truth and tenderness of his love. We have the history of their passion in some twenty short poems, as various as love itself, and in the most beautiful of them all he combines his love of flowers with his love for his mistress :

> ' The violet white I'll twine,
>   I'll twine the laughing lilies,
> And safran sweet combine
>   With languorous daffodillies.
>
> The hyacinth's crimson crest
>   I'll twine with myrtle posies,
> And then 'mid all the rest
>   I'll twine true lovers' roses.
>
> That so my falling wreath
>   For Heliodora fair
> May match with perfumed breath
>   The fragrance of her hair.'

159

It was probably the death of Heliodora that led
Meleager to leave the riotous splendour of Tyre for
the seclusion of Cos ; and there he completed the great
work of his old age, the *Stephanos*—or as we translate it,
the *Garland*, although the Greek word has wider and
different associations from ours, suggesting as it does
the triumph of victory in the games, the luxury of
voluptuous banquets, the perfumes of flowers offered
to a beloved mistress. Meleager's selection, which
began with Sappho and ended with his own poems, is
the original from which our present 'Anthology,'
whether in the Palatine manuscript or the Planudean
recension, has evolved. We can still see plain traces of
his handiwork in the overgrown collection that we
possess, although it is now very far from being in the
shape that he gave it. His text, probably much shorter
than ours, was arranged alphabetically according to the
first word of each poem. Ours is divided into sixteen
books, according to subject-matter, love poems, dedications, epitaphs, etc., and there is a tendency for poems
to run in series according to their author, the two
arrangements creating a sense of monotony which
Meleager's system insensibly avoided. The methods
of his criticism are not ours, for they are imaginative
rather than scientific ; but his preface is perhaps the
greatest *tour de force* in all the history of appreciation,
so exquisitely are flowers and poets blended together.
The choice of the myrtle for Callimachus, the honey-
suckle for Anacreon, and the thorn for Archilochus
takes the place of pages of laborious criticism. Nor is
it without interest that in an age like his Meleager gives
the two fairest flowers, the lily and the rose, to the
three women poets whom he places first in his list.

Parthenius (fl. 45 B.C.)

The Syrian poets were not only notable in themselves but they also had a great influence on the Roman elegists. A humbler but equally useful part in the development of Roman poetry was played by their contemporary Parthenius of Nicæa. Parthenius, like the historian Alexander of Miletus surnamed Polyhistor, was taken prisoner in Bithynia when the Romans were fighting Mithradates, brought to Rome, and there set up as a teacher by his master, Cinna. He was himself a poet, choosing his wife Aretê as the subject of his verse, and among his pupils was Virgil, who is said to have inserted a translation of one of his master's lines in the *Georgics* :[1]

'Glauco et Panopeæ et Inoo Melicertæ.'

Another pupil was the ill-starred Cornelius Gallus, Prefect of Egypt, to whom he dedicated his prose *Love Romances* in the following terms :

'I thought, my dear Cornelius Gallus, that to you above all men there would be something particularly agreeable in this collection of romances of love, and I have put them together and set them out in the shortest possible form. The stories, as they are found in the poets who treat this class of subject, are not usually related with sufficient simplicity ; I hope that, in the way I have treated them, you will have the summary of each : and you will thus have at hand a storehouse from which to draw material, as may seem best to you, for either epic or elegiac verse. I am sure you will not think the worse of them because they have not that polish of which you yourself are such a master : I have only put them together as aids to memory, and that is the sole purpose for which they are meant to be of service to you.'[2]

The *Love Romances* consists of thirty-six short tales, told in rather halting prose and drawn from the obscurer byways of Greek history and legend. Three of

---

[1] Georgics I. 437.
[2] Translations by S. Gaselee, Loeb Library.

them introduce historical characters in Cyrus, Periander, and Cleonymus of Sparta; two are much to the discredit of Odysseus; four are variations of the story of Tarpeia; and six are concerned with the incestuous loves of father and daughter, mother and son, and brother and sister. Although they were ostensibly written to supply subjects to the budding poets of Rome, they seem to have been little used, and only four of the tales appear in Latin literature. The legend of Daphnis, the Sicilian shepherd beloved by a nymph, who broke his vows and was punished with blindness, occurs in places, and Ovid introduces the tales of Œnone and of Byblis. But even Ovid preferred the ordinary version of the Daphne myth to the strange variant which Parthenius gives:

'This is how the story of Daphne, the daughter of Amyclas, is related. She used never to come down into the town, nor consort with the other maidens; but she got together a large pack of hounds, and used to hunt, either in Laconia, or sometimes going into the other countries of the Peloponnese. For this reason she was very dear to Artemis, who gave her the gift of shooting straight. On one occasion she was traversing the country of Elis, and there Leucippus, the son of Œnomaus, fell in love with her; he resolved not to woo her in any common way, but assumed women's clothes, and in the guise of a maiden joined her hunt. And it so happened that she very soon became extremely fond of him, nor would she let him quit her side, embracing him and clinging to him at all times. But Apollo was also fired with love for the girl, and it was with feelings of anger and jealousy that he saw Leucippus always with her; he therefore put it into her mind to visit a stream with her attendant maidens, and there to bathe. On their arrival there, they all began to strip; and when they saw that Leucippus was unwilling to follow their example, they tore his clothes from him: but when they thus became aware of the deceit he had practised and the plot he had devised against them, they all plunged their spears into his body. He, by the will of the gods, disappeared; but Daphne, seeing Apollo advancing upon her took vigorously to flight; then, as he pursued her, she implored Zeus that she might be translated away from mortal sight, and she is supposed to have become the bay-tree which is called *daphne* after her.'

162

PART II

ROME
(31 B.C.–A.D. 313)

Chapter I

THE WORLD AT PEACE

(31 B.C.–A.D. 117)

IN 31 B.C., the last of the Greek kingdoms went down
in blood and fire at Actium, and for the next two
centuries the Mediterranean world enjoyed the blessings
of universal peace. There were certainly a few frontier
wars and an occasional outburst of military violence,
such as that which in A.D. 68 set the armies of the East
and West marching on Rome ; but speaking generally
the ' Pax Romana ' remained unbroken until the time
of Marcus Aurelius. A system of state socialism was
also introduced under bureaucratic management, and
life proceeded everywhere upon calm and orderly lines.
The result, however, was not encouraging for those
who believe that peace and socialism are good things
for the combative animal Man. There was a general
weakening of energy, a general desire for the lower
forms of amusement, a general disinclination to regard
life as a serious matter. It is true that there was a great
increase in material prosperity ; but in answer to that
a religion arose which affirmed that material prosperity
was a danger to the soul and that the best use to make
of money was to give it away.

Here we are only concerned with literature, and in
the first century A.D. Latin writers overshadow the
Greeks. The results of the patronage extended to men
of letters by Augustus and by Mæcenas, the Roman
counterpart of Demetrius, and their founding of the
Palatine Library, were exactly the same as those which

the Ptolemies had obtained. There was a first quick flowering with Virgil, Horace, Propertius, Livy, and Ovid; a second blooming, due chiefly to a reaction against the imperial system, with Tacitus, Juvenal, and Martial; and then a sudden and complete cessation of literary production. But here again it is with Greek and not with Latin literature that we are dealing; and we must now take up the tale of Greek writers under the Early Principate.

The epigrammatists

The most striking feature in the Greek literature of this period is the almost total absence of poetry. So slender indeed is the stream of Greek verse and so entirely confined to the channel of the epigram that it will be convenient to take all its practitioners together. The first in order of time is Crinagoras, the best of the contemporary poets who appear in the *Garland* which Philip of Thessalonica published some time about the beginning of our era. The duality of Greek and Latin which ran through all the imperial administration extended even to poetry, and under Augustus Crinagoras and Horace shared between them the post of poet laureate, official commemorators in Greek and Latin verse of the triumphs of the new régime. Crinagoras is of course overshadowed by his great rival but his occasional pieces are very graceful. One celebrates the birth of the child of Drusus Germanicus and Antonia, the child who was to unite the fortunes of the Julian and Antonian families :

> ' Great Queen, whose daughters bless the bridal bed,
> By whose strong power the child to life is led ;
> And thou most Mighty father of us all,
> Hear me when for Antonia I call.

Grant that her travail may be quickly stayed
And let the Healer lend soft hands to aid,
That so the mothers of our royal pair
May greet the child she to her lord shall bear.'

A.P. vi. 244.

In another piece he refers to one of the defeats that chequered the course of the German campaigns whose, victories Horace celebrates in the fourth book of the Odes :

' E'en though fierce Ocean lift his waves on high,
E'en though the Germans drink their Rhine flood dry,
The might of Rome shall still unshaken stand
While she confides in Cæsar's high command ;
Strong as the oak whose trunk stays rooted fast
Though autumn gales its leaves to heaven cast.'

A.P. ix. 291.

Crinagoras is of much finer temperament than most of his contemporaries : he is neither coarse, lascivious, nor self-seeking ; and it is hardly to be expected that he should have found the atmosphere of Roman society congenial. We find sufficient evidence in his poems of the painful difference there can be between a poet's ideals and the realities of life, and the spirit of pessimism that drives Omar to his wine jug appears in Crinagoras in a more plaintive form :

' How long, poor heart, these dreams of wealth ?   How long
These empty hopes that to the clouds belong ?
    Dost think at ease to gather riches in !
Leave gold to fools and take God's gift of song.'

A.P. ix. 234.

While Crinagoras occupied a public and quasi-official position, Marcus Argentarius is only known to us by his poems. His name, if we may use the evidence, implies that he was a manumitted slave and that, like two of our greatest Hellenists, he combined the profession of banking with a devotion to the softer art of

167

literature. Such of his verse as has come down to us is chiefly amatory and in some cases derives its inspiration from Meleager.

But Marcus possesses a vein of delicious humour that distinguishes his verse from the over-luscious productions of many amorists. He has a very light touch, and in the little poem to Pyrrha—perhaps the same Pyrrha for whom Horace wrote ' quis multa gracilis '— the joke takes a literary form :

> ' The other day I did espy
> My darling Pyrrha walking by,
> Just as within my hands I took
> Old master Hesiod's musty book.
> I threw the scroll upon the floor
> And vowed I'd read in it no more.
> What do I want with " Works " to-day
> When with my Pyrrha I can play.'
>
> A.P. ix. 161.

Humour is largely a matter of taste, and some may consider that Marcus is more successful than the professional humourists Lucilius and Nicarchus whose poems were published in Nero's reign and now appear in the tenth and eleventh books of the Anthology. To tell the truth their satirical epigrams—' On misers,' ' on philosophers,' ' on athletes '—make rather tedious reading and are chiefly interesting as the models on which Martial so vastly improved. Still, such as they are, here are some specimens. One from Lucilius on misers :

> ' When Stingy has the stomach-ache
> He does not pennyroyal take,
> But draws a penny from his purse
> And sniffs it till the pains disperse.'
>
> A.P. xi. 165.

Another from Lucilius on the statue of a professional pugilist :

> ' He never hurt a living thing,
>   His hands with blood were never wet ;
>   So we who fought him in the ring
>   His statue here have set.'
>   *A.P.* xi. 80.

The third has been frequently adapted in English :

> ' Old Stingy chanced a mouse to see
>   And cried " What want you, miss, with me ? "
>   The mouse replied, with civil sneer
>   " There's nothing, friend, for you to fear.
>   I shall not put you to expense ;
>   I seek not board but residence." '
>   *A.P.* xi. 391.

Puritans and vegetarians were familiar figures even in Rome, and one of the funniest pieces in Book XI, by Ammianus, is aimed against the latter sect :

> ' He went among his garden roots
>   And took a knife and cut their throats,
>   Then served us green stuff heap on heap
>   As though his guests were bleating sheep.
>   Rue, lettuce, onion, basil, leek,
>   Radishes, chicory, fenugreek,
>   Asparagus and peppermint
>   And lupines boiled—he made no stint.
>   At last in fear I came away :
>   I thought the next course would be hay.'
>   *A.P.* xi. 413.

In a graver vein Ammianus is equally effective :

> ' Dawn follows Dawn until the Dark One come
>   To drive us scattered to our Common Home.
>   Heedless we play, while Water, Wasting, Fire
>   To this one and to that he gives for Doom.'
>   *A.P.* xi. 13.

In a strain of similar sadness writes his contemporary Besantinus, the author of the curious acrostic poem *The Altar* (*A.P.* xv. 25) :

' " Alas for cruel Age ! " I heard One sigh.
" Alas for Youth ! " soft Echo made reply.
No hour for blissful Tarrying may we know.
Youth swift has flown and swift Age draweth nigh.'

A.P. ix. 118.

So much then for the satirists. It may be argued
that humorous verse, like humorous painting, is a
mistake, and that the proper medium for a literary joke
is prose as the proper medium for a pictorial joke is
black and white. But be that as it may, this Græco-
Roman humorous verse is not very exhilarating. It is
rather coarse, rather monotonous, and rather brutal,
the three adjectives which may well be used of Rufinus,
the next considerable poet of this period.

Of Rufinus himself we know as little as it is possible
to know of an author. When and where he lived, who
he was and what position he held, are all questions that
admit of no certain answer. It has been conjectured
that he is the same person as the Rufinus Domesticus,
one of the officials of the Byzantine court to whom a
single epigram in the latter part of Book V is attributed.
But this is altogether unlikely and it is far more probable
that the first third of Book V containing the forty poems
of Rufinus, mingled with the work of minor poets of
the first century A.D., is what remains of the anthology
that he brought out in Trajan's reign. In any case his
amatory verse—and all his surviving poems are concerned with this one subject—show that strange mixture
of sentiment and grossness which is the true mark of
decadence in literature and morals. Some of Rufinus
sinks very low and is almost grotesque in its indelicacy,
but yet, when he likes, as in the letter to Elpis, he can
write charming verse. But Rufinus, even at his best,
is somewhat mawkish. It is only when compared with
Strato, his immediate successor in time, that he appears
bearable. With Strato we descend to the nadir of

corruption, to depths far lower than those Rufinus reaches. The compiler of the *Musa Puerilis* is one of the least estimable of poets and the twelfth book of the Anthology, which bears his name, reveals only too plainly the anarchy of morals which preceded the anarchy of government in the third century A.D. As it stands now the twelfth book has Strato's work only as its basis, for Cephalas or some other Byzantine editor incorporated with it many pieces of the same character taken from previous anthologies and also, by a somewhat ludicrous mistake, a few of Meleager's most beautiful love poems addressed to women. This last editor too, whoever he was, prefixed to the book the following apologetic words :

' What sort of man should I be if, after setting forth for your knowledge all that precedes this, I should now conceal the *Puerile Muse* of Strato of Sardis, which he himself used to recite in jest to his companions, taking his own special pleasure not in the meaning of the epigrams but in their style. Receive then what follows ; for as the tragic poet says " If a woman be chaste, she will not be corrupted at the theatre." '

It may well be considered that some apology is needed, and Strato, speaking in his own person in prologue and epilogue, gives both warning and defence.

PREFACE

' You will not read of Priam here,
Of Niobe, and of Medea ;
No Itys here his mother grieves
Nor nightingales among the leaves.
The bards of old have done enough
With all that solemn tragic stuff.
I sing of Love, I sing of Wine,
And Graces gay with both combine,
Nor dismal faces wish to see ;
For frowns and I do not agree.'

A.P. xii. 2.

But when every allowance is made for Strato ; when we take into account that he was born at Sardis, the capital of the old Lydian kingdom where this particular vice was endemic and whence probably it was imported into Greece ; even when we know that Hadrian, the reigning emperor of his day, was so infatuated with his young favourite Antinous as to claim for him the honour due to a god ; in spite of all it is impossible to acquit the poet of a very considerable amount of personal responsibility. In the great revival of Greek culture that was the glory of the second century A.D., it was perhaps inevitable that the darker side of Greek life should appear in literature, but for the mixture of grossness and triviality which he uses in treating his subject Strato alone is to blame.

Still, in spite of his deplorable errors in taste and his flagrant offences against morality, Strato is an ingenious and graceful versifier. *The Little Florist* is a fair specimen of his best manner :—

> ' The other day, as I passed by
> A florist's shop, I chanced to spy
> A face within that seemed more fair
> Than all the flowers assembled there.
>
> My heart beat fast : I rushed inside
> And to my charmer quickly cried :
> " Roses like you I just adore ;
> Pray how much may I have one for ? "
>
> At that there came a sudden blush
> More red than any rose, and " Hush,
> Hush, sir " ; soft whispered, " go away.
> My father is at home to-day ! "
>
> I bought some flowers, to save my face,
> And backward went with lagging pace.
> But from that shop I'm hoping yet
> The fairest flower of all to get.'

A.P. xii. 8.

Diodorus Siculus (fl. 30 B.C.)

We must now return to chronological order and to the prose writers of the Augustan age. First among them is Diodorus of Sicily, who is as good a link between the Alexandrian and the Roman periods as his favourite authors Ephorus and Timæus are between the Athenian and the Alexandrian. Diodorus was born at Agyrium in Sicily about 80 B.C., and after learning Latin in his youth travelled for many years in Europe and Asia, preparing himself for the great historical work which he had conceived. This time of preparation lasted for some thirty years, and it was probably soon after the battle of Actium in 31 B.C., that he published his *Historical Library*. In his preface Diodorus himself gives us a summary of this immense work. Divided into forty books it covered a period of 1138 years from the Trojan War in 1183 down to the death of Julius Cæsar in 44 without counting the mythical period before exact chronology begins. To this prehistoric age the first six books were devoted, three dealing with Egypt, Assyria, and Ethiopia, and three with Greece. The next eleven carried on the tale from the Trojan War to the death of Alexander, the tenth book ending with the Persian War 480, and the next seven embracing the most important period of Greek history from 480 to 323. These seven we still have complete together with five of the first six, and we also have Books XVIII, XIX, and XX, which contain the history of the successors of Alexander : the last twenty books, which extended from 302 to 44 B.C., only now exist in fragments.

It will be seen that Diodorus' scheme is not lacking in grandeur, and if his execution had corresponded with his idea he might have written a great book. But unfortunately he has no originality, no critical method, and no sense of style. When we have him speaking in his own person, as he does in the first five chapters of the first book, he uses an awkward jargon of long words and clumsily constructed sentences; but in most of his history Diodorus himself hardly appears. His system is to take some previous author, generally one whose flat style appealed to his own taste, and following him closely to flatten him still further. His principal sources seem to have been Hecatæus of Abdera and Ctesias for Egypt and Persia; Ephorus, Theopompus and Callisthenes for Greece in the fifth and fourth centuries; Philistus and Timæus for Sicily; and Cleitarchus and Douris for Alexander and his successors. Thucydides and Xenophon he uses hardly at all; but he gives some extracts from two writers of great interest of whom otherwise we should have nothing, Iambulus and Hieronymus of Cardia.

As for consulting inscriptions, monuments, and city archives, Diodorus does not appear to have even conceived the idea; and it is in vain to look in him for any philosophy of history or general view of the rise and fall of nations. Nor is it often that he draws on his personal knowledge. He tells us, it is true, that at the time of his visit to Alexandria, probably about 50 B.C., a Roman who killed a cat by accident was murdered by an angry mob, and that he saw over the doorway of a library in Egyptian Thebes the inscription ' This is a sanatorium for the soul.' But anything so actual as this is rare, and it is seldom that we get a lifelike picture of place or person. One of the best is the portrait of Demetrius Poliorcetes in Book XX: ' His beauty and stature were such that people would follow him in the streets for the mere pleasure of looking at him. His spirit was haughty and proud, contemptuous of all men small or great. In peace he was a second Bacchus in his love of wine and riotous feasting, in war the most sober and energetic of men and of surpassing vigour.' Passages like this, however, are rare and it is for his facts that Diodorus is now read. In his earlier books and in his account of Sicilian affairs there are many curious tales, such as the discovery of barley and wheat by Isis in Egypt (I. 14) and the expedition of Minos of Crete against Kokalos in Sicily (IV. 66), and historians find in him a mine of information. But it is a pity that he is not a better writer.

Nicolaus of Damascus (fl. 25 B.C.)

The writing of universal history, as we have seen in our own days, is a tempting proposition whether it be done by one man or by a syndicate, and Diodorus had a contemporary rival in Nicolaus of Damascus. Nicolaus was born of a rich Syrian family, and according to his own account was one of the most brilliant youths of his time. His talents recommended him to the notice of Herod, whom Mark Antony in 40 B.C. had made King of the Jews, and he became at first Herod's secretary and then his confidential adviser. In this latter capacity he was sent to Rome to justify to Augustus Herod's conduct towards the Arabs; a mission which, he says, he performed with complete success. Later in Herod's reign he was commissioned by his master to accuse his eldest son Antipater before the governor of Syria, and after Herod's death, 4 B.C., he made a second journey to Rome in the interests of Archelaus, and at Rome probably died.

Nicolaus wrote his history to please one autocrat, and the preservation of such parts of it as remain is due to another, Constantinus Porphyrogenitus, Emperor of Byzantium, A.D. 912–959, who had copious extracts made from the first eight of its 144 books. These now fill a hundred pages in Dindorf's *Historici Græci*

Minores, and we have also a short autobiography and a *Life of Julius Cæsar.* Nicolaus' style is rather Asianic, but it is not lacking in vigour, and his long account of Cæsar's assassination is full of vivid details :

> ' Meanwhile the assassins made ready, taking their places for the ambush, some at his side, some in front, some behind. Before he entered the senate house the priests brought in the sacrifice, the last indeed which he was to offer ; and plainly in that offering he was not blessed. The soothsayers found the omens unfavourable, and kept on changing the victims, in the hope that some better sign might be vouchsafed them ; but at last they had to confess that the heavens were hostile and that they saw an avenging spirit hidden in the sacrifice. Thereupon Cæsar in annoyance turned from them towards the sun which was just setting : and, of course, that at once became a fresh omen.'

Juba (fl. 10 B.C.)

Another encyclopædist of the Augustan age is Juba II, son of the king of Numidia who fought for the Pompeians against Julius Cæsar at Thapsus in 46 B.C., and committed suicide after his defeat. As a child Juba was brought to Rome to grace Cæsar's triumph, and as a young man he fought for Octavian against Antony. As a reward he was restored to his father's throne, given Cleopatra Selene, daughter of the great Cleopatra, as his wife, and as king of Numidia and Mauretania lived peacefully in his new capital of Cæsarea until his death in A.D. 20, his days being fully occupied with literary pursuits. According to Plutarch he was the most cultured of all kings and the most learned in history, while Athenæus calls him the perfect polymath. Among his works were a *Roman History* and two books on Libya and Arabia, from which that other great compiler Pliny the Elder drew much doubtful information. More valuable perhaps were his two long treatises, the *Art of Painting* and the *History of the Theatre,* of which latter much has passed without acknowledgment into the *Onomasticon* of Julius Pollux.

Strabo (63 B.C.–A.D. 21)

Juba's encyclopædias, constructed probably by a free use of scissors and paste, have passed away; but we possess a more valuable and a more practical collection of facts in Strabo's *Geography*. Strabo, who is quoted by later writers simply as 'the geographer' as Homer is 'the poet' and Aristoxenus 'the musician,' was born at Amasia in Pontus in the year of Cicero's consulship when Pompey with a Roman army was marching up and down Asia Minor. By race he was half an Asiatic, for his mother's ancestors were natives of Pontus, one of them priest of Ma under Mithradates the Great; but by education he became completely Greek, being a pupil at first of Aristodemus of Nysa, then of Tyrannion, tutor to Cicero's son, finally of Xenarchus of Seleucia. Under Tyrannion and Xenarchus he studied at Rome about the year 44 B.C., and it was probably Tyrannion who first turned his attention to geography, a further stimulus perhaps being given by Poseidonius, whose acquaintance he also then made. Another of his friends was the Stoic philosopher Athenodorus, the teacher of Augustus, and it was to the Stoics that Strabo eventually turned, their doctrine of conformity to nature being set forth at length in his seventeenth book, while in his political opinions he follows Polybius, and frequently expresses his admiration for the Roman imperial system : 'It would be difficult,' he says, ' to administer so great an empire except by handing it over to one man as to a father; and never have the Romans enjoyed such peace and plenty as Augustus Cæsar gave them and Tiberius is giving them now ' (Bk. VI. 4. 2).

M   177

It was once thought that Strabo wrote the *Geography* at Rome between the years A.D. 18 and 19 at the instigation of his powerful Roman friends. But Ettore Pais has recently argued that it was put together chiefly in the interest of Pythodoris, Queen of Pontus, and that it was meant not so much for the Romans as for the Greeks of Asia Minor. Pais also considers that although much of the material was collected earlier, the actual writing of the book was done at Amasia about 7 B.C., and that it was only a revised edition which appeared in A.D. 18. These theories are supported by the fact that no Roman author, not even Pliny the Elder, shows any knowledge of Strabo, and they are also in harmony with those dates in Strabo's life which are known to us. In 44 B.C., and again in 35, 31, and 29, we find him visiting Rome ; in 25 B.C. he was in Egypt as adviser to Ælius Gallus and accompanied him up the Nile to Syene ; he was still living in Egypt in 20 B.C., and probably during those five years made in the Alexandrian Library the excerpts from his predecessors which fill such a large part of his book. Just before 7 B.C. he was again in Rome, being then about fifty-six years old, and we have no evidence that he visited Italy again, nor is he acquainted with the map of Agrippa which was made some little time after.

Strabo considered himself a great traveller :

' I have travelled westward from Armenia as far as the regions of Tyrrhenia opposite Sardinia, and southward from the Euxine Sea as far as the frontiers of Ethiopia. You will not find any geographical writer who has travelled over greater distances than I have ' (Bk. II. 5. 11) ;

but it is only of the Southern and Eastern Mediterranean lands that he has extensive first-hand knowledge. It cannot be proved that even in Greece he visited any place except Corinth, and in Italy his journeys were usually confined to the main roads. His book, in fact, is quite as much the work of an historian as of a traveller, and it is inspired not so much by a love of science as by a vague moral purpose :

> 'After I had written my *Historical Sketches*, which have been useful, I suppose, for moral and political philosophy, I determined to write the present treatise also ; for this work itself is based on the same plan, and is addressed to the same class of readers, and particularly to men of exalted stations in life. Furthermore, just as in my *Historical Sketches* only the incidents in the lives of distinguished men are recorded, while deeds that are petty and ignoble are omitted, so in this work also I must leave untouched what is petty and inconspicuous, and devote my attention to what is noble and great, and to what contains the practically useful, or memorable, or entertaining.' [1]

The *Geography* is divided into seventeen books, and it is rather unfortunate that the first two are both in manner and matter the least inviting of all. After a general introduction and defence of Homer as a source of geographical knowledge Strabo attempts to refute Eratosthenes and Hipparchus, but as he is not himself an expert mathematician he only succeeds in being tedious. But it is worth while ploughing through these two books—or skipping them—in order to come to the rest. Books Three to Ten are a description of the European countries, Spain in Book Three, Gaul and Britain in Book Four, Italy and its islands in Books Five and Six, N.E. Europe in Book Seven, and Greece in Books Eight, Nine, and Ten. We then pass over to Asia and in Books Eleven to Fourteen have an account of the countries in Asia Minor ; Book Fifteen treats of India and Persia, Book Sixteen of Assyria, Syria and Arabia, and Book Seventeen deals very fully with Egypt. The descriptions that Strabo gives of the different countries vary greatly in interest and in length, depending, as they do, on his own knowledge and the

---

[1] Bk. I. i. 23. tr. H. L. Jones, Loeb Library.

authorities at his disposal. Of Britain he has not much
to say : 'It is triangular in shape and its longest side
stretches parallel to Gaul and is of the same length,
4300 furlongs. Most of the island is flat and overgrown
with forests although many parts are hilly. It produces
grain, cattle, silver and iron, hides, dogs, and slaves.
The Britons are taller than the Gauls but bandy-legged
and ill proportioned. Their forests are their cities, and
they have more rain than snow. Even in clear weather
it is so foggy that the sun only appears for three hours
in the middle of the day.' This is a summary of Strabo
on Britain, and on Ireland he is even less instructive :
'Ierne is a large island inhabited by a savage people.
They eat their fathers when dead and have intercourse
with their mothers and sisters.'

As regards Britain and Ireland Strabo is not at his
best : but his account of Spain, based on Poseidonius
and Artemidorus, is extremely interesting. South-west
Spain, the ancient Turdetania, lying between Cape
St Vincent and Gibraltar, is described in rapturous
terms as a land of plenty, abounding in grain, wine,
oil, wax, honey and pitch, rich in cattle and free from
all destructive animals except 'burrowing hares.' Here,
too, all the metals are to be found ; iron, copper, silver,
and gold in nuggets weighing half a pound ; while off
the coast there is a profusion of oysters, mussels, conger-
eels and tunny fish, 'which feed on stunted oaks
growing at the bottom of the sea and producing large
fruit.' On the other parts of Spain Strabo is equally
full of information. The Atlantic coast is inhabited
by a slovenly race who bathe in urine matured in cisterns
and with it wash their teeth : they think that to walk
for exercise is a proof of madness. The Cantabrians
are a most ferocious people, impossible to subdue : once
when some of them had been taken prisoners a small
boy got hold of a sword and at their command killed

his father and his brothers. The men of Gades fit out the largest of all the merchant ships which ply in Our Sea and the Outer Sea, Gades itself being equal in size to any city save Rome. The Lusitanians drink water, eat acorn bread and goat's flesh, sleep on the ground, dress in black, let their hair grow over their eyes, and are excellent fighters.

These are but a few details from the third book, for Strabo is an inexhaustible mine of information. In Book XI, for instance, on one subject only, ways of burial, he gives us the following facts. The Massagetæ consider the best kind of death when they are old is to be chopped up with the flesh of cattle and eaten in the mixture. The Bactrians when an old man becomes feeble throw him out as a prey for the dogs which they keep on purpose and call in their tongue ' undertakers.' The Caspians starve anyone over seventy to death and place his body in the desert, keeping watch over it from a distance. If they see it dragged off the bier by a vulture they deem it fortunate, if by a wild beast or dog less happy, but if it is left untouched they think it accursed.

While Strabo is interested in the disposal of dead bodies, he is even more interested in the killing of animals, and he is one of the few ancient authors who can be described as a sportsman. With him we can spear swordfish off Sicily, stalk ostriches in Nubia, and ferret rabbits in Spain ; and his account of the different ways of elephant hunting in India is especially good. The last method he describes is this : ' The hunters note the trees against which the elephants are wont to rest, and approaching them from the other side cut the trunks low down. So when the elephant comes and leans against it, the tree falls and the elephant falls too. And since the elephant is unable to rise because its legs have only a continuous and unbending bone, they leap down from the trees and cut it to pieces. And these hunters are called " Untouchables." '

Strabo, indeed, has almost as keen an eye for the curious as Herodotus himself, although he scarcely possesses the historian's narrative skill, as may be seen in the stories of Polycrates and of the gold digging ants which occur in both authors. But he has many good tales of his own. In his pages, for example, we may read how Piasus, king of the Pelasgians, becoming enamoured of his daughter Larisa, was punished for his unnatural passion when the girl tipped him into a cask of wine over which he was carelessly leaning : how the Sicilian tyrant Dionysius invited the young girls of Locri to a banquet, made them dance naked, and then let loose among them a flock of doves which they had to chase in odd sandals, one with a high heel and one with a low : how, finally, the Arabian princess, wearying of the attentions of her fifteen brothers, put their walking-sticks outside her boudoir, as a lady might now hang up a visitor's hat, and was discovered when all fifteen happened to meet.

Nor does Strabo in his many digressions from geographical matters confine himself to the lighter side of history. He gives us in his fifteenth book a long and very interesting account of the Brahmins and fakirs of India, an account which shows how little that great continent has changed since Alexander's day. In Book X we have an elaborate discussion of the origin of religion and myth, and in Book XVI the following portrait of Moses :

' Moses was one of the Ægyptian priests, and held a part of Lower Ægypt ; but he went away from there to Judæa, since he was displeased with the state of affairs there, and was accompanied by many people who worshipped the Divine Being. For he said and taught that the Ægyptians were mistaken in representing the Divine Being by the images of beasts and cattle, and that the Greeks were also wrong in modelling gods in human form ; for according to him God is this one thing alone that encompasses us all and encompasses land and sea—the thing which we call heaven, or universe, or the nature of all that exists. . . . Now Moses, saying things of this kind, persuaded not a few thoughtful men and led them away to this place where the settlement of Jerusalem now is; and he easily took possession of the place, since it is not a place that would be looked on with envy, nor yet one for which anyone would make a serious fight.'[1]

Dionysius of Halicarnassus (fl. 10 B.C.)

History, even literary history, has a curious way of repeating itself, and searchers after coincidence may find in the service done to Greek letters by Dionysius in the first century A.D. a presage of the part which was to be played by Petrarch in Latin thirteen centuries later. Greek prose after the death of Demosthenes passed through a slack period. Aristotle set the fashion of indifference to artistic form, and during three centuries there was hardly a prose author who followed the canons of Attic style. A few indulged in tasteless rhetoric but most were merely dull and flat. The mass of their work accordingly was allowed to perish, and although the value of their material has preserved Polybius, Diodorus, and Strabo, even they gain rather than lose by translation. At last with Dionysius there came a reaction, and from a literary standpoint he is as truly the morning star of one renaissance as Petrarch is of the other.

We have said 'from a literary standpoint'; for Dionysius was very far from playing a brilliant part in society or from having the authority over the outside world in matters of taste which Petrarch exercised. Coming to Rome from Asia Minor about 30 B.C., an unknown scholar without a patron, he earned his living as a private tutor to some Roman nobles of literary tastes, such as Rufus Melitius and Ælius Tubero; and eventually became a well-known figure in a small circle

[1] Tr. H. L. Jones, Loeb Library.

of Greek professors who had for various reasons taken up their home in the great capital, Cæcilius, Zeno, Demetrius and Ammæus. It is to this company that we must look for the first signs of the Attic revival, and the writings of Dionysius are the best expression we have of the literary discussions which occupied most of their energy.

The list of these writings is a fairly long one, the first in time probably being the *On the Ancient Orators*, six essays of which we now have only the first three, on Lysias, Isæus, and Isocrates. These are all written on the same plan; a short life followed by a critical estimate of the speeches and a series of illustrative extracts. Lysias is praised for his purity of diction, his truth to character, and his powers of persuasion, ' even if he says what is untrue you are compelled to believe.' Isæus, on the other hand, is too clever, ' although he is telling the truth you suspect him '; while Isocrates in spite of his smoothness is tame, and ' strives laboriously to attain the charm which with Lysias is a gift of nature.'

After the *Ancient Orators* come two studies of a more elaborate nature, one on the orator Deinarchus, the other on Demosthenes. In the *Deinarchus* our author is concerned chiefly with facts of literary history and seeks to draw up a true list of the genuine speeches; but the other essay *On the eloquence of Demosthenes* is a glowing tribute of enthusiastic praise. ' When I take up one of his speeches, I am entranced and carried hither and thither. I feel distrust, anxiety, fear, disdain, hatred, pity, good-will, jealousy. I am agitated by every passion in turn which can sway the human heart.' To Dionysius Demosthenes is what Cicero was to Petrarch, and even though the treatise is now sadly mutilated it has always been rightly regarded as a masterpiece of critical appreciation. Far less successful is the *On Thucydides*, in which the great historian is

THE WORLD AT PEACE, 31 B.C.–A.D. 117

taken to task both for the style of his speeches and for the treatment of his subject. Dionysius admits that his narrative is usually admirable, but he is clearly afraid that writers will try to imitate the speeches, and insists that from them Demosthenes has taken all the good points and avoided all the bad.

The three *Literary Letters* to Ammæus and Cnæus Pompeius are again chiefly occupied with Demosthenes and Thucydides, although the letter to Pompeius also deals with some points in Plato's style. In the first letter to Ammæus Dionysius undertakes to refute the statement, made by an anonymous critic, that Demosthenes owed his success as an orator to the precepts laid down by Aristotle in the *Rhetoric*, and points out that most of Demosthenes' speeches were delivered before the *Rhetoric* was written. The second letter to Ammæus deals at rather tedious length with the technical features of Thucydides' style, while the letter to Pompeius, after setting out the author's judgment on Plato, ' In this one respect Plato is inferior to Demosthenes, that with him elevation of diction sometimes lapses into emptiness,' in the third chapter compares Thucydides adversely with Herodotus. It must be remembered, however, that although Dionysius is a very good critic, he was also a very poor historian, and his longest work, to which he attached a high value, is the *Roman Antiquities*, a history of early Rome of which we now have about ten of its original twenty books. Of the *Roman Antiquities* the less said the better, for it is nearly as impossible as Petrarch's epic poem *Africa*, and like Dionysius' criticisms of Thucydides it is vitiated by the assumption that the first object of history is to please or to instruct rather than to tell the truth.

All the critical treatises we have mentioned contain much of literary value, but the best of Dionysius is to be found in the *On the arrangement of words*, which among other things has preserved for us the two finest pieces of Greek lyric, the *Ode to Aphrodite* of Sappho and the *Danaë* of Simonides. It begins by distinguishing between thoughts and words, and proceeds to a short account of the 'parts of speech,' the proper combination of which makes a sentence. Beauty of style is obtained by melody, rhythm variety, and propriety, and three modes of composition are enumerated, the austere, the florid, and the intermediate. Prose should be metrical, rhythmical, and melodious without actually becoming metre, rhythm, or poem; and this precept is illustrated in what is perhaps Dionysius' most eloquent passage. People have said that if Demosthenes had been a really great orator he would not have troubled about the arrangement of his words, and Dionysius, after citing the example of Plato and Isocrates, defends his hero :—

> 'What wonder, then, if Demosthenes also was careful to secure euphony and melody and to employ no random or untested word or thought ? For it appears to me far more reasonable for a man who is composing public speeches, eternal memorials of his own powers, to attend even to the slightest details, than it is for the disciples of painters and workers in relief, who display the dexterity and industry of their hands in a perishable medium, to expend the finished resources of their art on veins and down and bloom and similar minutiæ. These arguments seem to me to make no unreasonable claim ; and we may further add that though when Demosthenes was a lad, and had but recently taken up the study of rhetoric, he naturally had to ask himself consciously what the effects attainable by human skill were, yet when long training had issued in perfect mastery, and had graven on his mind forms and impressions of all that he had practised, he henceforth produced his effects with the utmost ease from sheer force of habit.' [1]

It is easy to point out Dionysius' weaknesses, his narrowness of view, his love of rhetoric, and his absorption in questions of style. But his weakness is

[1] 'De Compositione Verborum,' Ch. xxv. trans. W. Rhys Roberts.

also his strength. Style was just the thing which for three centuries had disappeared from prose, and it is chiefly owing to the *On the arrangement of words*, and its fellow treatises *On the Sublime* and *On Style* that nearly every Greek author in the second and third centuries A.D. is acquainted with the principles of good writing and can still be read with pleasure.

' On the Sublime '

The authorship of the treatise *On the Sublime*, formerly attributed to Cassius Longinus, who flourished at the court of Zenobia, queen of Palmyra, in the third century A.D., is a matter which in default of fresh facts cannot be decided. But internal evidence, and especially the mention of Cæcilius, a critic contemporary with Dionysius, whose works are now lost, fix the date of its composition with some certainty as early in the first century A.D. It is brief and incomplete, and its existence was unknown until it was published by Robortello at Bonn in 1554, but ever since it attracted Boileau's notice in 1674, and was translated by him, it has been recognized as one of the most illuminating pieces of criticism in world literature. ' Till now,' says Gibbon in his *Journal*, ' I was acquainted only with two ways of criticizing a beautiful passage, the one to show by an exact anatomy of it the distinct beauties of it and whence they sprung ; the other an idle exclamation or a general encomium, which leaves nothing behind it. Longinus has shown me that there is a third. He tells me his own feelings upon reading it, and tells them with such energy that he communicates them.'

The treatise is in fact the beginning of modern appreciative criticism, as an analysis of its contents will show. The author begins by defining ' the Sublime ' as 'a certain distinction and excellence of language,' and remarks that although a lofty style may be the gift of nature it is yet controlled by art. The faults that are inconsistent with sublimity are bombast, puerility, misplaced emotion, and bad taste, and to avoid these we must know what the Sublime really is, which is difficult owing to the fact that a just judgment is the final fruit of much experience. The Sublime depends on five things; grandeur of conception, intensity of emotion, the proper employment of figures of speech, nobility of expression, and dignity of composition; and the rest of the book is devoted to a consideration of these five qualities.

Grandeur of conception, which can only be obtained by 'nourishing a soul to greatness,' comes first and is illustrated from Homer's Iliad, from Sappho's Ode to Anactoria, and from the Jewish lawgiver, 'no ordinary man,' who said : 'God said—what ? "Let there be light," and there was light. "Let there be earth," and there was earth.' It is also seen in Demosthenes who resembles a thunderbolt, and in Cicero who is more like a spreading fire. Intensity of emotion is reserved for another treatise, and figures of speech, such as the oath of Demosthenes 'by the men of Marathon,' are then discussed at length, many examples being given from Herodotus, Thucydides, and Xenophon. Nobility of expression comes next, 'for beautiful words are in deed and in fact the very light of the spirit,' and after some remarks on metaphors there is a digression on the question whether grandeur with some faults is to be preferred to a faultless mediocrity, the decision being that Homer comes before Apollonius, Demosthenes before Hypereides, and Plato before Lysias. Dignity of composition is then briefly discussed and the treatise ends with a long and very interesting chapter on the decay of literature in the author's time, which he is inclined to attribute not to the loss of freedom but to the prevailing love of money and desire for pleasure.

> ' When the whole life of each one of us is governed by thoughts of petty gain and by hunting after other men's deaths and laying snares for legacies ; when we have enslaved ourselves to luxury and have sold our souls for gain at any cost, how can we expect in this ruinous pestilence to find even one impartial judge of the things that are great and last for ever ? For such as us it is perhaps better to have a master than to be free.'

' On Style '

The treatise *On Style* is somewhat later than the *On the Sublime*, and as regards authorship it is in much the same case. Its writer, Demetrius, was once supposed to be Demetrius of Phalerum, but this is an obvious mistake, and it has been suggested that he is the Demetrius of Tarsus who was a friend of Plutarch and in A.D. 80 was teaching Greek at York. Whoever the author may be, the book is a workmanlike production, and though it cannot be compared with the *On the Sublime*, it contains much sound criticism. Written in unpretending style and based on Aristotle's *Rhetoric* its main subject is the art of prose composition, but many quotations are also given from Homer, from Sappho ' in the texture of whose poetry every lovely word is inwoven,' and from Sophron. Four varieties of style are distinguished, the elevated, the elegant, the plain, and the forcible ; and although the author's own preference is for short sentences he shrewdly remarks— ' The clauses in the periodic style may be compared to the stones which support and hold together a vaulted dome : in the disconnected style they resemble stones flung down near to one another and not built into a structure.'

' The Tablet of Cebes '

The Tablet is another work, of much less importance than the previous two, which has like them often been wrongly dated and wrongly attributed. Its author is not the Cebes of Thebes who was one of Socrates' followers, but a Stoic philosopher of the same name who wrote towards the end of the first century A.D. In form it is a description of an allegorical picture seen by two strangers in the temple of Cronos and interpreted to them by a benevolent guide. As the picture is an image of human life and the figures in it comprise most of the Virtues and Vices, it may be imagined that the allegory is both long and complicated, nor is it lightened by any great amount of imagination. But as a popular presentation of the Pythagorean and the Stoic creeds it was widely read in ancient times and was one of the first school books used in England. In the sixteenth century it was studied by the sixth form of Norwich School, and Milton in his Treatise on Education speaks of it as ' easy and delightful ' : but of these epithets the first now seems more appropriate than the second.

' The Library of Apollodorus '

Still a fourth book of uncertain date and authorship is the ' Library ' of Apollodorus, a summary of the Greek myths and heroic legends, derived from books and written in a plain and unaffected style. The patriarch Photius, writing in the ninth century A.D., thought that its author was the Athenian grammarian who flourished about 140 B.C. and wrote a treatise *On the Gods*, but this has been shown to be impossible, and such evidence as we can get from style points to the first century of our era as its probable date. Until

1885 we only possessed three of its seven books, but in that year an epitome of the entire work was discovered in the Vatican Library at Rome, and this partly fills the gap. The first six chapters of Book I contain the Theogony, and then the narrative proceeds by families ; Deucalion, Inachus, Agenor with its two branches Europa and Cadmus, Pelasgus, Atlas, and Asopus. In the fourteenth chapter of Book III we come to the Kings of Athens and among them to Theseus, before we reach the family of Pelops. Then we have the events before the Trojan War, the War itself and its sequels, the return of the Greek leaders, and lastly the wanderings of Odysseus. All this is set out simply but in full detail, and if anyone wishes to get a knowledge of Greek mythology he will be well advised to neglect modern manuals and to read Apollodorus in Sir James Frazer's excellent translation.

Apollonius of Tyana

The four books we have just mentioned are of uncertain date and authorship, but some people deny that Apollonius ever existed, and consider the *Life*, written by Philostratus in the third century A.D., to be sheer fiction. It is certain that many of the details given by Philostratus of the ascetic wanderer are imaginary, but there is considerable evidence to show that Apollonius was a real man, that he lived in the reign of Nero, and that among other things he wrote a Life of Pythagoras which was used by Porphyry and Iamblichus. Moreover, the great Church historian Eusebius quotes one passage as definitely his which deserves citation :

'The only proper way to worship God and to win at once His surpassing favour and grace, is not to sacrifice at all, nor to kindle fires, nor to name by any sensible object Him whom I called the prime Deity, the one God, apart from and before all others. He

191

needs nothing even from beings superior to us ; and all the products
of earth and air, whether plant or animal, have a taint of pollution.
Let us only address God in the higher language—not the language
that proceeds from our lips—and ask blessings from the noblest of
existing beings by means of the noblest power in us. That power
is Reason, which needs no organ to express it.'

Philo Judæus (fl. A.D. 20)

We may now turn to the series of Jewish writers who
are so remarkable a feature in the Greek literature of
this period. Philo, commonly called 'the Jew' to
distinguish him from the many others of the same
name, was born about 20 B.C. at Alexandria, in whose
vicinity nearly a million Jews then resided. The
literary interests of this community during the first
century before and after the birth of Christ were
somewhat peculiar, and many of the forged histories,
forged letters, and forged oracles which we possess are
probably to be attributed to the misguided energy of
some of its members. But Philo is an author of a more
serious type, and as a link between Hellenism and
Judaism on the one hand, and between Judaism and
Christianity on the other, he holds a very important
position in the history of thought.

Philo writes in Greek, but it will be obvious to anyone
who reads him that in spite of his constant references
to the various schools of Greek philosophy, the Pytha-
goreans, the Platonists, and the Stoics, he is always at
heart a Hebrew. He may borrow at times from Plato's
theory of ideas, but the central point of his theology
is that while God is absolutely removed from us and
incomprehensible, He is also infinitely close. This is
an antinomy, and Philo solves it by postulating as
intermediaries between the uncreated and the created
the *Logos*, and the two *Potencies* represented in the
Old Testament by the names of ' God ' and ' Lord.'

Philo's works fall into five divisions, the first and far the largest consisting of the twenty-two treatises in which he expounds what he considers to be the inner and spiritual meaning of various incidents and texts in Genesis. To him every word of the Pentateuch, even in the Septuagint translation which he used, is directly inspired ; and as he is also conscious that many passages in their literal sense are either trivial or incredible, he extracts from them the underlying thought which the unwary fail to perceive. One example may illustrate his method. In the treatise *On the Creation* he is explaining why we are told that a serpent tempted Eve :

'Following a probable conjecture one would say that the serpent spoken of is a fit symbol of pleasure, because in the first place he is an animal without feet sunk prone upon his belly ; secondly because he takes clods of earth as food ; thirdly because he carries in his teeth the venom with which it is his nature to destroy those whom he has bitten. The lover of pleasure is exempt from none of these traits, for he is so weighted and dragged downwards that it is with difficulty that he lifts up his head, thrown down and tripped up by intemperance ; he feeds not on heavenly nourishment, which wisdom by discourses and doctrines proffers to lovers of contemplation, but on that which comes up out of the earth with the revolving seasons, and which produces drunkenness, daintiness, and greediness. These, causing the cravings of the belly to burst out and fanning them into flame, make the man a glutton, while they also stimulate and stir up the stings of his sexual lusts.' [1]

The second section of Philo's writings contains the lives of Abraham, Joseph, and Moses ; the third the books dealing with the Mosaic legislation ; the fourth the essays *Goodness is Freedom, The Contemplative Life, Rewards and Punishments* and *The Virtues* ; the fifth the two political treatises *Against Flaccus* and the *Embassy to Caius.* These last two were both written in Philo's old age, but they are extremely vigorous and

[1] 'On the Creation', Ch. lvi.   Translation, G. H. Whitaker, Loeb Library.

of considerable historical importance. From them we
see that the Jews in spite of their many excellent
qualities were not too popular in Alexandria, and
Philo's main charge against Flaccus, the Roman
governor, is that he never tried to check the insolence
of the mob, ' an idle and lazy crowd, accustomed to
licence of speech and bursting with envy and ill-will.'
One such incident is related at length. When Herod
Agrippa arrived in Alexandria, on his way to take the
throne in Judæa which Caius had given him, some
rascals got hold of a harmless maniac, who usually lay
naked in the roads, dressed him up with a papyrus
crown, a door-mat cloak, and a stick for sceptre, and
hailed him as ' King of the Jews ' : and Flaccus let
them go unpunished. Other similar misdeeds occupy
forty pages and the piece ends with the governor's
death at the Emperor's order, ' a plain proof of God's
providence watching over the Jewish people.'

The *Embassy to Caius* is even more interesting, for it
contains a full and first-hand account of one of the
strangest figures in Roman history, the mad Emperor
Caius Caligula. Caius, among his other eccentricities,
was convinced of his own godhead, and issued orders
that he should receive divine honours from all the
peoples of the Empire. Thereupon the Alexandrian
Jews sent Philo and four others to Rome asking to be
excused, and the story of their experiences fills nearly
a hundred printed pages. They found it almost
impossible to get an interview with the Emperor, for
he was always occupied with some mad prank, and one
day, when they were awaiting his pleasure at his seaside
villa, a Jew came rushing up to them ' with bloodshot
eyes and sobbing for breath,' and told them that Caius
had just decreed that his statue should be placed in
the Holy of Holies at Jerusalem. At last the unfortunate ambassadors succeeded in entering the imperial

presence, and followed Caius as he went from room to room in his new palace with a train of architects and contractors at his heels. But all they could get from him was ' Why do you not eat pork ? ' and they were finally dismissed with the remark that they seemed rather foolish than wicked, in that they did not gladly accept Caius as a god.

Josephus (c. A.D. 37–102)

Josephus shares with Plutarch the distinction of having been with us for many years one of the most popular of Greek writers. Half a century ago if an English household possessed six books five of them were apt to be the Bible, Shakespeare, Bunyan, Plutarch's Lives, and Whiston's Josephus. Popular education has altered all this, and it is possible that Whiston to-day has but a small sale ; but in spite of the attractions of the daily press, the *Jewish War* and the *Antiquities* are still books that may be read with pleasure and profit.

Joseph ben Matthias, son of a priest and of royal descent, was born in Palestine four years after Caius' attempt to place his statue in the Temple almost brought about a religious revolt. He showed his precocious talents early, when at the age of fourteen he was consulted by learned rabbis, and after spending three years as an ascetic in the wilderness returned to Jerusalem in early manhood to become a leader among the Pharisees. In 64, when under Nero the Christians were made responsible for the burning of Rome, he visited Italy, and on his return to Judæa did his best to check the feeling against Rome which was rising high among his countrymen. The slackness of the Roman governor, however, and the attack on Roman troops at Bethhoron in 66 made war inevitable, and Josephus was given an important command in Galilee. When

Vespasian advanced from Antioch he threw himself into the fortified town of Jotapata and stood a siege of forty-seven days. Then the town surrendered and Josephus for the next two years was a prisoner in Roman hands. In July 69 Vespasian was proclaimed Emperor by his soldiers, and Josephus, who had prophesied Vespasian's rise to imperial power, was released and accompanied Titus to the siege of Jerusalem, serving him there as interpreter and conducting the difficult negotiations between the Romans and the Jews. After the fall of Jerusalem in 70 he came to Rome, and was given Roman citizenship, a place on the civil list, and rooms in Vespasian's private house. There he stayed for the rest of his life occupied chiefly with his writings and even in the dangerous times of Domitian still retaining the imperial favour.

The foregoing account of Josephus' life is based upon his own *Autobiography*, the latest and by far the least satisfactory of the four works that have come down to us. It was published about A.D. 101 in answer to attacks made upon the author by a rival Jewish historian, and consists largely of a defence of his conduct during his half year's command in Galilee in 67. To this a brief account of his youth in Palestine and his later years in Rome is added, in which Josephus indulges his vanity to the full, and the whole book, whether we regard its taste, its veracity, or its literary style, is a very poor production.

The second of the minor works, *Against Apion*, is much more attractive : it is well designed, shows considerable knowledge of classical Greek literature, is inspired by a sincere enthusiasm for the Jewish religion, and is written with a fair amount of literary skill. The reason of this superiority seems to be that in the *Autobiography* Josephus depended upon himself, but in the *Against Apion* and also in his other two books he had the assistance of Greek collaborators. He himself reveals the fact that he ' employed helpers for the sake of the Greek,' and the ingenuity of modern editors has revealed the personality of two of these ghosts, one of them a slavish imitator of Thucydides, the other a more cultured writer with a great love of the Greek poets and especially of Sophocles. The treatise is a defence of Judaism against its enemies and would be better called ' Against the Greeks,' for Apion, who was an Alexandrian Greek teaching at Rome, nicknamed by Tiberius 'the cymbal of the world,' only appears in the second book and is regarded merely as a typical detractor of the chosen people. One of the libels spread abroad by Apion and refuted by Josephus may be taken as an example of the rest. When Antiochus Epiphanes forced his way into the Temple sanctuary he found a man reclining before a table laden with good things, who told him that he had been kidnapped by the Jews and was being fattened for sacrifice ; ' a tale,' as Josephus says, ' which is not merely packed with tragic horrors but is also replete with impudent cruelty.' He goes on to show its incredibility :

' All who ever saw our temple are aware of the general design of the building and the inviolable barriers which preserved its sanctity. It had four surrounding courts, each with its special statutory restrictions. The outer court was open to all, foreigners included; women during their impurity were alone refused admission. To the second court all Jews were admitted and, when uncontaminated by any defilement, their wives ; to the third male Jews, if clean and purified ; to the fourth the priests robed in their priestly vestments. The sanctuary was entered only by the high-priests, clad in the raiment peculiar to themselves, and into it no vessel whatever might be carried.' [1]

All that Josephus wrote is propaganda, and the chief purpose of the *Jewish War* is to prove to his com-

---

[1] ' Against Apion ', II. 102. This passage is from the Latin version of Cassiodorus. Trans. H. St J. Thackeray, Loeb Library.

patriots the futility of further opposition to Rome:
' My intention is not so much to extol the Romans as to
console those whom they have vanquished and to deter
others who may be tempted to revolt ' (Bk. III, 108).
It was composed at Rome under the patronage of
Vespasian and Titus and published by their authority :
' So anxious was the Emperor Titus that my volumes
should be the sole authority from which the world
should learn the facts that he affixed his own signature
to them and gave orders for their publication.' This,
of course, refers to the Greek text as we have it now,
but there was also a previous version written in Aramaic,
while the Russian translation, entitled ' On the Capture
of Jerusalem,' contains many details of the life of Jesus
which do not appear in our manuscripts. With this,
however, we cannot now deal, and the reader must be
referred to the highly important work of Dr Eisler,
' The Messiah Jesus and John the Baptist ' (London,
1931).

The *Jewish War* is in seven books and covers a period
of over two centuries. The first book extends from
the time of Antiochus Epiphanes of Syria (c. 170 B.C.)
to the death of Herod the Great, the second goes down
to the outbreak of war in Judæa in A.D. 66. Book III
tells the story of Vespasian's campaign in Galilee
A.D. 67, and includes the siege and capture of Jotapata.
In Book IV we have the conclusion of the Galilean
campaign, the investment of Jerusalem, and the
proclamation of Vespasian as Emperor at Alexandria
in July A.D. 69. Books V and VI describe the siege and
capture of Jerusalem by Titus in A.D. 70, and the
history ends in Book VII with the triumphal return of
the victors to Rome. Whether we regard it as history
or as literature the book has conspicuous merits, and
it is one of the few cases where the writer himself
played a prominent part in the events which he relates.

It should be too well known to need quotations, but as examples of Josephus at his best we may refer to the vigorous account of the siege of Jotapata in Book III and to the poignant narrative of Herod's domestic tragedies in Book I, in which we may suspect that the ' Sophoclean ' assistant rendered considerable help.

Lastly we come to Josephus' *magnum opus*, the *Jewish Antiquities*, dedicated, like the *Against Apion* and the *Autobiography*, to a certain Epaphroditus, probably the wealthy scholar mentioned by Suidas who possessed a library of 30,000 books in Rome. The *Antiquities*, modelled on the similar work of Dionysius of Halicarnassus on ancient Rome, is an attempt to prove to the western world the greatness of Judæa, just as the *Jewish War* was an attempt to prove to the eastern world the greatness of Rome. It is in twenty books, the first ten, going down to the captivity in Babylon, being an expansion of the biblical narrative ; the last ten, based on Nicolaus of Damascus and the author's own knowledge, continuing the history to the reign of Nero. Speaking generally the *Antiquities* is not so interesting as the *Jewish War* ; it has many dull passages and is very uneven in style : indeed, the author seems himself to have grown weary of his long task and to have handed over the latter books entirely to the worse of his two chief assistants, the ' Thucydidean ' scribe. For the brighter parts the ' Sophoclean ' helper is probably responsible, and his hand may certainly be seen in the story of Joseph and the wife of Pentephres (Potiphar), which is expanded into a long narrative, with many arguments on both sides :

' By these words and yet more to like effect Joseph endeavoured to curb the woman's impulse and to turn her passion into the path of reason ; but she displayed only a more violent ardour and, flinging her arms about him, despairing of persuasion she would have had resort to force. Joseph fled from her in indignation, leaving with her his cloak, by which she had held him, and which he abandoned when he leapt from the chamber ; then, terrified lest he should inform her husband, and smarting under this affront, she resolved to forestall Joseph by falsely accusing him to Pentephres : this method of avenging herself for so grievous a slight and of accusing him in advance seemed to her alike wise and womanly.'

The Writers of the New Testament

It has been the habit of pedants in all ages to depreciate the literary qualities of the New Testament and to imagine that because the Apostles and St Paul do not use the Attic idiom they are unworthy of the attention of classical scholars. In the sixteenth century Cardinal Bembo could seriously warn his colleague Sadoleto against reading St Paul's Epistles, lest their barbarous language should corrupt his taste: 'Omitte has nugas, non enim decent gravem Virum tales ineptiæ'; and in our own days Nietzsche's gibe is well known : ' It is strange that God found it necessary to learn Greek in order to communicate with men, and that he learnt it so badly.' Such men, being themselves but half alive, have always chosen to regard Greek as a dead language and have refused to see that the New Testament writers, so far from writing bad Greek, achieve lucid narrative, close reasoning, and impassioned poetry in a living tongue. If this folly needed refutation, it has been supplied by Bishop Lightfoot's Commentaries on the Pauline Epistles, and the discovery of the Egyptian papyri has given the words of that great scholar, spoken in 1863, a new significance : ' If we could only recover letters that ordinary people wrote to each other without any thought of being literary, we should have the greatest possible help for the understanding of the language of the New Testament.' Since Lightfoot's day his wish has been fulfilled, and we see now that in the New Testament we have a particularly good example of the *Koinê*, the 'common language,' which was the usual medium of intercourse in the Eastern part of the Roman Empire. Therefore in the following pages an attempt will be made to give a brief account of the various books, regarding them solely as literature written by plain men for plain men.

Of the three Synoptic Gospels it is now generally agreed that the 'Good News' of St Mark was written first, and is the basis from which St Matthew and St Luke built up their longer narratives. Its author, if we may trust the statement of Papias, Bishop of Hierapolis in the second century A.D., quoted by Eusebius in his *Ecclesiastical History*, was the John Mark of the Acts, and he derived his information from St Peter, whose companion and Greek interpreter he was. He wrote his Gospel about the year A.D. 70 after Peter's death, and he depended on his memory to recall the details which Peter had given him, using also perhaps a narrative of the Passion which was already in existence. He begins not with a statement, but with a triumphant fact, and his Gospel is above all a record of events arranged in chronological order, supported by many marks of concrete truth, and emphasizing the acts of Jesus rather than His teaching. In style Mark recalls the historical books of the Septuagint even more plainly than the other Evangelists, and his sentences are joined together in the most simple fashion. But he is transparently clear, and his very simplicity gives his language a majestic dignity and even a kind of rhythm.

The Gospel of St Matthew has St Mark for its foundation, but it contains many additions, some peculiar to itself, others drawn from the *Logia*, the 'Sayings of Jesus,' which both Matthew and Luke use. Its author was probably, but not certainly, the apostle who is called in this Gospel only a 'publican,' and its date is some time after A.D. 70 : all else is uncertain.

The chief points in which it differs from St Mark are three. Firstly, although this is of little importance, it is slightly more elaborate in style and composition. Secondly, St Matthew stresses the connection between the old dispensation and the new, he quotes much more frequently from the Old Testament and in his first chapter emphasizes the descent of Jesus from David and Abraham, and he twice refers to the new community of Jesus' followers as a Church. Thirdly, St Matthew gives far more of the teaching of Jesus. Not only are the parables more numerous, but we find long continuous discourses, such as the instructions given to the disciples, the invective against the Pharisees, and above all the Sermon on the Mount. It has been said that the Sermon, which we owe to Matthew alone, is in its beauty, simplicity, and truth purely Hellenic; and certainly in all these three qualities it is unsurpassed in Greek literature.

St Luke, author of the Gospel which bears his name and also of the Acts of the Apostles, is a writer of a different kind from Mark and Matthew. He is by way of being a professional, and his preface has a distinct literary flavour :

'Forasmuch as many have taken in hand to set forth in order a declaration of those things which are most surely believed among us, even as they delivered them unto us, which from the beginning were eyewitnesses, and ministers of the word ; it seemed good to me also, having had perfect understanding of all things from the very first, to write unto thee in order, most excellent Theophilus, that thou mightest know the certainty of those things, wherein thou hast been instructed.'

This preface, however, is perhaps a concession to the weakness of some wealthy convert, and the rest of the gospel is written in a much more natural style. But St Luke is always an artist, and while it is hard for us to discover what manner of men Mark and Matthew were, Luke, like all artists, reveals himself in his books. It is to the poet in him that we owe the *Magnificat* and the *Nunc dimittis*; the physician is revealed in his intense sympathy with the poor and suffering; the imaginative writer appears in the wonderful episode of the pilgrims of Emmaus.

The Gospel was written by St Luke sometime between A.D. 80 and 90; the Acts, again with a preface to Theophilus, came some years later. They fall into two parts, the first twelve chapters giving the history of the early church at Jerusalem where Luke depends for his facts on others, the last sixteen narrating the missionary journeys of St Paul in which Luke played a personal part. In the Gospel the nature of his material and the example given by Matthew and Mark more or less fixed the character of Luke's account; but in the Acts he is his own master and we have a book which when compared with profane histories even in a literary sense at least holds its own. The narrative, with its mixture of the real and the miraculous, is a very subtle blend of simplicity and art, while the speeches, undoubtedly composed by Luke himself, that of Peter after the Pentecost, that of Stephen before his martyrdom, and above all that of Paul at the Areopagus in Athens, serve to sum up a period or a personage as well as does the Funeral Oration of Pericles.

Of the fourth Gospel, and of the Apocalypse, which also bears the name of John, it is difficult to give a brief account. The Gospel begins with the doctrine of the *Logos*—' In the beginning was the Word, and the Word was with God, and the Word was God,' and in the eighth chapter we have another mystic utterance: ' I am the Light of the World '; both ideas common in later Alexandrian theology but hard to attribute to the simple fisherman who was a disciple of Jesus. The whole trend of the Gospel is towards mystical theology, and in the Apocalypse addressed to the seven churches of Asia, with its visions and obscure historical allusions, this is accentuated. The language of the Gospel does not differ greatly from that of the three Synoptic narratives, but the Apocalypse is written in the strangest of styles. Epithets do not agree in gender with their nouns, words are used in other senses than the usual, phrases like ' From He who is and was and shall be ' are common, and generally speaking it may be said that although the author writes in Greek he is plainly not in the habit of thinking in Greek. As for the date of the two compositions and the personality of their writer, both subjects of much dispute, all that can be said here is that the Apocalypse was probably written by a prophet called John about A.D. 70, that he was identified by the early church with John the son of Zebedee, and that the fourth Gospel, composed A.D. 100, and the three Epistles were also attributed to him.

Besides the three Epistles of John there are four other so-called General Epistles. The two by St Peter and the Epistle of Jude are of no great importance and by some are considered apocryphal, but the Epistle of St James is of great literary interest. Renan thought it the best written of all the New Testament books, and its language follows classical models so closely that although the sentiments are those of James the actual composition may be due to his Greek secretary. Its doctrinal value lies in the importance given to works over faith, but it is best known by the many moral maxims in its pages. ' Pure religion and undefiled before our God and Father is this, to visit the fatherless and widows in their affliction, and to keep himself unspotted from the world.' ' The tongue is a little member, and boasteth great things . . . the tongue is a fire . . . the tongue can no man tame ; it is a

restless evil full of deadly poison.' 'Swear not, neither
by the heaven, nor by the earth, nor by any other
oath : but let your yea be yea, and your nay, nay.'
These and many other pregnant sayings are to be found
in its five short chapters.

We have left the greatest of the New Testament
writers to the last. Saul of Tarsus, afterwards called
Paul, was born about A.D. 10, his father being a Jew
who had gained Roman citizenship and probably a tent-
maker by trade. At Tarsus, which was a university
town and the chief centre in Cilicia of Greek civilization,
Paul received his early education before going to
Jerusalem to study under the rabbi Gamaliel. As an
ardent supporter of militant Judaism he was present at
the martyrdom of St Stephen, and was on his way to
persecute the Christians at Damascus when he was
converted by a vision, and after a conference at Jerusalem was admitted into the new church to become the
Apostle to the Gentiles. Of the tribulations he endured
for the next years he himself has spoken with incomparable force [1] :

> ' Of the Jews five times received I forty stripes save one. Thrice
> was I beaten with rods, once was I stoned, thrice I suffered ship-
> wreck, a night and a day I have been in the deep ; in journeyings
> often, in perils of waters, in perils of robbers, in perils by mine
> own countrymen, in perils by the heathen, in perils in the city, in
> perils in the wilderness, in perils in the sea, in perils among false
> brethren ; in weariness and painfulness, in watchings often, in
> hunger and thirst, in fastings often, in cold and nakedness.'

In his early missions Paul was accompanied by
Barnabas and John Mark, in his later by Silas, Timothy,
and Luke. The church in Galatia was his first founda-
tion, followed in Greece by Philippi, Thessalonica, and
Corinth. He was living in Corinth in the years
A.D. 50–51 when the Jews accused him before the

---

[1] II Corinthians, xi. 24–27.

Roman governor Gallio, ' who cared for none of these things ' ; and then after three years' travels he returned to Jerusalem in 54, to be seized by the Jews and brought before the governor Felix. Felix handed him over to his successor Festus, and Festus, after keeping him for two years in Cæsarea, sent him for trial to Rome. At Rome he stayed under free custody ' in his own hired dwelling ' until 58, and after that date we know nothing certain. It is possible that he visited Spain in the following years, and it was the tradition of the early church that both he and St Peter suffered martyrdom on the same day in A.D. 68.

These are the main facts of Paul's life ; but here we are concerned with him not as the second founder of Christianity, but only as a figure in Greek literature. In that literature the fifteen Pauline Epistles have a place of their own, and a list of them at least must be given. The four masterpieces are Romans, Galatians, and First and Second Corinthians. Of the others the first Epistle to the Thessalonians is a simple message of encouragement, the second is of doubtful authenticity. Philippians and Colossians have incurred criticism for doctrinal reasons but are now generally accepted, but Ephesians is doubtful. So also is the Epistle to the Hebrews, which almost certainly is not by Paul; and of the four letters to individuals, to Philemon, to Titus, and the two to Timothy, only Philemon is above suspicion. It will be seen that the Epistles are of unequal value, but in the great four, although they are written in colloquial Greek, and although the writer has no thought for art, there are pages which are as moving and as impressive as the finest flights of Demosthenes. Paul never studied rhetoric, but with him genius takes the place of training, and the flowing periods of Attic orators do not surpass his short anaphoric sentences in effect :

'Love suffereth long and is kind; love envieth not; love vaunteth not itself, is not puffed up, doth not behave itself unseemly, seeketh not its own, is not provoked, taketh not account of evil; rejoiceth not in unrighteousness, but rejoiceth with the truth; beareth all things, believeth all things, hopeth all things, endureth all things. Love never faileth.'

Epictetus (c. A.D. 50–120)

The New Testament gives us one example of the *Koinê*; another is supplied by the *Discourses* of Epictetus. Indeed, these are even nearer to the spoken language, for Epictetus himself never wrote anything, and the book which goes by his name consists of the verbatim notes of his lectures made by one of his pupils, Arrian, the man who afterwards became famous as historian and administrator. In his preface Arrian makes this plain:

'I have not composed these *Words of Epictetus* as one might be said to "compose" books of this kind, nor have I of my own act published them to the world; indeed, I acknowledge that I have not "composed" them at all. Whatever I heard him say I used to write down, word for word, as best I could, endeavouring to preserve it as a memorial, for my own future use, of his way of thinking and the frankness of his speech. They are, accordingly, as you might expect, such remarks as one man might make off-hand to another, not such as he would compose for men to read in after-time.'[1]

But before we consider the *Discourses* and the *Manual*, some facts concerning the life of Epictetus must be given. Epictetus was born at Hierapolis in Phrygia about A.D. 50, the son of a slave woman, and was for many years a slave himself. He was of feeble health and had been lamed by the brutality of one of his masters before he was brought to Rome and entered the household of Nero's agent, Epaphroditus. His new owner seems to have been fairly humane and perhaps it was he who gave Epictetus his liberty. At any rate

[1] Translations, W. A. Oldfather, Loeb Library.

he became a free man, and after attending the Greek lectures of the great Stoic, Musonius Rufus, set up himself as a teacher in Rome. By the time of Domitian he was well known, and when that perverse reformer in A.D. 89 banished all philosophers from Italy he was compelled to leave Rome and establish his school at Nicopolis in Epirus. There he remained for the rest of his life, taking a wife in his old age to help him bring up a little child whom he had saved from exposure. His pupils were many and the Emperor Hadrian was his friend, but his life was of the utmost simplicity, as one anecdote in the *Discourses* shows.[1] He is telling his pupils that the best way to avoid loss of property is to have none, and says : ' I too until lately had an iron lamp which I kept by the side of my household gods. Well, one day I heard a noise at my window, and running down found that my lamp had been stolen. I reflected that the thief's motive was not altogether unreasonable, and " To-morrow," said I, " you will find an earthenware lamp there." '

Of the two records of Epictetus which Arrian has left us the *Enchiridion*, or ' Manual,' is far the best known. It is quite short, a compilation made by Arrian from the *Discourses*, and one quotation must suffice :

' As on a voyage, when your ship has moored off shore, if you go on land to get fresh water, you may pick up as an extra on your way a small mussel or a little fish, but you have to keep your attention fixed on the ship, and turn round frequently for fear lest the captain should call ; and if he calls, you must give up all that, if you would escape being thrown on board tied up like the sheep. So it is also in life. If there be given you, instead of a little fish or a small mussel, a little wife or a small child, there will be no objection. But if the captain calls, give up all that and run to the ship, without even turning to look back. And if you are an old man, never even get far away from the ship, for fear that when He calls you may be missing.'

[1] 'Discourses', I. xviii. 15.

208

The *Manual*, although it proved invaluable in the Middle Ages as a guide to the main principles of the monastic life, is too formal and systematic to give an adequate idea of Epictetus himself. To see how lovable the man was and how great his influence over his pupils we must turn to the *Discourses*. There we find the born teacher, sure of himself and sure of the doctrine which it is his business to impart.

'And so now I am your teacher, and you are being taught in my school. And my purpose is this—to make you a perfect work, secure against restraint, compulsion, and hindrance, free, prosperous, happy, looking to God in everything both small and great; and you are here with the purpose of learning and practising all this. Why, then, do you not complete the work, if it is true that you on your part have the right kind of purpose and I on my part, in addition to the purpose, have the right kind of preparation? . . . Cannot the matter be taught? It can. Is it, then, not under our control? Nay, it is the only thing in the whole world that is under our control. Wealth is not under our control, nor health, nor fame, nor, in a word, anything else except the right use of external impressions. This alone is by nature secure against restraint and hindrance. Why, then, do you not finish the work? Tell me the reason. . . . Only let us begin, and, take my word for it, you shall see.'

It may be asked what was this work which he strove to achieve in his pupils; and the answer may almost be given in the one word—Freedom. To him, who had been a slave, liberty and independence seemed the greatest of all possessions, and with the utmost intensity he forces home the truth that a man can only be free when he breaks himself loose from worldly ties. Nothing can compensate for the loss of freedom : wealth, fame, riches, love, the pleasures of sense, the acquisition of knowledge, all these when compared with freedom are as nothing.

'To one man it is reasonable to hold a chamber-pot for another, since he considers only that, if he does not hold it, he will get a beating and will not get food, whereas, if he does hold it, nothing harsh or painful will be done to him ; but some other man feels that it is not merely unendurable to hold such a pot himself, but even to tolerate another's doing so. If you ask me then, " Shall I hold the pot or not ? " I will tell you that to get food is of greater value than not to get it, and to be flayed is of greater detriment than not to be : so that if you measure your interests by these standards, go and hold the pot. " Yes, but it would be unworthy of me." That is an additional consideration, which you, and not I, must introduce into the question. For you are the one that knows yourself, how much you are worth in your own eyes and at what price you sell yourself. For different men sell themselves at different prices.'

In this passage Epictetus speaks with a touch of ironical indulgence ; but usually he allows no paltering with weakness. To read the *Discourses* is as bracing as to take a cold bath on a frosty morning. Some may find the first shock painful, but the plunge once taken is followed by a marvellous sense of moral and spiritual vigour.

Plutarch (c. A.D. 45–125)

Plutarch from a purely literary point of view is something of a phenomenon. Of all Greek prose writers he is the most widely read, and he has been the favourite author of innumerable great men, not only of men of action like Napoleon and Frederick the Great, but also of men of letters like Rousseau and Schiller. Montaigne called the *Lives* his ' breviary,' Madame Roland styled them ' the pasture of great souls,' and Emerson says ' Plutarch will be perpetually rediscovered from time to time as long as books last.' And yet he cannot be called a good writer in the strict sense of the word. He is the last of the Alexandrians, untouched by the influence of Dionysius and his school, and his style has all that peculiar flatness which is the mark of Alexandrian prose. In translation, of course, this is not so obvious, and Plutarch has been fortunate in his translators, for both North and Amyot are classics in English and French literature. But as a general rule, when a translation is as good as its original, the original itself from the point of view of style falls far short of perfection. Therefore, in giving Plutarch the praise which is his due, it must be remembered that it is upon his matter rather than his manner that his greatness depends.

Plutarch was born at Chæronea in Bœotia about A.D. 45, just at the time when Greece was beginning to revive after the disasters of the Roman civil wars. His family was of an old Greek stock established in Bœotia from time immemorial, and in his childhood from the lips of his grandfather Lamprias he listened to tales that went back to the days of Antony and Cleopatra. His youth was passed in a genial atmosphere of simple refinement, and he was already familiar with the masterpieces of Greek literature when at the age of nineteen he left home to finish his education at Athens. There he spent several years, studying rhetoric, mathematics and philosophy under Ammonius, and after a visit to Egypt settled for a time in Rome, where his lectures on philosophy were attended by many of the leading Romans of Vespasian's reign. He travelled extensively in Italy but never acquired a thorough knowledge of Latin, for, as he says, ' I had no leisure to practise myself in the Roman language, owing to my public duties and the number of my pupils in philosophy,' and finally decided to leave Rome and practise virtue in his native town, which, small though it was, was the smaller for his absence. At Chæronea he remained for the rest of his long life, only leaving it for an occasional visit to Athens or Delphi, and there he died peacefully about A.D. 125.

All his life through Plutarch was a rapid and prolific writer, and the list of his works is a very long one. They fall into two divisions, the *Parallel Lives,* and

the *Morals*, and it will be convenient to take the latter
first. In spite of the title the *Morals* are really a
collection of miscellaneous pieces, for Plutarch is the
first essayist, the direct ancestor of Montaigne and
Hazlitt, and in the eighty subjects which it pleased
him to call ' Ethical ' he ranges over as wide a field as
either of his descendants. There are literary essays
such as the ' Comparison between Aristophanes and
Menander,' the ' Malice of Herodotus,' and ' How
young people should study poetry.' There are discourses on religion, the ' Slowness of God's vengeance,'
the ' Pythian oracle,' and the ' Isis.' There are
attempts at popular science : ' The face in the moon,'
' Is fire or water the more useful element,' ' The
sagacity of animals,' ' On the eating of meat ' ; and
beside all these ' The Table Talk ' and the long collections of disputed questions in Greek and Roman
antiquities which are rather miscellanies of information
than formal compositions. But it is in moral questions
that Plutarch takes most interest, and it is as a moralist
teacher, ' a physician for the soul ' as he has been
called, that he is most valuable. Sometimes he writes
on the theory of virtue, ' Can virtue be taught,' ' On
the nature of moral virtue,' ' Of the difference between
virtue and vice.' But more often he deals with such
practical subjects as ' Envy,' ' Superstition,' ' Indis-
cretion,' ' False-shame,' ' Gossip,' ' How to cure anger,'
' How to praise oneself without offending others.' On
all such topics he has real advice to give : he points out
men's weakness and shows the remedy ; to the feeble
he gives encouragement and to the unhappy consolation. He is, moreover, a constructive moralist and
puts forward his teaching on the organization of the
family and society in what is perhaps the most attractive
of all the divisions of the *Morals* : there is the dialogue
' On love,' the ' Precepts for marriage ' ; the ' Love of

children'; and lastly, the essay on education which comes first in our manuscripts.

The *Education of Children*, a treatise of some thirty pages, is considered by some critics to be of doubtful authenticity; but it so well embodies Plutarch's teaching as we find it in his other works that one extract, on the choice of a teacher, must be given here:

> 'The schoolmaster must be a man blameless in his life and of irreproachable character, one who has acquired virtue by experience. Honest schooling is the root of gentlemanly conduct; it is the fountain-head of virtue. As husbandmen prop up their vines with stakes, so honest schoolmasters prop up youth with careful admonition and precepts, so that they may grow up men of straight character.'

Therefore a teacher should be carefully chosen and only his personal merits should be considered. No regard is to be paid to advertisements, or even to the recommendation of friends: the teacher's functions are as vital as those of the physician, and in both cases the cheap quack should be avoided. Many parents love their gold more than their children's welfare and rather than pay an honest fee they purchase ignorance cheap. They invest money on slaves instead of on education, and as a result their children grow up with servile minds. So Plutarch advises:

> 'In brief then I say (and I may fairly be thought here to be " speaking as an oracle rather than as a mere adviser ") that the one chief thing in these matters, the first thing, the middle, and the last, is good education and sound instruction. These, I say, both lead to virtue and conduce to happiness. Compared with knowledge, all other human advantages, birth, wealth, glory, strength are unstable. Sound, wholesome learning is a permanent possession. And because it is valuable it cannot be acquired without effort: mere idle fluency of speech should be avoided as rigorously as narrow specialization; the study of philosophy is the essential part of education.'

It is impossible to give more than brief quotations, and one passage from a practical essay, that on Superstition, must suffice. Plutarch is discussing the difference between atheism and superstition, and by many examples shows that the latter is the more dangerous of the two :

'When an atheist is distressed and miserable without cause, one can dry his tears, cut his hair, and change his dress. But how is one to comfort the superstitious man ? In what way can one help him ? He sits outside his house, girt about with filthy rags, and often rolls naked in the mire, and proclaims his sins and errors—how he ate this, or drank that, or walked on a path which his conscience forbade him to take. At best, if his superstition takes him in a mild form, he sits at home fumigating and purifying himself, and the old women, in Bion's words, " bring anything that turns up and fasten it on to him as though he were a peg." '

Plutarch disapproves of superstition, but he is strongly drawn to the mystical side of religion. In the essay *De sera numinum vindicta* he gives an elaborate picture of the next world, based upon the Orphic doctrines of purification, rebirth, and future rewards and punishments, which may be compared with Plato's 'Dream of Er,' and Dante's *Divina Commedia*. In another piece *On the decay of the oracles* he tells how a certain Demetrius, landing on an island near Britain, found the air disturbed by fiery blasts and sudden gusts of wind, caused, as the people said, by the death somewhere 'of one of the mightier ones,' whose end is always followed by storm and tempest. From the same essay comes this tale :

'It was evening when the breeze died down and our ship drifted towards Paxi. Most on board were awake, and many were still drinking after supper. Suddenly a voice was heard from the island ; some one was calling loudly "Thamous." Now Thamous was our steersman, an Egyptian not even known by name to many of the passengers. Twice he was called and remained silent ; the third time he answered, and then the caller raising his voice cried : " When you reach the Palodes, tell them that Great Pan is dead." '

A contrast to these romantic stories is to be found in the homely and sensible *Advice on health*, in which, among other sound remarks, Plutarch informs us that milk is a food and not a beverage ; that wine is the most beneficial of drinks, the pleasantest of medicines, and the least cloying of appetizers ; and that everyone should drink two or three glasses of water each day. As regards eating he reminds us of the saying ' Leave room for the cake,' and suggests that conversation at dinner is as good as a second meal. Of what conversation at his own table was we learn from the nine books of *Table Talk*, where some of the topics are these : ' Why is A the first letter of the alphabet ? Why does fresh water wash clothes better than salt ? Why are signet-rings worn on the fourth finger ? Do the Jews abstain from pork because they worship pigs or because they detest them ? '

The *Table Talk* deals with a variety of matters, grave and gay : the more serious questions of religion and archæology which from time to time attracted Plutarch's attention are to be found in the *Quæstiones Romanæ* and the *Quæstiones Græcæ*. Here are six problems, three Latin and three Greek, from the 172 in the two volumes : ' Why do women kiss their kinsmen on the mouth ? Why do Romans who are supposed to be of particularly noble birth wear crescents on their shoes ? Why do Romans never marry in the month of May ? Who is the rider on the donkey at Kymê ? Why was it the custom of the Bottiæan maidens to call as they danced, " Let us go to Athens " ? Who are the Perpetual Sailors among the Milesians ? '

We have quoted from the *Moralia* at some length : the *Lives* are so well known that they may be dealt with more briefly, and it can be said at once that the qualities which make Plutarch the most delightful of all biographers are just those whose absence makes Thucydides the most valuable of all historians, a taste for moralizing and a love of anecdote. Plutarch puts his own case in the first chapter of his *Life of Alexander* :

> ' As preface I must ask my readers not to complain if I do not tell of every famous action or go exhaustively into each detail, but rather give an epitome of most events. I am not writing Histories but Lives, and in the most illustrious deeds there is not always a manifestation of virtue or vice. Frequently a slight thing, a word or a jest, gives a better impression of character than battles where ten thousand fall, or the greatest armaments, or sieges of cities. As painters get their likenesses from the face and the expression of the eyes, by which character is revealed, and take little notice of the other parts of the body, so I must be permitted to concentrate on the signs of the soul in men, and by them to picture each life, leaving to others the tale of greatness and glorious contests.'

A phrase, as Plutarch says here, will often reveal the man, and the number of pithy sayings scattered among the *Lives* is one of their most attractive features. It is to Plutarch that we owe such examples of old Cato's wisdom as ' There are three things I regret : I told my wife a secret ; I let myself be carried when I might have walked ; I lived one day without having made my will.' ' Wise men profit more from fools than fools from wise men : the wise man shuns the fool's mistakes, the fool does not imitate the wise man's successes.' ' Old age is ugly in itself ; do not make it worse by vice.' From the Greek *Lives* come these : ' Someone asked the elder Dionysius if he had any leisure. " Heaven forbid," he replied, " that I ever should." ' ' When the Spartan allies asked Archidamus to fix a regular quota he declined, saying " War has a very irregular appetite." ' ' Agesilaus was urged to hear a man who imitated a nightingale. " No, thank you," he answered ; " I have heard a nightingale." '

The fifty Lives form a gallery of the great characters in ancient history. Four of them, Aratus, Artaxerxes, Galba, Otho, stand by themselves ; the remaining forty-six are arranged in pairs, one Greek and one Roman, with a comparison at the end.

Plutarch's purpose, as he tells us, was a moral one, to illustrate virtue by concrete examples, and all the early lives are those of good men. The probable order of composition is Sertorius and Eumenes, Cimon and Lucullus, Lysander and Sulla, Demosthenes and Cicero, Agis and Cleomenes and the Gracchi, Pelopidas and Marcellus, Phocion and Cato Uticensis, Aristides and Cato the Censor. A second series consists of Pericles and Fabius, Nicias and Crassus, Dion and Brutus, Timoleon and Æmilius Paulus, Philopœmen and Flamininus, Themistocles and Camillus, Alexander and Julius Cæsar, Agesilaus and Pompey, Pyrrhus and Marius, Solon and Publicola. Then Plutarch saw that a useful moral lesson might also be drawn from the errors of great men, and wrote the lives of Demetrius Poliorcetes and Mark Antony, Alcibiades and Coriolanus, finally rounding off the whole series with Lycurgus and Numa, Theseus and Romulus.

We have said that one of Plutarch's most striking qualities is the knack of seizing a happy phrase. But he has also a very keen insight into character, a wonderful power of visualizing a scene, and a strong sense of dramatic effect. With one example of this last, taken from the *Life of Agis*, our account must end. The Ephor Amphares after killing Agis and his grandmother orders his mother also to be executed :

‘ So she went into the chamber of execution, and when she saw her son lying dead upon the ground, and her mother's dead body still hanging in the noose, with her own hands she helped the officers to take her down, laid her body out by the side of Agis, and composed and covered it. Then, embracing her son and kissing his face she said : “ My son, it was thy too great regard for others, and thy gentleness and humanity, which has brought thee to ruin, and us as well.” Then Amphares, who stood at the door and saw and

217

heard what she said and did, came in and said angrily to her : " If, then, thou hast been of the same mind as thy son, thou shalt also suffer the same fate." And Agestrata, as she rose to present her neck to the noose, said : " My only prayer is that this may bring good to Sparta." ' [1]

[1] 'Life of Agis,' Ch. xx.   Trans. B. Perrin.   Loeb Library.

CHAPTER II

THE GREEK RENAISSANCE
(A.D. 117–193)

IT is always difficult to fix an exact date for the beginning of a long process, and there are many signs to be found even in the writers of the first century A.D. that a revival of the Greek spirit was approaching. The literary criticism of Dionysius, the moral teaching of Epictetus, and the historical studies of Plutarch all bear witness to the growth of a new spirit of confidence. It only remained for some Roman Emperor to appear who should be a lover of Greek literature, willing to extend to the Greeks that measure of material support which the conditions of Roman life rendered necessary. That Emperor was found in Hadrian who succeeded Trajan in A.D. 117, and with his accession to power the Greek Renaissance may definitely be regarded as an established fact. Hadrian, both in his strength and in his weakness, was as much a Greek as a Roman. His insatiable curiosity, his capriciousness, his love of travel, and his romantic temperament made him an object of suspicion to his fellow-countrymen, and it was in Greece that he found his spiritual home. Nero imagined that he was an artist, Hadrian really was one, and the lines which he wrote upon his death-bed show that he might have been one of the most original of Roman poets :

> ' Animula vagula blandula
> hospes comesque corporis,
> quæ nunc abibis in loca
> pallidula rigida nudula,
> nec ut soles dabis jocos.'

To the patronage which Hadrian gave them the prodigious vogue of the great Greek sophists in the second century A.D. must at least partly be attributed. But before we describe their well-paid eloquence, we must touch upon the more varied fortunes of their precursor, the first Greek writer for some centuries whose prose it is a true pleasure to read.

Dion of Prusa (A.D. 42–c. 125)

Dion, sometimes called Chrysostom, was born at Prusa in Bithynia, the modern Broussa, in A.D. 40, about the time when the disciples were first called Christians at Antioch. His father was a man of importance, and Dion had both inherited a competence and himself gained some renown as a teacher of rhetoric when at the age of forty he was involved in the ruin of a Roman protector and banished from his home by imperial decree. For the next fourteen years he tramped the world with only a Plato and a Demosthenes in his wallet, and in the school of adversity framed for himself a philosophy of life based on the Cynic creed, to limit your wants and to look for happiness not in possessions but in your own soul. The death of Domitian in A.D. 96 brought his exile to an end, and under Nerva he visited Rome before returning to take up his career again in his native town. Henceforth he travelled, not as an unknown beggar but as a popular lecturer, addressing enthusiastic audiences in Asia Minor and in Egypt, and was finally called to Rome by Trajan, before whom he delivered two of his best-known speeches, *On the duty of a prince*. Trajan's favour he enjoyed until the Emperor's death, and he himself probably died early in Hadrian's reign.

His works, the Orations of Dion Chrysostom, fill two stout volumes in the Teubner series and consist of eighty separate items in the form of dialogues, lectures, and speeches. The earlier in date are chiefly on fanciful or literary themes, such as the *Praise of Baldness*, the *Comparison of Æschylus, Sophocles, and Euripides*, and the *Speech to the Trojans*, where he shows that Homer was wrong and that Troy was never taken by the Greeks. A second group contains his political speeches, addressed to the people of Prusa, Nicæa, Tarsus, and Apamea, in which he appears as a sound and practical adviser, preaching peace and harmony to the turbulent assemblies of these Eastern cities. The third and most important division consists of the moral discourses, ' diatribes ' in the Cynic fashion, such as the *Borysthenite*, a reminiscence of his years of exile, the *Alexandrian Oration*, in which he tells the Egyptians many shrewd home-truths, the *Olympic Discourse* where Phidias is made to give his views on God, and the *Eubœan*. All these four are charming, and the last will serve as a specimen of the others :

' I happened to cross the sea from Chios with some fishermen in quite a small boat, after the summer season was over. A violent storm came on, and it was with difficulty that we reached the Hollows of Eubœa alive. My companions ran their craft on to the rugged shore beneath the cliffs and let it break up, while they themselves made their way to some shell-fishers, who were lying up under the neighbouring breakwater, and decided to stay there and join forces with them. I was left to myself, and not knowing to what city I should go for shelter, wandered aimlessly along the shore, hoping to find some coasting-vessel or party taking shelter from the storm. I had gone a good way without seeing a human being, when I suddenly came upon a stag which had fallen over the cliff on to the beach, and still panting was being buffeted to and fro by the waves. A little afterwards I fancied I heard the barking of dogs above my head, but the sound came faintly because of the noise of the sea.

' So I went on, and climbing with great difficulty to higher ground, saw the dogs running about at a loss, whereby I inferred that the stag, being hard pressed, had leapt over the cliff. Soon afterwards I saw a man, a hunter by his looks and dress, with healthy cheeks and a generous shock of hair at the back of his head, worn in the same fashion as Homer describes with the Eubœans at Troy, making fun and mock of them because, while the other Achæans had a full head of hair, they only allowed half theirs to grow. " Pray, stranger," he asked, " have you noticed a stag anywhere about here trying to escape ? " " Yes," I replied, " there he is in the waves." And then I took him to the place and showed him. So he dragged the creature out of the water, and flayed its skin with his hunting-knife, I helping him to the best of my ability, and then cut off the hind-quarters, which he carried away, together with the skin, inviting me to come with him and partake of the meat.

' As we walked along, he told me on the way about his affairs and the manner of life he led with his wife and children. " There are two of us, my friend," he said, " and we live close together. Our wives are sisters and we both have a family of sons and daughters. We live for the most part by hunting, although we cultivate also a small piece of land. The place does not belong to us ; we do not own it, nor did our fathers. They were freemen, but they were as poor as we are, herdsmen working for hire, tending the cattle of one of the rich landowners of the island, who possessed many herds both of horses and cattle, and many flocks of sheep, and many fine farms also, and much property of every kind as well as all the hills that you see. Their master, however, was put to death and all his estate confiscated—people say that it was because of his money that the Emperor had him killed—and then all the cattle were driven off to the slaughter-house, and with them some poor beasts of our own, for which no one ever paid us a penny." '

['The hunter explains to Dion how his father and his comrade, having no other means of existence, settled down in the deserted pastures with such few cattle as were left, and there maintained themselves by grazing and hunting. The two families intermarried and, although the elder men were now dead, the sons still followed their fathers' mode of life.']

' " One of us, although he is now fifty, has never yet been to town. I have only been there twice, once when I was a lad with my father, in the days when we had the herd of cattle. Some years after that, a fellow came here one morning demanding money, as though forsooth we had any, and bade me follow him to the city. We have no money, and to that I took my oath, declaring that if we had we would have given it to him at once. We entertained him as well as we could, and gave him two deer-skins ; and I went back to town with him, for he said there was no help for it, but that one of us two should come and explain our position," '

222

['The hunter then says how he was brought before the Assembly and accused of holding land without paying taxes, and moreover of pursuing the trade of wrecker. He tells the people the truth; that he has no money and gains nothing but a bare subsistence; and, so far from luring ships on to the rocks by false signals, he has always helped shipwrecked sailors to the best of his ability.']

' " While I was saying this, a man got up in the middle of the Assembly. 'Here is another fellow,' thought I to myself, ' of the same sort, I suppose, going to tell lies about me.' But what he said was this : ' Gentlemen, for some time I have half recognized our friend here, although I felt doubtful. I am sure of him now, and I think it would be unfair, nay even impious, not to tell you what I know of him, and so repay him in words the very great service that he rendered me in deeds. I am a citizen of this town, as you know ; and so is my neighbour '—with that he pointed to the man at his side, who also rose to his feet—' and two years ago, as it happened, we both made a voyage in Socles' ship. Our craft was wrecked off Cape Caphereus, and only a few of our number got to shore. Some, who had money in their purses, were taken in by shell-gatherers. But we, who were stripped quite bare, had to plod our way up the cliff path, hoping to find shelter in some shepherd's hut, and running a good chance of dying from hunger and thirst. At last, after a struggle, we came to some shanties, and standing still shouted for help. Our friend here came out at our cries, and led us indoors, and gradually got a fire to burn, although it was not a very large one. Then he himself rubbed one of us down, while his wife did the same for the other, using fat instead of oil, which they did not possess. Finally, when the water was warm, they poured it over us to revive us after the cold. Our bath over, they gave us what clothes they had, and setting us down to table, served us with wheaten bread, while they themselves ate boiled pulse. We, too, had wine to drink, although they were content with water, and with the wine, venison in abundance, both roast and boiled. When we wanted to go away the next morning, they insisted on keeping us for three days, and then escorted us down to the level country ; and at our final departure we were presented, each of us, with a piece of meat and a very fine skin. As for myself, seeing that I was still weak from exposure, our host took his daughter's tunic and gave it to me, the girl putting on some other piece of stuff. That, however, I returned when we got to the village. So, gentlemen, it was to our friend here, after heaven, that we owed our lives.' " '

223

['As a result of this testimonial the hunter was allowed to leave the city unpunished; and the tale ends with preparations for a marriage between his daughter and his partner's son.']

The Great Sophists: Herodes Atticus and Polemon

Dion heralds in the 'Age of the Sophists,' and it may be well to state briefly the nature of the sophist's profession. Rhetoric, the invention of a Sicilian, Corax of Syracuse, had at first been an art like music and poetry. But the conditions of life in Athens, where the good speaker was all-powerful, required that rhetoric, once introduced, should descend to the level of science and be taught on fixed rules. This was done in the fifth century B.C. by Protagoras, who invented formal laws of style and composition and applied them to the two chief instruments of his educational method, the controversial theme and the sententious essay. In the theme his pupils were encouraged to take a subject and consider it in all aspects; the literary process being thus made a preparation for the practical difficulties that life brings. The essay, on the other hand, was pure theory and was intended to develop clearness of thought and fertility of language by a gradual accumulation of new ideas and phrases. To Protagoras rhetoric meant a training in all the affairs of life, and he, with his great contemporaries Gorgias, Hippias, and Prodicus, undertook not only to make orators but also to make good citizens. They taught rules of conduct as well as rules of style and endeavoured to turn out men who should be both mentally and morally perfect. Protagoras said 'Culture does not flourish in the soul unless one reaches to the depths'; and the success of his method may be judged by the fact that four of his pupils were Pericles, Thucydides, Hippocrates and Euripides.

In Athens, the law courts and the public assembly

had offered a real field for the exercise of the precepts taught by the masters of rhetoric. Under the Roman Empire political and forensic orations in the Greek tongue were seldom possible, and the art of speaking was taught and practised for itself alone. Art for art's sake was the true motto of the Empire sophist, and the higher teaching aimed almost exclusively either at producing the finished orator or at training an audience capable of appreciating the refinements of the orator's art. The names of the great artists in words who spent their lives in the practice of composition, and to whom form was even more important than matter, are legion. Polemon, Herodes Atticus, Aristides, Maximus of Tyre belong to the class of sophists proper ; Lucian, Alciphron and the Philostrati should perhaps be regarded as literary men. But whether they were speakers or writers, whether their chief aim was to instruct or merely to interest their audience, all these men made it their life's work to revive the glories of Greek literature, and if eventually this renaissance did not yield all the fruits that might have been expected from it, its failure was due rather to political than intellectual causes.

It is difficult for us to realize the fascination which the sophistic oratory exercised over Greek audiences, for we do not know the rules of the game and they did. A great speaker passed first through a long and arduous course of training : he had to possess a thorough knowledge of the poets and prose writers of antiquity, so that he could introduce appropriate quotations at the fitting moment ; he had also to be well acquainted with the history of Greece, for patriotism played a large part in exciting popular enthusiasm, and at any time he might be required to assume the character of Themistocles or Pericles and deliver an extempore oration on the victory of Salamis or the building of

the Parthenon. His bearing had to be majestic, his
voice melodious, and his oration was composed according
to elaborate rules with which we are as unfamiliar as
we are with the methods used by Æschylus in composing a tragic chorus. To the Greeks, it must be
remembered, music was the music of words, and they
felt much the same emotion in listening to the delivery
of one of Polemon's speeches as we do in listening to
the performance of a Beethoven symphony.

Of all the Empire sophists Dion comes nearest to
the Hellenic ideal, and in his insistence on the simple,
self-sufficient life he recalls the great Hippias who
appeared on one occasion at the Olympic games
wearing garments of which every part—oil-flask, rings,
and girdle included—had been made by his own hands.
But Dion is not so typical of his age as are Polemon
and Herodes Atticus, whose brilliant careers are
narrated at length by Philostratus in his *Lives of the
Sophists* (A.D. 103–179). Herodes Atticus had the
advantage of being born with the soul of an artist and
the wealth of a millionaire, and he lived his life in a
blaze of glory and munificence. The buildings which
he gave his native city, the Stadium and the Odeum
theatre, are still among the most prominent sights of
Athens; under Hadrian he was put in charge of the
free cities of Asia and spent over a quarter of a million
on the water-supply of Troy, defraying half the cost
from his own purse; Antoninus Pius gave him the
rank of consul, and although under Marcus Aurelius
he was accused of having caused his wife's death, he
continued to enjoy the imperial favour and received
a public funeral, 'where the whole population of
Athens came to meet the bier with tears and cries, like
children who have lost a good father.'

He received his first training from Scopelian and
Favorinus of Gaul, one of Dion's pupils, and passed

most of his life in travelling from town to town making public speeches. In his latter years his magnificent villa at Cephisia was the chief literary centre of Greece, and there he both gave lessons in rhetoric and displayed his own powers of oratory. His writings included a *Journal*, a collection of speeches, and a large number of letters : but of these nothing remains but one speech, which is generally regarded as spurious.

Of Polemon (A.D. 85-141) also we now only have two speeches, which seem hardly adequate to his reputation ; but he was an even more remarkable character than Herodes, for in his case the immense sums he spent were earned by his own exertions. His fee for a private lesson was £2400, and when Herodes sent him £6000 after attending one of his lectures he sent it back as inadequate, but agreed to accept £10,000 in its place. Emperors he treated as equals, and both at Smyrna and at his native Laodicea he was regarded almost as a god. He used to travel in his own yacht with a retinue of slaves, horses, and hounds ; his carriage was profusely adorned with silver trappings, and his arrival at a town was made the occasion of a public holiday. Philostratus quotes a letter of Herodes which describes his methods :

' He would come forward to deliver his speech with a calm and confident face, although, as he was crippled by rheumatism, he used to be carried in to the hall in a litter. When a theme had been proposed, he did not meditate on it in public but would withdraw for a few minutes. His voice was clear and powerful, and an amazing sonority thundered from his lips. Herodes says that he would reach such a pitch of excitement that he would leap up from his chair when he came to the climax of his argument, and as he rounded off a period would deliver the concluding phrase with a smile, to show the ease with which he spoke, stamping the ground at certain points in his speech like a horse in Homer.'

Ælius Aristides (A.D. 129–189)

Polemon practised the flowery Asianic style of oratory which may eventually be traced back to Gorgias, who said of those who choose science in preference to philosophy that they were 'suitors of Penelope dallying with her hand-maidens,' and ended a funeral oration with ' Victories won over barbarians call for pæans of triumph ; victories wrung from the Greeks call for dirges of lament.' Aristides preferred to take pattern from the cool sobriety of Protagoras, and in style is the most perfect of all the writers of his time. But in him we see all the weakness of the artistic temperament. He has an intense love of beauty and a passion for perfection, but he values emotion for its own sake and puts it above reason ; sensibility takes the place of sense. No one has ever understood the technique of writing better ; he uses the purest Attic, indistinguishable from the style of the great Athenians of the fifth and fourth centuries B.C., and his sentences have a rhythm which was the result of the most sedulous care. But unfortunately his matter is by no means equal to his manner, and it has been well said of him that he is a wasted genius.[1] 'One of the great masters of the Greek language, he used it to record what no one cares to read. An acute dialectician, he employs his gift to prove with entire sincerity and seriousness what is either false or not worth proving.'

Publius Ælius Aristides, son of a priest of Zeus, was born at Adriani in Mysia about A.D. 129. In his youth he studied rhetoric at Pergamum under Aristocles and at Athens under Herodes Atticus, and when he was about twenty, conceiving a romantic enthusiasm for Egypt, spent five years in that country, where he delivered his first public speeches. At the age of

[1] R. W. Livingstone. *The Mission of Greece*, p. 239.

twenty-six he went to Rome; and this journey, accomplished in winter under very bad conditions, brought on a nervous malady which tormented him for the next seventeen years. This period he spent chiefly as a patient in search of health at the temples of Asclepius, but he never abandoned his enthusiasm for literature or his literary pursuits. At last, about the year A.D. 172, he regained his strength and had the honour of addressing an oration to Marcus Aurelius at Smyrna in 176. Two years later, when Smyrna was partly destroyed by an earthquake, he was successful by a letter which moved Marcus to tears in enlisting the help of the Emperor for the devastated town, and until his death in A.D. 189 he continued to pour out a stream of writings which have mostly come down to us.

His fifty-five extant works may be classed as follows. Firstly, the public speeches, in which he himself considered that he had surpassed Demosthenes, written for some actual ceremony or dealing with some contemporary event. The most famous of these was the *Panathenaic Oration* delivered in Athens at the feast of the Panathenæa, where all the history of Athens is summarized in glowing words, and the *Praise of Rome*, from which one extract may be given:

‘ Now the whole world keeps holiday and, laying aside its ancient dress of steel, has turned in freedom to adornment and all delights. The cities have abandoned their old quarrels, and are occupied by a single rivalry, each ambitious to be most pleasant and beautiful. Everywhere are playgrounds, fountains, arcades, temples, workshops, schools. To use a metaphor from medicine, the world sick from creation has recovered its health. Gifts never cease flowing from you. One cannot find one place more richly endowed than another, for your beneficence is equally shown to all. Cities are ablaze with brightness and beauty, and all the earth is adorned like a king’s garden. The beacon fires of friendship rise on her plains, and those of war are gone as though a wind had blown them beyond land and sea : in their place has come every beautiful spectacle and an endless number of games. . . . To-day Greek or foreigner may travel freely where he will, with full or empty hands, as though he was passing from homeland to homeland. The Cilician Gates have no terrors for him, nor the narrow sandy passes through Arabia to Egypt, nor difficult mountains nor inhospitable savage tribes nor rivers broad beyond measuring. To be safe, it is enough to be a Roman, or rather a subject of yours. You have made into a reality the saying of Homer, that earth belongs to all, for you have meted out the whole world, bridled rivers with many a bridge, cut mountains into carriage roads, filled the deserts with outposts, and civilized all things with settled discipline and life.' [1]

Even more effective than this in their vividness of description are the accounts he gives of the earthquakes at Smyrna and at Rhodes in A.D. 155.

' Who even now can be calm when he remembers that awful midday hour when the mischief first began and swooped down upon us ? The sea stood still awaiting what was to come, the air was silent, the birds were mute, the sun cast one final gleam upon his city, and then in a moment all the fury of the earthquake was let loose. The sea went back, the harbour was left dry, houses were flung down, tombs burst open, towers fell on towers, sheds on galleys, temples on altars, offerings on statues, men on men, everything on everything.'

A second division contains his two technical treatises on rhetoric, and the speeches composed on set subjects and put into the mouths of imaginary persons, such as Orations XXIX and XXX, which are arguments, supposed to be delivered in the Assembly at Athens 414 B.C., for and against sending reinforcements to the Sicilian expedition. To the same class belong his critical and historical essays, of which the most famous was the *Apology for Four Statesmen*, the four being Miltiades, Themistocles, Cimon and Pericles. In all these literary art is united with historical knowledge and dialectical skill, and they were the delight of Byzantine scholars who ranked them with the greatest writings of the classical age.

[1] Translation, R. W. Livingstone, *op. cit.*, p. 256.

In his speeches and essays Aristides displays his talents to perfection, but the most curious of his works are the six books, the *Sacred Orations*, in which he describes his seventeen years of physical suffering. His illness began with his calamitous winter journey to Rome. He travelled in haste, inns were scarce, and more water came through their roofs than fell from the sky; the cold was intense, the country round the Danube was flooded, and at last he was in such a condition that he expected his teeth to drop out. The Roman doctors treated him with aperients, blood-letting, and poison antidotes, and he determined to escape home before it was too late. At Smyrna his physician advised hot baths, and when these proved useless he put himself under the care of the god Asclepius and passed from temple to temple, trying now drugs and now a milk diet, now treatment by suggestion and now an open-air life. His malady was nervous in origin with symptoms continually changing, and the advice that the god gave him in dreams was often both drastic and paradoxical. At one crisis, soon after he had been ordered hot baths, this was the prescription vouchsafed in a vision :

' He told me to go down to the river in front of the city and bathe. A beardless boy, whom he pointed out, should be my guide. . . . It was mid-winter, and a black north wind and frost. The stones were so frozen together that they resembled a continuous surface of ice; the water was what you would expect in such weather. . . . There was a considerable crowd and everything was in full view from the bridge. When we reached the river, no encouragement was needed, but still full of warmth from the sight of the god, I threw off my clothes and, without asking anyone to give me a rub, I plunged into the deepest part of the stream, where I amused myself as though it had been a swimming bath and the water temperate and mild.'

Maximus of Tyre (fl. A.D. 160)

Far less talented than Aristides is the other great popular lecturer of this age, Maximus of Tyre, of whose discourses forty-one are now extant. It might be thought that writings so numerous would give us some information about their author, but that is not so, and all that we know of Maximus is that he was born at Tyre, and that he was living for some years at Rome in the reign of Commodus. He professes to be a philosopher and an earnest student of Plato, and several of his lectures are concerned with Socrates, two on the *Dæmon of Socrates* and four on *Socrates and Love*. But even on such likely subjects as these he has nothing very striking to say, and philosophy for him is chiefly an excuse for rhetoric. The titles of his lectures are often attractive, *On Pleasure*, *How to win friends*, *Should we repay injuries?*, *How can one escape pain?*, but the titles are their best part, and Maximus for us is chiefly important as an example of the eloquence that attracted a cultivated audience in his day. It must be allowed that his style is easy and flowing, in spite of the weakness of his thought, as the beginning of his lecture *On the Cynic's Life* may show:

'I want to tell you a story in the manner of Æsop. My speakers will not be a lion or an eagle or things still less vocal such as oaks, but this is how I shall tell my tale. Zeus, the heavens, and the earth existed. The gods were citizens of the sky. But earth's children, men, had not yet seen the light of day. Zeus summoned Prometheus and directed him to colonize earth with two-footed creatures. Their minds, he said, are to be closely allied with ours, their bodies slight, upright, symmetrical, their looks mild, their hands apt to labour, their steps firm. Prometheus obeyed, created man and colonized the earth. When they came into being, men lived easy lives. The earth gave them sufficient food, deep meadows, leafy mountains, an abundance of fruits, all that she loves to bear when untroubled by the farmer's hand. The nymphs gave them clear fountains, transparent rivers, a rich and generous variety of waters. Their limbs were lapped in the temperate and comforting warmth of the sun ; in summer the winds blowing off the streams refreshed their frame ; and in the lavish and natural abundance of their life nothing was a subject of strife.' [1]

The Rhetoricians

Thus far we have only spoken of the great sophists, the men at the head of their profession, whose fame was as world-wide as that of a great singer in our time. But the charm of their oratory, which entranced a crowded assembly, depended eventually on the humbler efforts of the rhetoricians who turned out thousands of pupils, to produce occasionally one great artist in speech. Of these technical writers a few must at least be mentioned. The chief of them was Hermogenes of Tarsus (fl. A.D. 190), in his youth a famous orator, who, losing his skill, became a teacher and writer on rhetoric. His works, which we still possess, are the best manual of the art as it was understood in his time. On grammar we have books of some value by Apollonius, surnamed the 'Difficult,' and by his son Herodian, who lived in the reign of Marcus Aurelius ; on Attic style the treatise by Phrynichus (fl. 190), known chiefly by the summary in Photius. Finally, there are the writers on metre such as Hephæstion, whose manual has come down to us, and the compilers of lexicons, Harpocration and Julius Pollux. A brief account of Pollux will serve to exemplify the whole class.

Julius Pollux (fl. A.D. 170)

Pollux, born at Naucratis in Egypt, owed his first success, like Hermogenes, to his oratorical skill. Coming to Rome about A.D. 170, he became tutor to the young

---

[1] Trans., R. W. Livingstone, *op. cit.*, p. 184.

Commodus, whom he delighted with such imaginary discourses as that which Philostratus quotes :

> 'A boy on the mainland writes from Babylon to his father on an island : " I am a king's slave ; I was given to him as a present from a satrap ; yet I never mount a Median horse nor handle a Persian bow ; nay, I never go forth to war or to the chase like a man, but I sit in the harem and wait on the king's concubines ; and the king does not mind, for I am a eunuch." '

The favour of his royal pupil secured Pollux one of the professorial chairs which Marcus Aurelius founded at Athens, and henceforth he was a man of distinction in the academic world. As such, and as a pedant to boot, he incurred the wrath of Lucian, who attacks him fiercely in the *Lexiphanes* and in the *Rhetorician's Vade Mecum*. He is not indeed mentioned by name, but Lucian leaves no doubt when he says, 'My father had been a slave south of Xois and Thmuis, my mother was a common sempstress. I took the short cut of rhetoric, and was able to change my name to one that puts me on a level with the sons of Zeus and Leda.'

This passage comes from the *Rhetorician's Vade Mecum*, where Lucian's victim is made to explain 'how you may become a rhetorician and win for yourself the imposing title of Professor.' In the other piece the unfortunate Pollux is Lexiphanes, who suffers from a flux of words and delivers a long speech in this style : 'My eyes are disordered ; my pupils are turbid ; I wink and blink, the tears come unbidden, my eyes crave the ophthalmic leech's healing drug, mortar-brayed and infused, that they may blush and blear no more, nor moistly peer.'

The motive of Lucian's attack is to be found in two facts. Firstly, Pollux had made his way to a high position with very dubious qualifications, and secondly, he had written a short guide to success for budding rhetoricians. This was the *Onomasticon*, which we still possess, although it is not often used now for its original purpose, a lexicon containing long lists of unusual words, with explanations appended, warranted to give colour to any speech. It is in ten books, the first ranging from gods to bees, the third from relatives to travelling, the sixth from meals to crimes. The ninth book treats of games, and in default of better authorities is one of our chief sources for the technical arrangements of the ancient theatre. But such information as Pollux gives is both confused and confusing. Here is a specimen. One of his useful words is *eklaktismata*, 'women's dances, for one had to kick up over the shoulder.' The explanation does not seem very illuminating, and Bentley conjectured that *gynaikon* 'womanish' was a misreading for *gymnikon* 'gymnastic.' But whether the mistake is due to the copyist of Pollux' manuscript, or was made by Pollux himself in transcribing from his original authority, is a question which can hardly now be decided.

Lucian (A.D. 125–c. 195)

We have said in a previous chapter that Dionysius of Halicarnassus in the first century A.D. offers some points of resemblance with Petrarch in the fourteenth; and the parallel may be extended, if we wish, to Lucian and Erasmus, who both came into the movement, which their predecessors started, at the time of its full fruition, and in their writings expressed its spirit perfectly before the inevitable reaction began. There are, moreover, other points of likeness between Lucian and Erasmus besides this one of point of time. Erasmus was a Dutchman by birth, Lucian was a Syrian; but they put aside their native tongues and succeeded in writing, the one a Latin, and the other a Greek, which is equal in style to the best of the great classical authors.

There are curious resemblances also in their mode of thought and in their outlook on life. Both of them are destructive forces, sending the cool light of common sense into the dark places of folly and superstition ; they criticize but they do not create ; and when they are faced by a definite choice between the old and the new they are apt to lapse into inconsistencies. Finally, even in the outward form of their works they have the same preferences. They both naturally incline to the dialogue ; they both are adepts at cloaking satire in the disguise of a simple story ; they both love, while keeping in the background, to bring their own personality into their books. They may indeed both be described as novelists who never found the literary form which would have exactly suited their talents.

The facts of Lucian's life are known to us chiefly from his own writings. *The Vision* is direct autobiography ; he appears in the thinnest of disguises in the *Portrait-Study*, in the *Defence of the Portrait-Study*, in *The Double Indictment*, and in the *Menippus*, and there is intentional but veiled autobiography in over twenty of the other pieces. He was born A.D. 125 at Samosata, a Syrian town on the Euphrates. His parents were humble folk, and when it became necessary for him to earn his living he was apprenticed to his mother's brother to learn the sculptor's trade. The apprenticeship lasted one day ; for when his uncle chastised him with a stick he ran off home, and, abetted by his mother, resolved to become a rhetorician. How he found the means to pay for his training we do not know ; but mothers sometimes have a way of achieving the impossible. At any rate, he left home for one of the great cities of Asia Minor where the sophists were then at the height of their glory, and made his first appearance as an advocate at Antioch in A.D. 150.

Lucian was now fairly launched upon a career, in

which the law was to be but the first stage. He was too much of an artist and too little of a business man to take much interest in his pleadings, and he soon abandoned the law courts for the lecturer's platform ; and then, like most of the sophists, he started on a world tour. For ten years he travelled, lecturing in Ionia, in Greece, in Italy, and in Gaul, where he stayed for some time and perhaps held a professorial chair. He claims to have been one of the leading rhetoricians there, but in 160 he gave up his position and returned to Antioch, where he was living in A.D. 163, when Lucius Verus visited the town and Lucian wrote for his mistress, Panthea, the glowing panegyric of *The Portrait-Study*. This is one of the last of his purely rhetorical pieces, for in the next year he changed his home and profession once more, and taking his father with him migrated to Athens and set up there as a man of letters.

His early years at Athens form the third stage in his literary progress. As he says himself, he then abandoned his old mistress, Rhetoric, and took up with Dialogue in her place. In other words, it is to these years that his philosophic dialogues belong, the *Toxaris*, a collection of stories on friendship, the *Anacharsis*, a treatise on physical training, the *Pantomime*, an elaborate eulogy on the actor's art, the *Hermotimus*, an exposition of true philosophy, and lastly the *Parasite*, where for the first time satire and dialogue are mingled together. This last piece leads to his final manner, the fusing of Comedy and Dialogue, a new literary form, meant like Comedy for purposes of entertainment, but intended like Dialogue to be read and not acted. Lucian regarded this as his own original invention ; in it nearly all his best things are written ; and on it his claim to immortality depends.

Between A.D. 165 and 175 is Lucian's great period,

the period of *The Liar*, *The Dialogues of the Gods*, *The Fate of Creeds*, and of *Zeus Tragœdus*. All these are in that particular form of the dialogue which he made his own and they were probably written at Athens. But although Athens had become his permanent home, Lucian made frequent visits abroad. In 165 he went to Ionia, where the Parthian war gave him the occasion for *The Way to write History*. In 169 he attended the Olympic Games and wrote the *Death of Peregrine* and its sequel, *The Runaways*. To other places he went to give readings from his books, and the *Zeuxis* and similar pieces were written to serve as introductions.

Then there followed a time of quietude, broken only by the two contrasting studies, the life of Demonax, prince of philosophers, and the life of Alexander of Abonytichus, prince of impostors. Finally, in his old age, Lucian was appointed by Commodus to a well-paid legal post in Egypt, and there he died, perhaps from gout, towards the end of the century.

In the course of this narrative the names of some of Lucian's writings have been given. But these form only a small proportion of his eighty-two pieces, most of which may be read in the four volumes of the excellent translation by H. W. and F. G. Fowler ; and of the most important of these some particulars must now be given. The best known of them all is the *True History*, a parody of the traveller's tales which the Greeks so greatly enjoyed, and itself the model for countless fantasies in modern times. 'The only true statement in all the book,' says Lucian, 'is this : I am a liar' ; and he then proceeds to relate his wonderful adventures. Starting from the Pillars of Heracles, his ship was carried for eighty days into the Atlantic and finally caught up by a waterspout and lifted to the moon. He finds a war raging between the Sunites and the Moonites, in which he plays a gallant part, and describes some of the singular habits of his hosts :

> ' In the Moon when a man becomes old, he does not die, but dissolves in smoke into the air. There is one universal diet ; they light a fire, and in the embers roast frogs, great numbers of which are always flying in the air ; they then sit round as at table, snuffing up the fumes which rise and serve them for food ; their drink is air compressed in a cup till it gives off a moisture resembling dew. Beauty with them consists in a bald head and hairless body ; a good crop of hair is an abomination. . . . They have beards, however, just above the knee ; no toe-nails, and but one toe on each foot. They are all tailed, the tail being a large cabbage of an evergreen kind, which does not break if they fall upon it.'

From the Moon he returns in his ship to the Ocean and is swallowed by a huge whale, from which he escapes by lighting fires in its interior, and next visits the Island of the Blest and the Island of Dreams. In these delectable lands he interviews a number of well-known characters, Ajax, Homer, Alexander, Helen, Epicurus ; and his travels end with a visit to Calypso and the Donkey-legged Sirens.

The *True History* is the most good-tempered of Lucian's writings and may be read purely for amusement like *Gulliver's Travels* without regard to its satirical purpose. Equally interesting as a tale, although here the moral purpose is more explicit, is the account of the charlatan Alexander, one of the many religious impostors who were then preying on the credulity of the mob. Alexander had the brilliant idea of reincarnating the god Asclepius for his own profit and arranged as follows. He procured a large tame snake and made a serpent's head of painted linen. He then inserted a small reptile in a goose egg which he buried in the mud close to a temple of Asclepius then being built, and one day rushed into the market-place, naked except for a gold-spangled loin-cloth, and called the people to come with him and see the birth of a god. Amid an excited crowd he extricated and broke the egg, took out the reptile, and hastened back to his house. A few days passed, and then sitting in a dark room with the tame snake coiled about him and the linen head under his control, he invited all who wished to consult the god at the trifling charge of one shilling a head. How Lucian himself unveiled the imposture closes the account, which, as he says, may not be unserviceable, since it is not only destructive, but, for men of sense, constructive also.

As a descriptive writer Lucian shows his full powers in the real scenes of the *Alexander*, and the word pictures of celebrated paintings scattered among his writings are equally effective. There is the well-known account of Apelles' allegory ' Slander ' with which the essay on that subject begins, and even better the description of ' The Centaurs ' of Zeuxis :

> ' On the fresh sward appears the mother Centaur, the whole equine part of her stretched on the ground, her hoofs extended backwards ; the human part is slightly raised on the elbows ; the fore feet are not extended like the others, for she is only partially on her side ; one of them is bent as in the act of kneeling, with the hoof tucked in, while the other is beginning to straighten and take a hold on the ground—the action of a horse rising. Of the cubs she is holding one in her arms suckling it in the human fashion, while the other is drawing at the mare's dug like a foal. In the upper part of the picture, as on higher ground, is a centaur who is clearly the husband of the nursing mother ; he leans over laughing, visible only down to the middle of his horse body ; he holds a lion whelp aloft in his right hand, terrifying the youngsters with it in sport.'

In every branch of art, indeed, Lucian is keenly interested, and his account of the *Pantomime*, the actor who expressed everything by gesture, as the sophist expressed everything by words, conceals a real appreciation under its cloak of humour. A first-rate pantomime, he says, needs the highest qualities of mind and body :

he must have memory, sensibility, shrewdness, rapidity of conception, tact, and judgment : he must be capable of discerning good music and rejecting bad. Like Calchas in Homer, he should know ' all that is, that was, that shall be,' and faithfully to represent his subject he must make plain all that might be obscure ; clearness in his case depending solely on clearness of gesticulation. His work must be one harmonious whole, avoiding exaggeration, perfect in balance and proportion, and based on human sympathy. The spectator must see in him, as in a mirror, the reflection of his own feelings until audience and actor become one. Above all he must be a man of extraordinary versatility, such a one as Paris, who would at times dispense even with the aid of chorus and orchestra. Time beaters, flutes, singers were ordered to preserve a strict silence ; and the dancer left to his own resources would represent the whole story of Ares and Aphrodite. In turn he would be the tell-tale Sun, and crafty Hephæstus, the Gods surrounding the captured lovers, the blushing Aphrodite and the guilty Ares. It is not to be wondered at if even stern philosophers cried out in admiration, ' This is not seeing, but hearing and seeing together : 'tis as if your hands were tongues.'

Up to this point we have only quoted from pieces in the narrative form, and good though they are they might conceivably have been written by some one other than Lucian himself. It is in the dialogue, and especially in the *Dialogues of the Gods* that Lucian stands beyond imitation, and here the only difficulty is to know what passage to select. The conversation between Zeus and Hera on the subject of Ixion's presumptuous love-making is delightful ; so is the account given to Hephæstus by Apollo of the tricks of the baby Hermes ; so is the elaborate picture of the Judgment of Paris. And as an example of feminine malice—an engaging quality of which Lucian has a full dose in his own composition, it would be difficult to find anything better than the two dialogues between the sea-nymphs Doris and Galatea and the goddesses Hera and Leto. The girls scratch one another lightly like kittens, but the elder ladies use their claws without compunction :

' HERA. I must congratulate you, madam, on the children with whom you have presented Zeus.

LETO. Ah, madam ; we cannot all be the proud mothers of Hephæstuses.

HERA. My boy may be a cripple, but at least he is of some use. He is a wonderful smith, and has made Heaven look another place ; and Aphrodite thought him worth marrying, and dotes on him still. But those two of yours !—that girl is wild and mannish to a degree ; and now she has gone off to Scythia, and her doings *there* are no secret. . . . Apollo, too, who pretends to be so clever, with his bow and his lyre and his medicine and his prophecies ; sensible people know that most of it is claptrap.

LETO. Oh, of course ; my children are butchers and impostors. I know how you hate the sight of them. You cannot bear to hear my girl complimented on her looks, or my boy's playing admired by the company.

HERA. His playing, madam !—excuse a smile ;—why, if the Muses had not favoured him, his contest with Marsyas would have cost him his skin. . . . As for your charming daughter, when Actæon once caught sight of her charms, she had to set the dogs upon him, for fear he should tell all he knew : I forbear to ask where the innocent child picked up her knowledge of obstetrics.

LETO. You set no small value on yourself, madam, because you are the wife of Zeus, and share his throne ; you may insult whom you please. But there will be tears presently, when the next bull or swan sets out on his travels, and you are left neglected.' [1]

This is very light stuff ; but in many of the dialogues Lucian is more serious. The *Sale of Creeds*, for example, where the principal philosophers of the past are put up for auction, contains much acute criticism of the different systems current in Lucian's day. The *Runaways* is a vigorous defence of philosophy against pretenders ; the *Timon* deals with the proper use of

[1] Tr. H. W. and F. G. Fowler.

money; the *Charon* with the proper employment of life. In *Zeus as Tragedian* the question of Providence is raised, and in the *Zeus cross-examined* the vital problems of Predestination and Fate, which also are more lightly touched upon in the last of the *Dialogues of the Dead*.

' MINOS. Sostratus, the pirate here can be dropped into Pyri-phlegethon, Hermes.

SOSTRATUS. A word with you, sir. See if there is not some justice in my plea.

MI. What, more pleadings? Have you not been convicted of villainy and murder without end?

Sos. I have. Yet consider whether my sentence is just.

MI. Say on, but be brief; I have other cases waiting for me.

Sos. The deeds of my life—were they in my own choice, or were they decreed by Fate?

MI. Decreed, of course.

Sos. Then all of us, whether we passed for honest men or rogues, were the instruments of Fate in all that we did?

MI. Certainly; Clotho prescribes the conduct of every man at his birth.

Sos. Observe, then, your injustice. You punish us who are but the slaves of Clotho's bidding; for it will never be said that it was in our power to gainsay the irresistible ordinances of Fate.

MI. Ah, Sostratus : look closely enough, and you will find plenty of inconsistencies besides these. However, I see you are no common pirate, but a philosopher in your way. Let him go, Hermes; he shall not be punished after that. But mind, Sostratus, you must not put it into other people's heads to ask questions of this kind.' [1]

Alciphron (fl. A.D. 170)

Of Alciphron we know nothing except that he was a friend of Lucian; and this is merely an inference from the *Letters* of Aristænetus, an author of the sixth century, who in his book makes the two men correspond with one another. There are, however, sufficient resemblances between them to make friendship probable, and several of the letters from parasites and

[1] Tr. H. W. and F. G. Fowler.

courtesans in Alciphron seem to be founded on reminiscences of passages in Lucian. In any case, Alciphron is one of the most attractive products of sophistic, and in ease of style and vividness of phrasing comes next after Lucian. Unlike most of his contemporaries he is a sheer realist, and in the evolution of the prose novel he plays an important part, for many of the imaginary letters of which his book consists approach very closely to our idea of a short story. They would perhaps have been even more interesting if they had dealt with the life of Alciphron's own time, but they are so far literary that they are based on the New Comedy of Menander, and the picture they give us, a series of light dramatic sketches, is one of Athens in the fourth century B.C.

The *Letters*, as we have them in Schepers' edition, one hundred and twenty-two in number, fall into four main divisions,—the Sea, the Country, Society, Love— and the style changes from gay to serious, from pathos to jest, from moralizing to frivolity, as swiftly as in the pages of the *Sentimental Journey*. The Fishermen's and the Farmers' letters present to us two small communities near Athens, one busied with the sea, the other with the land. These two sections may be compared—*mutatis mutandis*—with Mr Bernard Gilbert's ' god's-eye view ' of an English village in *Old England*. With Alciphron as with the English author, each character is introduced separately, and then their relations one to the other gradually emerge. Alciphron sees the possibilities of the method, and in some cases by letter and reply—or even letter, reply, and counter-reply—we have an intrigue started. Unfortunately he does not push the method far enough : the intrigue no sooner starts than it ends.

The next section, the forty-two letters of *Parasites*, is perhaps less interesting to modern readers, for it is difficult to feel much sympathy for the woes of these unfortunates who, having no money of their own and being too idle to work for a living, were forced to gain the rich food they coveted by submitting to the capricious insults of a rich patron. But in his variations on this one theme Alciphron is amazingly fertile, and his invention of names for his characters shows a comic verve worthy of Aristophanes himself. As in the previous letters the scene is still Athens and the period towards the end of the fourth century B.C., but there is a strong Roman flavour about many of the episodes, and for his names Alciphron does not shrink from an anachronism, so that some of his most prodigious creations are a blend of Latin and Greek.

In the *Parasites* Alciphron draws near to Lucian ; in the *Courtesans* he is triumphantly himself, and his heroines are presented to us with far more sympathy and understanding than Lucian could ever command. In this section the persons are no longer pure imagination ; many of them are historical characters imaginatively treated—the method of our historical novel. We have Philemon, Diphilus, and Menander, the three chief writers of the New Comedy, together with the latter's mistress, Glycera, from whom he drew his delightful heroine, ' The girl with the clipped hair.' Phryne, the most famous of beauties, appears with her sculptor, Praxiteles, and her advocate, Hypereides. Leontion, the friend of Epicurus, gives us a very different account of her relations with the great philosopher than that which we gather from Landor's *Imaginary Conversations.* Finally, as an ornament to these simple civilians, we see the two most notable of Alexander's successors, Ptolemy, the cautious king of Egypt, and Demetrius, the young and gallant ' Sacker of Cities.'

The ladies, real and imaginary, belong all to one profession and have the gratification of men as their chief purpose in life ; but they exhibit very different shades of character. There is the practical and sagacious Glycera, the proud Phryne, and the wanton Megara : Petale and Philumena are excessively business-like, Thaïs and Myrrhina go to the other extreme : Leæna writes spitefully, Lamia lovingly, and each letter tells its own story. All these portraits of women are life-like, but perhaps the most effective of all is the picture of his dead mistress, drawn by Euthycles for his friend, Bk. IV. 11. Here Alciphron reaches to the true spirit of romance ; parallels to various passages might be found in the elegiac poets of Greece and Rome, but there is nothing like it in prose before his time.

Menecleides to Euthycles

' She is gone, my Bacchis, my beautiful : she has passed away and left me nothing but tears—tears and the bitter-sweet memory of our love. Never, never will the day come when I shall forget Bacchis. Ah, what sympathy was hers ! " A plea for frail women "; it would not be amiss to make that the title of her life-story. If all the beauties of every land came together and set up her statue in the temple of Aphrodite or the Graces, methinks they would do a seemly deed. The common gossip of women's faithlessness and mischief, that they look only for gain and fall to the highest bidder, that they are the cause of every sort of trouble to those who come their way, all this in herself she has shown to be an unjust libel : so effective a contrast was her character to the scandal of the mob. . . . But she is gone ; she has left me, and now she is lying alone, my Bacchis. Dear God, how unjust it is ! I ought to be lying by her side this hour ; but I am alive and putting out my hand to food, and soon I shall be talking with my friends again, while she——. Ah, never more will she look at me with a smile in those bright eyes, never more will her gracious love gladden my nights with the sweetest of all pleasures. To think how soft her voice was, how fair her eyes ; what siren charms dwelt ever in her company, how sweet and pure the nectar that her kisses distilled. The very spirit of persuasion sat upon her lips : it was a magic girdle that clasped her breast, and all the charms of love were hers to greet love's queen. But now they are gone, the pretty songs that she would sing at our toasts : gone, too, the lyre which her ivory fingers used to strike.

She whom all the graces loved is lying dead, dust and ashes and a dull stone.

'Dear Euthycles, I am easier now that I have poured out all my grief. Even to talk and write about her seems a pleasure now, for nothing is left me but her memory. Farewell.'

Christian Literature

While the sophists were dazzling the world with their brilliant eloquence, writers less skilful but more sincere were striving patiently to spread the truth, and often suffering martyrdom for their faith. An adequate account of them here is impossible, and readers must be referred to the master work of Aimé Puech, *Histoire de la littérature grecque chrétienne*, but a few details may be given of the five Apostolic Fathers, as they are called, Barnabas, Clement of Rome, Hermas, Ignatius, and Polycarp. Of their writings Clement's *Epistle to the Corinthians* comes first in time, for it was probably composed in the last years of the first century. It is a moving and eloquent appeal for harmony between the churches of Rome and Corinth, and for moderation on the part of the Corinthians, and as literature it stands on a much higher level than the Epistle of Barnabas, so called, written early in the second century, which comes next. The pseudo-Barnabas is a poor writer and his importance is chiefly doctrinal, but the Epistles of Ignatius, martyred in the reign of Trajan and perhaps parodied by Lucian in the *Life and death of Peregrine*, are of a very different class. Ignatius is an Eastern mystic who approaches St Paul in vigour of language and intensity of feeling, and his letters to the churches of Magnesia, Tralles, Ephesus, and Rome contain passages which might almost have been written by the great apostle. Here are some sentences from his *Epistle to the Romans*, written just before his martyrdom:
'The possession of the earth to its last limits, the

247

kingdoms of this world can serve me for nothing.
Better is it for me to die in sight of Jesus Christ than
to reign over the confines of earth. It is He whom
I seek, He who died for us; it is He whom I crave,
He who for us was born again. The hour of my birth
is drawing near.' Polycarp, Bishop of Smyrna, martyred
soon after Ignatius, is a more simple character, and his
one surviving work, the *Letter to the Philippians* was
written in his youth and is of no great literary value.
More significant of his greatness is the answer he made
to the Roman governor who bade him curse Christ:
'For eighty-six years I have served Him and He has
never done me wrong. How can I blaspheme my
Saviour and my King.'

Finally we come to Hermas, whose *Shepherd*, written
about A.D. 145, almost won its way into the scriptural
canon. *The Shepherd* is altogether different from the
Epistles we have just described, for Hermas is a Greek,
and his book has all the fresh simplicity of early Greek
or early Christian art. It is of some length and is
divided into three parts, the *Visions*, the *Commandments*, and the *Parables*. Its main purpose is to call
men to repentance, and in the first vision Hermas tells
us how he come to write. He was a freed slave, and
one day, seeing his mistress Rhodê bathing in the
Tiber he said to himself, 'O that I had such a wife.'
Soon after this Rhodê appeared to him in a vision and
smilingly reproached him, and that same night in a
second dream the Church, personified as a majestic
dame, bade him redeem his fault by warning others.
The *Visions* are a delightful mixture of allegory and
instruction, and while the *Commandments* are more
strictly doctrinal, we return to the first manner in the ten
Parables, which, like the *Visions*, have an introduction.
While the Tower, which is the Church, seen by Hermas
in the third vision, was building, the writer passed the

night with twelve virgins, who were the twelve virtues. ' I was ashamed,' says Hermas, ' to remain in their company. But she who seemed first among them began to kiss and embrace me ; then the others, seeing her doing this, kissed me in their turn and sported with me and led me round the Tower. I felt myself young again, and began to sport with them : some made a ring, others danced, and others sang. I kept silence, and walking with them round the Tower took part in their joy.'

Justin Martyr (A.D. c. 100–165)

The Apostolic Fathers are chiefly concerned with doctrine, and address their own flocks. Another class of Christian writers, among whom Justin is chief, propose rather to justify Christianity to the outer world. Born of a Greek family in Judæa about A.D. 100, Justin was converted to Christianity in his early manhood and came to Rome in the reign of Hadrian. At Rome he remained for the rest of his life, teaching his new religion to which he had adapted some of Plato's doctrines, and there in the first years of Marcus Aurelius he suffered martyrdom for his faith. Of his authentic writings three now remain, the two *Apologies for Christianity* and the *Dialogue with Tryphon the Jew*, although a number of other writings, such as the *Exhortation to the Gentiles* and the *Letter to Diognetus*, have been wrongly attributed to him.

Justin is not a great writer, and his thought and language both suffer from lack of orderly arrangement ; but in spite of that he is very interesting. The *Dialogue with Tryphon* endeavours to refute the arguments against Christianity used by the Jews, and shows that the Christian belief is not really at variance with Jewish monotheism and that, as a universal religion, it can realize all the promises made to the chosen people in the Old Testament. The two *Apologies* have a wider scope, and while they explain to the Roman government the principles of Christian worship, they also seek to reconcile Greek philosophy with Christianity. Justin recognizes that even the pagans had some knowledge of the truth : ' All those who have written have been able, thanks to the seed of reason naturally inborn in them, to perceive obscurely that which is. Those who have lived with the Word are Christians, even though they have been considered atheists ; Socrates and Heraclitus, for example, among the Greeks, and those who were like to them.' That he then attributes their wisdom partly to the influence of demons and partly to the use they made of the writings of Moses rather detracts from the justness of his views, but it is something that he goes even as far as he does.

Marcus Aurelius (A.D. 121–180)

Justin was martyred in the reign of Marcus Aurelius ; but it would not be just to put any responsibility for his death upon the philosopher Emperor, author of the little book which is usually known as the ' Meditations of Marcus Aurelius ' but in Greek is called simply ' Marcus Aurelius to himself.' Marcus Aurelius Antoninus, son of Annius Verus, was born at Rome in 121, and while still a boy attracted the notice of the Emperor Hadrian, who called him in jest Verissimus, and a little before his death in 138 instructed his successor Antoninus Pius to adopt him as his son. He then for twenty-three years lived in the imperial palace as heir-presumptive, and in 161 became in his turn Emperor, ruling until his death in 180. With the events of his reign, except in so far as they bear on his book, a literary history is not concerned ; but it is worth remembering that the *Meditations*, which belongs to his last ten years, was written in the midst of arduous campaigns on the Danube frontier against the barbarians who were just beginning to take the offensive against Rome.

We can imagine the toil-worn Emperor—he speaks of himself as old at fifty—in his tent at night, after he had written the army orders for the next day in Latin, turning to his other language and putting down his intimate communings in the familiar Greek of the Stoic philosophy which was his sure haven and refuge throughout life. How this private journal came to be published after his death we do not know. It certainly was not done by his worthless son Commodus, but it may have been due to the loving care of his daughter Cornificia, for her last words before she was put to death by Caracalla in 215 are reminiscent of her father's teaching :

'O wretched little soul of mine, imprisoned in an unworthy body, go forth, be free.'

But published it was, to the great benefit of the world ; and for many years the writer was regarded by pious Romans not merely as a god but as one of the intimate divinities of the household to whom offerings every day had to be made.

The *Meditations* is too informal to admit of analysis. If one wishes to appreciate its quality, it should be read through from beginning to end ; but some quotations may be useful. Of the twelve books into which it is now divided the first was probably written after the others, and serves as an introduction. In it Marcus renders thanks to all those to whom he is under obligation : briefly to his parents ; more fully to his tutors ; at much greater length to Antoninus Pius, who set him a pattern of simplicity, calmness, generosity, and an inflexible determination to give every man his due ; lastly to the gods from whose hands all his good fortune has come. The second book, written among the Quadi and probably after the 'miraculous victory' of 174, begins thus : [1]

'Say to thyself at daybreak : I shall come across the busybody, the thankless, the overbearing, the treacherous, the envious, the unneighbourly. All this has befallen them because they know not good from evil. But I, in that I have comprehended the nature of the Good that it is beautiful, and the nature of Evil that it is ugly, and the nature of the wrong-doer himself that it is akin to me, not as partaker of the same blood and seed but of intelligence and a morsel of the Divine, can neither be injured by any of them—for no one can involve me in what is debasing—nor can I be wroth with my kinsman and hate him. For we have come into being for co-operation, as have the feet, the hands, the eyelids, the rows of upper and lower teeth. Therefore to thwart one another is against Nature : and we do thwart one another by showing resentment and aversion.

'This that I am, whatever it be, is mere flesh and a little breath and the ruling Reason. Away with thy books ! Be no longer drawn aside by them : it is not allowed. But as one already dying disdain the flesh : it is naught but gore and bones and a network compact of nerves and veins and arteries. Look at the breath too, what sort of thing it is : air : and not even that always the same, but every minute belched forth and again gulped down. Then thirdly, is the ruling Reason. Put thy thought thus : thou art an old man ; let this be a thrall no longer, no more a puppet pulled aside by every selfish impulse ; nor let it grumble any longer at what is allotted to it in the present or dread it in the future.'

Another passage of equal vigour occurs at the beginning of Book VII :

'Empty love of pageantry, stage plays, flocks and herds, sham-fights, a bone thrown to lap-dogs, crumbs cast in a fish-pond, painful travail of ants and their bearing of burdens, skurryings of scared little mice, puppets moved by strings. Amid such environments thou must take thy place graciously.'

[1] Translations, C. R. Haines, Loeb Library.

Amid these vanities the good man must always examine his own life :

> 'To what use am I putting my soul ? Never fail to ask thyself this question and to cross-examine thyself thus : What relation have I to this part of me which they call the ruling Reason ? And whose soul have I got now ? The soul of a child ? Of a youth ? Of a woman ? Of a tyrant ? Of a domestic animal ? Of a wild beast ? '

The Stoic doctrine produced in some men a stern and rigid virtue inclined to intolerance ; but not so with Marcus :

> ' It is a man's especial privilege to love even those who stumble. And this love follows as soon as thou reflectest that they are of kin to thee and that they do wrong involuntarily and through ignorance ; and that within a little while both they and thou will be dead ; and this, above all, that the man has done thee no hurt ; for he has not made thy ruling Reason worse than it was before.'

It is tempting to continue, but with two of the many short reflections we must conclude : ' Put an end once for all to this discussion of what a good man should be, and be one ' ; and shorter still : ' Neither tragedian nor harlot.'

Marcus makes no pretensions to elegance of style, as perhaps these translations may show : if he had, his book would have lost half its reality. Its beauty consists in the sincerity and truth of its emotion, and its effect is due, not to any literary artifice, but to the nobility of the ideas which it sets forth and to the revelation of a great spirit.

Sextus Empiricus (fl. A.D. 180)

Another philosopher in this period whose works we possess, Sextus Empiricus, is of a very different type from Marcus Aurelius, both in himself and in the doctrines which he professes. In Marcus we see Stoicism at its strongest, in Sextus Scepticism at its weakest, and his two books *Pyrrhonic Sketches* and *Notes on Scepticism* are monuments of barren pedantry. The latter of the two is by far the longer and is divided into eleven sections. The first five of these attempt to show that dogmatic philosophy is absurd and that neither logic, physics, or ethics can be taught. The next six deal in the same way with science in its six branches, grammar, rhetoric, geometry, arithmetic, astrology and music. The arguments he uses are the commonplaces of the Sceptic school, and the only value of the book lies in such information as it gives us of the sciences which it seeks to destroy.

Celsus (fl. A.D. 180)

Far more interesting than Sextus is the Platonist Celsus, whose treatise against Christianity *The true word* was refuted by Origen in the third century A.D. The treatise itself is lost, but Origen's long quotations enable us both to reconstruct its arguments and to appreciate its satirical style. To Celsus Christianity seemed a denial of reason ; its fundamental idea, that of God made man, was to him an absurdity ; the government of the world by a deity biassed in favour of one nation appeared grossly unfair ; and the elevation of religion over patriotism offended all his notions of civic duty. His chief weapon in combating these new ideas is satire, and he compares Christianity to one of those Egyptian temples, magnificent in outward adornment but containing in their sanctuary a cat or a monkey or a crocodile. Equally severe is the following passage :

'When I see these Jews and Christians I think of a swarm of bats, or of ants coming out of their hole, or of frogs croaking in a marsh, or of worms wriggling about on a manure heap—and saying to one another : "God has revealed to us all that has to be ; He cares not for the rest of the world ; He lets heaven and earth roll on as they will, He only thinks of us. We are the only creatures to whom He sends his messengers; with us alone He wishes to associate, for He has made us in his likeness. Everything is subordinate to us, the earth, the sea, the air and the stars; all has been made for us and destinied for our use; and because it has happened that some of us have sinned God Himself will come or will send his own son to burn the wicked and give us the enjoyment of eternal life." '

The Historians : Arrian (fl. A.D. 140)

After the philosophers come the two historians, Arrian and Appian, writers who, though they do not reach the highest place in literature, are yet possessed of striking merits and devoid of any glaring defects. They are both typical men of their age, imperial functionaries trained in affairs and sure of judgment, suited in every respect for the historian's task except that they lack the precious gifts of independence and imagination. One gives us a history of Alexander in which nothing is wanting save a sense of Alexander's overpowering greatness; the other writes a history of Rome in which there is everything except the spirit of Rome herself.

Arrian was born at Nicomedia in Bithynia towards the end of the first century A.D., and received the most valuable of all trainings from Epictetus, the memory of which he celebrates in the records of his great teacher to which we have already referred. For him Epictetus was a second Socrates, and on the life of the most practical of Socrates' disciples he modelled his own career so closely that his contemporaries often speak of him as ' the new Xenophon.' Entering the army he quickly rose through all the grades, and in 131 was appointed by Hadrian imperial legate of the province of Cappadocia. He was not more than forty when he thus reached the highest office open to a Roman, but after the death of Hadrian in A.D. 138 he seems, like his Athenian exemplar, to have retired into private life, and to have passed his time either at Nicomedia or at Athens, where he was a civic official in 171, either hunting or engaged in literary work. Of his last years we know little and he probably died about A.D. 180.

The writings of Arrian are numerous and include works on philosophy, travel, military tactics, and history. To the first class belong his records of Epictetus' teaching; to the second his description of the coast of the Black Sea, written briefly first in Latin and then at Hadrian's request enlarged in Greek, and also his version, the *Indica*, of the *Periplus* of Nearchus, commander of Alexander's fleet. In the third section we have the treatise *On Tactics* written in 137 and the short *Plan of campaign against the Alans*. To the last belongs his most important book, the *Anabasis of Alexander*, which begins as follows: 'When the histories of Alexander son of Philip written by Ptolemy son of Lagus and by Aristobulus son of Aristobulus agree, I follow them as giving the exact truth; when they differ, I choose from them that account which seems to me the more credible and of the greater historical interest.' The narrative starts with a brief account of the destruction of Thebes, and as early as the thirteenth chapter we come to the battle of the Granicus, the results of which occupy the rest of the First Book. The remaining six books narrate the campaigns of Alexander, and the last six chapters of Book VII tell us of the great king's death. This passage is an excellent example of Arrian's method, exact in details, with constant references to his authorities, and even more picturesque and convincing than Plutarch himself. After describing the course of Alexander's sudden malady Arrian proceeds thus:

'Such is the account given in the royal gazette. We are told furthermore that the soldiers yearned to set eyes upon him, some that they might see him while he was still alive, others because the news was getting about already that he was no more, and they suspected, I imagine, that his death was being concealed by the body-guard : but most of them were moved by grief and a yearning for their king to force their way into his presence. They tell us that Alexander lay speechless as the army defiled before his bed, but that he greeted individual soldiers, lifting up his head with difficulty and making signs to them with his eyes. The royal gazette also says that Peithon and Attalus and Demophon and Peucestas passed the night in the temple of Serapis, and that Cleomenes and Menidas and Seleucus also asked the god if it would be better for Alexander to be brought into the god's shrine and as a suppliant to receive treatment at his hands ; and that a voice came from the sanctuary— " Bring him not to my temple ; it will be better for him to stay where he is." The Companions brought back this message and soon afterwards Alexander died, that indeed being then the better thing for him. The accounts given by Aristobulus and by Ptolemy closely coincide with this. And they also record the fact that the Companions asked him to whom he was leaving his kingdom, and that he replied " To the strongest." Others add that he also said " I see that there will be a big funeral contest over my body." '

Appian (A.D. 95–165)

What little we know of Appian is gleaned from his own writings and from the letters of Fronto, tutor to Marcus Aurelius. He was born at Alexandria about A.D. 95 and was a lawyer by profession, although he took some part in the operations against the Jews in 116 when Trajan suppressed the Jewish insurrection. As a pleader he rose to distinction in Egypt, and after a time migrated to Rome, became a Roman citizen of at least equestrian rank, and practised as fiscal advocate in the imperial court. A letter of Fronto to the Emperor Antoninus Pius is extant asking for the appointment of Appian as procurator and vouching for his friend's honour and integrity. We know from Appian's preface that the appointment was conferred upon him and also that it was in the reign of Antoninus that the preface was written ; but further information we have none ; for though he says ' If anyone has a desire to learn further details of my life, there is a special treatise of mine on the subject,' that treatise is now lost.

Photius, patriarch of Constantinople († A.D. 891) and author of the *Myriobiblon,* knew of twenty-four separate books of Appian, of which eleven have come down to us almost complete. These are the histories of the Spanish, Hannibalic, Punic, Illyrian, Syrian, and Mithradatic Wars, in one book each, and the five books of the Civil Wars of Rome. Extracts from his other writings are also to be found in the compilation made by Constantine Porphyrogenitus, to which we have referred in our account of Nicolaus of Damascus ; and from these and from a few other sources we know something of books ' On the early kings of Rome,' ' On Italy,' ' On Sicily and the other islands ' as well as of a Samnite and a Gallic history. In all these works Appian's method is the same ; he narrates the facts clearly and on the whole correctly, although he has been censured by modern critics for inaccuracy in details, but he never rises to any philosophic view of events, and we get from him no impression of the general character of the Roman people or of the lines on which Roman policy moved. His style, however, is simple and pleasing, devoid of rhetorical ornament in its narrative portions but rising occasionally in the speeches to real eloquence, and even if he cannot be called a writer of the highest class, the value of this subject-matter renders him indispensable to all students of Roman history.

In two of its sections Appian's history is especially important, as giving a continuous account of two vital periods in the history of Rome. One of these is the first book of the *Civil Wars,* which begins with the tribunate of Tiberius Gracchus in 133 B.C. and ends with the defeat of Spartacus by Crassus in 71 B.C., thus bridging the gap between Polybius and Cicero. There are omissions and on many points Appian is unsatisfactory, but his narrative is clear, and in the case of the Gracchi quite impartial. ' So perished Tiberius,' the historian says, ' the son of that Gracchus who was twice consul, and of Cornelia, daughter of that Scipio who robbed Carthage of her supremacy. He lost his life in consequence of a most excellent design too violently pursued ; and this abominable crime, the first perpetrated in the public assembly, was seldom without parallels thereafter.'

The other section is chapters ten to twenty in the history of the *Punic Wars*, a narrative of some sixty printed pages, containing our only detailed account of the destruction of Carthage in 146 B.C. Here Appian rises to the greatness of his theme and the final stages of the desperate fighting in the city are related with dramatic vigour :

> ' Scipio's main object of attack was Byrsa, the strongest part of the city, where the greater part of the inhabitants had taken refuge. There were three streets ascending from the Forum to this fortress, along which on either side were houses built closely together and six storeys high from which the Romans were assailed with missiles. But they captured the first few houses, and from them attacked the occupants of the next. When they had become masters of these, they put timbers across over the narrow passage-ways, and crossed as on bridges. While one war was raging in this way on the roofs, another was going on among those who met each other in the streets below. All places were filled with groans, shrieks, shouts, and every kind of agony. Some were stabbed, others were hurled alive from the roofs to the pavement, some of them falling on the heads of spears or other pointed weapons or swords. No one dared to set fire to the houses on account of those who were still on the roofs, until Scipio reached Byrsa. Then he gave orders to set fire to the three streets all together.' [1]

[1] Translation, H. White, Loeb Library.

The Military Writers

A sidelight on history is to be found in the military writers of this period. The Greeks of the fifth and fourth centuries B.C., in spite of their frequent wars, were not really a military people, as Philip of Macedon eventually showed them. Even less warlike were the Greeks of the first and second centuries A.D., who lived under the assured peace of the Roman Empire, but for all that the production of treatises on strategy and tactics went on busily. It is true that they were usually written by philosophers with no experience of warfare, but a Greek philosopher took all life for his province and was never deterred from writing by lack of practical knowledge. None of these works has much literary or military value ; still, as they have come down to us, they must be at least mentioned.

The first author in point of time is Asclepiodotus, who is sometimes considered to be merely passing on notes taken at the lectures of Poseidonius, and is himself an arm-chair strategist of the most theoretical type. He considers that the proper number of men in a phalanx is 16,384, since that number is evenly divisible by two down to unity. Next comes *The General* by Onosander, who flourished about A.D. 50, and also wrote a commentary on Plato's *Republic*. Of Onosander's book opinions vary : some critics in the past have regarded it ' as the most learned and valuable treatise to be found upon the art of war ' ; others, less favourable, describe it as ' a useless and pedantic wilderness of generalities.' Then we have Ælian the tactician, not to be confused with Ælian the third-century sophist, who wrote in the time of the Emperor Trajan and dedicated to him an extremely literary production. And lastly there is Polyænus, author of *The Ruses of War*, dedicated to Marcus Aurelius and

Lucius Verus, a collection of nine hundred and nine military anecdotes, whose only value lies in the fact that it tells us of a certain number of incidents otherwise unrecorded.

Pausanias (fl. A.D. 160)

From these amateur warriors it is a relief to turn to an author who knows what he is talking about, one who, though he did not write history, gives us a full account of many historical episodes, and is moreover our most precious source for the knowledge of the mythology, the topography, and the monuments of ancient Greece. Pausanias was born in the first half of the second century in Lydia, his native town possibly being Magnesia at the foot of Mount Sipylus. He travelled widely in the Mediterranean and visited Syria, Jerusalem, Greece, Italy ; and using the experience thus gained began to write the *Description of Greece*. The *Description* seems to have taken some twenty years of his life, for the first of its ten books was certainly finished by A.D. 160, if not earlier, the fifth can be definitely assigned to 174, and the last five were probably not published much before 180. Of Pausanias himself we know nothing, except in so far as he reveals himself in his book.

The *Description of Greece* is a plain account by an eye-witness of the state of Greece in the Age of the Antonines, a period when new temples and theatres had sprung up under the sunshine of imperial favour and when the monuments of the glorious past still existed in a fair state of preservation. The narrative is divided into ten books and begins abruptly thus : ' Cape Sunium, in the land of Attica, juts out from that part of the Greek mainland which faces the Cyclades and the Ægean Sea. When you have sailed past the cape you come to a harbour, and there is a temple of

Sunian Athena on the summit of the cape.' In the second chapter we arrive at Athens, but there is then a long digression on Greek history from Ptolemy I to Pyrrhus. A description of the chief buildings of Athens fills fourteen chapters, and then we pass to Marathon and Salamis, and following the Sacred Way to Eleusis finally reach Megara.

The second book deals in the same method with Corinth, Sicyon, Argos, and the neighbouring districts ; the third with Laconia, the first ten chapters being historical, the last sixteen descriptive. The fourth book, on Messenia, consists chiefly of the romantic story of Aristomenes and the Messenian Wars ; the fifth and sixth, on Elis, contain a very full account of Olympia, the offerings—especially the chest of Cypselus—and the statues of athletes. ' Many a wondrous sight may be seen, and not a few tales of wonder may be heard in Greece ; but there is nothing on which the blessing of God rests in so full a measure as the rites of Eleusis and the Olympic games.' In the seventh book, on Achaia, ten chapters are given to the history of the Achæan League ; the remainder are topographical, as is most of the eighth book on Arcadia. The ninth book takes us into Bœotia, first to Thebes and then to Tanagra, Lake Copais, Orchomenus and Chæronea. Finally, in the tenth book, on Phocis, we have a description of Delphi, a long narrative of the attack on the shrine made by the Gauls in 287 B.C., and a full account of the paintings by Polygnotus in the temple club-room.

This summary only gives the framework of the *Description of Greece*, and to appreciate its value the book should be read through from beginning to end. Pausanias is one of the few second-century authors whose style is distinctly bad, and of it his translator says :

' Pausanias was neither a great man nor a great writer. He was an honest, laborious, plodding man of plain good sense, without either genius or imagination, and his style is a faithful mirror of his character. It is plain and unadorned, yet heavy and laboured, as if the writer had had to cast about for the proper words and then fit them painfully together like the pieces in a Chinese puzzle. There is a sense of strain and effort about it. The sentences are devoid of rhythm and harmony. They do not march, but hobble and shamble and shuffle along. At the end of one of them the reader is not let down easily by a graceful cadence, a dying fall; he is tripped up suddenly and left sprawling, till he can pull himself together, take breath, and grapple with the next. It is a loose, clumsy, ill-jointed, ill-compacted, rickety, ramshackle style, without ease or grace or elegance of any sort.'

But fortunately for English readers Sir James Frazer's edition and translation of Pausanias is one of the master works of modern scholarship, and in it Pausanias can be studied to greater advantage than in the original Greek. His matter rather than his manner is what gives him value, and, as Sir James points out in his exhaustive introduction, his matter is of the most lively interest :

' We see sick people asleep and dreaming on the reeking skins of slaughtered rams, or dropping gold and silver coins as a thank-offering for recovered health into a sacred spring ; lepers praying to the nymphs in a cave, then swimming the river and leaving, like Naaman, their uncleanness behind them in the water ; holy men staggering along narrow paths under the burden of uprooted trees ; processions of priests and magistrates, of white-robed boys with garlands of hyacinths in their hair, of children wreathed with corn and ivy, of men holding aloft blazing torches and chanting as they march their native hymns ; women wailing for Achilles while the sun sinks low in the west ; Persians in tall caps, droning their strange litany in an unknown tongue ; husbandmen sticking gold leaf on a bronze goat in a market-place to protect their vines from blight, or running with the bleeding pieces of a white cock round the vineyards while the black squall comes crawling up across the bay.'

The catalogue of strange religious rites might be continued indefinitely, and religion is only one of the topics on which Pausanias loves to dilate. His interests are mainly antiquarian, and on superstitious customs, folk-tales, myths, and local legends he is an inexhaustible store of information. Scenery does not particularly attract him but in describing monuments, especially the ancient monuments of religious art and architecture, he is at his best. At Athens, Olympia, and Delphi he has only to choose from an abundance of material ; but even at small towns like Tanagra he finds things worthy of notice. His account of the Triton statue he saw there is very characteristic :

'I saw another Triton among the marvels of Rome, but it was not so big as the one at Tanagra. The appearance of the Tritons is this. On their heads they have hair which resembles the hair of marsh frogs both in hue and in this, that you cannot separate one hair from another. The rest of their body bristles with fine scales like those of a shark. They have gills under their ears and a human nose, but their mouth is wider, and their teeth are those of a beast. Their eyes, I think, are blue, and they have hands, fingers, and nails like the shells of mussels. Under their breast and belly, instead of feet, they have a tail like a dolphin's.' [1]

And even if for the moment we exclude art and archæology, myth and religion, there are still in Pausanias the numerous passages of history, some of which are really vivid pieces of writing. His account of the repulse of the Gauls at Delphi, for example, is even in the Greek a most dramatic narrative :

'At first, despite the cross-fire of missiles and the bitter cold which told on them, and especially on the wounded, not less cruelly than the arrows of the enemy, the Gauls made a gallant stand, notably Brennus' own company, the tallest and most stalwart of them all. But when Brennus himself was wounded and carried fainting from the field, the barbarians, beset on every side, fell sullenly back, butchering as they went their comrades, whom wounds or sickness disabled from attending the retreat. They encamped on the spot where night overtook them ; but in the night a panic fear fell upon them. (Causeless fears, they say, are inspired by Pan.) It was late in the evening when the confusion arose in their army, and at first it was a mere handful who lost their heads, fancying that they heard the trampling of charging horses and the onset of foemen ;

---

[1] Translations by J. G. Frazer, 'Pausanias.'

but soon the delusion spread to the whole host. So they snatched up their arms, and, taking sides, dealt death and received it.'

The Scientists : Claudius Ptolemæus (fl. A.D. 170)

This chapter must conclude with an account of the revival of science which coincided with the revival of literature, and produced in Ptolemy and Galen two masters whose influence extended almost to modern times. Claudius Ptolemæus, astronomer and geographer, was, like so many of these Greeks, a native of Alexandria and flourished in the reign of Marcus Aurelius. Of his life we know little except that his astronomical observations were made at the temple of Canopus in Egypt. In astronomy his chief work is the *Compendium* in thirteen books, mainly a summary of Hipparchus, which, translated into Arabic in the eleventh century under the title of *Almageste*, became *the* authority on all astronomical matters until the time of Copernicus. In geography, where just before his time we have the didactic poem of Dionysius Periegetes describing the Mediterranean lands, Ptolemy is more original, and in his *Introduction to Map reading*, after a general view of the subject, he gives in a series of tables the latitude and longitude of the principal places in the world from the tenth degree south to the sixtieth degree north of the Equator.

Artemidorus (fl. A.D. 170)

Ptolemy belongs perhaps rather to the history of science than to the history of literature ; his contemporary, Artemidorus of Daldis, so called to distinguish him from the geographer Artemidorus of Ephesus (fl. 100 B.C.), has more definitely literary qualities, even if the science on which he writes, the interpretation of dreams, is now regarded with some suspicion. Times change, and in ancient days the dream interpreter received the same respect as is now given to weather experts, and dreams were held to be due not to the faulty working of the digestion but to the direct action of divine providence. The interpretation of these warnings was a science of the same nature as augury and astrology, and Artemidorus is its chief representative in literature. By profession he was a priest of Apollo, but as he tells us in his preface, he was also an enthusiastic student of dream lore, spending many years in collecting books on the subject and recording in tabulated form all those dreams that came to his knowledge. The result of his investigations he gives us in the *Oneirocritica*, a treatise which in Hercher's edition extends to some three hundred pages with a subject index of another sixty.

The *Oneirocritica* is a delightful book, and whether Artemidorus is quite in earnest is immaterial : we can smile with him or at him as we please. It is arranged in four sections dealing exhaustively with every aspect of the science and illustrated by copious examples, and there is an appendix of ninety-five typical dreams such as this : ' The fuller's wife dreamed that she put on a black dress and then, altering her mind, changed into a white one. She lost her son, and found him three days later. So white things in a dream are better than black.' In the seventeenth and eighteenth centuries it was in Robert Wood's translation extremely popular, and when ' Thy loving friend R. W.' penned his preface in 1640, he could say : ' After I had compared these things with experience I could not but reverence both the work and the author.' Wood's ideas of translation are extremely fantastic, and his book, *The Interpretation of Dreams*, contains almost as much of himself as of Artemidorus. But the following passage is so exactly in the spirit at least of the Greek that it deserves quotation :

> 'There was one that dreamed she was walking in a greenish mead, all fragrant with beautiful flowers and flourishing plants, who whilst she wondered and stood as amazed at the glory of the Spring, an ancient fir all withered and lean faced with Oldness, the very Emblem of death, made towards her with a green bough in his hand, sharping at the end, who as she fled away from his pursuit, darted it often at her. . . . Now mark the sequel of it ; within Three Days after she was for her recreation sake walking in a green closure, hard by a pond side, and on a sudden her brain was so intoxicated and distempered, whether with a spice of the vertigo, or what amazing disease soever I know not, but she was hurried into the deep, with her head forward, in great peril of drowning, and if she had not caught fast hold by chance of a branch, that hung over the water, she had been drowned.'

Galen (A.D. 131–c. 200)

If Ptolemy falls short in art and Artemidorus in science, Galen excels equally in both, and is a perfect example of the scientist who is also a man of letters. Claudius Galenus was born at Pergamum in A.D. 131, his father Nicon giving him his second name 'Peaceable' for reasons which we may infer. ' I had the great good fortune,' says Galen, ' to have as a father a highly amiable, just, good, and benevolent man. My mother, on the other hand, possessed a very bad temper ; she used sometimes to bite her serving-maids, and she was perpetually shouting at my father and quarrelling with him—worse than Xantippe with Socrates. When, therefore, I compared the excellence of my father's disposition with the disgraceful passions of my mother, I resolved to embrace and love the former qualities, and to avoid and hate the latter.'[1]

Pergamum was a great educational centre, and his

---

[1] 'On the affections of the mind,' p. 41. Trans. A .J. Brock, Loeb Library.

father saw to it that Galen received a thorough training in philosophy and rhetoric before he began his medical studies at the age of seventeen. These he pursued at first in his own town and then at Smyrna and Alexandria, returning to Pergamum to become surgeon to the gladiatorial school there. This post he held for some years, and then about A.D. 160 migrated to Rome. There he remained for eight years, acquiring a brilliant reputation as a public lecturer and practitioner, the Emperor himself being one of his patients; but in 168 professional jealousy, exasperated by his own sharp criticisms, obliged him to leave the capital, and he went back to Pergamum again. His retirement, however, was of short duration, for within a year he was recalled by Marcus Aurelius, who wished for his company on the Danube expedition for which he was then preparing. How Galen managed to escape this uncongenial duty we do not know; but avoid it he did, and was left behind in Rome in charge of the young Commodus. In the following years he probably wrote most of his extant works, and died towards the end of the century.

In Galen's time physicians were divided into three schools. There were the Dogmatics, who followed Hippocrates and trusted to the healing power of nature; the Empirics, who concentrated their attention on the symptoms of disease; and the Methodists, who were satisfied if they could fix a label on any particular malady. All three schools propagated their doctrines vigorously both in lectures and in books, and we possess a long treatise by Dioscorides (fl. A.D. 100) on materia medica, another by Rufus of Ephesus (fl. A.D. 110) on the terminology of the human organs, a third by Soranus (fl. A.D. 120) on gynæcology. Even more effective in rousing popular interest were the public lectures, in which sometimes the audience took a part which would scarcely be allowed to-day. Galen tells

us how once he was proving by demonstration that
it is impossible for the bladder to regurgitate into
the ureters, when a sophist 'a thoroughly hardened
disputer and a skilful master of language,' got up and
disputed his conclusions :

> ' " For," said he, " one may clearly observe any day in the case
> of any bladder, that, if one fills it with water or air and then ties
> up its neck and squeezes it all round, it does not let anything out
> at any point, but accurately retains all its contents. And surely,"
> said he, " if there were any large and perceptible channels coming
> into it from the kidneys the liquid would run out through these
> when the bladder was squeezed, in the same way that it entered ? "
> Having abruptly made these and similar remarks in precise and
> clear tones, he concluded by jumping up and departing—leaving
> me as though I were quite incapable of finding any plausible answer.' [1]

Galen's writings are so voluminous that in his old
age he felt constrained to supply readers with a guide
to their contents and published the two pamphlets
which we still possess, *On the order of my writings* and
On my genuine works. These latter in Kühn's monu-
mental edition fill twenty large volumes, and embrace
medicine in all its aspects, as well as a very small
selection from the many treatises which he wrote on
philosophy, rhetoric and logic. His medical works fall
into three divisions, the first dealing with the technique
of medicine, the second with medical theory, and the
third containing books of general interest. To the
first class belongs the *Commentary on Hippocrates*,
which, though it has come down to us incomplete, may
be said to be the beginning of exact scholarship as
applied to science ; the *Functions of the parts of the
body*, a treatise of one thousand printed pages, which
was for centuries the foundation of medical knowledge ;
and, not to mention minor works, the *Art of Medicine*
and the *Therapeutic Method*, which, under the titles of

---

[1] 'On the natural faculties,' 34, 35. Trans. A. J. Brock, Loeb Library.

'Microtechnum' and 'Megalotechnum,' were the favourite text-books of the medieval physician.

In the second class we have, among many other treatises, the short essay *The best physician is also a philosopher;* the long book *On the dogmas of Hippocrates and Plato,* in which the eclectic system, which is the basis of Galen's philosophy, is expounded; the guide for young doctors *On the Sects,* in which he sets out the doctrines of the three chief medical schools; and, most important of all, the *On the Natural Faculties,* which contains the essence of his teaching and is a perfect example of his dialectical method and of the clearness of his style. Both this section and the last, it will be seen, are purely scientific; but in spite of that they are never dull. With Galen philosophy always treads hard on the heels of physics, and in an early chapter of the *Parts of the Body,* we have the following characteristic passage :

> 'As man is the wisest of all creatures, so the hands are instruments made for a wise creature's use. It is not because he has hands that man is wise, as Anaxagoras said, but because he is wise therefore he has hands, as Aristotle with sound sense remarks. Reason, not hands, taught man the arts; the hands are but an instrument, as the lyre is for a musician and the tongs for a blacksmith.'

The third section contains essays on various subjects, treated usually from the physician's standpoint, such as the *Thrasybulus,* debating the question whether health is a matter of medicine or of exercise, the *States of the Mind* and its sequel the *Defects of the Mind,* the very interesting treatise *That mental powers depend on bodily temperament,* and the *Exercise by means of the small ball.*

This last treatise is an enthusiastic account of the small ball game, pictured on the statue base discovered at Athens in 1922, and its conclusion may be given :

> 'In addition to all the other advantages which the small ball possesses, there is one more which I should not like to omit. It is

free from all the risks to which most other athletic exercises are liable. Before to-day many a man has died of a broken blood-vessel after a violent race : and so also the practice of loud and furious shouting, if pursued without intermission for some time, has often proved the cause of very serious mischief. Continuous horse-riding ruptures the parts about the kidneys and often injures the chest, besides in some cases doing harm to the generative organs. I say nothing of the mistakes that horses make, whereby frequently their riders have been unseated and killed on the spot. Many men have also been hurt while jumping, or throwing the discus, or turning somersaults. As for the frequenters of the wrestling school, what need I say of them ? They are all scarred more shamefully than the Curse-hags of whom Homer tells us. The great poet describes them : " Lame and wrinkled and with eyes askance." And so with the wrestling master's pupils, you will find them lame, distorted, battered, and maimed in some part at least of their body. Since then, in addition to the other advantages, this freedom from danger is the particular attribute of small ball games, they must be regarded as the best of all inventions, so far as actual utility is concerned.'

CHAPTER III

THE THIRD CENTURY

(A.D. 193–313)

TOWARDS the end of the second century storm-clouds began to gather over the Mediterranean world, and the structure of the Roman Empire, which had seemed to be based on so firm a foundation, showed ominous signs of disruption and decay. In the sphere of government the theory that the Senate appointed the Emperor, a theory which had worked with fair success for two hundred years, was definitely abandoned, and the armies nominated whom they wished. In social life all classes alike were tending to a state of apathy and indifference under the weight of crushing taxation, and when Caracalla in 212 made the whole world citizens of Rome, and therefore subject to the Roman death-duties, he laid the last straw on an overburdened back. In religion Christianity was steadily growing, but by its side new creeds were continually springing up like weeds, flourishing for a time, and then disappearing, so that men were left more uncertain than ever.

Still, in spite of wars, tumults and economic depression, during the Age of the Severi A.D. 193–235 a certain level of artistic accomplishment was maintained, and under the patronage of that remarkable woman, Julia Domna, wife of the Emperor Septimius Severus, a large amount of attractive light literature was produced. But after the Age of the Severi there followed fifty years of military anarchy which were only brought to an end by the iron rule of Diocletian, and in that half century there would be little for the literary historian to record were it not for the Christian theologians and the Neoplatonic philosophers. With the second generation of the Empire sophists this chapter will begin.

The Philostrati

Of all the literary men, in whose company Julia Domna found some consolation for her husband's neglect, the Philostrati are perhaps the most brilliant. It is not often that literary talent passes from generation to generation in the same family, although we have the example of the four Ekkehards in medieval Latin and the Huxleys in our own day. When it does, it is apt to cause trouble for later historians, and the exact relationships of the Philostrati and their dates have been a fruitful source of argument. The learned Olearius in the great edition of the whole Philostratean 'corpus' which he published in 1709 dismissed as a mere error the statement of Suidas that the first Philostratus lived in Nero's reign, and himself only acknowledges three persons, father, son and grandson, living under Severus and Caracalla. Modern research has partly confirmed, partly refuted his conclusions and it is now usually supposed that the first Philostratus, son of Verus, was the father of the most celebrated member of the family, Flavius Philostratus, sometimes called 'the Athenian.' Flavius was the author of *In Honour of Apollonius of Tyana* and of *The Lives of the Sophists*, but not, as Olearius wrongly thought, of the three books of *Eikones*. These are the work of his nephew or son-in-law, Philostratus, 'the Lemnian,' born A.D 191, who is responsible for the first two books, the third book being probably written two generations later by his grandson.

Flavius Philostratus was born 170, perhaps at Lemnos, and studied at Athens and Ephesus before being introduced to Julia Domna by the Syrian sophist Antipater. With Julia, who was a great traveller as well as a great reader, he probably visited Gaul and Britain, and when the dowager empress took up her home at Antioch as virtual regent for her son Caracalla, he became a prominent member of her circle and was given senatorial rank. After Julia's downfall and death Philostratus went first to Tyre, where he wrote his book on Apollonius of Tyana, and then to Athens, where he wrote the *Lives of the Sophists* dedicated to Gordian, consul in 230 and proconsul of Africa in A.D. 231. Of his later career we know nothing except that he was still alive in the reign of Philip the Arab, A.D. 244–249.

From the *Lives of the Sophists* we have already quoted at some length and it is unnecessary to say more of that book, unless indeed we point out that it is not really biography but anecdote, that the author intentionally disregards any orderly arrangement of time or place, and that even his discussions of style are capricious and superficial. The other book, however, *In Honour of Apollonius of Tyana* requires fuller notice. Julia Domna was a Syrian by birth and an eclectic in religious matters like her husband Severus, who set up in his private chapel statues of Abraham, Christ, Alexander the Great, and Apollonius of Tyana. These two last were similar in one respect : by the third century a mass of fables had gathered round them and they had become almost as much figures of legend as our King Arthur. Alexander already had his Malory in the pseudo-Callisthenes, and it seems that Julia suggested—and a suggestion from her was perilously near to a command—that Philostratus should perform the same service to Apollonius. She herself supplied him with some materials, written by a disciple of the master, and bade Philostratus polish them up. This the unfortunate sophist attempted to do by inserting bright passages from his own *Lives* and by borrowing from travellers' tales, and the result is a book which bears a close resemblance to the curate's egg. It is very, very long ; for Apollonius is imagined by Philostratus to be a sophist of a religious turn of mind, and his conversations with disciple Damis and with Emperor Vespasian are related with unsparing prolixity. These conversations, it need hardly be said, are pure inventions : but they are not amusing, while many of the invented stories are. One of dozens is the account of how Apollonius hunted dragons in India. 'It is utterly absurd,' says Philostratus, ' when amateur sportsmen spin out yarns about hare hunting, that I should hesitate to describe a chase as bold as it is wonderful, of which too the sage was careful to leave a record.' India, it appears, is completely surrounded by enormous dragons, some living in the marshes and some in the mountains. The marsh kind are sluggish and have black backs, as Homer knew, but

' the dragons of the mountains have scales of a golden colour and in length excel those of the plain, and they have bushy beards which are also of a golden hue ; and their eyebrows are more prominent than those of the plain, and their eye is sunk deep under the eyebrow and emits a terrible and ruthless glance. And they give off a noise like the clashing of brass whenever they are burrowing under the earth, and from their crests, which are all fiery red, there flashes a fire brighter than a torch. . . . The Indians catch them thus. They embroider golden runes on a scarlet cloak, which they lay in front of the animal's burrow after charming the runes to cause sleep ; for this is the only way to overcome the eyes of the dragon, which are otherwise inflexible, and much mysterious lore is sung by them to overcome him. These runes induce the dragon to stretch his neck out of his burrow and fall asleep over them : then the Indians fall upon him as he lies there, and despatch him with blows of their axes, and having cut off the head they despoil it of its gems. . . . This is all I know about dragons.'

With that naïve confession we may leave dragons, Apollonius, and Flavius Philostratus.

Of the lives of the other two Philostrati we know little, but their *Eikones* are among the most typical products of third-century sophistic, and are written in a style deftly fashioned for a definite purpose ; ' descriptive writing ' we should call it, the sort of thing which, if it were possible, would be taught in schools of journalism to-day. Based on Lucian it is more varied, more poetical, more picturesque than its exemplar— the style of Ruskin as compared with that of Hazlitt— and in the hands of the two Philostrati it is an admirable implement of art-criticism. The elder Philostratus writes descriptions of sixty-four paintings, the younger of seventeen. No dates or painters' names are given and the pictures are all of one class, figure subjects single or in small groups, usually either gods or heroes, Poseidon, Aphrodite, Herakles, Pelops. Occasionally they seem to be suggested by some well-known episode in literature, *e.g.* the group of Ganymede, Eros, and the three goddesses by the passage in Apollonius' Argonautica ; but usually they are merely the stock figures of the ancient legend. Their interest is chiefly literary, for it is obvious that the authors are more interested in sounds and words than in shapes and colours, but they give us also a definite idea of what an ancient critic thought important in painting. This clear impression of course depends partly upon the cumulative effect of the eighty-one pieces ; here it must suffice to give one specimen of each writer. From the Lemnian we will take the *Narcissus at the Fountain* :

' The fountain is a picture of Narcissus, the picture of the fountain and all Narcissus' body. The lad has just returned from hunting and as he stands by the spring, the brightness of him, as you see, strikes upon the water and he begins to fall in love with his own beauty, deriving from himself the yearning of desire. . . .

'The lad is not listening to us : he is rapt, eyes and ears, in the water ; so let us describe him as the picture reveals him to us. He is standing upright, resting with his legs crossed ; his hand leans upon his spear which is fixed in the ground on his left. His right arm bends round to his waist which is raised on that side, the right part of his body rising to correspond with the left part, which drops. At the bend of the elbow you can see the light through his arm and where the wrist turns there are dimples in the flesh. The inside of the hand is mostly in shadow as the light slants obliquely through the closed fingers. His breast is heaving either with the excitement of the chase or with the thrill of love, and his eyes reveal his longing, as a look of yearning passion softens their natural bold gleam. Perhaps he thinks that his love is already returned, for his shadow is looking at him with the reflection of his own gaze.

'As to his hair, we should have had much to say about it, if we had met him in the actual chase ; for as he ran and the wind caught it, its movements must have surpassed all counting. Even now some description it must have. Luxuriant is it and bright as gold ; the neck claims some locks for its own, the ears divide others ; some play upon his forehead, some fall down his cheeks. There are two figures of Narcissus here and each shows a like beauty, save that the one stands out from the surrounding air, the other is sunk beneath the spring. By the standing water stands the boy with fixed gaze, all athirst for the loveliness before him.'

From the younger Philostratus comes *Marsyas*, a description which will bear comparison with Matthew Arnold's poem :

'The Phrygian has been beaten ; there is despair in his eyes for he realizes what will be his fate. He has piped for the last time ; full well he knows ; his boasts against Latona's son have failed. His flute is flung down in disgrace ; never more will he play ; its weakness has been made manifest. He stands beside the pine tree wherefrom he knows that he will hang, flayed alive to make a wine skin, for that was the penalty which he adjudged against himself. He steals a look at the Scythian who is whetting the edge of his knife for him : (notice how the arms strain against the whetstone and the blade) and the savage looks back at Marsyas, his eyes agleam, his hair standing erect, rough and stiff. There is a red flush upon his cheek, as of one, methinks, who thirsts for blood ; his over-hanging eyebrows are contracted in anger and give a touch of character to his fury. His lips have an angry snarl at the thought of what he is going to do, perhaps a snarl of joy, perhaps it is his heart swelling at the idea of murder. As for Apollo, he is pictured resting on a rock ; his harp lies by his left side and his left hand is still upon it, striking softly and plucking now one string, now another. Note the God's quiet pose and the smile that lights up his face, and how his right hand rests near his bosom, gently holding the quill, lulled to quietude by the joy of victory. There is the river, too, soon to change its name ; and mark me lastly the band of Satyrs, their sorrow as plainly shown as their wanton love of movement, how they are depicted mourning for their dear Marsyas.'

Ælian (fl. A.D. 210)

Of Claudius Ælianus, born at Præneste in Italy, whom Suidas calls the ' honey-tongued,' his contemporary Philostratus gives this notice. ' Ælian was a Roman, but he wrote Attic as correctly as the Athenians in the interior of Attica. This man in my opinion is worthy of all praise, in the first place because by hard work he achieved purity of speech though he lived in a city which employed another language ; secondly, because, though he received the title of sophist at the hands of those who award that honour, he did not trust to their decision, but neither flattered his own intelligence nor was puffed up by this appellation, exalted though it was, but after taking careful stock of his own abilities, he saw that they were not suited to declamation, and so he applied himself to writing history and won admiration in this field.'

History is hardly the word which we should use of Ælian's surviving works, *The nature of animals* and the *Various History*, unless history is held to consist entirely of anecdotes ; but both books are full of amazing information set out in a clear and lively style and make very good reading. *The nature of animals* is far from being as scientific as Aristotle but it is more amusing, for the author's main purpose is to show that animals possess the same virtues and vices as men. At Susa, for example, cows possess some knowledge of arith-metic, and the fish called ætnæos is a model of conjugal fidelity ' though he is not restrained by the laws of Solon or by the attraction of a marriage dowry.' The heron for his part is a Philhellene, and Ælian opens his narrative thus :

' There is an island called the isle of Diomede and it has many herons. These birds, men say, never hurt the natives nor come near to them. But if a Greek voyager lands, by divine dispensation they put their wings together like hands and fly up to greet them. When the Greeks touch them they do not fly away but keep quite still, and will settle in the folds of their gowns as though they were invited to share in a meal.'

Dolphins also possess good qualities which are not always recognized :

' The dolphin is an animal with strong family feelings. Here is a proof. There is a certain town in Thrace called Ænus. It happened that a dolphin was caught there and hurt, but not seriously. He lost some blood, however, and those dolphins who had not been caught scented it, and came in herds into the harbour, and started leaping about as though they meant to do something un-pleasant. So the people of Ænus were afraid, and let the captured dolphin go ; and the other dolphins then went away carrying their injured kinsman with them. Seldom does a human being show such zeal and care for his relatives, male or female, when trouble comes.'

On the other hand even virtue in an animal, when carried to excess, may lead to disaster, as witness the story of the too affectionate horse :

' There was a certain Athenian named Socles, with whose history few people seem to be acquainted, a youth beautiful in reality and by repute. Well, Socles bought a horse, which was also a handsome creature, and of a particularly loving disposition, and more intelligent in a way than ordinary horses are. The animal conceived a violent passion for its master, and when he came near would snort, and when he patted him whinny loudly. If the youth mounted him he obeyed every touch ; if he was standing in sight he cast languishing glances. All these signs of amativeness were charming at first, but when he became bolder and seemed as if he wished to take liberties, people began to talk. Accordingly Socles, disliking scandal and feeling annoyed at the horse's intemperate affection, got rid of him ; and the horse, unable to bear this separation from the beloved, then starved himself to death.'

The *Various History* is composed on the same model, and English readers will find the seventeenth-century translation by Thomas Stanley as amusing as the original. The first book begins with a series of short chapters on animals, 'polypusses, Spiders, Ægyptian Frogs, Pismires ' ; the climax of brevity being reached in the two-line chapter on lions—'When a Lion is sick, nothing will cure him but to eat an Ape.' Then follows a series of anecdotes on persons known and unknown : ' I have heard of a woman that could sound a Trumpet, which art was her way of living, by name Aglais daughter of Megacles ; she wore a Periwig and a plume on her head, and at one meal ate twelve pounds of meat and four quartern loaves, and drank a gallon of wine.' So Ælian prattles on for fourteen books, telling us now of people, now of places, and now of things. He is usually brief, but at the beginning of Book XII he gives us quite a long history of the virtuous Greek maiden, Aspasia of Phocæa, who became the mistress, first of Cyrus and then of his brother Artaxerxes : ' Of hair yellow, locks a little curling, she had great eyes, somewhat hawk-nosed, ears short, skin delicate, complexion like Roses. Her lips were red, teeth whiter than snow, small insteps, her voice sweet and smooth.'

It will be seen that Ælian has a keen eye for beauty and his description of the valley of Tempe shows an appreciation of nature rare in Greek literature :

' Come then and let us now describe the so-called Valley Land of Thessaly, and picture it in words. It is a district lying between Olympus and Ossa. These mountains are exceedingly lofty and

THE THIRD CENTURY, A.D. 193-313

being separated by divine providence as it were admit an intervening space, whose length extends for some forty furlongs, and its breadth in some places for thirty yards, and in others a little more. Through the middle of it runs a stream called the Peneus and into it the other rivers fall joining their waters and so make Peneus the great river we know. The district contains many charming spots of various kinds wherein to linger, not made by man but straight from the hand of Nature, who, when this land came to birth, was ambitious to produce a thing of beauty. There are masses of shaggy ivy growing in abundance, which like the best kind of vines creep up the high trees from below and cling closely to them, while smilax also in profusion runs up the cliff face and overshadows the rock. You do not see the plant itself, but you notice that everywhere is verdant ; and it is a cynosure for all eyes.'

Diogenes Laertius (fl. 220)

As Ælian in history, so Diogenes Laertius in biography depends almost entirely upon anecdote. Of the author of the *Lives and Opinions of Eminent Philosophers*, who he was and where he was born, little is recorded. Even the form of his name is doubtful for Eustathius calls him Laertes and other authorities Laertius Diogenes, while his date, though fairly certain, is only obtained by inference. The last philosopher he mentions is Saturninus, pupil of Sextus Empiricus who flourished in the reign of Marcus Aurelius, and he never alludes to the Neoplatonists of the middle decades of the third century A.D. : he himself therefore may safely be placed as living about the time of Caracalla. In any case the book is far more important than the man, and into it the personality of the writer scarcely enters. It is, of course, a compilation from earlier authors, such as Antigonus, Hermippus, Sotion, Apollodorus and Demetrius, and its interest varies according to the character of the original authority whom Diogenes is at any one time using.

Still, taking it as a whole and looking at it as a

contribution to literature rather than to philosophy, the *Lives* must be pronounced to be a success, and in Latin translations it introduced the early Greek thinkers to medieval Europe. It is true that Diogenes himself never seems to have studied philosophy seriously nor to have attached himself to any one school; but from a literary standpoint this is scarcely a defect, and his multifarious reading, amazing industry, and insatiable curiosity produced a book which has survived while all the authorities on which it is based have perished.

The *Lives*, divided into ten books, fall into two parts, the first tracing the succession of Ionian philosophers in the East, the other that of the Italian Greeks in the West. In Book I we have the sixth-century physicists, Solon and Thales being the chief figures. Book II begins with Anaximander and Anaxagoras and continuing with Socrates ends with Menedemus of Eretria. In Book III we return to Plato who has a book to himself, while Book IV is given to his followers, Book V to Aristotle, Theophrastus and the later Peripatetics, Book VI to the Cynics, and Book VII to the Stoics and especially to Zeno. Then in Book VIII the Italians appear with Pythagoras and Empedocles, Book IX is a medley of the minor schools, and Book X is devoted entirely to Epicurus.

As we have said, the value of the individual accounts varies considerably. The best Lives perhaps are those of Pythagoras, Solon, Plato, Aristotle, and Zeno; the most amusing are those of Menedemus, Diogenes, Arcesilaus and Pyrrho. The Life of Epicurus has an especial importance in that it includes long extracts from Epicurus' own writings. Generally speaking, Diogenes is most interesting when he follows Antigonus of Carystus, and to Antigonus the following account of the sceptic Pyrrho is expressly referred:

' Pyrrho at first was a poor and unknown painter, and there are still some indifferent torch-racers of his in the gymnasium at Elis. He would withdraw from the world and live in solitude, rarely showing himself to his relatives ; this he did because he had heard an Indian reproach Anaxarchus, telling him that he would never be able to teach others what is good while he himself danced attendance on kings at their courts. He would maintain the same composure at all times, so that, even if you left him when he was in the middle of a speech, he would finish what he had to say with no audience but himself, though in his youth he had been hasty. Often, our informant adds, he would leave his home and, telling no one, would go roaming about with whomsoever he chanced to meet. And once, when Anaxarchus fell into a slough, he passed by without giving him any help, and, while others blamed him, Anaxarchus himself praised his indifference and *sang-froid*.'

Athenæus (fl. A.D. 220)

The Greeks of the Empire may not have produced any work to equal the great achievements of the classical age, but in the art of combining instruction with amusement they reached a very high level. As bedside books it would be difficult to surpass Strabo, Plutarch, Lucian, Pausanias, and Ælian ; and to these five Athenæus, author of the *Deipnosophists*, may fittingly be added. Athenæus was a Greek born at Naucratis in Egypt and he lived in Rome after the death of the Emperor Commodus : with that our information ends, for though he is lavish in anecdotes of other men he tells us almost nothing of his own life. As for his great work, the *Deipnosophists* (commonly mistranslated the ' Banquet of the Learned,' although the word rather means ' Experts at dining ' than ' Experts at dinner ' and is equivalent to our ' Epicures Club ') it unfortunately now survives only in an abridged form, even though in its present shape it extends to over 1000 closely printed pages. Originally in thirty-one books it was reduced in Byzantine times to fifteen and these fifteen were again condensed and

shortened. To the final epitome the 1st, 2nd, 3rd,
11th, and 15th, books of our present manuscript belong ;
the other ten representing the second and fuller revision.

In all antiquity there is no collection of general
information which can be compared in richness to the
Deipnosophists. On every page, under a mass of gossip
and trivial detail, interesting facts abound. It purports
in the form of a conversation to give the topics discussed
at a banquet which has lately taken place at the house
of a noble Roman, Laurentius, and the characters are
introduced with some dramatic skill. There is the
magnificent host, a man of learning who guides the
conversation from subject to subject, age to age, and
country to country, until at the end there is scarcely
a topic unmentioned. Among the guests are the great
names of Galen, the chief scientist, and Ulpian, the
most learned lawyer of the age, and after them a host
of smaller men including of course the indispensable
cynics, satirists by profession, buffoons at need. The
nearest analogy of Athenæus in English literature is
Robert Burton's *Anatomy of Melancholy*, and it would
be difficult to say which of the two miscellanies is the
most captivating. But Athenæus has a great advantage
in range of subject, for he deals not with one single
emotion but with all social life, and he extends his
survey over some ten centuries. Like most of the
Greeks of his day he continually recurs to the great age
of his country's glory in the fifth century, and of Rome
and Latin literature he tells us very little. Nor does
he concern himself much with the formal politics into
which Greek history too often degenerates, and from
some of our most familiar Greek authors he scarcely
quotes. Demosthenes, for example, supplies only
sixteen citations, Diphilus the comic poet nearly a
hundred : Theopompus is quoted sixty-four times,
Thucydides five. The social life that the great historian

neglects is Athenæus' chief subject : of music and banquets, of theatres and dancing, of wine and food, of courtesans and jesters he discourses at length. The luxury of the Greek cities through the ages, Sybaris, Tarentum, Miletus, Alexandria under the Ptolemies, Antioch under the Romans, is illustrated by countless anecdotes and by such long descriptive passages as the account of the Feast of Caranus, Hiero's ship, and the Procession of Ptolemy Philadelphus. The talk covers the widest possible range, although the subject of edibles, fruit, vegetables, hors-d'œuvre, fish, and the various kinds of wine has, of course, a much larger share of attention than any other topic. A Greek dinner, however, included many things besides eating and drinking, and the most interesting parts of the *Deipnosophists* are concerned with the concomitants of the feast, the riddles, the merry tales, the music, and the dancing. These two last subjects are continually recurring, and some extracts will show the richness of Athenæus' store of information :

'Music contributes both to the exercise of the body and the keenness of the mind, and that is the reason seemingly why all the Greeks and every foreign nation we know practise it. Damon's pupils at Athens were right when they said songs and dances are a law of nature, whenever the mind is in any way aroused. Gentlemanly and honourable feelings result in honourable dances, feelings that are the opposite of honourable produce dances that are also the opposite. It was this that led to the witty saying of Cleisthenes, tyrant of Sicyon, whereby he gave plain proof of a well-educated mind. The story goes thus : " One of his daughter's suitors (it was Hippocleides the Athenian) danced in a vulgar fashion and Cleisthenes saw him. Judging apparently that the man's mind was as vulgar as his dancing, he said to him, ' You have danced away your marriage.' " Indeed, both in dancing and in walking decorum and grace are good, disorder and vulgarity bad. So originally poets rather than dancing-masters arranged the movements of the dance and free-born men, not slaves, took part in it. The gestures were used merely as visible signs of the words that were sung, and the principles that guide a manly gentleman were always strictly

observed. . . . The movements of these gesture dances they transferred to the dramatic chorus, and from the chorus they were
transferred once more to the gymnasium. In music and in bodily
fitness they sought an examplar of courage, and with a view to
motion under arms they practised gymnastics to the accompaniment
of song. This is the origin of the various steps called Pyrrhic and
all such military kind of dancing, with their different titles—the
Cretan " Quick-step," for example, and the " Front-face."

' The dance called the " Shake-off "—of which Cratinus speaks
in his *Nemesis* as well as Cephisodorus in the *Amazons* and Aristophanes in the *Centaur* and many others also—this was afterwards
called " The Kneading dance." It was danced by a number of
women together and these women I have been told were called
" The Kneaders." Some dances are comparatively sedate, some
are rapid and in some the steps are more simple than in others.
There are the dactyl-dances, where one long step is followed by
two short, the iambic dance where one short step is followed by a
long and the Molossian harmony where three long steps are taken.
There is the Kordax, the Sicinnis and the Persian dance. Then
we have a Phrygian dance called the Nibatismos, a Thracian dance
the Colabrismos, and finally the Telesias. This latter is a Macedonian
dance of which Ptolemy's men took advantage to murder Alexander
the brother of Philip (as Marsyas tells us in the third book of his
Macedonian History). There are also some dances of an hysterical
character—the " Dish-carrier," the " Poker-and-tongs," and the
" Shrieker." And in everyday life there was a dance called " The
Offering." As people danced it they used to repeat these words :

> *A.*   Where is my lovely parsley, say ?
>   My violets, roses, where are they ?
> *B.*   Your parsley, roses, violets fair,
>   You see before you. All are here.

' The people of Syracuse have a special dance—performed in
honour of Artemis with a flute accompaniment—and there was an
Ionian dance called " The Banquet " : they also practised a third
convivial measure called " The telling of the News." There is
again another dance which is styled " The World-conflagration,"
the steps showing how everything may take the shape of burning fire.

' Then there are the comic dances, the " Pestle and mortar,"
" the Kneading trough," " the Shake-off," " the Parade " ; and
besides these " The Grimace " dance, the " Spilling of the flour,"
the " Way to pay off debts," the " Owl and the Lion," the " A.B.C.,"
and the " Red-King's " dance. They also danced with a flute

accompaniment, the " Boatswain's hornpipe " and " the Plank."
Among the postures used in dancing there is the sword step, the
basket step, the cock's comb, the look-out, and the watcher. Other
figures are the " Poker-and-tongs," the " Double kick," " the
Target," the " Hand-down," the " Hand-up," the " Two foot,"
the " Touch-wood," the " Elbow hold," the " Basket," and
" The Top." '

These extracts come from the longest single passage
in Athenæus dealing solely with dancing but this by
no means exhausts the information he possesses. The
song and the gesture-dance always in Greece went
together in ancient times, as they do to-day, and when
our author is treating of music he gives a further
catalogue of dance songs. He tells us of the Dances of
the Revellers, one in single and one in triple time, the
Dance of the Herdsmen and the Dance of the Satyrs.
There are National dances, Spartan, Sicilian, Cretan,
Ionian, and Mantinean : dances that are forms of
athletics and required acrobatic skill—the ball dance,
the somersault dance and the clapping dance ; dances
for special occasions—the War dance, the Phallic dance
and the Dance of Triumph, and fantastic dances whose
name suggest boisterous humour—the Tickler, the
Squeaker, and the Clown. Then there are the song
dances with which working folk lightened their toil ;
some for men, the millers' dance, the reapers' dance,
the dance of the weavers and the dance of the bath-
men : others for women, the dance of the spinning
women and the wool workers, the nurses and the cooks.
In all these dances words, music and gesture made one
inseparable whole as they did in those folk-songs and
village plays which, both in ancient and modern Greece,
play so great a part in the life of the people. On the
François vase of the sixth century B.C., we see Theseus
with a band of youths and maidens hand in hand
dancing the Crane dance to celebrate his victory over

the Minotaur. And Athenæus gives us the words of
two other simple dramas; the Dance of the Crow and
the Dance of the Swallow, as they had been played
from time immemorial in Colophon and Rhodes. The
words alone now remain : we must picture for ourselves
the bands of children disguised with black and white
feathers as they dance from door to door and collect
their doles of cake and wine, while with merry gestures
they mime, now the swift flight of the swallow, now
the fierce attack of a robber band :

> ' The swallow comes winging
> His way to us here !
> Fair hours is he bringing,
> And a happy new year !
> White and black
> Are his belly and back.
> Give him welcome once more,
> With figs from your store,
> With wine in its flasket,
> And cheese in its basket,
> And eggs—ay, and wheat if we ask it.
> Shall we go or receive ? yes, we'll go, if you'll give ;
> But, if you refuse us, we never will leave.
> We'll tear up the door,
> And the lintel and floor ;
> And your wife, if you still demur—
> She is little and light—we will come to-night
> And run away e'en with her.
> But if you will grant
> The presents we want,
> Great good shall come of it,
> And plenty of profit !
> Come, throw open free
> Your doors to the swallow !
> Not old men but children we
> And the swallow says " Open to me." '

The Poets : Babrius and Oppian (fl. A.D. 220)

Greek poetry, outside the epigram, for three centuries
suffered an almost total eclipse, but the age of the

Severi produced two authors who even if they are not great poets at least write tolerable verse of some length. Both of them strangely enough were Romans who preferred Greek to their native tongue and both of them had a practical purpose. Babrius is eminently suitable for a school book, and in Oppian those who wish will find much useful information on fishing and hunting.

The text of Babrius' *Fables* depends mainly on the manuscript discovered by Menas in the monastery of St Laura on Mt. Athos in 1840, which is now in the British Museum. This contains 122 fables arranged alphabetically according to the first letter of the first word, and although other sources have brought the number up to 137, several are of doubtful authenticity. Babrius, whose name is connected with the Latin Barbatus, writes in choliambics after the model of Martial rather than of Hipponax, and mediocre poet though he is the student will find in his book the most attractive presentment of the so-called Æsopic fables which we possess. The best is No. 84, *The sick lion, the fox and the stag*, but that is too long to quote, and two shorter fables will serve as examples of Babrius' style. One is the well-known story of the wolf and the heron:

'Once a wolf got a bone fixed inside his gullet and arranged to give a heron a suitable reward if he would sling down his neck and by extracting it relieve the pain. The heron did so and at once claimed the reward. Then the wolf with a jagged smile said, " It is a sufficient wage for your services to have drawn your head out safe from a wolf's throat." '

The other is perhaps less familiar :

'A squirrel lying in wait for some house fowl hung himself from a peg and pretended to be a bag. But a clever crook-beaked cock saw him and in a shrill voice jeered at him thus : " Many bags do I remember to have seen ere now, but none of them had a live squirrel's teeth." '

T

Oppian, author of the two poems *On Fishing* and *On Hunting* seems to have had a long literary career, for the first is dedicated to Marcus Aurelius, the second to Caracalla, and the reigns of these two emperors are separated from one another by over thirty years. Either, then, there were two poets of the same name nearly contemporary who wrote on similar subjects, or else the first poem is the work of the author's youth, the second that of his old age. The piece on hunting is distinctly the inferior, but that in itself is indecisive, and it is perhaps best to leave the question open.

The *Halieutica*, the 'Compleat Angler,' in about three thousand five hundred hexameter lines, is in its own way a really remarkable work. It is not the highest kind of poetry, but it is vastly clever and full of the most varied information, not only on methods of fishing but on the habits and morals of the fish themselves. The first book treats of their ways of breeding : how, for example, the lamprey mates with a serpent :

> ' The bitter serpent, goaded by hot lust,
> Creeps to the shore and leaves his native dust,
> And voids his venom on some hollow stone
> Until he feels the deadly store has gone
> And he may go, rid of his load of hate,
> Serene and calm to meet his destined mate.
> Rising upon the beach he whistles clear
> His mating call : the lamprey hastens near
> And swifter than an arrow darts to land.
> He speeds to meet her on the wave-washed strand
> And brings his body close : the panting bride,
> Opens her mouth and takes his head inside.'

The second book tells how fish prey upon each other, the strong using force, the feeble, like the fishing-frog, using fraud :

> ' Slow is the fishing-frog and soft withal,
> Wide-mouthed and foul : on cunning he must call
> When he is hungry, and it is by skill
> That he contrives his greedy maw to fill.

Wrapped in the slimy mud inert he lies
And lets a fleshy fibre gently rise
Which grows from out his chin ; 'tis thin and bright
And has a fetid smell; the fishes sight
The bait, and to his mouth the quivering snare
Is gently drawn ; of danger unaware
His victims follow in, nor feel afraid
Till the jaws snap and they are prisoners made.'

In the third book we come to fishing proper, with hooks, nets, and creels ; in the fourth to more curious methods, such as by using the lure of a female fish, by poisoning the water, and by catching in the hand. The fifth book opens with a surprisingly vivid account of a whale-hunt, proceeds to a glowing description of the righteous dolphin whom it is immoral to hunt, and ends with shellfish and sponges.

The *Cynegetica*, ' The Chase,' is rather more than half the length of its companion poem and is less ingenious. It begins with a dialogue between the poet and Artemis, and the first book is concerned with the huntsman's helpers, his horses and hounds. The remaining three books describe the various kinds of wild animals, ranging from the lion to the hare, and the methods used in their chase. The most diverting passage perhaps is the digression on the ichneumon :

' This is the subtle device which the ichneumon weaves against the crocodile. With eyes askance he watches the huge beast until he is confident that it is deep asleep. Then, having rolled himself in sand and mud he swiftly springs and flies with daring heart through the gate of death and passes through the wide throat. Then the wretched crocodile wakes from his heavy sleep and carrying in his belly such an evil unlooked for, everywhere he roams in helpless rage, now going to the farthest reaches of the river, now rolling shoreward in the sand, gasping wildly and tossing in his agony. But the ichneumon heeds not but enjoys his sweet repast ; and mostly by the liver he sits to banquet ; then late and last he leaps forth and leaves the empty body of the beast.' [1]

[1] 'Cynegetica,' III. 415. Trans. A. W. Mair, Loeb Library.

The Novelists

Thus far we have considered Sophistic in all its
branches, and have traced its progress from the theatrical
harangues of Polemon and the elaborate discourses of
Aristides to the dialogues of Lucian, the letters of
Alciphron, and the descriptive prose of the Philostrati.
It is time now to turn to its most remarkable product,
the prose romance, as we find it in the pages of Longus
and Heliodorus. Tales there had been in plenty before,
realistic tales, imaginary tales, traveller's tales; but
this was a new thing, and perhaps it may be well to
explain the difference. A definition of romance would
be easy if there were general agreement on the meaning
of the word. Unfortunately there is not. Most people
if asked, 'What is Romance?' would answer, as
Augustine did of Time: 'I know when you do not
ask me.' A definition of the novel is a more simple
task. We may call it, with the English eighteenth-
century master, 'a large and diffused picture, com-
prehending the characters of life, disposed in groups.'
Or, we may follow the French critic—'a reflection of
a corner of the world seen through a temperament.'
Perhaps the main difference between a novel and a
romance is that the interest of the latter depends
eventually on the mystery of sex. That mingled sense
of attraction and repulsion, idealized by emotion and
kept, as far as may be, free from all gross elements is
the foundation of romance. Bishop Huet gave the
essentials when he said of the French 'roman' that it
is 'une histoire feinte d'aventures amoureuses, écrite
en prose avec art pour le plaisir de lecteurs'; and
Dr Johnson follows him in his blunt description: 'a
novel is a short tale of adventures, mostly dealing with
love.'

It is with the romance in this sense that we are now

concerned, and before we come to Longus and Heliodorus a brief account of some earlier and imperfect essays in that form may be given. The papyrus fragment dealing in prose with the loves of Ninus and Semiramis, found recently in Egypt and apparently written about the middle of the first century A.D., is too short to admit of classification, but it was probably a free treatment of history rather than a romance. Similarly the *Marvels beyond Thule* by Antonius Diogenes, written about the same time, of which we have a summary in Photius, was really a traveller's tale with some love episodes inserted. The anonymous *Apollonius of Tyre*, now only existing in a Latin translation, makes a definite step forward, and the adventures of the young Tyrian prince, who marries the daughter of the king of Cyrene, throws what he believes to be her corpse into the sea, and then after many trials finds his wife and daughter alive in Ionia, have a great deal of the true romantic spirit in them.

The loss of the *Drama* of Iamblichus, save for a few fragments and a summary by Photius, is even more disappointing than the disappearance of the Greek original of *Apollonius of Tyre*. It would seem, as far as we can judge, that Iamblichus put real life into his story, and his characters, the hero Rhodanes, the heroine Sinis, and the villain Garmus are moved not by external accidents but by their own emotions, Rhodanes by love, Sinis by jealousy, Garmus by lustful desire. The plot briefly is this. The two lovers escape from King Garmus, and pursued by Damas, one of his servants, pass through various adventures, partly due to the malignity of Garmus and his minions, partly to the jealousy of Sinis who suspects Rhodanes of loving another woman. Finally all ends happily, the lovers are reconciled and reunited, and Rhodanes becomes king in Garmus' place. But although the plot is

293

conventional, Iamblichus appears to have given it a psychological interest. A few isolated sentences survive : ' When love has taken jealousy to himself, he turns from king to tyrant.' ' A lover's wits are very keen, swift to suspect, ready to conjecture, and inspired to foretell what is to be.' ' Love takes all men out of themselves, and makes eunuchs as bloodthirsty as wine makes Scythians. A Scythian when he is drunk and a eunuch when he is in love are both ripe for murder.' Even more illustrative of the sophistic method is the long fragment which relates how a husband accused a youthful slave of adultery, his evidence being that his wife had told him that in a dream she had had intercourse with the lad. His speech to the judge concludes thus :

> ' A dream is but the image of a woman's activities. In sleep the good wife keeps house, the breeder feels the pangs of childbirth, the bustler is hard at work, the wanton sports with a lover : this woman had intercourse. Let each one of us remind himself of his dreams, what he dreams about usually, and what he sees. The archer sees a bow, the horseman a horse, the king a throne : this woman saw a lover. Base jade, you have been caught in the act. I have taken you lying by the stripling's side. Your nightly kisses are but reminiscences of your daytime embraces. What you do in your waking hours you practise again in your sleep. You lie in my bed but you keep your leisure for him. I have your body, he has your heart. I find you asleep, not so he.'

Of Iamblichus scarcely enough remains to form a definite judgment, but the *Ephesian History* of Xenophon has come down to us complete. It is comparatively short and relates the story of Habrocomes and Antheia, a young married couple separated and exposed to many perils by the anger of the god Eros whom Habrocomes had offended. Having to take a sea voyage husband and wife are captured by pirates ; the chief of the band immediately becomes enamoured of Antheia, his daughter of Habrocomes. The pirates are soon captured and slain by Pirothous, governor of Cilicia, but he in his turn falls violently in love with the young wife. To escape from him she takes poison and is left for dead ; but before she can be buried she revives and is carried off to Egypt, whither Habrocomes by another series of misfortunes has also been taken. The faithful pair however do not meet, and fresh disasters for both follow. Antheia is buried alive and then sold to a pander in Sicily, from whom she is rescued by Hippothous, a bandit with some good qualities who is continually appearing in the story. He takes her to Rhodes, and there at last her husband finds her and they are united. If abundance of incident could make a romance, the *Ephesian History* would be a great success ; but it is not. Xenophon's style is flat and dull, his characters are wooden, and the constant recurrence of calamity becomes wearisome. The best that can be said of him is that he prepares the way for two greater writers.

Longus (fl. A.D. 220)

So far the books we have mentioned have been either imperfect examples of the romance, or they have been fragmentary, or their authors have been lacking in skill. With Longus we come to the first romantic novelist, an artist in words and a man of original genius. It was once thought that Longus was one of the last figures in Greek literature, and Anatole France imagined him as a Byzantine of the sixth or seventh century, writing for the blasé courtiers and merchants of the great capital. ' Le Chloé du roman grec ne fut jamais une vraie bergère et son Daphnis ne fut jamais un vrai chevrier : pourtant ils nous plaisent encore. Le grec subtil qui nous conta leur historie ne se souciait point d'étables ni de boucs. Il n'avait souci que de poésie et d'amour.' But both the style and the manner of the book are decisively against a late date, and what real evidence we have would put Longus about A.D. 220, and make him a contemporary of the Philostrati. His book, however, alone is of importance, and in spite of one or two lapses it is a masterpiece ; in Amyot's translation a French as well as a Greek classic.

'There is a city in Lesbos, Mytilene, large and beautiful. Inlets of the sea run up and divide the town, while bridges of white polished stone adorn it. You would think you were looking not at a city but an island. About two hundred furlongs away a certain rich man had a farm, a beautiful estate : mountains, where wild creatures lived, plains that produced wheat, rising ground for vines, pasture land for flocks. And the sea washed a broad open beach of white sand.'

So the story begins. It was on this estate that one day a shepherd Lamon found a boy child whom he took home and called Daphnis ; here, also, that two years later his neighbour Dryas found another lost babe to whom he gave the name of Chloë. The children were brought up together, and in the springtime when lambs were skipping, bees humming, and birds singing in every bush, they also would skip, sing, and gather the honey-flowers ; together they tended their flocks and shared the pleasures and pains of a shepherd's life. At last one day Daphnis pursuing a wolf falls into a pit whence a friendly shepherd, with the help of Chloë's waistband, extricates him, all besmeared with mud. Lest their parents should be alarmed, they wash the stains away, and while so doing Chloë for the first time feels the smart of love. 'What ailed her she knew not, but soon her heart was full of pain : she cared not for food, she lay awake at nights, she neglected her flock, all her talk was of Daphnis : she could not keep her eyes still : now she would laugh, now cry : at one moment she would doze and then again start up from her sleep : her face was now pale, now all afire with red.' Such are the phases of the malady as Longus describes them.

Daphnis for his part is at first untouched, but when a rival youth, Dorcon, comes a-courting and the maiden, queen of the contest, gives Daphnis the prize of a kiss, his heart too is set on fire. ' It was as though he had been not kissed but stung : he could not stop the quick beating of his heart : he longed to look at Chloë, and when he looked he turned all rosy red. Then for the first time he marvelled at her hair, how golden it was and her eyes wide open like a heifer's and her face more white than goat's milk.' Once a chatterer the lad now falls silent ; his face is paler than the grass in summer : he cannot understand how every-thing about him, flocks, birds, and flowers, seems indifferent to his pain. Nature indeed conspires to increase the young lovers' torments—' It was now the end of spring and the beginning of summer : everything was at its prime, the trees were full of fruit, the fields of grain. Sweet the sound of the cicada, pleasant the bleating of the flocks, lovely the scent of the ripe fruit. One might fancy that the rivers were singing softly as they ran, that the breezes were piping as they blew among the pine trees, that the fruit fell to the ground for love, and the sun, amorous of beauty, stripped men of their clothes.' Dorcon tries in vain to secure Chloë's hand in marriage ; some Tyrian pirates land and capture Daphnis for a moment, but these are only episodes to the main theme—the influence of love on virgin hearts.

The time of vintage brings strangers to the country-side who vex the young people with unsought atten-tions ; among others a certain old man, Philetas, tells them that he has had a dream—they are destined to be slaves of Love. 'And what is Love?' Daphnis asks. 'Love is divine,' Philetas answers, 'and from him there is no way of escape save one.'

But before the old man's precepts can take effect, the quiet course of life is again disturbed. Some youths from Methymna attack Daphnis because of an imagined wrong, and when condemned before a rustic arbitrator, carry Chloë away in their ship. The god Pan interferes, and she returns unharmed ; but autumn is now over, and in the winter the lovers have little opportunity of meeting. Still love finds a way : Daphnis waits outside Dryas' cottage under pretext of snaring birds, until he is invited in. 'And when they saw one another again they almost sank to the ground : it was with an effort that they kept their feet and spoke and kissed.' The lovers, of course, have to separate soon, but Daphnis finds other pretexts for an occasional visit ; always, when leaving, he embraced his hosts first, so that Chloë's kiss may remain undisturbed upon his lips. So the winter passes ; with the spring the flocks go back to the fields, and life and love return. A young married woman, Lycænium, becomes enamoured of Daphnis, and soon he is no longer wholly innocent ; but he remains constant with a pure love to Chloë, and is himself endangered by the schemes of a disgusting parasite, Gnatho. So real is his peril that Lamon discloses to his master the circumstances of his birth ; the tokens discovered with him are examined, and he is found to be the master's own lost son. Chloë in her turn recovers her father, a rich merchant, and the tale ends, as all romances should, with a marriage. In a postscript the author tells us that they lived happy ever after, and had two children.

The style of Longus is perfect, for it is exactly suited to his subject. Apparently simple and artless, it really follows the most elaborate laws of prose rhythm : the passages that seem the most natural are the result of endless polishing and pains ; but the art is so success-fully hidden that it needs a trained ear to detect the subtle harmonies of a prose which is as musical as the lightest lyric. It is impossible to reproduce these melodies in English, for they depend on transpositions which are foreign to our usage ; but even in our rough tongue they sometimes may be faintly heard.

' Dost see how like the hyacinth is his hair, and how beneath his eyebrows his eyes flash forth like a jewel in a setting of gold ! His face is all one rosy flush, his teeth are white like ivory. . . . Anchises was a neat-herd, and yet Aphrodite took him for her own. Branchus tended goats, and yet Apollo kissed him. Ganymede was a shepherd, and the lord of all things ravished him away. Let us not despise the lad ; we see the goats obedient like lovers to him. Nay, rather, let us be grateful to the eagles of Zeus that they allow such beauty to remain on earth.'

Altogether different from this is the effect of quaint simplicity which appears in the sixteenth-century French translation, and in some of the early English versions, such as that of G. Thornley, London, 1657. ' Adorned with cutts, a most sweet and pleasant pastorall for young ladies.'

Longus is not simple ; indeed, he is often, though unjustly, called a decadent both in style and morals. He comes towards the end of one period of the world's history, but he is the harbinger of a new age. And as it is with the style, so it is with the subject and general character of the book. To those familiar with the grandeurs of epic and tragedy, the tale of Daphnis and Chloë has often seemed of a simplicity scarcely worthy of the dignity of Greek literature. A boy and girl, humble peasant folk living in the country, fall in love, and after a few simple adventures, marry. That is all the plot, but Longus knew that exciting incidents are not always needed. Like Richardson, he concerns himself almost entirely with the human heart ; the externals of life he disregards. Chloë, like Pamela, is only a humble country lass ; but, like Pamela also, she is the universal woman : both books have an appearance of simplicity which in reality they are very far from possessing.

Heliodorus (fl. A.D. 225)

Longus is a psychologist, and although the psychology of love is of permanent interest, for as he says ' no one has ever escaped Love or will escape, so long as beauty is and eyes see,' yet the average man prefers the romance of adventure to the close analysis of sentiment and emotion. Longus is the master of all those who from Richardson to Proust have tried to fathom the mysteries of the human heart ; but the great majority of writers choose rather the externals of life, its accidents and escapes, and find their model in Heliodorus. Of Heliodorus, author of the *Æthiopica*, we know a little more than we do of Longus. The statement of the fifth-century historian, Socrates, that he was the Christian Bishop of Tricca who flourished about 400 B.C. is for many reasons highly improbable, and the story that being given his choice between his bishopric and his book he preferred the latter is just one of those anecdotes which are suitable enough for prose fiction but quite out of place in critical history. But fortunately we have two pieces of evidence which, if taken together, may give us a clue to his real personality. At the end of the *Æthiopica* the writer tells us that he is ' Heliodorus, son of Theodosius, a Phœnician of Emesa, of the race of the sun.' Now the last sophist but one mentioned by Philostratus in the

Lives of the Sophists is Heliodorus the Arab, ' who is now spending his old age at Rome, neither greatly admired, nor altogether neglected.' The novelist was plainly acquainted with Philostratus, for his account of the Gymnosophists is based upon the other's *Life of Apollonius of Tyana*, and we shall probably not be mistaken if we identify him with the sophist of whom Philostratus gives a somewhat cool account.

But whoever Heliodorus may have been, the *Æthiopica* is a masterpiece, and it may be doubted whether any novel has a more vigorous beginning :

> ' One morning at the first smile of dawn, just when the sun was lighting up the mountain tops, some robbers, sword in hand, came creeping over a hill which stretches by the mouth of the Nile called Heracleotis, where the river runs into the sea. For a moment they halted and surveyed the waters beneath them ; their eyes ranged over the ocean but nothing that could be prey for pirates was visible sailing there. Then their looks turned to the beach hard by and this is what they saw.'

A vivid description of the scene upon the beach follows : men, dead and dying, lie about a pirate galley, their revels interrupted by a drunken brawl ; near them sit their two captives, a maiden wondrous fair and a wounded youth, Chariclea and Theagenes. The robbers seize them and carry them off to a lair among the marshes, but who the unfortunate pair are we only learn as the romance proceeds, for Heliodorus is a master of the art of construction and knows full well the advantage to be gained from suspense. From the first the plot is intricate, but never confused : each thread of the story is held firmly in the author's guiding hands and the central incident, the secret of Chariclea's birth, is reserved for the middle of the book. But it will perhaps be convenient to give the tale in chronological order.

One day the queen of Æthiopia by a strange accident

301

gives birth to a white-skinned child. Fearing her
husband's suspicions she entrusts the baby to one
Sisimithres, who in turn consigns her to Charicles,
priest of Delphi. Chariclea, for so she is now called,
spends her childhood in Greece, and when approaching
womanhood receives as tutor an aged Egyptian named
Calasiris, whose duty it is to prepare her for marriage
with the nephew of Charicles. But these plans are
interrupted by the arrival at Delphi of Theagenes ' a
young man ' (to quote Underdown's translation) ' of
Achilles' courage indeed, who in countenance and
stomache appeared no lesse, with a straight neck, hie-
foreheaded with his hair in coomely sort rebending
down, his nose and nosthrilles wide enough to take
breathe, which is a token of courage and strength :
his eyes not very grey but grey and blacke which made
him looke somewhat fiercely and yet very amiably, not
much unlike the sea which is newe calmed after a
boysterous tempest.'

Chariclea naturally becomes enamoured of this
paragon and in company with Calasiris the lovers fly
from Delphi. But they are captured first by pirates
and then by the Egyptian robbers ; Chariclea, it is
needless to say, suffering much vexation from the
amorous advances of the bandit chiefs. Finally they
are rescued by the governor of Egypt, and Thyamis,
the captain of the robbers, now discovered to be the
son of Calasiris, is elected high priest of Memphis,
whither all parties repair. The lovers for a moment
see happiness before them, but unfortunately the
beauty of Theagenes inflames the passions of Queen
Arsace who in her husband's absence rules at Memphis.
On his virtuous refusal to accede to her advances the
queen orders his torture and Chariclea's death, but
before her command is executed a dispatch arrives
announcing that the absent monarch has discovered his

wife's intrigue. Arsace hangs herself and the lovers are escorted to King Oroondates. On their way, however, they are captured by the Ethiopians, whose king, Hydaspes, Chariclea's father, defeats Oroondates in a great battle. The prisoners are about to be sacrificed as a thank-offering to the Sun, when a ring and fillet fastened to Chariclea's body reveal her as the long-lost child. Charicles opportunely arrives to explain all further details, Chariclea is recognized as heiress to the throne, and the young couple are at last united.

As regards the style in which the *Æthiopica* is written, some critics have complained that it is over-ornate, fantastic and poetical, composed of tags from Homer and the tragedians. As a matter of fact, those who will consult the Greek and forget for a moment the quaintness of Amyot and the conceits of Underdown, will find a simple prose, plain yet picturesque, admirably suited for imaginative narrative. There are certainly many reminiscences and occasional quotations from the poets, but these are no great blemish in a romance which might be called poetical history. The style has not the graceful charm of Longus but it is perfectly adequate. When all is said, Heliodorus is a great author : no one can reproach him with poverty of invention : he sows from a full sack : incident follows incident, character character, and not a person appears on the scene without having his own story first to divulge. His heroine too is beyond cavil : that when she was still only seven she seemed almost of marriage-able age may be imputed either to the warmth of the climate or the miraculous circumstances of her birth ; as a woman in the book Chariclea is a wonder of beauty, virtue, and courage. In the opening scenes there are some reminiscences of Euripides' Electra, the purest type of sisterly love—and indeed the sisterly relation-ship is used several times as a subterfuge by the lovers—

but in all essentials she is Heliodorus' own invention and a most significant proof of the change that was coming over men's minds as regards women.

No, when the account is cast up, the merits of the *Æthiopica* far outweigh its defects. Achilles Tatius, Chariton, and the later Greek romancers follow closely on the lines that Heliodorus lays down. His influence on modern literature has been equally great. Tasso, Racine, and Mme de Scudery are only a few of the authors who have acknowledged their indebtedness. Our own Elizabethan novelists, Lyly and the rest, borrow incessantly, and even Sidney, as we know now by manuscript evidence, completely remodelled his best work after reading Heliodorus. The *Æthiopica* is a book far more elaborate in its structure than *Daphnis and Chloë*, although Longus beneath his apparent simplicity conceals the finer art. *Daphnis and Chloë* is unique, and in its own 'genre' has never been surpassed; the *Æthiopica* owes its importance partly to its position in history. It is the first example of a type which has, since the days of Heliodorus, attracted authors far greater than he. Fielding, Scott, Dumas, Balzac, are all his spiritual sons, and they have left their father far behind. Still Heliodorus is the first begetter of the clan, and deserves at least the veneration that children should give to age. To him belongs the credit of inventing the romance of adventure, and those who write and read our modern novels should at least once in their lives peruse the pages of the *Æthiopian History*.

Achilles Tatius (fl. A.D. 260)

The third novelist of this period is Achilles Tatius, author of the *Adventures of Leucippe and Clitophon*, whom the later Byzantines regarded as one of the chief masters in this kind of writing. In powers of invention, however, he is greatly inferior to Heliodorus, from whom indeed he borrows the main features of his plot. His hero, Clitophon, who tells the story in the first person, is tempted, like Theagenes, by a rich and amorous dame ; but with the exception of one lapse remains faithful to his first love. Leucippe, for her part, like Chariclea, is taken captive, and as a slave finds her chastity threatened by her master, but finally emerges with her honour and person intact. Even the dangers which the young couple continually have to face resemble those in the *Æthiopian History*, and once more we have a succession of shipwrecks, abductions, and fights with brigands in the Delta.

All that we know of Achilles Tatius is that he was a native of Alexandria, and until quite recently it was generally considered that he lived in the fifth or sixth century A.D. This, however, is impossible, for a papyrus fragment found by Grenfell and Hunt in Egypt contains a portion of his novel. Palæographical evidence fixes the date of the papyrus as the first half of the fourth century, and we may therefore safely place Achilles in the latter half of the third. With this date also every other indication agrees, for it is plain that Achilles was well acquainted with the sophistic literature of the third century, and borrows from many other authors besides Heliodorus. The tale of the lamprey and the viper, for example, which we quoted from Oppian appears again in his pages ; his zoological digressions are strongly reminiscent of Ælian ; the long discussion on the respective delights of male and female love in the second book is based on the pseudo-Lucian *Amores* ; and the elaborate descriptions of pictures, by which the narrative is continually being interrupted, are exactly in the style of the Philostrati.

These descriptions of pictures and places are quite the best things in the novel. As a creator of characters

Achilles is negligible, and the few incidents in the plot which seem to be his own invention are ludicrous. His heroine is twice killed before her lover's eyes ; but on the first occasion the knife that rips her body open is a stage weapon and the streams of blood which he sees come from a bladder concealed beneath her dress ; on the second, the headless body which the pirates throw to him is not that of his mistress but of another woman wearing her clothes. His psychology also is very lacking in finesse, and one cannot feel much sympathy for his virgin heroine, whose troubles begin by her mother finding her in bed with a man. Still, in spite of all these defects, Achilles possesses the one essential quality of a novelist ; he is never dull, and sometimes, without always meaning it, he is very amusing. His elaborate rhetoric is not in all cases quite appropriate to his subject, but in a description, such as that of the picture of Europa and the bull with which the novel opens, it can be extremely effective :

'The sea had two different tinges of colour ; towards the land it was almost red, but out towards the deep water it was dark blue : and foam, and rocks, and wave crests had been painted in it. The rocks ran out from the shore and were whitened with foam, while the waves rose into crests and were then dashed into foam by breaking upon the rocks. Far out in the ocean was painted a bull breasting the waves, while a billow rose like a mountain where his leg was bent in swimming : the maiden sat on the middle of his back, not astride but sideways, with her feet held together on the right : with her left hand she clung to his horn, like a charioteer holding the reins, and the bull inclined a little in that direction, guided by the pressure of her hand. On the upper part of her body she wore a tunic down to her middle, and then a robe covered the lower part of her body : the tunic was white, the robe purple : and her figure could be traced under the clothes—the deep-set navel, the long slight curve of the belly, the narrow waist, broadening down to the loins, the breasts gently swelling from her bosom and confined, as well as her tunic, by a girdle : and the tunic was a kind of mirror to the shape of her body.'[1]

[1] Tr. S. Gaselee, Loeb Library.

Chariton (fl. A.D. 260)

The fourth of this group, Chariton, to whom we owe the *Chæreas and Callirrhoë*, although less entertaining than Achilles Tatius, is more suitable for family reading. He tells us that he was born at Aphrodisias, 'Venus town,' and that he served as copyist to one Athenagoras, 'Attic eloquence'; but it is probable that both statements are merely cryptic references to the love theme of his novel and its elegant language, and have no foundation in fact. The book itself derives a certain interest from its historical setting, but otherwise shows little originality. The events of the story are supposed to take place in the early years of the fourth century B.C., and we are introduced to such real persons as Artaxerxes, king of Persia, and Hermocrates, the Syracusan general who fought against the Athenians in 413 B.C. Hermocrates is the father of the heroine, Callirrhoë, and the tale begins with his reconciliation to his political adversary, Ariston, by the marriage of his daughter to Ariston's son, Chæreas. After that, however, we have a repetition of the stock incidents of Greek romance, *crambe repetita*, which in Chariton have lost all the freshness which they ever possessed. Callirrhoë, whose beauty stupefies all beholders, has a cataleptic fit, and in that state is entombed. Robbers break into her sepulchre, find her alive, and carry her off to the slave-market at Miletus, whence after various adventures she finds her way to the harem of Artaxerxes. Meanwhile Chæreas, by the agency of the goddess Rumour, has learned of his wife's existence, and goes to look for her. He in his turn is taken prisoner and sold as a slave to the Persian satrap of Caria, in whose retinue he also arrives at Artaxerxes' court. Then, by a slight anachronism, the Egyptian revolt breaks out, and Chæreas, escaping from his

master, becomes one of the rebel leaders. At the head
of their fleet he captures Arados, where he finds his
wife again, and with her returns in triumph to Syracuse.

Cassius Dio (A.D. 155–230)

Almost as attractive as the sophistic novelists are the
two sophistic historians, Dio and Herodian. Cassius
Dio Cocceianus, otherwise known as Dion Cassius, was
born in Bithynia about A.D. 155. His father, Cassius
Apronianus, was governor of Cilicia under Marcus
Aurelius, and Dio himself became a senator at the age
of twenty-five. During the reign of Commodus
(180–193) he was living in Rome and actively engaged
in public affairs, and when the tyrant was succeeded
by Septimius Severus he became prætor. The year of
his prætorship was also the year of his first literary
work, for in 194 he wrote a short account of the dreams
and portents which had foretold the future greatness
of Severus. The emperor gave the book his gracious
approval, and Dio was vouchsafed another dream in
which he was admonished to write a narrative of the
events leading up to his accession. This proved equally
successful, and it seems that Dio then resolved to write
the history of Rome from the landing of Æneas in
Italy down to his own time. For this purpose he
retired from public life to his country house near
Capua, and spent the next twenty years in studying
his subject, collecting his materials, and writing a large
part of his narrative. In 216 he was recalled from his
retirement by Caracalla and compelled to attend the
emperor on his eastern expedition, while under
Alexander Severus he was made proconsul of Africa,
and then governor of Dalmatia and Upper Pannonia
in succession. In Pannonia his discipline was so strict
that he became unpopular with the soldiers, and in 230

he prudently sought permission to retire to his native town of Nicæa, where he probably soon afterwards died.

Dio's *Roman History*, originally in eighty books, covered a period of nearly a thousand years and was divided into three main sections. The first part, as he tells us, contained the history of the republican period, when power rested with the senate and the people, and the facts were public property. The second part dealt with the early principate from Julius Cæsar to Marcus Aurelius, and here the historian had to rely on such official accounts as the emperors allowed to be published. The third part, a descent from the golden to the iron age, narrated the events of his own day, in many of which he himself played a part, and consequently there was here much more of detail than in the earlier history. Of the whole work only about one-third has come down intact, the extant portions being Books 34 to 60, which carry us from 70 B.C. to A.D. 46, Books 78 and 79, and the Paris fragments describing the events of the years 207–200 B.C. We have, however, a certain number of excerpts and quotations made by later writers, and especially the epitome of Books 1–30 made by Zonaras in the twelfth century A.D., and the epitome of Books 61–80 made by Xiphilinus towards the end of the eleventh century.

In style and diction Dio modelled himself upon Thucydides, and his history is as typical a product of sophistic in the third century A.D. as that of Thucydides is of sophistic in the fifth century B.C. Thucydides, it is true, submits everything to the clear light of reason, Dio does not : Thucydides does not repeat anything that is obviously incredible, Dio does : but in other respects the later historian follows his great exemplar as closely as he can. He follows him, indeed, somewhat too closely for modern taste in his habit of diversifying the narrative with long formal speeches ; but it should be remembered that both writers were trained in rhetoric, an art with which we are quite unfamiliar, and that although we cannot appreciate their efforts, ancient readers could.

It has been the habit to disparage Dio, largely on this ground of his love for speeches, and to disregard the fact that he is a writer who can be read with pleasure. The two long discourses in Book 52, for example, in which Mæcenas and Agrippa state the case for and against the imperial system, may not please those who think that history should confine itself to facts, but they are extremely valuable as political pamphlets. The device of the inserted speech, moreover, is very useful in heightening the interest of a critical situation, and it is so used in Book 50, the whole of which is given to the Battle of Actium, 31 B.C. The first fifteen chapters give the preliminaries of the fight, concluding with an account of the omens unfavourable to Cleopatra, and then we have the two set speeches delivered to their men by Antony and Octavian. Antony declares that his opponent is a weakling who wishes to be a tyrant ; Octavian replies that Antony is the slave of an Egyptian woman. Each speech fills six chapters ; and then comes the battle where ' Cleopatra, true to her nature as a woman and an Egyptian, grew impatient and hoisted the signal for retreat.'

But even if the speeches give a certain air of artifice to the earlier part of the history, the later books, where Dio is writing of his own times, cannot be accused of any lack of realism. Dio lived through the reign of Caracalla, and his account of how the tyrant murdered his brother Geta in their mother's presence is extremely vigorous. Equally striking is his picture of that strange figure, the emperor Elagabalus :

' He would go to the taverns by night, wearing a wig, and there ply the trade of a female huckster. He frequented the notorious brothels, drove out the prostitutes, and played the prostitute himself. Finally, he set aside a room in the palace, and there committed his indecencies, standing nude at the door of the room, as the harlots do, and shaking the curtain which hung from gold rings, while in a soft and melting voice he solicited the passers-by. . . . The " husband " of this " woman " was Hierocles, a Carian slave, but certain other men also were honoured by being allowed intercourse with the emperor. For he wished to have the reputation of committing adultery, so that in this respect also he might imitate the most lewd women ; and he would often allow himself to be caught in the very act, in consequence of which he used to be violently upbraided by his " husband " and beaten, so that he had black eyes.' [1]

Herodian (fl. A.D. 220)

Habent sua fata libelli. Herodian to-day is practically unknown to English readers, unless they be professional historians, and those who wish to consult him must do so in the original Greek. But in the seventeenth and eighteenth centuries he was almost a popular author with us, and translations of his *History of the Roman Emperors* were numerous. The Latin version made by the great Renaissance scholar, Angelo Poliziano, was put into English by N. Smythe in 1550 ; James Maxwell translated the Greek into prose in 1629, and C. B. Stapylton turned it into 'an heroick poem,' in 1652. A 'gentleman of Oxford' followed in 1705, J. Hart in 1749, and in 1789, the year of the French Revolution, Richard Graves published a translation of the life of Commodus under the significant title of *The Heir-Apparent.*

Herodian would probably be equally attractive to-day, for his history of Rome from the death of Marcus Aurelius in A.D. 180 to the time of the Gordians, A.D. 240, is full of good things, and as the Oxford gentleman says, ' His language is clear and masculine, and flows from him with so much ease that he seems

[1] Bk. LXXX. xv. Trans. E. Cary, Loeb Library.

311

to have taken no Pains to adorn it : Yet as careless of Ornament as he appears, he still preserves a Majesty suitable to the Greatness of the Subject which he Treats, and has something in him so pleasing and so comely, as perhaps all the Art and Labour of other Men can never reach.' Of his method a condensed version of his account of Commodus' death will give some idea. The tyrant had been criticized by his concubine Marcia and his minister Eclectus, and had noted on a tablet that both should be put to death that night :

'Now there was about the Court one of that sort of Boys that go naked and are tricked up with Gold and Jewels, being kept by Persons of Quality in Rome for their diversion. The boy found the tablet and handed it to Marcia, who, calling in Eclectus, resolved to give Commodus poison in a cup of wine, for he drank anything with a peculiar Rellish that was prepared by that dear Creature. The poison was given ; but Commodus had already drunk so much that soon afterwards he began to vomit, and the conspirators, when they saw him disgorge at this rate, fearing lest he should cast up all the Poison, and recover, and consequently put them all to Death, perswaded *Narcissus*, a young *Desperado*, to strangle him in his Chamber. Thus dy'd Commodus, after he had reign'd thirteen years from his Father's Death. He was the Noblest Prince and goodliest Person of his Age ; and if we may admit Valour to consist in Skill in Shooting, or Levelling at a Mark, no man was more eminently possessed of that Vertue ; but the whole Tenor of his Life was made up of base Actions and dishonourable Practises, as is before related.'

Clement of Alexandria (A.D. c. 150–212)

We must next return to the Christian authors. The writings of the great Irenæus (125–202) now only exist in a Latin translation, but of all the Greek Fathers Clement is the most attractive to the general reader. Clement was born about the middle of the second century A.D., possibly at Athens, where he may have studied under Herodes Atticus. It is clear that he was originally a pagan and probably he had been initiated into the Eleusinian Mysteries before he set out on the usual student travels which led him to S. Italy, Asia Minor, and finally about A.D. 180 to Alexandria. Here he met Pantænus, the first head of the Catechetical School; and if he had not been converted before by any of the five 'blessed and memorable' preachers whom he had met on his travels, under the guidance of Pantænus he became a Christian. In the church of Alexandria he soon rose to the office of presbyter, and when Pantænus died he succeeded him as head of the school. For twenty years he taught at Alexandria, but in 202 the persecution of the Christians by Severus began and he left Egypt never to return. We know that he was alive in A.D. 211, for in that year he brought a letter from his old pupil Alexander to the church at Antioch, but he probably died soon after that date.

In the early Christian church the writer's trade was regarded with suspicion, and to the believer the Old and the New Testament formed a sufficient library. The importance of Clement in history lies in the fact that he, together with his great Latin contemporary Tertullian, faced this prejudice boldly, and by producing work which is in the strict sense literary enabled Christians to meet their pagan adversaries on their own ground. In the opening lines of the *Stromateis* Clement raises the whole question :

'Is writing books admissible ? If it is not, what is the good of letters ? Who should write them, good men or bad ? It would be absurd to reject good men's books and to accept productions of the other kind. Shall Theopompus and Timæus, who composed fables and slanders, shall Epicurus, that fountain-head of impiety, shall Hipponax and Archilochus be allowed to write shameful stuff, while the man who preaches the truth shall be prevented from leaving benefits to future ages ? '

313

Of the works that Clement wrote in pursuance of this aim the *Sketches*, a commentary on the Scriptures, is now lost ; but we possess the eight books of that wonderful miscellany, *Stromateis*, 'Hold-alls,' the *Protrepticus*, an admonition to the Greeks to abandon the follies of paganism and turn to the true faith, the *Pedagogue*, a guide to conduct for those who have been converted, and lastly a sermon on riches, *What rich man shall be saved?* Of these the *Stromateis*—the word properly means the striped sacks in which bedding was stored—is by far the longest and most discursive, but throughout it is inspired by one idea, to show the use which devout Christians may make of Greek philosophy. 'All sects of philosophy,' says Clement, 'contain a germ of truth. Greek philosophy, as it were, purges the soul and prepares it beforehand for the reception of faith on which the Truth builds up the edifice of knowledge.' The first book states this position clearly and also contains a comparison between sacred and profane history. The second insists on the superiority of faith over reason and combats the Gnostic heresy. The third and fourth books treat of sexual purity and of the love of God which leads Christians willingly to accept martyrdom. The fifth attempts to show that Greek philosophy has a symbolic truth and that it borrows largely from Jewish sources, the sixth and seventh enlarge upon its practical value, and argue that there is a true Christian Gnosticism of which the heresy is only a perversion. The eighth book is unfinished and is of doubtful authenticity. Such is a brief summary of the *Stromateis* ; but, as the title indicates, each book contains a large number of digressions, and to appreciate its variety the whole work must be read through.

The *Protrepticus* or *Exhortation to the Greeks* is really an apology for the Christian faith and should be read

314

together with Tertullian's great oration. In it Clement shows, as Plato before him had done, the absurdity and immorality of much of Greek religion. The legends of the gods are passed in review, and Clement cries :

> ' Still, there was some life in Zeus when he was a man : but by this time even your tales appear to me to have grown old. He is no longer a god who flies, or corrupts boys, or kisses, or ravishes ; and yet there are still many beautiful women left, fairer even than Semele. Yes, Zeus is dead (take it not to heart) like Leda, like the swan, like the eagle, like the amorous man, like the snake.'

In the same way he shows that the ritual of the mysteries was a mixture of barbarism, frivolity, and obscenity, whether it was performed in honour of Dionysus or of Demeter :

> ' What manifest shamelessness ! Formerly night, which drew a veil over the pleasures of temperate men, was a time for silence. But now, when night is for those who are being initiated a temptation to licentiousness, talk abounds, and the torch-fires convict unbridled passions. Quench the fire, thou priest. Shrink from the flaming brands, torchbearer. The light convicts your Iacchus. Suffer night to hide the mysteries. Let the orgies be honoured by darkness.' [1]

While the *Exhortation* is meant for the unconverted Greeks, the *Pedagogue* is addressed to the richer members of the Christian church in Alexandria and gives us a very interesting view of social life in Clement's time. The main point of conduct on which the writer insists for his people is simplicity : the Christian man or woman should be known by plain white clothes and an absence of all luxury. Christians may go to the public baths but they must not forget their modesty. As for the theatre, the circus, and the drinking-shop, they should never be seen in such haunts of vice, and if they drink wine at all they must do so in moderation.

---

[1] 'Protrepticus,' I. 2. Trans. G. W. Butterworth, Loeb Library.

In contrast are the pictures of pagan society which Clement paints. There are the courtesans, 'Helens' as he calls them, with their painted faces and their yellow-dyed hair, thronging the streets and the amphitheatre. There are the ladies of fashion, scarcely to be distinguished from their unfortunate sisters, so strongly scented that their husbands are stupefied by their perfumes. Dressed in transparent silk and the finest linen with purple veils they spend hours on their toilet and pass the rest of the day in idle games and frivolity. Their male counterpart is the dandy in his flowing gown, with a garland on his head and jewelled rings on his fingers. He dyes his hair, and not only is he clean shaven but he uses depilatories, and prefers the bath to the gymnasium. Finally there is the vulgar millionaire, in whose house everything is made of gold or silver or ivory, and whose banquets are the last word in luxury. At his table everything is to be found except good manners : the world is ransacked for dainties, but the guests snatch at their favourite dish and seldom open their mouths except to eat or to make some immodest jest.

Clement was a great reader, like Athenæus and Diogenes Laertius, and some of these details may come from books, for he cites by name over three hundred authors of whom otherwise we should know nothing. The great library of Alexandria was open to him, even if his quotations may partly be drawn from anthologies ; but there can be no doubt of his thorough knowledge of Homer and Plato. Unfortunately, although he borrows largely from Plato's thought he is intentionally indifferent to Plato's charm of speech. His own style is very variable, and though under the influence of moral indignation or religious fervour he sometimes writes with point and vigour, his sentences are apt to be long and involved, he can be guilty of serious lapses in good taste, and too often he is painfully diffuse. He says himself, 'the search for style is not my business'; and his readers have to suffer.

Origen (A.D. 185-254)

Clement's leaning towards Gnosticism exposed him to some suspicion from the strictly orthodox; but his greatest pupil went much farther in striking out a path for himself. Origenes, sometimes called Adamantius, 'The man of adamant,' because of his invincible industry, was born at Alexandria A.D. 185, and at the age of eighteen was already so zealous a Christian that he urged his father, Leonidas, to face martyrdom when the persecution under Severus began. Leonidas suffered death, and on Clement's prudent retirement Origen was appointed by Demetrius, Bishop of Alexandria, as head of the Catechetical School. About this time a too literal interpretation of St Matthew xix. 12 induced the young professor to castrate himself, and the friendship which he formed with Ammonius, the founder of Neoplatonism, increased his natural tendencies to mystic exaltation. He thought it best, however, to leave Alexandria in 215 during Caracalla's sanguinary persecution of the Christians, and after visiting Julia Mammæa, mother of the future emperor Alexander Severus, at Antioch in 218, he was in 230 ordained priest at Jerusalem.

By this time Bishop Demetrius had scented heresy in some of the many books which Origen with the help of his rich friend Ambrosius had published, and calling a synod together he declared the offender's ordination invalid and forbade him to teach in Alexandria. Accordingly in 232 Origen transferred his activities to Cæsarea, and soon made his school there the most famous centre of Christian philosophy. At Cæsarea during the persecution of Maximinus in 236 he wrote his fervid *Exhortation to Martyrdom*, and when Decius in 250 began his fierce attempt to crush Christianity by force, his reputation marked him out as a certain victim. Eusebius, his ardent admirer, who consecrated to him the sixth book of the *Ecclesiastical History*, tells us how he heroically endured every form of torture and still refused to recant. The final test of martyrdom however, he escaped, although his strength was completely shattered, and after lingering on for some time he died either at Cæsarea or at Tyre in 254.

The works of Origen were too voluminous, as Jerome remarks, for any one man to read them all, and it is said that the total number of his treatises amounted to six thousand. Most of this immense production has now disappeared, although the remnants fill nine volumes in Migne's *Patrologia Græca*, and some part of it only survives in the Latin translations made by Rufinus and St Jerome. The most remarkable perhaps of them was the *Hexapla*, an edition of the Old Testament with six columns on each page, the first column containing the Hebrew text, the second the same written in Greek characters, the third, fourth, and sixth the translations made by Aquila, Symmachus, and Theodotion respectively, and the fifth the Septuagint. For its composition, Eusebius says, Ambrosius furnished Origen with more than seven amanuenses who relieved each other at stated times and with an equal number of transcribers, along with young girls who had been practised in calligraphy, and it is probable that there was never more than one manuscript, which disappeared when Cæsarea was sacked by the Saracens in A.D. 638.

Of Origen's other books, many of which were banned by the Church as heretical, the following divisions may be made. First, the exegetical works, the *Scholia*, notes on passages in Scripture, the *Tomi*, commentaries on Matthew, John, etc., and the *Homilies*, two hundred of which, mostly in Latin translations, are to be found in Migne. Second, the *Stromateis* in ten books, a miscellany of the same character as Clement's, now only existing in fragments. Third, the two discourses *On Prayer* and *Exhortation to Martyrdom*. Fourth, the Letters, many of them preserved in Eusebius, the most important being the *Letter to Africanus*, written in A.D. 240. Fifth, the dogmatic treatise *De Principiis*, of which large fragments in the original Greek remain as quoted by Basil and Gregory of Nazianzus. Sixth, the apology for Christianity known as *Against Celsus*.

Of the exegetical books little need be said here, for their importance is theological rather than literary, and Origen's method, which consists in maintaining that a text says two things at the same time or that it does not say what it seems to say, has long ago been superseded. More practical is the *Against Celsus*, a defence of the Christian faith in answer to the attack made upon it by the pagan philosopher in the second century A.D.[1] Its length is somewhat against it—it runs to six hundred closely printed pages—and like all Origen's work it seems to have been written in haste without much care for style and orderly arrangement ; but its subject-matter gives it still an interest, for most of Celsus' arguments are those which rationalists are inclined to use to-day. It was apparently written at the suggestion of Ambrosius, and in his preface Origen says :

‘ When false witnesses testified against our Lord and Saviour Jesus Christ, He remained silent ; and when unfounded charges were brought against Him, He returned no answer, believing that His whole life and conduct among the Jews were a better refutation than any reply to the false testimony or any formal defence against the accusations. And I know not, my good Ambrosius, why you have

[1] See p. 254.

wished me to write an answer to the false charges brought by Celsus against the Christians and to his accusations directed against the faith of the churches in his treatise ; as if the facts themselves did not furnish a manifest refutation, and the doctrine give a better answer than any writing.'

The *Against Celsus* suffers from the circumstances of its composition ; far more important is the *De Principiis*, the first systematic account of Christian theology and the most profound work of serious philosophy which the third century produced. Of its four books the first treats of God and the celestial beings ; the second of the world, mankind, the Incarnation, and the eternal life ; the third of free-will and predestination ; the fourth of the inspiration of the Scriptures. On all these vital subjects Origen discourses with marvellous subtlety, and proposes solutions for many of the difficulties that were then troubling the minds of believers. He suggests, for example, that the souls of men existed previously and are here now because of past sin ; that our human bodies shall be changed to ethereal at the resurrection ; and that all men and even devils shall finally by Christ's mediation be saved. These and similar expressions of Origen's own belief were somewhat unjustly regarded by the later church as dangerous heresies, and in the edict of Justinian, published 543, nine of Origen's statements were stigmatized as definitely false. But Jerome in the fourth century, a man far more learned and far more broad-minded than the later theologians, held a contrary opinion, and in his considered judgment Origen as a Christian teacher ranked only second to St Paul.

The Neoplatonists, Plotinus and Porphyry

From Origen the transition is easy to Neoplatonism, for its founder, Ammonius, a Christian before he became a pervert to Paganism, was Origen's intimate friend, and Porphyry, through whom we know Plotinus, was for a time one of his pupils at Cæsarea. Moreover, between the Christian philosophy of Origen and the mystical philosophy of Plotinus there are many points of resemblance, and both men develop in varying degree ideas which have in Plato their ultimate origin.

Of Plotinus we have a vivid picture in the *Life* written by his disciple Porphyry. He was born in Egypt A.D. 204, and studied philosophy under Ammonius at Alexandria for eleven years. In 243, wishing to gain knowledge of the wisdom of Persia and India, he accompanied the emperor Gordian III on his disastrous eastern expedition and was fortunate to escape with his life. In the next year, Philip the Arab having now succeeded Gordian, he came to Rome and there remained for the last twenty-six years of his life, surrounded by a circle of loving disciples and entirely absorbed in his philosophical studies. The emperor Gallienus and his consort Salonina were often among his audience, but he maintained a strict simplicity, and died quietly in his house at Puteoli, A.D. 270.

Such are the bare facts of Plotinus' life : Porphyry supplies the intimate details. ' Plotinus the philosopher, our contemporary, seemed ashamed of being in the body. So deeply rooted was this feeling that he could never be induced to tell of his ancestry, his parentage, or his birthplace, nor to sit to a painter for his portrait.' These are the first two sentences of the *Life*, and the rest is written in the same familiar style. Plotinus was the typical enthusiast : ' When he was speaking his intellect illuminated his face : always of winning presence, he became at these times still more engaging : a slight moisture gathered on his forehead : he radiated benignity.' The moisture may sometimes have been due to embarrassment, for, like Dr Spooner, Plotinus was inclined to slips of the tongue, and would say

' rimend ' when he meant ' remind ' ; but we may be
sure that even then he remained benign. Some other
weaknesses also, not unknown in scholars, Plotinus
possessed : ' His handwriting was slovenly ; he mis-
joined his words ; he cared nothing for spelling ; his
one concern was for the idea.' So absorbed, indeed, was
Plotinus in pure thought, so intent, as he said on his
death-bed, in giving back the Divine in himself to the
Divine in the All, that he never prepared his lectures
for publication, and it is to Porphyry that we owe the
Enneads in its present form.

The *Enneads*, which contain the essence of Neoplatonic doctrine, are now available for English readers
in the five volumes of Mr Mackenna's excellent translation, and may even by scholars be thus more
conveniently read than in the original, which is by
necessity rendered difficult owing to the number of its
technical terms. The book owes its title, ' Nines,' to
Porphyry, who collected his master's rough lecture
notes, and arranged them to the best of his ability in
six books, each book containing nine dissertations, the
two numbers each having a mystical signification. The
first Ennead is chiefly concerned with ethics, the
second and the third with the world regarded philo-
sophically and the manner in which it is governed.
These three books form the easier half of the work ;
the second portion is more esoteric. The fourth
Ennead deals with the soul, the fifth with the mind
and the primal hypostases, the sixth with the nature
of being and the authentic existent.

An account of the contents of the *Enneads* would be
more appropriate to a history of philosophy than of
literature, but the titles of the nine treatises in the
first book may be given. The first is on the animate
and man, and then come virtue, dialectic, happiness,
time, beauty, good primal and secondary, evil its

source and nature, and finally the reasoned withdrawal from life. As a specimen of style, a short passage from the dissertation on beauty shows Plotinus at his best :

> ' This is the spirit that Beauty must ever induce, wonderment and a delicious trouble, longing and love and a trembling that is all delight. For the unseen all this may be felt as for the seen ; and this the souls feel for it, every soul in some degree, but those the more deeply that are the more truly apt to this higher love—just as all take delight in the beauty of the body but all are not stung as sharply, and those only that feel the keener wound are known as Lovers.' [1]

The chief point that emerges from the reading of Plotinus is the force and sincerity with which he seeks to liberate men's souls from the ties of this world. Although he is imprisoned in the bonds of matter, man has the gift of reason, and the best use which he can make of that reason is to unite himself with God, ' who has neither form nor outward shape, but is set firm beyond the bounds of sense and all thought.' By reason and by constant purification man can rise to God and live in God ; and even when reason fails, intuition and ecstasy come to our aid. In the last resort an intense concentration of the soul will make the material world disappear and bring us into the presence of God who is Light—' this is the true end for the soul, to lay hold upon that light, and by it itself to have vision, not by the light of something else but itself through that whereby it sees.'

It is unnecessary to stress the resemblance between these ideas and those of the medieval Christian mystics, and with one more quotation from the fifth Ennead we must conclude :

> ' Before all let every Soul remember that itself is the creator of every living thing, having breathed the life into them : into all that the earth nourishes and the sea ; all that are in the air and all the

[1] Trans. S. Mackenna.

divine stars of the heavens ; itself has formed the sun and this vast firmament of sky ; itself has given them their stately ordering and leads them around in their ranks ; and it is a Nature apart from all to which it gives the order and the movement and the life, and it must of necessity be more honourable than they ; for they are things whose being has had a beginning and they perish when the soul that leads the chorus dance of life departs, but the soul itself has ever-being since it cannot suffer change.' [1]

We have said that Porphyry is chiefly responsible for the form in which we now have the Enneads, but he was also the author of many original works. Born in 233 at Tyre he studied first under Origen and then with Longinus, the most celebrated rhetorician of his age, and in 263 joined Plotinus at Rome. His health was then so bad that he contemplated suicide but was dissuaded by his master, whom eventually he long survived. A visit to Sicily restored his strength, and in his old age he married a poor widow with seven children, dying finally at Rome in the early years of the fourth century.

Of Porphyry's historical works we have still extant the *Life of Plotinus* already cited, and a *Life of Pythagoras* which formed part of a history of philosophy which is now lost. His philosophical treatises, excluding the *Enneads*, are represented by the *Introduction to the Knowledge of the Intelligible*, a long and rather difficult summary of Neoplatonic doctrine ; four books, now incomplete, of the discourse *On abstinence from meat* ; and the very curious essay, *The cave of the nymphs in the Odyssey*, where Porphyry with abundant learning and many quotations applies to Homer the same method of allegorical interpretation which Origen had used in the Old Testament. His most famous work, however, was the *Discourse against Christianity*, which earned him the title of ' The Enemy ' from the early church ; but of that now nothing remains.

[1] 'Enneads,' V. i. 2. Trans. S. Mackenna.

PART III

BYZANTIUM
(A.D. 313–565)

CHAPTER I

THE CHRISTIAN WRITERS
(A.D. 313–527)

THE third century witnessed the break-up of Græco-Roman civilization, and when Constantine recognized Christianity as a state religion and removed the seat of government to Byzantium a new era began. It is true that at first Christianity was only put on an equality with the other religions, but in a very short time it had the doubtful advantage of imperial favour, and before the fourth century was over there was a definite alliance between Church and State. Christian literature accordingly takes now a different tone ; it ceases to be apologetic and becomes militant, its militancy being directed both against those who still clung to the old beliefs and with even more vigour against its own heretical children.

Eusebius of Cæsarea (A.D. 265–340)

Eusebius, the great historian of the early Church, forms in Greek letters a link between the two periods, just as Lactantius does in Latin. He was born about 265 and was probably of Greek origin, and some have thought that he was originally the slave of Pamphilus. In any case Pamphilus, the most learned of Origen's pupils, was his first master, whether in a legal or a philosophical sense, and in his library at Cæsarea Eusebius received his first training. When the great persecution of Diocletian broke out in 303 Pamphilus was one of the victims, but Eusebius escaped, and in 313 became bishop of Cæsarea. For a few years we hear little of him ; but as soon as Constantine began to take an interest in theological matters he appears as his chief adviser. At the Council of Nicæa he sat on the Emperor's right hand, and supported him in his efforts to find a formula which would be acceptable both to the Arian party and to their orthodox opponents. In the end, however, he sided with the majority, but still remained at heart a semi-Arian, using all his influence to secure such a modification of the Athanasian Creed as would leave room for differences of opinion on metaphysical questions. In 331 he attended the Council of Antioch which deposed the orthodox bishop Eustathius, in 335 he was at Tarsus, where Athanasius himself was condemned, and in the same year he was chosen to represent the Church at the festival held to celebrate the thirtieth year of Constantine's reign. In 337 Constantine died and Eusebius did not long survive him, the probable date of his death being 30th May 339.

Eusebius was a mediocre theologian and perhaps something of a time-server ; but his chronological and historical work is of the highest value. His *Chronological Tables*, which we possess partly in an Armenian version and partly in Jerome's Latin translation, consists of a brief outline of world history and then in parallel columns the dates of the chief events in Jewish and pagan records. Abraham is put 2016 B.C. ; Moses comes fifty years before the Trojan War ; Isaiah is contemporary with the first Olympiad, 776 B.C. These calculations, although they are to some extent based upon a similar compilation by Julius Africanus in the preceding century, must have involved an immense amount of patient labour, and are the foundation of our chronological knowledge for a large part of Greek

and Roman history. Why we date events as B.C. or
A.D. is chiefly due to Eusebius.

The *Ecclesiastical History* is more definitely a work
of literature, and in its ten books contains a history of
Christianity from the birth of Christ down to 323, the
date of the victory of Constantine over Licinius being
taken as the end of the period of persecution. Its
object is stated in the preface : [1]

> ' I have purposed to record in writing the successions of the
> sacred apostles, covering the period stretching from our Saviour to
> ourselves ; the number and character of the transactions recorded
> in the history of the Church ; the number of those who were
> distinguished in her government and leadership in the provinces of
> greatest fame ; the number of those who in each generation were
> the ambassadors of the word of God either by speech or pen ; the
> names, the number and the age of those who, driven by the desire
> of innovation to an extremity of error, have heralded themselves as
> the introducers of knowledge, falsely so-called, ravaging the flock
> of Christ unsparingly, like grim wolves.'

This, as Eusebius says, is pioneer work, and the
History was in process of writing from 311 to 324, four
separate editions probably appearing in that time. It
owes nothing to rhetoric, and no attempt is made to
draw a picture of society or to trace the general current
of ideas. Eusebius' method was to collect his authorities,
go through them carefully, select such passages as
suited his general plan, and then by means of copious
quotations combine them into one narrative. His own
contribution is often quite small—the seventh book,
for example, consists almost entirely of extracts from
Dionysus of Alexandria—and he has no great charm
of style ; but his flatness is counterbalanced by the
interest of the quotations from earlier writings. One
extract from the long account of Polycarp's martyrdom
issued by the church of Smyrna will serve as example :

---

[1] 'History,' I. 1. Tr. K. Lake, Loeb Library.

'Now when he had uttered his Amen and finished his prayer, the men in charge of the fire lit it, and a great flame blazed up, and we, to whom it was given to see, saw a marvel. And we have been preserved to report to others what befell. For the fire made the likeness of a room, like the sail of a vessel filled with wind, and surrounded the body of the martyr as with a wall, and he was within it not as burning flesh, but as gold and silver being refined in a furnace. And we perceived such a fragrant smell as the scent of incense or other costly spices. At length the lawless men, seeing that his body could not be consumed by the fire, commanded an executioner to go up and stab him with a dagger, and when he did this, there came out much blood, so that the fire was quenched, and all the crowd marvelled that there was such a difference between the unbelievers and the elect.'[1]

Eusebius' other works include a *Panegyric on Constantine*, an historical geography represented now by the *Onomasticon*, and various exegetical and controversial writings. More important than these are the two apologetic books, the *Evangelical Preparation* and the *Evangelical Demonstration*, in the first of which he proves to the pagans by a review of ancient philosophy that reason is on the side of the Christian faith, while in the second he shows the Jews that the prophecies of the Old Testament are all fulfilled by the facts recorded in the New.

Socrates and Sozomen (fl. A.D. 450)

The new path of Church history which Eusebius had opened out was followed in the fifth and sixth centuries by a succession of writers, Socrates, Sozomen, Theodoret, and Evagrius, this last ending his narrative with the year A.D. 594. Of them the first two, who continue Eusebius and deal with the period 324-439, are the most important ; for after 450, when the fierce conflicts caused by Arianism were appeased, church affairs for a time offer little of interest save the comparatively

[1] 'History,' IV. 15. Tr. K. Lake, Loeb Library.

insignificant disputes of the Monophysites and the Nestorians. All four, however, are writers of very modest talent, and it is the facts which they record which give them their chief value. Here is one anecdote from Socrates :

> 'The emperor Julian ordered the arrest of Athanasius, and he thereupon fled again from Alexandria, saying to his intimates, "Let us retire for a little while, friends : it is but a small cloud which will soon pass away." So he embarked on the Nile and hastened away, closely followed by his pursuers. When he saw that they were drawing close, his boatmen urged him to take refuge in the desert, but he had recourse to artifice. He persuaded them to turn the craft round and go back to meet his enemies, which they did ; and on approaching they were simply asked " where they had seen Athanasius " ; to which they replied " he was not a great way off " and " if they hastened they would soon overtake him." Being thus deluded the others started off again at full speed, and Athanasius returned secretly to Alexandria ' (*History* III. 14).

Athanasius (A.D. 295-373)

Eusebius is one type of churchman, a learned scholar with an aptitude for affairs of state and a talent for compromise, but possessed neither of eloquence nor of any inclination for metaphysics. Athanasius is a man of different character, a great preacher, a great thinker, and a theologian who regarded his faith as the most important thing in life. Born about 295 in Alexandria he showed an early interest in theological questions, and was ordained deacon long before the usual age. He accompanied Bishop Alexander as adviser to the Council of Nicæa in 325, and was largely responsible for drawing up the formula of ' homoousia ' ' like substance,' which was adopted by the council as the orthodox belief against the Arian heresy that Christ was a creature, and in defence of that belief he spent the rest of his long and troubled life.

In 326 he was appointed Bishop of Alexandria, but

in 335 at the synod of Tyre he was deposed. He was accused there of having cut off the hand of an Arian bishop, and the hand was produced but not the bishop, whom he discovered afterwards in possession of both his hands. On the death of Constantine he returned to Alexandria, but the next emperor, Constantius, was an Arian, and although his people and the western church of Rome were in his favour, another bishop held the see until 346, when by the help of Constans he again took his rightful place. Constantius, however, was still his determined enemy, and in 356 he was again expelled and took refuge with the hermits in the desert. George the Cappadocian succeeded him, only to be burned alive in a popular riot, and then he was restored to office by Julian, who recalled all those bishops whom his predecessor had banished. But Julian's favour did not last long, and in 362 he narrowly escaped being put to death at his order. Under Jovian there came a brief period of quietude, but with Valens trouble began again, and in 365 for the fifth time he went into exile. Then once more the people of Alexandria, deprived of the leader whom they loved, broke out into a fierce riot : Valens thought it wiser to allow him to return, and he was left in peace until his death in 373.

The writings of Athanasius, composed for the most part in the enforced leisure of exile, fill four volumes in Migne's *Patrologia Græca*. They consist chiefly of dogmatic treatises, of apologies, and of homilies and episcopal letters. In the first class the most important are the two books *Against the Pagans* and the three *Against the Arians*. In the second come the *Apology against the Arians*, the *Apology for his flight*, and the *History of the Arians*, this last containing some very fierce passages of invective. To the third belongs the *Letter to the bishops of Egypt and Libya*, the *Letter to Serapion*, the four *Letters on the Holy Spirit,* and the series of *Paschal Letters* which we possess only in an incomplete form.

There still remains one book ; and although everything that Athanasius wrote is of interest to theologians, for the general reader the *Life of St Anthony* stands out from the rest, and from it Flaubert drew the materials for his greatest novel. Its authenticity has been disputed, but there is little doubt that it is genuine ; and though it has been called ' the most dangerous book which was ever written,' its moral purpose is beyond reproach. Athanasius believed that the devil had a real existence and that the Arians were his emissaries, and when he describes the torments which Anthony endured in the tomb where he braved the infernal powers, he gives his assailants a visible form :

'All the night the demons made such an uproar that the whole district was shaken. It seemed as though they had burst through the walls and made their way in, changed into the shape of wild beasts and reptiles. The place was filled with lions, bears, leopards, bulls, serpents, aspics, scorpions, and wolves, each moving in its own fashion. The lion roared as though about to spring ; the bull tossed its horns ; the serpent crawled slowly ; the wolf sprang madly forward. All these phantoms together made a terrible uproar and showed a mad rage, but Anthony, although his body was troubled, kept a fearless heart. His body trembled, but his spirit kept its freedom and he mocked them : " If you had any power it would have been enough for one of you to come : but the Lord has robbed you of your strength. You try to frighten me by numbers, and it is a proof of your weakness that you have taken the shape of beasts." . . . But the Lord was not forgetful of Anthony, and looking up he saw the roof as it were opened and a ray of light descending. The demons vanished, his pains ceased, and he besought the vision, saying " Where wert thou ? Why didst thou not appear at the beginning ? " And a voice came to him, " Anthony, I was here but I waited to see thy fight. Wherefore since thou hast endured to victory, I will ever be a succour to thee." '

Basil (A.D. 330–379)

The second defender of the Church against Arianism is Basil, the first of the three great Cappadocian preachers. Basil was born at Cæsarea about 330 B.C., his father being a rhetorician by trade, his grandmother Macrina and his mother Emmelia both devout Christians. A delicate youth he received his first education at Cæsarea, and then proceeded to Athens. There he attended the lectures of Himerius, and on his return to Cæsarea himself taught rhetoric, until the day came when, as he says, he ' awoke from a deep sleep and saw the marvellous light of Gospel truth.' His baptism by Bishop Dianios was followed by a period of quiet meditation in the retreat at Pontus, which he describes to his friend Gregory of Nazianzus in one of his letters :[1]

> ' There is a high mountain, covered with a thick forest, watered on its northerly side by cool and transparent streams. At its base is outstretched an evenly sloping plain, ever enriched by the moisture from the mountain. A forest of many-coloured and multifarious trees, a spontaneous growth surrounding the place, acts almost as a hedge to enclose it, so that even Kalypso's isle, which Homer seems to have admired above all others for its beauty, is insignificant as compared with this. For it is, in fact, by no means far from being an island, since it is shut in on all sides by barriers. Two deep ravines break off abruptly on two sides, and on a third side, at the bottom of a cliff, the river which glides gently by forms a wall, being itself a continuous and impassable barrier ; and since the mountain stretches along the fourth side, and is joined to the ravines through bending sides which take the shape of a crescent, the passes at the base are blocked off. However there is one entrance here, and we are in control of it. Adjoining my dwelling is another neck of land, as it were, which supports at its summit a lofty ridge, so that from the former the plain below lies outspread before the eyes, and from the elevation we may gaze upon the encircling river.'

In this fair spot Basil lived, with some periods of absence, for the seven years between 358 and 365, and

---

[1] Letter 14. Trans. R. J. Deferrari, Loeb Library.

here he established the first monastic society. Before his time ascetics had lived either completely alone or in small groups where the eldest hermit might perhaps give counsel but had no permanent authority. At Annesi Basil organized a disciplined community of monks in which each hour of the day had its allotted duty and even the smallest details of food and clothing were regulated. For it he wrote the two sets of Rules which we still possess, the longer rules fifty-five in number, the shorter three hundred and thirteen. There are also many references to his monastic system in the treatises *On the Judgment of God* and *Concerning the Faith*, and in the *Letters*, such as the following passage :[1]

> 'The humble and abject spirit is attended by a gloomy and downcast eye, neglected appearance, unkempt hair and dirty clothes ; consequently the characteristics which mourners affect designedly are found in us as a matter of course. The tunic should be drawn close to the body by a girdle ; but let the belt not be above the flank, for that is effeminate, nor loose, so as to let the tunic slip through, for that is slovenly ; and the stride should be neither sluggish, which would argue a laxity of mind, nor, on the other hand, brisk and swaggering, which would indicate that its impulses were rash. As for dress, its sole object is to be a covering for the flesh adequate for winter and summer. And let neither brilliancy of colour be sought, nor delicacy and softness of material ; for seeking after bright colours in clothing is on a parity with women's practice of beautifying themselves by tinting their cheeks and dyeing their hair with artificial lustre. However, the tunic ought to be of such thickness that it will require no auxiliary garment to keep the wearer warm. The sandal should be inexpensive, yet completely adequate to one's needs.'

In 365 Basil was compelled to leave Annesi, for his presence was required at Cæsarea where the bishop had shown himself unable to cope with the Arian heresy ; and after labouring there for five years he was himself appointed to the archiepiscopal throne. In that high

---

[1] Letter 11. Trans. R. J. Deferrari, Loeb Library.

position he remained for nine years, preaching and writing, administering his diocese, founding charitable institutions, and above all combating the Arians who were at that time supported by the Emperor Valens. Valens, who had strongly opposed Basil's appointment, tried a counter-stroke by dividing Cappadocia into two provinces and making the see of Tyana equal in importance to that of Cæsarea. But Basil held his own against this and other imperial interference, and when he died in 379, worn out by his ascetic discipline and by his episcopal duties, he had the satisfaction of knowing that the great heresy was crushed in his country and that the Eastern Church was united in its adherence to the doctrine of the Trinity.

Basil only lived for fifty years, and those years were filled with occupations and anxieties very unfavourable to literary pursuits. But in spite of that his writings fill four volumes in Migne's *Patrologia Græca* and are among the most attractive in that great series. They fall into four main sections, Sermons, Ascetic Rules, Dogmatic Treatises, and Letters ; and of these four the first and last have a considerable literary as well as theological interest, for Basil's style has all the good qualities of fourth-century sophistic, while the earnestness of his thought saves him from the triviality which is the Sophist's besetting weakness. Of the Sermons the best known are that series of nine homilies on the creation of the world, the *Hexaemeron*, delivered to the working men who formed the majority of his congregation at Cæsarea. They accept the Mosaic account in its literal sense, for, as he says, ' in cases of difficulty the simplicity of faith should override logic,' but in their combination of picturesque description with religious fervour they form a wonderful work. Equally striking also are the three homilies, numbered Six, Seven, and Eight in Migne, the first addressed to the rich, the second to money-lenders, and the third written on the occasion of the great famine in Cappadocia, A.D. 368, when Basil sold all his possessions to buy food for the poor.

For the general reader, however, Basil's letters will be even more attractive than the sermons. There are three hundred and sixty-five of them in the Benedictine edition, and although two quotations have been made already, the conclusion of the letter addressed to a virgin who had broken her vows is so good an example of pious eloquence that it must be given here. Basil has faithfully declared to the erring nun the heinousness of her sin and ends with this fervent call to repentance : [1]

> 'The Father stands awaiting your return from your wandering. Only come back, and while you are still afar off, He will run and throw Himself upon your neck ; in embraces of love He will enfold you, already purified by your repentance. He will first put a robe upon you, a soul which has put off the old man and all his works ; He will place a ring on the hands which have been cleansed of the blood of death ; and He will bind sandals to the feet which have turned from the road of evil to the path of the Gospel of peace. And He will proclaim a day of happiness and joy for His own, both angels and men, and in every way will celebrate your salvation. For He says, "Amen, I say to you, that there is joy in heaven before God upon one sinner that doth penance." And if someone of those who think they stand finds fault because you have been quickly received, the good Father Himself will speak in your defence, saying, "It was fit that we should make merry and be glad, for this My daughter was dead, and is come to life again ; she was lost, and is found."'

Gregory of Nyssa (A.D. c. 341 –395)

From Basil we may pass to his brother Gregory of Nyssa, before we come to the more famous Gregory of Nazianzus who was his lifelong friend. Gregory was about ten years younger than Basil, whom he calls

[1] Letter 46. Trans. R. J. Deferrari, Loeb Library.

Y 337

'father' and 'master,' and while his brother was alive he was somewhat overshadowed by his masterful personality. But after 379 he became more prominent, and in the struggle against Arianism he holds a place of his own. He was not a great preacher nor a great writer, but he supplied the Church with a basis of philosophic thought, and it has been said of him that he was the first divine who sought to establish by rational consideration the whole complex of orthodox doctrines. His writings are not very numerous, but the longest of them, *Against Eunomius*, in thirteen books contains the fullest defence which we possess of orthodoxy against the logical arguments of the Arians, which it refutes by declaring boldly that God is incomprehensible. His other works include the dialogue *On the soul and the resurrection*, which has been called the Christian *Phædo*, the speakers being himself and his sister Macrina ; and a discourse on virginity where the little miseries of married life are described with great vigour. But the two best-known passages in his works occur in two less familiar treatises. One of them is the account of Arianism in Constantinople :[1]

> 'Every part of the capital is filled with this kind of talk, the alleys, the cross ways, the market places, the squares : old clothes men, money changers, costermongers, they are all the same. If you ask them for change for a shilling, they start at once ranting about the Begotten and the Unbegotten ; if you say " What is the price of that loaf ? " they reply " The Father is the greater, the Son is inferior " ; if you inquire whether your bath is ready the man solemnly informs you that the Son was made from nothing.'

The other is interesting as a proof of the veneration of relics in the early church.[2]

> 'When he has delighted his eyes with the elaborate pictures which appeal to the senses, he desires to approach the tomb itself, believing that to touch it will bring him a blessing and an increase

[1] 'Oratio de deitate Filii.'   [2] 'Encomium Sancti Theodori.'

of holiness. And if he is allowed to take away a little of the dust that lies on the martyr's resting place, he regards it as a precious trophy to be stored away as a treasure. As for touching the relics themselves, if any such stroke of good fortune should come his way, that indeed is the height of his ambition and the crown of all his prayers.'

Gregory of Nazianzus (A.D. 330-390)

From a purely literary point of view Gregory is the most remarkable of the four great Christian writers of the fourth century, for he was an eloquent preacher, a charming letter-writer, and also a poet of considerable skill and immense productiveness. But in his life, at least when compared with the other three, he was a failure. Athanasius was a born theologian, Basil a born administrator, and John Chrysostom a born orator ; and all three found ample opportunity for the exercise of their talents in the service of the Church. Gregory for his part was born with the artistic temperament, and although circumstances made him a bishop, he was never really happy in his episcopal functions and remained a man of letters to the end.

Gregory was born at Nazianzus in south-west Cappadocia about A.D. 330, the first son of an aged pair, Nonna and Gregory, bishop of the little town. His mother, an ardent Christian, regarded him as sent in answer to her prayers, and from the first destined him for the church ; but Gregory himself was ' in love with eloquence,' as he says, and after studying under Carterius at Cæsarea with Basil, set off to Egypt for further training in rhetoric. From Egypt he sailed to Athens, and during a violent storm which he met on the way remembered his mother's wishes and vowed himself to a clerical life. He reached land safely, however, and deferred matters for some ten years while he studied under Himerius. During part of that time Basil was with him, and when Basil returned home, Gregory after an interval reluctantly followed, and found himself faced by the necessity of choosing definitely his path in life. His father was now a very old man and needed help in his bishopric, and Gregory tells us that he was ' tyrannized ' by him into being ordained, and later by Basil into being ordained bishop of Sasima, a miserable little place in the middle of Cappadocia. For a lover of beauty this was an impossible home, and in 375 he escaped and lived for the next years in quiet seclusion at Seleucia in Isauria, where early in 379 he received news of Basil's death.

The loss of Basil was one blow to Gregory's serenity, and another came soon after when he was invited to take charge of the small community of orthodox Christians at Constantinople. The capital under Valens was at that time a stronghold of Arianism, but Gregory felt that it was his duty to go, and although he was never very successful in church politics he remained there for two years. At first he preached to his small congregation in the little chapel of Anastasia, but when Theodosius became emperor in 380 his situation changed. The Arians were driven out and Gregory, now recognized as patriarch of Constantinople, delivered his sermons in Santa Sophia itself. His appointment, however, had never been regarded as valid by one section of the Church, and when its legality was again challenged he determined to resign, and took a final leave of the city in May 381. He then retired to his native country, and devoted himself to his literary studies until his death in 390.

Gregory's prose writings consist of orations and letters. Of the orations we now have forty-five, which may be divided into three main sections. First come the five theological orations which won him the title of ' The Theologian.' These were delivered at Constantinople in defence of the doctrine of the Trinity, the first and second discourse treating of the nature and attributes of God, the third and fourth of the divinity of Christ, and the fifth of the influence of the Holy Spirit. Secondly, we have the moral orations, which include an apology for his reluctance to accept ordination, a farewell speech describing his work at Constantinople, and sermons on peace, the love of the poor, and the indissolubility of marriage. The two invectives against Julian form the third class, in which, as a contrast, may be included the funeral panegyrics on Gregory's father, brother, and sister, and on Basil. This last speech, with its vivid pictures of student life at Athens, shows Gregory at his best, and the peroration has been justly praised by all critics :

'Come hither to me, ye companions of Basil, ministers of the altar, servants of the temple, citizens and strangers together. Help me to complete my eulogy, each of you telling of one of his virtues and describing one feature in his life. Mourn, ye great ones, for a lawgiver ; ye people, for a guide ; ye men of letters, for a master ; ye wives, for your virtue's defender ; ye simple, for a helper ; ye inquirers, for a light ; ye fortunate, for a corrector ; ye unfortunate, for a consoler ; a staff for old age, a rule for youth, a benefactor for the needy, and an almoner for the rich. Widows, methinks, will celebrate their protector, poor folk the friend of the poor, all men him who made himself all things to all, that he might gain all men's souls.'

In oratory Gregory is surpassed by John Chrysostom and in letter-writing by Basil ; but in poetry he has not to stand comparison either with Basil or with John, and probably both of them thought that any time spent on writing verse was lamentably wasted. Gregory himself tells us that he had four reasons : (1) the exigencies of metre are a useful restraint ; (2) young people are attracted by poetry, which can guide them gently to the truth ; (3) poetry should not be left entirely in pagan hands ; (4) the writing of verse is an innocent and effective solace for old age. This last reason in Gregory's case has more justification than the first, for he has left us nearly seventeen thousand lines, and his poems in Migne with the commentaries on them fill as much space as his prose works. The Benedictine editors have arranged them in four divisions : theological, subdivided into dogmatic and moral verse ; historical, subdivided into poems about himself and poems on other people ; and two shorter sections consisting of epigrams and epitaphs.

It is impossible in a brief space to give an analysis of this huge mass of verse, written in hexameters, elegiacs, iambics and various lyric metres ; but a reader with abundant leisure will find the moral and the personal poems both edifying and instructive. One extract from the iambic poem *On his Life*, a little thing of just under two thousand lines, must serve as a specimen :

> ' What time I parted from Egyptian shores,
> Whence I had somewhat culled of ancient lore,
> We weighed, and under Cyprus cut the waves
> In a straight course for Hellas, when there rose
> A mighty strife of winds, and shook the ship ;
> And all was night ; earth, seas, and darkened sky ;
> And thunders echoed to the lightning's shock.
> Whistled the rigging of the swelling sails,
> And bent the mast ; the helm had lost its power,
> For none could hold it in the raging seas.
> The ship was filled with overwhelming waves ;
> Mingled the shout of sailor and the cries
> Of helmsman, captain, and of passenger,
> And those who till that fearful hour had been
> Unconscious of a God.'

John Chrysostom (A.D. 344–407)

The last and greatest of the fourth-century divines is John, to whom in the sixth century the name of Chrysostom was given, the golden-mouthed orator who in power of eloquence comes nearest of all the later Greeks to Demosthenes. Of his life and character Gibbon in his own incomparable style gives the following account :[1]

'Born of a noble and opulent family, in the capital of Syria, Chrysostom had been educated by the care of a tender mother, under the tuition of the most skilful masters. He studied the art of rhetoric in the school of Libanius ; and that celebrated sophist, who soon discovered the talents of his disciple, ingenuously confessed that John would have deserved to succeed him, had he not been stolen away by the Christians. His piety soon disposed him to receive the sacrament of baptism ; to renounce the lucrative and honourable profession of the law; and to bury himself in the adjacent desert, where he subdued the lusts of the flesh by an austere penance of six years. His infirmities compelled him to return to the society of mankind ; and the authority of Meletius devoted his talents to the service of the church ; but in the midst of his family, and afterwards on the archiepiscopal throne, Chrysostom still persevered in the practice of the monastic virtues. The ample revenues, which his predecessors had consumed in pomp and luxury, he diligently applied to the establishment of hospitals ; and the multitudes, who were supported by his charity, preferred the eloquent and edifying discourses of their archbishop to the amusements of the theatre or the circus. The monuments of that eloquence, which was admired near twenty years at Antioch and Constantinople, have been carefully preserved, and the possession of near one thousand sermons, or homilies, has authorized the critics of succeeding times to appreciate the genuine merit of Chrysostom. They unanimously attribute to the Christian orator the free command of an elegant and copious language ; the judgment to conceal the advantages which he derived from the knowledge of rhetoric and philosophy ; an inexhaustible fund of metaphors and similitudes, of ideas and images, to vary and illustrate the most familiar topics ; the happy art of engaging the passions in the service of virtue ; and of exposing the folly as well as the turpitude of vice, almost with the truth and spirit of a dramatic representation.'

To this a few dates and some further details may be added. John was born at Antioch about 344, his father being *magister militum Orientis*, and was baptized by

[1] Gibbon, *Decline and Fall*, ch. 32.

343

Meletius, Bishop of Antioch, in 369. Under Meletius and Diodorus, afterwards Bishop of Tarsus, he completed the education which he had begun with Libanius, and then from 374 to 380 he retired into the desert. Returning to Antioch he was ordained deacon and preached his first sermon there about 386. The great series of homilies, *On the Statues*, delivered after the riots at Antioch, followed in 387 together with one hundred and eighty homilies on the Gospels of St Matthew and St John ; and for the next ten years his eloquence attracted crowds of worshippers to the Great Church which Constantine had built in the Syrian capital. Then in 397 his time of trial began, when the eunuch Eutropius, who was all-powerful with the feeble Emperor Arcadius, induced him to accept the bishopric of Constantinople.

On his arrival John found that his predecessor, Nectarius, had permitted abuses of every kind to become established in the Church. Priests were cohabiting openly with virgins, and competing with the civil magistrates in the luxury of their private life. The money which should have been given to the poor was used by these clerics for their own purposes, and Arian heretics were allowed to parade in procession about the streets. All this John put down with a stern hand, and soon incurred the hostility both of his own subordinates and of Eutropius, who went so far as to violate the right of sanctuary which was one of the most cherished privileges of the Church. Eutropius fell from power and was only saved from death by John's intervention, but the Empress Eudoxia proved an even more dangerous enemy. Using Theophilus, Bishop of Alexandria, as her tool, she involved John in theological disputes, and in 403 at a synod of bishops held at The Oak, a suburb of Chalcedon, he was deposed from office and sent into exile.

In two days, however, he was recalled ; for the people rose in tumult and massacred Theophilus' supporters, an earthquake opportunely occurred, and Eudoxia gave way. For the moment justice triumphed, but peace did not last for long. In the autumn of 403 a silver statue of the Empress was set up in the city and inaugurated with festivities which John considered pagan in character. A violent sermon followed, and Eudoxia, resolving now to finish with her presumptuous critic, arranged for a second synod to be held, which declared that John had illegally resumed his bishopric and that the first sentence must stand. A strong force of soldiers was brought into the city to overawe the people, and John was arrested and sent off under guard to Cucusus in Armenia. There he remained for three years; but in 407, by a refinement of cruelty, orders were given to remove him to Pityus, a remote township on the east shore of the Black Sea. By that time, however, his strength was exhausted, and on the way he died.

Of John's homilies nearly a thousand have come down to us : they fill fourteen large volumes in Migne's *Patrologia Græca*, and even Gibbon confesses in a footnote that he is *almost* a stranger to their contents. It is too much to expect that many readers to-day will follow the example of the learned de Tillemont, who in the seventeenth century made a minute study of the whole collection ; but there are three short series among them which no lover of Greek literature can afford to neglect. One of them is the set of twenty-one homilies *On the Statues*. In 387, when extra taxes were imposed on Antioch, the people broke into a furious riot and tore down the imperial statues before order could be restored. Two commissioners were sent by Theodosius to take vengeance for the insult, and while their judicial investigation was proceeding John in these addresses endeavoured with moving eloquence to comfort his terror-stricken flock and to appease the Emperor's resentment. Another side of his talent is shown in the two treatises written at Constantinople, *Against those who have introduced virgins into their houses*, and *That Christian virgins must not cohabit with men*. Here John shows the greatest skill in dealing with a very delicate subject and the good sense of his admonitions is fully equalled by the grace of his language. Finally we have the two orations on Eutropius, highly dramatic in themselves and delivered in the most dramatic circumstances. The fallen minister had sought refuge in the very church whose sanctity he had once violated, and John, mounting the pulpit, began thus :

'It is always seasonable, and to-day it is more seasonable than ever, to cry "Vanity of vanities, all is vanity." Where is now the consul's splendour ? Where the applause, the dances, the banquets and the festivals ? Where is the noise of the crowd, the greetings in the circus, the flattering welcome of the theatre ? Where are the crowns and embroidered robe ? All that has passed away ; a sudden storm has brought down the leaves and devastated the tree ; behold it now, a trunk stripped bare, whose very roots have been shaken in their place. The wind's attack has been so fierce that it has threatened to tear it from the ground, roots and all, and has broken all its powers of life. Where are now the false friends ? Where are the dinners and feasts ? Where is the swarm of parasites, the wine poured out in streams all day long, the dainty dishes which the cooks unceasingly prepared, and the flatterers of power ready in its service to do and to say all things ? It was the dream of a night, and it has vanished with the day ; the flowers of spring, and the spring has fled and the flowers are faded. It was a shadow, and it has gone ; a fruit, and it has rotted ; bubbles, and they are broken ; a spider's web, and it has been torn to pieces. Therefore we now repeat the word of the Holy Spirit and once more we say, " Vanity of vanities, all is vanity." '

Synesius (A.D. 370–403)

After the end of the fourth century Christian eloquence lost its vigour and inspiration, and the writings of Cyril of Alexandria and Theodoretus are of no great merit. But before we leave Christian literature there are two authors, Synesius and Nonnus, standing on the confines between Christianity and paganism, of whom a full account is necessary.

Synesius was born about A.D. 370 at Cyrene in North Africa. His family claimed to be descended from the original founders of the town, and although his father died when he was a child, Synesius even in early manhood was one of the most important citizens of the Libyan Pentapolis. Cyrene was too poor to possess good teachers, and his education was obtained at Alexandria under Theon and Hypatia, for whom he always retained a deep affection. When he came back home he found his city in financial straits and in 397 was chosen by the people to go to Constantinople and ask the Emperor Arcadius for a remission of taxation.

At Constantinople he remained for three years— ' three bad years taken from my life '—often sleeping in the imperial offices on the big Egyptian rug he had brought with him and waiting in vain for an audience. But at last his opportunity came ; he delivered his speech, gained the remission for which he pleaded, and returned to Cyrene. On his country estate there he lived for the next nine years, hunting, cultivating his land, repelling attacks from barbarian invaders, and occasionally writing a book. Sometimes he travelled, going once to Athens and often to Alexandria, where in 403 he met the Christian lady who became his wife.

And then in 409 his whole life changed. Up till that year he had called himself a Hellenist ; that is, his sympathies had been with the old religion, he guided his life on the principles of philosophy which he had learned from Hypatia, and he was not a member of the Christian church. But in 409 the bishopric of Ptolemais, the most important city of the Pentapolis, fell vacant, and the people begged him to take office, and as bishop to defend them against the tyranny of the civil government. Synesius was in a difficult position ; his own inclinations called him one way, patriotism called him the other ; but patriotism prevailed, he accepted office, was baptized by Theophilus, Archbishop of Alexandria, and without passing through the lower grades of clerical rank, entered at once upon his new duties.

Synesius had expected trouble in his bishopric, and trouble he found in plenty. Preaching sermons was an uncongenial task, and even more uncongenial was the condemnation of heretical teachers and the settlement of the fierce quarrels which were constantly occurring among his Christian flock. He had, moreover, to repel a barbarian invasion, fighting side by side with his soldiers; and, worst of all, he was faced by a new governor, Andronicus, a man of the vilest character who used torture to extract money from the unfortunate people and violated the rights of sanctuary. Him Synesius was at last compelled to excommunicate : ' Let Andronicus of Berenice, born and bred to be the curse of the Pentapolis, who has by corrupt means obtained the rule over his native land, be held and accounted of no man for a Christian ; but let him and all his be shut out from the whole Church, as those that are hateful to God.'

Domestic misfortunes also came upon him, for his three sons died in quick succession, and he fell into the state of dejection which he expresses in a letter to Hypatia :

' Fortune cannot rob me of everything, but she does her best; and now " Of my noble sons she has bereft me." Still, she shall not rob me of a good conscience, nor of the will to help the injured, and I pray that she may never overpower my judgment. I hate injustice ; that I can do still : and I wish I could prevent it. But that power has been taken from me. I lost it before I lost my children :—" Long, long ago was I a man of might." There was

a time when I could help my friends, and you used to call me
" Other people's providence," since I would use for others my
influence with the great, who were indeed my hands. But now
I am left destitute, unless you can do something : for I count you
and virtue the sole blessings whereof I cannot be deprived.'

However, in spite of all he struggled on for three
years, doing his best for his unhappy country ; and
then he died, happy at least in that he did not live to
see Hypatia murdered.

Synesius is a very attractive writer both in verse and
in prose, and unlike most of his contemporaries he is
not too verbose. His poetry consists of ten hymns,
written in the short eight-syllable line, one of them
over seven hundred lines in length, the others much
shorter. But these, in spite of Mrs Browning's praise,
are not his best work, although they have a literary
charm which is too often lacking in productions of this
kind. Much more important is the *Oration on Kingship*,
addressed to the Emperor Arcadius, which is remarkable
both for its real eloquence and for the boldness of
its language : ' The fear that you emperors may
become men if you are often seen keeps you close
prisoners besieged by yourselves. You never see or hear
anything which could give you knowledge of realities.
You have no pleasures but those of the body, and
of them only the most sensual, such as taste and
touch give. You live the life of a mollusc, and dis-
daining manhood you can never reach manhood's
perfection.'

After the Oration come four long essays. The first,
On Providence, is a mixture of romance, philosophy, and
history ; for under the guise of an ' Egyptian tale,' the
conflict between the good Osiris and the bad Typhon,
we have in reality an account of events which happened
in Constantinople, 397–400, and an explanation of the
existence of good and evil in this world. The second,

349

Dion, is ostensibly an account of the great second-century sophist, but it is also a defence of Synesius himself against the pedantic scholars of his day, the 'men in white,' who accused him of frivolity, and against the ignorant monks, the 'men in black,' whose virtue seems so unintelligent that it is scarcely virtue at all. The third, *On dreams,* is pure Neoplatonism and suggests means of communion with God in sleep ; but it is less successful than the fourth essay, *In praise of baldness,* which is quite a good example of the humorous paradox on which the sophists loved to display their wit : 'Hair is the mark of beasts ; the less men have the better.' 'The bald head forms a sphere, and the sphere is the most perfect of all shapes.' 'Wanton youths always have long hair ; if they were bald they would not seduce our wives and daughters ' : and so on and so on.

But his *Letters* are Synesius' best memorial, and they give us a vivid picture both of the man himself and of his times. We have just over one hundred and fifty ; but some are very short. 'Need and longing draw me to you. I wonder if you too are expecting my arrival ' (Ep. 39). 'Some villainous strangers are vexing the church. Confront them boldly, for nail is driven out by nail ' (Ep. 45). 'Friendships with the great should be used but not abused ' (Ep. 63). Others, of course, are much longer. No. 3, for example, to his brother contains a full and very lively account of his voyage home from Constantinople. No. 57 to the bishops describes at length his conflicts with the tyrant Andronicus. No. 67 to Theophilus narrates the difficulties he encountered in his pastoral visitation. Most significant of all, as regards the writer's character, is No. 105, in which he gives his brother the reasons for and against accepting the bishopric. From it some sentences may be quoted :

'You know that philosophy is in many ways opposed to these common dogmas. I certainly will never consent to believe that the soul is born after the body. I will never say that the universe and all its parts are doomed to destruction. The doctrine of the resurrection which is preached to the people I consider a sacred mystery, and am far from agreeing with popular ideas on the subject. A philosophic mind which has contemplated truth concedes the usefulness of falsehood. Light is to the eye as truth is to the mind. Therefore as the eye would be injured by the enjoyment of immoderate light, and darkness is better for those of weak sight, so I count falsehood beneficial for ordinary folk, and truth harmful to those who are not strong enough to gaze steadfastly at the bright light of reality.'

Nonnus (fl. A.D. 420)

Of Nonnus himself we know nothing except that he was born at Panopolis, the ancient Chemnis, a town of the Thebaid in Egypt. The date of his birth can only be guessed, but it was probably some time in the latter half of the fourth century. It is also likely that he lived in Alexandria and had access to the great library : but the only certain fact about his life is that he produced two long poems. One of them is a paraphrase of St John's Gospel in hexameter verse, and is a work of the same class as the epics drawn from the Bible which a pious father and son named Apollinaris composed when Julian forbade Christian teachers to read the pagan authors. The other poem is less edifying but in a literary sense of considerably greater importance.

The *Dionysiaca*, 'Adventures of Dionysus,' an epic in forty-eight books, about twice the length of the Iliad, would be a wonderful work for any period, but written in the fifth century A.D., when literature was at its lowest ebb, it is something of a miracle. Nonnus may be described as an Ovid writing in Greek, and in fertility of invention, richness of description, and, it must be confessed, in absence of decorum, he is fully the equal of the author of the *Metamorphoses*. In verse technique he is even more interesting, for his hexameters come very close to the original form of the metre. In the early epic chanted to the lyre the dactyl was predominant, the spondee only a relief ; and this is exactly the method which Nonnus follows. He never has two spondees together, he avoids hiatus, and he frequently employs the trochaic cæsura in the third foot. Moreover, the tonic accent on one of the two last syllables in the line is invariable, and so Nonnus initiates the rhythmic versification which the Byzantines after him developed.

A summary of the *Dionysiaca* will run somewhat as follows. Before coming to his main subject Nonnus describes from what chaos the advent of Dionysus saved the world, and relates first the struggle between Zeus and Typhon, the opposing principles of Good and Evil. He then tells of Cadmus who, with his wife Harmonia, came to Greece, bringing with him the arts of Egypt and Phœnicia. The Titans conspire to slay Zagreus, but he appears again in a second incarnation as Dionysus of Thebes, the child of the lightning, who, escaping from the jealous anger of Hera, grows to manhood under the care of the universal mother Rhea. He subdues the savage beasts, trains himself to battle, and creates in the vine a weapon to bring peace to the world. Next he assembles a host of divinities, and at their head sets out to subdue India. He crosses the defiles of Lebanon and marches along the gulf of Nicomedia till he reaches the Hydaspes, welcomed now in humble cottages and now in royal palaces. Then we have the great conflict in India, with its victories and defeats, its truces and its stratagems, until at last Dionysus wins the day and establishes his worship in the East. From India he returns with his triumphal cortège to the Mediterranean, and passing northwards through Lydia comes down from the Balkans into

Greece. There he has to struggle at Argos once more against Hera, his eternal enemy, and then makes his way through Thrace to Phrygia, whence he leaves earth for his throne in heaven.

Such is the *Dionysiaca* in bare outline ; but the main narrative is expanded by numerous episodes, most of them concerned with the god's amorous exploits. Books Ten, Eleven, and Twelve, for example, deal with his passion for the fair youth Ampelos, 'Vine,' who engages with him in wrestling, running, and swimming matches, all described with a profusion of detail, and is at last killed, like Adonis, while hunting, by a savage beast, the vine being then created in his memory. In Books Fifteen and Sixteen we have another long digression on the proud nymph Nicæa who despises the love of the neat-herd Hymnos and is herself overcome by the god. Books Twenty to Forty are occupied with the Indian campaign, but then we return again to the love theme and have the tale of Beroë, daughter of Aphrodite and Adonis, the nymph who gave her name to the pearl of cities which lies under Lebanon. This delightful creature, whose charms are described in the warmest language, is beloved both by Dionysus and Poseidon, and three books barely suffice to tell the story of their rivalry. Next comes the tragedy of Pentheus, slain at Thebes by his mother Agave, which leads in Book Forty-seven to the discovery of Ariadne on Naxos, and so in the last book of all to the god's amours with Pallene and Aura.

The description of the wrestling match between Dionysus and Pallene, both stripped to the buff, descends to physical details which may bring a blush to the cheeks of modern readers, although the same pious Jesuit who finds in Dionysus a type of Moses sees in it only a reminiscence of the wrestling between Jacob and the angel. But in warmth of language it is surpassed by the tale of Aura which follows ; and this, the last long episode in the poem, is so typical of much of the rest that a brief summary may be given, the luscious descriptions being omitted. Aura, while swimming with Artemis one day, has the temerity not only to criticize the texture and contour of her mistress' breasts but also to make imputations on her chastity. Enraged at the affront the goddess hastens to Nemesis and begs her to punish the insolent nymph. Nemesis agrees, and Dionysus, the universal lover, is made the instrument of vengeance. Enflamed with passion he goes in search of Aura, and fearing to frighten her by too eager wooing creates a magic spring which seems to be water and is wine. Aura comes to drink, finds it delicious, and falls in a deep sleep on the grass, where the god takes her :

' On that nuptial couch fair Aura with a shuddering sigh awoke,
And from off her eyes the sleep that was her secret witness shook.
At herself she gazed bewildered, wondering at her snow-white breast
From its modest shelter ravished and her nakedness confessed.
On her thighs and on her tunic drops of red were plain to see
Telling of a stolen pleasure and a lost virginity.'

Dionysus has vanished, and in despair she storms about the country, wreaking havoc as she goes. But nature has her way and soon she finds that she is to be a mother. Artemis with cruel mockery tells her the father's name, and finally she brings forth Iacchus, to be after Zagreus and Dionysus the third incarnation of the god.

There are many better known poems which are far less entertaining than the *Dionysiaca*, and it is a pity that our best Greek text is now eighty years old and that there is no English translation. The great scholars of the past appreciated its charm, and Daniel Heinsius writes : ' I remember still the eager excitement which thrilled me when first I read Nonnus.' But it is to be feared that few readers give themselves that thrill of excitement to-day.

CHAPTER II

THE END OF PAGANISM

(A.D. 313–527)

DURING the fourth and fifth centuries A.D. Paganism was engaged in a hopeless battle ; but in literature at least it put up a good fight, and two striking achievements, the revival of sophistic eloquence and the revival of epic poetry, must be placed to its credit. It is true that Nonnus, the most original of the epic poets, embraced Christianity before his death, but it was the pagan Quintus who showed him that a long epic poem was still possible. The group of philosophers and rhetoricians, however, who gathered round the Emperor Julian were all strong adherents of the old religion, and with them we may begin.

Iamblichus and Himerius

The two first in order of time, the philosopher Iamblichus and the rhetorician Himerius, whose lives are told by Eunapius, have no great literary merit, but as typical figures of their time they have some import-ance. The date of Iamblichus is uncertain, but he was probably born about A.D. 280 and lived on to the reign of Julian, on whom he exercised a strong influence. It was he and his follower Maximus who perverted Neo-platonism, and turned their disciples from metaphysical speculation to the practice of divination. Neo-platonism, as taught by Plotinus and Porphyry, made communion with the Supreme its cardinal doctrine,

355

but Iamblichus substituted for spiritual contemplation the easier method of magic incantations, and it was as a magician that Maximus was put to death. Of the writings of Iamblichus we now only have the *Compendium of Pythagorean Doctrine* and some mathematical treatises of little value : the more important *On the Mysteries* is not from his pen, although it probably represents his teaching.

Himerius (c. 310–393) is the eldest and the least interesting of the three chief Sophists of the fourth century. He was a Bithynian, but after studying under Prohæresius at Athens he established his own school there, and had Basil and Gregory of Nazianzus among the pupils who listened to the theatrical displays of eloquence which he gave to an admiring audience. He joined Julian at Antioch in 362, delivering speeches at every important town on the way, and in 368 returned to Athens where he received a grant of Athenian citizenship and remained for the rest of his life. Of his Orations seventy-one were known and read by Photius, but of them twenty-three now only remain complete, and some of these are quite short. The best of them are the two which come first and last in our collection, and for most readers these two will be sufficient. The first, *On the marriage of Severus*, with its elaborate account of the primal wedlock of Earth and Heaven, is a typical piece of sophistic eloquence, charming in some parts, tedious in others. The last, *A monody on the death of his son Rufinus*, is equally characteristic, and its beginning and end may be quoted :

'I am doing wrong to speak at all when Rufinus lies dead. But since I have been left by fate merely to make lament over this tragedy, speak I will. It would be a sin not to sorrow in words for one who was the child of speech. And what a glorious subject !'

Himerius then tells us that his son was eloquent from the very moment that he began to make sounds and that the whole earth was enraptured by his infant cries, and ends thus :

> ' I will honour you with funeral games, and be in one respect at least more jealous of glory than the god of death. He may have your body, but heaven will have your soul, and all mankind your name.'

Themistius (A.D. c. 320–388)

Themistius is a deeper thinker and a more sober writer than Himerius, and has some importance both as a scholar and a rhetorician. His father, Eugenius, for whom he wrote a funeral oration, was a rich man with a taste for philosophy and literature, and Themistius had everything in his favour when he started his career. In 347 he was presented to the Emperor Constantius and delivered his first official speech before opening a school at Constantinople. In 355 he was made a senator, and gradually became one of the chief persons in the empire. Julian offered him various dignities, which he refused, but under Valens and Theodosius he played an important part in the government. The latter Emperor conferred upon him the title of Prefect of the City, and entrusted him with the education of his son Arcadius, and he probably died a few years before his pupil came to the throne.

Themistius prided himself on being a philosopher rather than a sophist, and his paraphrases of Aristotle have still a certain value. But he is best known by his Orations, of which thirty-four remain, many of them excellent specimens of official eloquence. A few treat of general subjects, such as the advantages of friendship, the duty of parents to their children, and the benefits of country life ; but the great majority are formal harangues composed on special occasions and addressed to the Emperor of the day. A good example is the *Oration to Jovian*, who on succeeding Julian had issued an edict of toleration for all forms of religion. The moderate pagans, of whom Themistius was one, had good reason to fear that the Christians would disregard this, and the orator makes an impassioned plea for liberty :

'You know full well, sire, that an emperor cannot force his subjects to do all things. Some matters escape compulsion and are stronger than threats or commands, as for example, virtue of every kind and especially the worship of the gods. You, most godlike sire, who are our sole ruler to-day and will be our ruler to the end, have by your law assigned equal rights of worship to all men, therein taking pattern by God, who has made it part of human nature to cherish piety but has allowed the mode of worship to depend on each man's will. . . . He who employs force in these affairs robs us of a power which God has bestowed upon us. The laws of Cambyses and the laws of Cheops have not survived their authors : but the law of God and your law, sire, will endure for ever, allowing each man's soul in matters of religion to follow that path which it thinks best. Against this law neither confiscation, nor the cross, nor the stake can prevail. You can break and kill the body if you will ; but the soul will escape, even though the tongue be constrained, taking with her the law and the freedom of her thought.'

Libanius (A.D. 314–393)

Himerius and Themistius both enjoyed a fair share of fame in their lifetime. But they were far outshone by Libanius, who in the fourth century occupied the same place that Polemon had filled in the second. Of the facts of his life, and of the influence of his chief divinity, we have a very long account by himself in the oration, *On his own Fortune*, which appears first in his collected works. Born in Antioch, 314, of a rich and illustrious family he went to Athens in 336 to complete his studies in rhetoric. There instead of joining the classes of the famous Christian teacher Prohæresius he was by a trick of his fellow-students handed over to the care of the very inferior Diophantus. But in spite

358

of this mishap his natural abilities quickly brought him to the front and in 342 he established his own school at Constantinople. Driven thence in 346 by the jealousy of rival professors he lived for the next years at Nicomedia, and then returned to Antioch, where he remained until his death in 393. During those fifty years, which cover the reigns of five Emperors, Constantius, Julian, Jovian, Valens and Theodosius, Libanius was the most famous of all literary men. In his own city he was little less than a god, and was in turn its patron, its panegyrist, and its defender. Pupils flocked to him from all the countries of the East, and when he consented to lecture his discourse was delivered in the Senate hall. The Emperor Julian was his devoted admirer, and had his reign been prolonged Libanius would probably have exercised a great influence on his government. But whether the combination of Julian and Libanius would have been an advantage to the world is a doubtful question.

The old religion had many more points of connection with ancient literature than had the new, and naturally Libanius was one of its most fervent supporters. But with the three great Christian orators of his day Libanius always lived in friendly relations. John Chrysostom was one of his pupils, Gregory of Nazianzus speaks of him as the ' prince of orators,' and even if the twenty-five letters that appear in his and Basil's correspondence are not all authentic some at least are genuine. The class of Christians that Libanius disliked was composed of the illiterate monks who thought to show their religious zeal by destroying statues and wrecking shrines, and of them he bitterly complains to the Emperor Theodosius in the Oration *For the defence of temples* written about A.D. 384:

' You, sire, have not ordered us to close our temples, you have not forbidden us to enter, you have not proscribed the fire, the incense, and the other rites performed on the altar and in the shrine. It is these men in black, more voracious than elephants, never satisfied with the cups which they drink to the sound of hymns, but concealing all that beneath an artificial pallor; it is they, sire, who, though your law exists and is still in vigour, run to our temples with faggots, stones, and crowbars, or sometimes without any other weapons but their legs and arms. The roof becomes the prey of Mysians; the walls are pulled down; the statues overthrown; the altars ruined; and the priests are compelled to remain silent under pain of death. Their work finished at one shrine, they rush to a second and then to a third, accumulating trophy after trophy.'

Libanius was not only a voluminous writer but was also held in very high esteem by the later Byzantines, who regarded him as equal to the great orators of the classical period, and they have preserved for us an enormous mass of his work. The Teubner edition by Richard Foerster (1903–1922) runs into twelve long volumes, four containing the orations, four the rhetorical works, two the letters, and two prolegomena and indices. Of the sixty-five speeches some are imaginary, but most were composed for real events, such as those on Julian's death, those on his own life and literary career, and those addressed to Theodosius to excuse the disorderly conduct of the people of Antioch. The rhetorical works consist of three volumes of *Declamations*, imaginary harangues supposed to have been delivered on various famous occasions in ancient history. There is, for example, an *Apology of Socrates*, a *Defence of his policy by Demosthenes*, speeches by Timon and Hyperides, and the counter-arguments of the Corinthians and the Athenians before the Peloponnesian War. Mythology supplies other subjects, as when Orestes answers the charge of matricide and Odysseus gives an account of his embassy. A third section consists of speeches of complaint, a surly man plagued by a talkative wife, a miser fleeced by a courtesan, a parasite cheated of his dinner, etc. Lastly comes one long volume of aids to young speakers, a collection of useful fables, stories, moral tales, refutations, confirmations, common topics, panegyrics, vituperations, comparisons, descriptions and character studies. And when the reader has finished these eight volumes, he has still before him nearly sixteen hundred letters, most of them mercifully short, which fill over fourteen hundred closely printed pages.

Perhaps the most interesting of Libanius' writings is the panegyric on his native city. Until the foundation of Constantinople Antioch was for centuries the third city of the world, ranking only after Rome and Alexandria as Paris now ranks after London and New York. Above all others it was the city of pleasure ; its ballet dancers, musicians and courtesans were famous all over the Mediterranean ; its chief street, over four miles long, with a covered colonnade on both sides and a broad carriage-way in the middle, was unsurpassed even in Rome ; and the garden of Daphne, ten miles in circumference, shaded by cypresses and laurel trees and adorned with fountains, was day and night alike thronged with crowds of holiday makers. In the serious life of the Empire, however, Antioch with her insolent and quarrelsome people played but a small part ; Libanius was almost the only writer whom she produced, and his description is her best memorial.

The speech, Oration XI, is, as usual with Libanius, rather too long and would gain in effect by compression, but towards the end Libanius gives some really valuable information about the water-supply of Antioch and about its system of artificial lighting, in which respect it seems to have been unique among ancient cities. Of it he says :

' With us Sleep, " the king of mortals," does not draw folk against their will under his thrall, nor lull them forcibly to rest. We alone of all men have shaken his tyranny from our eyes, and when the sun's torch goes out other lamps take his place, the only difference between night and day being in the kind of light. Our craftsmen find things by night just the same, and while some go on working diligently, others indulge in merry games or find relaxation in music. Some stay at the forge, others join in the dance, and so Hephæstus and Aphrodite share the night between them, whereas in other cities it is Endymion rather who is honoured.'

He is equally enthusiastic over the water-supply, and after describing the delights of Daphne and its fountains he proceeds thus :

'In other matters people may brazen us out, but when it comes to water all must yield to us. Some cities have beautiful fountains : we surpass them in number. Some have numerous fountains : we surpass them in beauty. Of our public baths each one has the proportions of a river ; of our private several are equally well supplied, and the others are not far behind. Anyone who has the means to build a new bath does so without having to trouble about water, and has no need to fear lest the supply should fail in summer, and his bath by lack of the Nymphs' presence be called " the thirsty one." Every district in the city prides itself on its baths, which are maintained at their own expense ; and although these district baths are smaller than the public ones, they are even more beautiful, for each district strives to outvie the others. The number of houses gives you an idea of our wealth in water : there are as many separate supplies as there are dwellings ; nay, sometimes there are several supplies to one house, and most of our workshops have the same convenience. Therefore we have no sparring matches at the public wells as to who shall draw before his neighbour—a common annoyance in many rich towns, where you will find crowds jostling round the wells lamenting over broken pitchers and broken heads. With us the public fountains are merely for display, since everyone has water laid on indoors. As for its clearness, you can test that easily if you fill a pail and then take it away. You will fancy that your receptacle is empty, so plainly can you see the shining bottom. Indeed I do not know whether the sight of our water rather excites thirst or abates it, for it both invites you to drink and also refreshes you before drinking.'

Julian (A.D. 331–363)

Our list of fourth-century rhetoricians must close with the name of the Emperor Julian ; for if Marcus

Aurelius was a born philosopher made by Fortune ruler of Rome, Julian even more truly was a born sophist whom the same goddess raised to the purple. Into the age-long controversy over his theological views and his reasons for abandoning Christianity and seeking to revive the old Pagan cult we need not in this book enter : here it will be sufficient to give the facts of his life and some account of his writings.

Flavius Claudius Julianus was born at Constantinople in 331, his father being half-brother of Constantine the Great, his mother, Basilina, who died when Julian was a few months old, a devout Christian. Soon after Constantine's death in 337, his successor, Constantius, murdered Julian's father, and in 345 sent Julian himself, who was then fourteen, together with his brother Gallus to the castle of Macellum in Cappadocia, where they were kept as virtual prisoners. This confinement lasted for six years, and as Julian says in his *Letter to the Athenians* he only escaped from moral degradation by the training which in his early boyhood he had received from the Christian eunuch, Mardonius, at Nicomedia, and by the love of literature which he had imbibed from the same excellent teacher.

In 351 Constantius relented, and raising Gallus to the rank of Cæsar sent him to Antioch as governor of the Eastern provinces, while Julian was allowed to follow his natural bent for study at Pergamum and Ephesus. In the latter city he met Maximus, the Neoplatonist wonder-worker, and was by him perverted from Christianity, although for ten years he never openly made profession of his change of faith. Then in 354 another turn of Fortune occurred. Constantius put Gallus to death as a traitor and summoned Julian to Milan, where he was only saved from a like fate by the intercession of the Empress Eusebia, whose virtues he commemorates in his *Third Oration*. Eusebia obtained permission for him to resume his studies at Athens, and during his two months' stay there in 354 he wrote the *Panegyric on Constantius* (Oration I), and also probably was initiated into the mysteries at Eleusis. In September he was again called to Milan, and made Cæsar by Constantius, who gave him his sister Helena in marriage, and sent him off to Gaul to expel the German invaders who were then ravaging the province.

Up till that time Julian had been a student immersed in books, and those who are inclined to underrate his capacities will find it difficult to explain how in the next five years he managed to defeat the Germans and Franks in many pitched battles, and finally brought the whole country back again to peace and prosperity. His success was so unexpected and his popularity with the army in Gaul had become in 359 so great that Constantius was alarmed, and sent him a peremptory order to dispatch half his troops at once for service in the East. The men, however, were most of them Celts who had only undertaken to serve in Gaul, and in February 360 they mutinied at Paris and proclaimed their reluctant general Emperor.

Hitherto Julian had been perfectly loyal to Constantius, and had written in his honour the second Oration, *The heroic deeds of Constantius*; but when on informing him of the soldiers' action he was sharply told that he must be content with the title of Cæsar, he determined to make a bid for the supreme power. Accordingly in 361 he marched eastwards with his army, and by October had reached the Danube, where he issued a proclamation, justifying his conduct and declaring his intention to revive Hellenism and the old religion. At that Constantius, who had been fighting against the Persians, started to return to Constantinople, but fell ill, and died in November, leaving Julian to enter the capital in triumph at the end of the year.

Julian had thus succeeded in a very perilous enter-
prise, and how great his danger had been may be seen
in a letter which he wrote to Hermogenes soon after
his accession : [1]

> 'Suffer me to say in the language of the poetical rhetoricians,
> O how little hope had I of safety ! O how little hope had I of
> hearing that you had escaped the three-headed hydra ! Zeus be
> my witness that I do not mean my brother Constantius—nay, he
> was what he was—but the wild beasts who surrounded him and
> cast their baleful eyes on all men ; for they made him even harsher
> than he was by nature, though on his own account he was by no
> means of a mild disposition, although he seemed so to many. But
> since he is now one of the blessed dead, may the earth lie lightly
> on him, as the saying is ! '

In February 362 Julian proclaimed religious freedom
in the empire, recalled the orthodox Christian bishops
who had been exiled by the Arian Constantius, and
ordered the restoration of any pagan temple that had
been destroyed. In spite of this last edict, however,
Hellenism made but slow progress, and Julian soon took
more vigorous measures. Pagans were to be preferred
to Christians for all public offices, the Christian clergy
were deprived of many of their privileges, and, most
important of all, Christian teachers were forbidden to
read pagan authors with their pupils. By this edict
all pretence of impartiality was discarded, and even
Julian's own supporters considered that a mistake had
been made. In June 362 Julian left the capital for
Antioch where he remained for nine months, and wrote
the *Misopogon*, 'Beard-hater,' a long invective against
the people of that city, who refused to show any
enthusiasm for paganism and made fun of the Emperor's
philosophic beard. He then decided to resume the
campaign against the Persians which Constantius had
begun, and setting out in March 363 sailed down the
Euphrates with 65,000 men. But although he won a

[1] Letters, No. 13. Tr. W. C. Wright, Loeb Library.

victory over Sapor near Ctesiphon, his Gallic soldiers suffered severely from the heat, and the Persians began to repeat the tactics which had proved successful against Crassus at Carrhæ. Finally, after a series of rear-guard actions, Julian himself was killed, June 26, 363, and in his place the soldiers elected the Christian general Jovian as Emperor.

Julian's writings fall into four classes, the Orations, the Hymns, the Satires, and the Letters. Of the Orations we have already mentioned the three most important ; the three others, less interesting, are the two scoldings addressed to the Cynics and the consolation to himself on the departure of his friend Sallust. Of the prose hymns there are two, the first, called by Cumont the official catechism of the pagan empire, to King Helios, beginning thus : [1]

> ' What I am now about to say I consider to be of the greatest importance for all things " that breathe and move upon the earth," and have a share in existence and a reasoning soul and intelligence, but above all others it is of importance to myself. For I am a follower of King Helios. And of this fact I possess within me, known to myself alone, proofs more certain than I can give. But this at least I am permitted to say without sacrilege, that from my childhood an extraordinary longing for the rays of the god penetrated deep into my soul.'

In this hymn and in its sequel, the Hymn to the Mother of the Gods, Julian expresses his deepest religious convictions and attempts to establish a harmony between the worship of the old gods and Mithraism. To appreciate the full significance of both hymns a knowledge of Neoplatonic doctrine is necessary, and for most they are rather difficult reading. The two satires on the other hand, the *Misopogon* and the *Cæsars*, are of a more popular kind, and the latter deserves description. Romulus gives a feast in heaven to the gods and to the Roman emperors, and a discussion

---

[1] 'Hymn to King Helios.' Trans. W. C. Wright, Loeb Library.

arises as to which of these latter is the greatest. Alexander joins the company, and the competition narrows down to six, Julius Cæsar, Alexander, Augustus, Trajan, Marcus Aurelius, and Constantine. Each one states his claims, and when Marcus Aurelius is adjudged the victor, they take their places next to their patron god :[1]

> 'As for Constantine, he could not discover among the gods the model of his own career, but when he caught sight of Pleasure, who was not far off, he ran to her. She received him tenderly and embraced him, then after dressing him in raiment of many colours and otherwise making him beautiful, she led him away to Incontinence. There too he found Jesus, who had taken up his abode with her and cried aloud to all comers : " He that is a seducer, he that is a murderer, he that is sacrilegious and infamous, let him approach without fear ! For with this water will I wash him and will straightway make him clean. And though he should be guilty of those same sins a second time, let him but smite his breast and beat his head and I will make him clean again." '

Lastly, we have the Letters, some of them formal productions, such as the *Letter to the Athenians*, the *Letter to a priest*, and the *Letter to Themistius* ; others shorter and of a more familiar style. A pleasing specimen is the letter to the rhetorician Evagrius, to whom he gave a small estate :[2]

> 'It is situated not more than twenty stades from the sea, so that no trader or sailor with his chatter and insolence disturbs the place. Yet it is not wholly deprived of the favours of Nereus, for it has a constant supply of fish, fresh and still gasping ; and if you walk up to a sort of hill away from the house you will see the Propontis and the islands. . . . Very peaceful it is to lie down there and glance into some book, and then, while resting one's eyes, it is very agreeable to gaze at the ships and the sea. When I was still hardly more than a boy I thought that this was the most delightful summer place, for it has, moreover, excellent springs and a charming bath and garden and trees. When I had grown to manhood I used to long for my old manner of life there and visited it often, and our meetings there

---

[1] 'The Cæsars.' Tr. W. C. Wright, Loeb Library.
[2] Letter 25. Tr. W. C. Wright, Loeb Library.

did not lack talks about literature. Moreover there is there, as a
humble monument of my husbandry, a small vineyard that produces
a fragrant, sweet wine, which does not have to wait for time to
improve its flavour. You will have a Vision of Dionysus and the
Graces. The grapes on the vine, and when they are being crushed
in the press, smell of roses, and the new-made wine in the jars is
a " rill of nectar," if one may trust Homer.'

Eunapius (A.D. 346-415)

Our knowledge of many of the men referred to in
this chapter is partly derived from Eunapius, who
wrote a history of the period from A.D. 270 to 404 and
also a series of *Lives of the Philosophers and Sophists*,
modelled on the work of Philostratus. The history,
which was in fourteen books with an enthusiastic
account of Julian's reign as its main subject, now only
exists in insignificant fragments ; but we have twenty-
three of the biographies and from them we can see that
the loss of the history is no very great disaster. The
Lives are entirely lacking in the critical spirit, in
composition, and in style ; and although many of the
stories in them are amusing, as a serious contribution to
history they are valueless. Themistius is not even
mentioned, and the accounts given of Himerius and
Libanius are extremely inadequate. On the other
hand, Eunapius has the greatest admiration for the
Neoplatonists Plotinus, Porphyry, Iamblichus, and
Maximus, and fills his pages with tales of the miracles
which the two latter were constantly performing. One
of them about Iamblichus may be given as an example
of his style :[1]

'There were two hot springs smaller than the others but prettier,
and he bade his disciples ask the natives of the place by what names
they used to be called in former times. When they had done his
bidding they said : " There is no pretence about it, this spring is
called Eros, and the name of the one next to it is Anteros." He at

---

[1] 'Lives.' Trans. W. C. Wright, Loeb Library.

once touched the water with his hand—he happened to be sitting on the ledge of the spring where the overflow runs off—and uttering a brief summons he called forth a boy from the depth of the spring. He was white-skinned and of medium height, his locks were golden and his back and breast shone ; and he exactly resembled one who was bathing or had just bathed. His disciples were overwhelmed with amazement, but Iamblichus said, " Let us go to the next spring," and he rose and led the way, with a thoughtful air. Then he went through the same performance there also, and summoned another Eros like the first in all respects, except that his hair was darker and fell loose in the sun. Both the boys embraced Iamblichus, and clung to him as though he were genuinely their father. He restored them to their proper places, and went away after his bath, reverenced by his pupils.'

Quintus Smyrnæus (fl. A.D. 400)

The second striking feature of pagan Greek literature towards the end of the fourth century is, as we have said, the revival of epic poetry. Since the time of Apollonius Rhodius the epic had been completely neglected by writers, and then suddenly we have Quintus, Nonnus, Tryphiodorus and the rest, who all go back to Homeric subjects and to the Homeric style. Of Nonnus we have spoken in the preceding chapter : the other poets may conveniently be grouped together here.

One day in the fifteenth century, when Cardinal Bessarion was travelling in Calabria he visited the monastery of St Nicholas at Otranto, and in its library found a Greek manuscript ' Ta Meth Homeron,' inscribed simply with the name Quintus. At first it was thought that Quintus was the original owner, but references in later grammarians show that he was the poet himself, and as he tells us that he spent his youth near Smyrna, he is now generally known as Quintus Smyrnæus. His date can be fixed fairly well by the evidence of style, but there are also two valuable pieces of evidence in the text. In the prophecy put into the

mouth of Chalcas,[1] Quintus says : ' It is decreed that
Æneas shall come to the Tiber's broad stream and build
there a sacred city, and his race after him shall be
Kings of all the lands from the rising to the setting of
the sun.' This is a plain reference to the Roman
Empire, and a simile in the Sixth Book brings us even
closer, for beast fights in the arena were abolished in
the early years of the fifth century A.D. : ' They turned
this way and that, like boars and lions in an enclosure,
who tear slaves to pieces when kings have gathered
men together.' [2]

From these passages we may conclude that Quintus
lived towards the end of the fourth century, and that
his home was once at Smyrna we know from the lines
in Book XII, 308–313 : [3]

> ' Tell, ye Queens of Song,
> Now man by man the names of all that passed
> Into the cavernous Horse ; for ye inspired
> My soul with all my song, long ere my cheek
> Grew dark with manhood's beard, what time I fed
> My goodly sheep on Smyrna's pasture-lea,
> From Hermus thrice so far as one may hear
> A man's shout, by the fane of Artemis,
> In the Deliverer's Grove, upon a hill
> Neither exceeding low nor passing high.'

This passage is plainly inspired by Hesiod, who says
that the Muses came to him as he fed his sheep under
Mount Helicon, and it is a curious fact that Homer,
Hesiod, and Apollonius Rhodius are the only poets to
whom Quintus can be said to be indebted. It would
seem that the literature of ten centuries passed over his
head unnoticed, and except for one or two slight
anachronisms, his poem, as far as historical allusions go,
might have been written by Homer himself.

His purpose is to bridge the gap between the Iliad

---

[1] 'Posthomerica,' XIII. 336.   [2] *Ibid.*, VI. 531.
[3] Trans. A. S. Way, Loeb Library.

and the Odyssey, and this he does in a series of episodes divided into fourteen books, the whole poem being about half the length of the Iliad. Book I tells how Penthesilea, Queen of the Amazons, came to the help of Troy, and after wreaking havoc among the Greeks was in her turn slain by Achilles. Book II relates the similar fate which befell Memnon, son of Aurora, when he led his Ethiopians into the fray :

> ' As when a mist enshrouds the hills, what time
> Roll up the rain-clouds, and the torrent-beds
> Roar as they fill with rushing floods, and howls
> Each gorge with fearful voices ; shepherds quake
> To see the waters' downrush and the mist
> Screen dear to wolves and all the wild fierce things
> Nursed in the wide arms of the forest ; so
> Around the fighters' feet the choking dust
> Hung, hiding the fair splendour of the sun
> And darkening all the heaven.' [1]

Book III describes the death of Achilles at the hands of Apollo and the laments made over his corpse by Ajax, Agamemnon, Briseis, and his mother Thetis, while in the next book we have an account of the Funeral Games held in his honour. Book V deals with the contest between Odysseus and Ajax for the arms of Achilles, which ended in the latter's madness and suicide ; and here Quintus at least holds his own with Ovid, who tells the same story in the *Metamorphoses*. Books Six to Eight are concerned with Eurypylus, grandson of Heracles, and Neoptolemus, son of Achilles, the first book telling how Eurypylus came to help the Trojans, the second how Neoptolemus was brought from Scyros in spite of Deidamia's prayer, and the third how he slew Eurypylus in battle. In Book Nine Philoctetes, possessor of the bow of Heracles, rejoins the Greeks after his long exile at Lemnos, and in the next book wounds Paris with a poisoned arrow. Œnone,

---

[1] 'Posthomerica,' II. 471. Trans. A. S. Way, Loeb Library.

who could have healed her husband, refuses her help and scornfully sends him back to Helen ; but after his death she repents :

> ' Not with them of Troy she wailed,
> But far away within that desolate home
> Moaning she lay on her lost husband's bed.
> As when the copses on high mountains stand
> White-veiled with frozen snow, which o'er the glens
> The west wind blasts have strown, but now the sun
> And east wind melt it fast, and the long heights
> With water-courses stream and down the glades
> Slide, as they thaw, the heavy sheets, to swell
> The rushing waters of an ice-cold spring.' [1]

In the next three books we have the last episodes of the siege ; the making of the wooden horse, the secret entry of the Greeks into Troy, the death of Priam, and the burning of his city ; scenes familiar to most in Virgil's majestic narrative. Finally, in Book Fourteen, the Greek leaders sail away, taking their captives with them, each man to his own fate ; and the poem ends with the great storm which by the wrath of heaven fell upon their fleet and scattered their ships to the four winds.

Such is the story of the *Posthomerica* in outline, and perhaps after this long account of fighting and battles it may be asked if Quintus is really worth reading. If those who ask that question admire Tennyson, the answer should be in the affirmative, for the two men have much in common. Quintus is not a great poet ; nor is the Englishman ; but they both are a very good imitation.

Coluthus, Tryphiodorus, The Orphica

The same can hardly be said of the other epic poets of the fifth century, interesting though they may be

---

[1] 'Posthomerica,' X. 412. Trans. A. S. Way, Loeb Library.

to students of literature. The *Rape of Helen*, by Coluthus (fl. A.D. 490), is a pleasant little poem and that is all. Beginning with an invocation to the Trojan nymphs, it tells the story of the golden apple and the judgment of Paris, who ' bent a gentle eye and quietly essayed to judge the beauty of each goddess. He looked at the radiance of their flashing eyes, he looked on their necks adorned with gold, he marked the bravery of each, the shape of the heel behind and the very soles of their feet.' He gives the prize to the Cyprian, and sails for Sparta where, meeting Helen, he tells her that Menelaus is not much of a man and that she is altogether superior to her company. Helen, chiefly from a desire to see a new country, flies with him that night, and the piece ends with the lament of the young Hermione when she finds her mother gone.

The *Taking of Troy*, by Tryphiodorus (fl. A.D. 470), is rather more elaborate, but suffers from the inevitable comparison with Virgil. It opens with the making of the wooden horse, which is elaborately described ; and then the Greek chiefs, encouraged by a speech from Odysseus, climb into its belly. The stratagem of Sinon follows, the horse is brought into Troy, and Cassandra in a long prophecy warns the Trojans of their fate. The Greek fleet returns, the signal being given both by Sinon and by Helen, the warriors come down from the horse, and scenes of massacre fill the rest of the poem : ' And birds and dogs this way and that about the city, the fowls of the air and the beasts that walk, feasted in company and drank the black blood and made a savage meal. The shrilling of the birds breathed carnage, and the barking dogs bayed fiercely over slaughtered men, pitiless and heeding not that they were rending their own masters.'

Of Coluthus and Tryphiodorus we know a few details, but we have not even the names of the poets responsible

373

for the pieces in the collection known as *Orphica*. The two chief of them, however, the *Precious Stones* and the *Argonautica*, seem to belong to the latter years of the fourth century and may be briefly mentioned here. In the first, a didactic poem of about eight hundred hexameter lines, the mythical Orpheus explains to Theodamas, son of Priam, the mystical value of jewels and the use which can be made of them in magic. The second, slightly more interesting, tells the story of the voyage of the Argonauts in fourteen hundred hexameters. It is natural to compare it with Apollonius Rhodius and the comparison is not in its favour. The love interest disappears, and so do all the dramatic and descriptive elements of the earlier poem. Orpheus becomes the chief character, but in spite of his long speeches, prayers and sacrifices he is not really brought to life. Indeed the author's main interest seems to lie in geography, and he brings the Argo home by way of the western Mediterranean and Central Europe, a complete change from the route which Apollonius describes.

Palladas (fl. A.D. 400)

From these shadowy figures we pass to a poet who has given us a mass of information about himself. Upon a certain day in a certain month at Alexandria some time between the years A.D. 350 and 360—we cannot be more exact, for even if the two events may have happened on the same morning they may have been separated by the space of those ten years—there were born two baby boys destined to be almost the last offshoots from the great tree of Græco-Roman poetry. One of them, although he began by composing in Greek a poem on the wars of the Giants, of which seventy-seven lines remain, left Alexandria for Rome

374

in 394, gained a place in the civil service there and, what was more important, the favour of the great general, Stilicho, and the puppet emperor, Honorius. Under the shelter of their patronage the Egyptian clerk abandoned Greek for Latin and wrote the *Epithalamium* for the marriage of Honorius, the poem *On the consulship of Stilicho*, and the wonderful *Rape of Proserpine* which definitely sets the name of Claudian among the glories of Roman literature. The other boy was less happy in his life and has been less fortunate in his posthumous fame.

Palladas lived apparently most of his days at Alexandria and by trade was a Grammaticus, a secondary schoolmaster ; his business being to take boys who had been taught by a Grammatistes to read and write, and force them to commit to memory as much of Homer and the Greek tragedians as they could be induced to stomach. It was a profession which, in ancient times at least, was regarded with humorous contempt, and those who followed it did so for no very obvious reason. They were, by definition, men of some intelligence, but they were overworked, badly paid, and usually held up to scorn both by their pupils and their pupils' parents. Palladas cries out with grim sarcasm on his prospects :

> ' Parsing has brought me to a pretty pass—
> I'll sell my books and turn my Muse to grass.
> For if I don't, I plainly see
> That one fine day she'll be the death of me.'
>
> *A. P.* ix. 171.

He draws us a vivid picture of the teacher's trials : how parents will arrange for a year's instruction and then withdraw the pupil in the eleventh month leaving the master unpaid : how in other cases the children's nurse comes reluctantly once a month to pay the fee, on the way changing the good coins for bad and putting in leaden pieces instead of bronze. And Palladas was not even an independent practitioner in his sordid trade. He was an usher, and an incompetent one at that, for his headmaster, Dorotheus, at last gave him the sack.

Poor and cynical, discontented and a schoolmaster, we need not be surprised if Palladas was unhappy in his married life. And he was unhappy. If we may believe him his wife was both ill-favoured and ill-tempered. 'He who has the misfortune to possess an ugly wife sees darkness when he lights the lamps in the evening,' he says, and again, with a reference to the first lines of the Iliad, the schoolmaster's text-book— ' I have married a wife who is herself " pernicious wrath," and so I am forced to consort with wrath for ever, in my trade as a schoolmaster and in my quarrelsome wife.'

Such utterances as these do not reveal a very happy household, and it is doubtful whether Palladas disliked his wife or his profession the more. But from the latter after long years of penury he broke free. To his marital partner, as he bitterly says, Roman law and the conditions of the marriage contract bound him, an unwilling prisoner. He probably had spent his wife's dowry and could not get a separation without repayment. So, not being able to escape from his wife, Palladas takes his revenge on womankind in general, and sums up the relations between the sexes in six lines :

> ' Wives are a curse,
> Some bad, some worse :
> Vexation beyond measure.
> When they're in bed,
> And when they're dead,
> Our only hours of pleasure.'

A. P. xi. 381.

Like many other poor men he is inclined to attribute his ill-success not to his own character but to the perverse malignity of Fortune, and against that goddess he aims his most venomous shafts. ' Fortune is a strumpet,' he cries, ' who plays with men as with a ball, now tossing them high in the air, now letting them fall at her caprice. She is always rather inclined to favour the wicked than the just : consequently the man of property is by inference a rogue.' Such views as these, expressed in pungent verse, were naturally popular, and the following piece is not only preserved in the *Anthology* but was found also some years ago by the Austrian School when they were excavating at Ephesus, inscribed upon the wall of a latrine :

> ' Life is but a flying slave,
>   Now escaped and now imprisoned,
> Fortune tossed by every wave,
>   Like some harlot gay bedizened.
> Jest at both, nor grieve to see
> The unrighteous in prosperity.'
>
> *A. P.* x. 87.

And for all these troubles Palladas has no remedy or consolation to offer, except such illusory aid as Bacchus and Aphrodite can give. The only doubt in his mind is as to whether life or death is the greater evil. At one time life with its constant expectation of sickness and sorrow seems the worse :

> ' I weep no more for those who pass away
>   To dreamless sleep.
> For those who live and look for death each day—
>   For them I weep.'
>
> *A. P.* x. 282.

But more often even life and its manifold miseries appear preferable to the nothingness that is to come :

> ' Away with grief, away with tears ;
>   This life is but a fleeting dream.
> Soon you must die, and these few years
>   Will but a moment seem.

377

> Vex not your heart while yet you live
> Before death's judgment on you fall.
> Soon to the tomb your corpse they'll give
> And worms about you crawl.'
>
> *A. P.* x. 78.

How active a share Palladas took with his friends
Theon and Hypatia in their struggle against the
Christians is uncertain. But we know that he took part
in the contest and that the contest was long and fierce,
and we know also that there is nothing which more
tends to embitter a man's mind than religious controversy. The atmosphere of Alexandria was charged
with sectarian hatred, a hatred intensified by the
personal animosity of the Christian bishop Cyril against
the Greek prefect Orestes, and there can be little doubt
that the triumph of the new faith was one of several
causes that drove Palladas to despair. To a convinced
Pagan like himself the victory of Christianity, with its
fierce temper of bigoted intolerance and its contempt
for ancient learning, was the victory of the worse over
the better cause. He had already seen the statues of
his gods destroyed by the Christian mob of Alexandria
in the episcopate of Theophilus, A.D. 389, and the murder
of Hypatia, A.D. 415, may well have seemed to him the
crowning stroke of infamy.

But Palladas does not acquiesce in God's will : he
rebels against it, and in the *Descent of Man* he pours out
all his bitterness :

> ' If thou would call to mind that deed of shame
> Thy father did before to life thou came,
> Methinks thou would not, friend, so haughty be,
> Or plume thyself as one of high degree :
> But reading Plato's dreams with pride thou art flown—
> " Immortal plant in heaven's garden grown,
> Of God's own clay begotten "—Prithee stay,
> And put these tales, these fancies vain away.
> Come, learn the truth and know : poor crawling worm,
> Thou art sprung from lust and one foul drop of sperm.'
>
> *A. P.* x. 45.

In grim intensity of thought and in bitter irony it would be hard to surpass these lines. This pessimism is not the product of satiety ; it springs from a real disgust with the facts of life, such a disgust as Hypatia seems also to have felt when she drove away her lover by thrusting under his eyes the evidence of her physical weakness. To indulge the feeling is to strike one's head against a brick wall, but Palladas was the child of his age and in his time a morbid abhorrence of the natural process of reproduction was filling the world with monks and celibates. It is not a feeling that is liable to afflict most Englishmen, but there is one of our greatest authors whose existence was poisoned by it, and perhaps we can best appreciate the tragedy of Palladas' life by recalling the memory of that most unhappy genius, Jonathan Swift.

Zosimus (fl. 450)

After Palladas there are few pagan authors of any importance. Orion and Hesychius, the lexicographers, belong rather to the history of scholarship than to the history of literature, and the anthologist Stobæus, valuable though his four books of selections are for what they preserve for us of classical authors, contributes little of his own. Zosimus, however, author of the *Contemporary History*, is a writer of some merit and requires a brief notice. His work was written in the reigns of Theodosius II and his successors, and consists of six books. The first gives a summary of Roman history from Augustus to Diocletian ; the second, third, and fourth deal in fuller detail with the period between the death of Diocletian in 304 and the death of Theodosius I in 395 ; the fifth and sixth, the most important, describe the reign of Arcadius and the early years of Theodosius II. In these two last books

379

Zosimus not only narrates events, but also seeks to discover the cause of the decadence of the Empire, which he finds to be chiefly due to the overthrow of the old religion. His style is clear and his narrative sensible, but the narrowness of his theological outlook renders his analysis of the situation of little value.

Proclus (A.D. 410–485)

The last pagan author whom we have to mention is Proclus, and with him we return for the last time to Athens, where this narrative began. Neoplatonism, which with Iamblichus and Maximus degenerated into witchcraft, was revived at Alexandria in a purer shape by Theon and his daughter Hypatia during the early years of the fifth century. After the murder of Hypatia in 415 the doctrines she had taught were taken to Athens by Nestorius, who established there a school which lasted for over two centuries in spite of Christian opposition and was finally closed by an edict of Justinian in 529. We know the names and have writings by several of its heads, Syrianus, Hermias, and Simplicius : but the only one of them who can be called a real genius is Proclus, and with him Neoplatonism takes its final and most precise form.

Proclus was born at Constantinople in 410, and at first intended to follow his father Patricius in an official career. But his natural vocation for philosophy was too strong, and arriving at Athens as a student about 430 he became eight years later head of the Neoplatonists. For half a century he remained in that position, devoting all his days to teaching, writing, and meditation. He never married, he slept as little as possible, his life was that of an ascetic : but he was a person of charming manners, and in spite of his austerities he continued hale and vigorous almost until the time of his death in his seventy-fifth year.

Proclus was a great thinker but hardly a great writer, and his surviving works are mostly commentaries on separate dialogues of Plato, the *Republic*, the *Timæus*, the *Parmenides*, or else general discussions of the master's theories, such as the treatise *On the theology of Plato*. Besides these we have six *Hymns*, devotional exercises in mediocre verse, and some writings on mathematics and astronomy. But all of them are more interesting to the student of philosophy than to the lover of literature.

CHAPTER III
THE REIGN OF JUSTINIAN
(A.D. 527–565)

THE last two chapters have abandoned chronological order and treated the Pagan and the Christian literature of the fourth and fifth centuries separately. But when we come to Constantinople in the reign of Justinian this distinction is no longer necessary; for the writers of Justinian's court, although they are nominally Christians, in outlook and expression are entirely Pagan, and their religion has very little influence on their literary work. They are amoral rather than immoral, and in some ways it is a relief to turn from Pagan bitterness and Christian intolerance to the blithe indifference of these Byzantines; but from the Puritan point of view there is in them much to seek. There are, of course, some serious writers among them, for a scientist and a lawyer finds it difficult to be frivolous even if he wishes; but they are in an insignificant minority, and it is the historians and the love poets who give this period its distinctive note.

The age of Justinian is marked by brilliant achievement. Justinian himself seems to have been one of those lucky rulers who, without pre-eminent intellectual gifts of their own, achieve by the help of capable subordinates the results that are sometimes denied to the most brilliant genius. Like Augustus, with whose career his life has much in common, a position was already made for him when he succeeded his uncle

Justin on the throne. Tribonian was another Mæcenas, Belisarius and Narses were as faithful to him as Agrippa and Tiberius had been to the Julian Emperor, labouring invincibly for another's glory ; and, like Augustus, Justinian had the good fortune to marry a woman who at least doubled his individual strength. At his court poets like Paul and Agathias stood side by side with scholars like Stephanus, Johannes Lydus, and Eutokios, and with the wonderful band of architects, sculptors and painters who, under the direction of Anthemius, built the great church of Santa Sophia. The Imperial Library, with its six hundred thousand volumes, con- tained all that was most valuable in ancient literature ; the Hippodrome and the city palaces were ornamented with the most famous statues and sculptures of the past. In one private house, we are told, there stood the Aphrodite of Praxiteles, the Hera of Lysippus and the Zeus of Phidias, together with a library of one hundred and twenty thousand books. Byzantium had inherited all the past splendours of Athens, Alexandria, and Antioch ; Rome had ceased to be the capital of the world ; and the chief memorials of Greek art were concentrated in one Greek city.

Of all this splendour two great memorials still survive. One of them is the conspectus of Roman law which Tribonian and his assistants arranged, the *Pandects* in Latin and the *Novellæ* in Greek ; the other is the mosque whose gilded crescent has taken the place of the Christian cross. In collecting materials for the building of Santa Sophia seven years were spent, and for eight years more 60,000 masons and artificers laboured at the work. The ancient gods were robbed for its profit, and the Temple of the Sun at Baalbek, the Temple of Diana at Ephesus, the Temple of Pallas at Athens, and the Temple of Phœbus at Delos, were among the world-famous shrines, some of whose columns yet stand beneath the cupola of Anthemius. The bricks were made of a special clay imported from Rhodes, the walls glowed with the rarest marble, the mosaic floor represented the four rivers of Paradise. Gold and silver by the hundredweight were used for the church furniture, and during the night services six thousand golden lamps shed their light around.

Procopius (A.D. c. 490-575)

Our chief knowledge of the events of Justinian's reign is derived from the narratives of two contemporary writers, Procopius and Agathias ; and Procopius is one of the most curious figures in literature. The first of his three works, a history of the Persian, Vandalic and Gothic wars, is a straightforward account in eight books of the campaigns of Belisarius, to whom he acted as private secretary. The second, the *Buildings of Justinian*, written perhaps by royal order, is an elaborate description of the Emperor's architectural creations in Constantinople and his fortifications throughout the Empire. The third, the *Anecdota*, or *Secret History*, is a malignant criticism of the whole imperial administration and seriously suggests that Justinian and Theodora are demons in human shape. It is true that even in his first book Procopius shows no great enthusiasm for his imperial master and gives most of the glory to Belisarius ; but there is a gap between indifference and hatred, and it is difficult to reconcile the flattery of the *Buildings* and the malignity of the *Secret History* without imputing a considerable share of duplicity to the author.

His military history is that one of Procopius' works which is least open to criticism, and of it Gibbon justly says :[1] 'His facts are collected from the personal

---

[1] *Decline and Fall*, Vol. IV., p. 210.

experience and free conversation of a soldier, a states-
man, and a traveller; his style continually aspires, and
often attains, to the merit of strength and elegance;
his reflections, more especially in the speeches which
he too frequently inserts, contain a rich fund of political
knowledge; and the historian, excited by the generous
ambition of pleasing and instructing posterity, appears
to disdain the prejudices of the people and the flattery
of courts.' In his historical method Procopius takes
Herodotus and Thucydides as his models, following the
first in his geographical digressions and in the importance which he attaches to dreams and portents of every
kind, the second in his prefaces, his inserted speeches,
and his descriptions of sieges and naval battles. His
political ideas, of course, are his own, and he shows
himself a fervent patriot who thinks that Græco-
Roman civilization is a thing apart and altogether
inaccessible to barbarians. He is also a staunch con-
servative, loving law and order and hating innovation in
all constitutional matters. As for religion, he writes as
a sceptic and regards Christianity with cool indifference.

Of the eight books into which the *History* is divided,
the first seven were written in 545 and published in
550, the eighth following in 554. Books One and Two
are chiefly concerned with the wars waged by Belisarius against the Persian king Chosroes, the fighting
being mainly on the Euphrates and the chief episode
the capture of Antioch by the Persian forces. Books
Three and Four describe the campaigns of Belisarius
in Africa against the Vandals and the Moors, the first
people, according to Procopius, 'a race who spend
their days at the bath or at luxurious feasts, dressed
in cloth of gold, and indulging in sexual pleasures of
every kind'; the second 'living in stuffy huts and
wearing the same clothes summer and winter alike,
sleeping on the ground and eating nothing but raw

barley grain.' In the last four books, the Gothic Wars, the scene shifts to Italy, and by the side of Belisarius we have the eunuch general Narses and the Gothic king Totila, into whose mouth Procopius puts his own criticism of Justinian's administration. In this case the acrimony is veiled, but something of the bitterness of the *Secret History* appears in the early chapters of Book One, which deal with affairs in Constantinople before the main narrative begins. Here, for example, is a sketch of Justinian's chief confidant, the prætorian prefect, John of Cappadocia :[1]

'John was entirely without the advantages of a liberal education ; for he learned nothing while attending the elementary school except his letters, and these, too, poorly enough ; but by his natural ability he became the most powerful man of whom we know. For he was most capable in deciding upon what was needful and in finding a solution for difficulties. But he became the basest of all men and employed his natural power to further his low designs; neither consideration for God nor any shame before man entered into his mind, but to destroy the lives of many men for the sake of gain and to wreck whole cities was his constant concern. So within a short time indeed he had acquired vast sums of money, and he flung himself completely into the sordid life of a drunken scoundrel; for up to the time of lunch each day he would plunder the property of his subjects, and for the rest of the day occupy himself with drinking and with wanton deeds of lust.'

Procopius' second book, *The buildings of Justinian*, published in 556, although it is disfigured by extravagant adulation, is still a valuable record of facts. It is in six parts, the first dealing with Constantinople, the other five with Mesopotamia, Armenia, Europe, Asia Minor and Palestine, and North Africa. In the first part the chief buildings described are St Sophia, the churches of Irene, Acacius, and the Apostles, the penitentiary for prostitutes, the senate house, the baths of Arcadius, and the aqueducts and water-cisterns. The next two parts consist mainly of descriptions of the

[1] 'History,' I. xxiv. 12. Tr. H. B. Dewing, Loeb Library.

386

forts erected in Mesopotamia and Armenia by Justinian, 'who is a king by nature, since, as Homer says, he is as gentle as a father.' The fourth part opens with an apology : 'I count it a perilous task to cross a great ocean in a crazy vessel ; and it is the same thing to describe the buildings of Justinian in a feeble narrative.' A list of the new forts in North Greece and the Chersonese follows, and then Procopius crosses to Asia Minor and to Palestine, where the New Church at Jerusalem is described at length. Africa comes last with the rebuilding of Carthage, Leptis Magna, and Adrumetum.

It is difficult to give an account of the *Secret History* without transgressing the limits of propriety. Its last half is comparatively decent, for there it is the meanness and cupidity of Justinian which form the subject of invective ; but the first twelve of its thirty chapters consist of scandalous details concerning the private lives of the Emperor and of Belisarius. The great general is represented as a despicable cuckold, who even when he catches his wife Antonina *flagrante delicto* is abject enough to kiss her feet and vow that henceforth he will be her slave, not her husband. Antonina herself in these pages appears as a shameless wanton, giving herself openly to her own servants, while the Empress abets her in her amours. As for the description which Procopius gives of Theodora's unfortunate youth, when as a circus girl she was prostituted to the pleasure of the Byzantine mob, a few sentences from Gibbon's paraphrase must suffice :

' She neither danced nor sang, nor played on the flute ; her skill was confined to the pantomime arts : she excelled in buffoon characters, and as often as the comedian swelled her cheeks and complained with a ridiculous tone and gesture of the blows that were inflicted upon her, the whole theatre of Constantinople resounded with laughter and applause. The beauty of Theodora was the subject of more flattering praise and the source of more exquisite delight. Her features were delicate and regular; her complexion, though somewhat pale, was tinged with a natural colour; every sensation was instantly expressed by the vivacity of her eyes; her easy motions displayed the graces of a small but elegant figure; and even adulation might proclaim that painting and poetry were incapable of delineating the matchless excellence of her form. But this form was degraded by the facility with which it was exposed to the public eye and prostituted to licentious desire. Her venal charms were abandoned to a promiscuous crowd of citizens and strangers, of every rank and of every profession; the fortunate lover who had been promised a night of enjoyment was often driven from her bed by a stronger or more wealthy favourite; and, when she passed through the streets, her presence was avoided by all who wished to escape either the scandal or the temptation.'[1]

For his tales of Theodora's youth Procopius had some foundation of fact; but his description of her cruelties as Empress is much exaggerated. Even less credible is the portrait drawn of Justinian in the later chapters. The Emperor is a fool and a knave, a faithless friend and a pitiless foe, a hypocrite who in the mildest of voices will order thousands of innocent men to be put to death. The son of a demon, he was seen on one occasion walking about without a head, on another with his face changed into a shapeless mass of flesh, on a third a monk came upon him sitting on his throne in Satan's own shape. Pages are filled with stories of his cupidity, and the book ends thus: 'As for the state treasure, no one knows where it is now. Not till Justinian—whether he be man or devil—shall have departed from this world, will those who are then living be able to learn the truth.'

Agathias (A.D. 536–582)

The other historian, Agathias, is a less vigorous writer, but a more likeable man; and thanks mainly to his own interest in himself we know enough of his life to draw a picture of a typical Byzantine man of letters. In the early years of the sixth century of our era there lived in the Mysian town of Myrina a married couple, Memnonius and Periclea. Memnonius was by profession a 'rhetorician'; a word which may be translated in this case as 'literary gentleman' or 'university extension lecturer.' His special business was to instruct and amuse an adolescent or adult audience by means of lectures; but anyone who contributed to the diffusion of knowledge, useful or useless, and was not a schoolmaster, came under this head. The rhetoricians were the lineal descendants of the sophists, and higher education in all its non-specialized branches was largely in their hands. A flourishing community would maintain several rhetoricians as our townships support two or three local newspapers, but Myrina was a small and insignificant place; and we may presume that Memnonius was not among the most successful practitioners of his art, for all the more eminent lecturers gravitated eventually to the great cities.

As with most members of his class, Memnonius had only a small family; the elder of his two was a daughter Eugenia, who showed considerable talent both in literature and jurisprudence, the younger was Agathias. In A.D. 539, when Agathias was only three years old, the father and mother made a journey to Byzantium, perhaps in connection with their daughter's career, since Byzantium was at that time the centre of legal studies, and the great jurisconsult, Tribonian, then was at the height of his fame. During their visit Periclea fell ill and died; and the little boy, who had been left behind at home, never saw his mother again. He too probably, like his sister, gave early promise of ability; for after learning all that his father could teach him he passed on to the renowned academy of

389

Alexandria and thence, now a young man, to Byzantium. The great government departments under Justinian offered an ambitious youth a brilliant career, and Agathias devoted himself to the legal studies that were then a necessary prelude to official life, combining, however, as many young advocates have done since, the pursuit of letters with that of law.

It was as a love poet that he made his first appearance and we still have the preface to his *Daphniaca*, so called from the famous pleasure gardens of Antioch :

> ' Behold the ninefold strain in Daphne's praise
> That to Love's Queen Agathias doth raise.
> For 'tis not of the Muses that he sings
> But of young Cupid and his wanton wings.
> And this his prayer—" May I be fancy free ;
> Or, if I love, may she, too, willing be." ' [1]

Whether the little volume was a public success we do not know ; but it served to introduce Agathias to the notice of Paul the Silentiary, the most brilliant figure in the literary circles of the court. The acquaintance soon ripened into friendship ; the young provincial found himself admitted into the intimacy of one of Theodora's favourites ; and his fortune was made. Paul was not only a poet, he was a man of wealth and position, able to advance the interests of any protégé. Moreover, he was considerably older than his young friend and had a daughter Aniceteia of marriageable age. What more natural than that Agathias, whose sister was already living with her husband in the city, should wish to draw still closer the ties between himself and his patron ? The progress of his courtship can be traced in the poems of the Anthology. From the beginning he seems to have had Paul's support, and our first document is a letter in verse addressed to his prospective father-in-law.[2] Agathias at the moment

[1] *A. P.* vi. 80.   [2] *A. P.* v. 292.

was immersed in legal business and detained upon the
opposite shore of the Bosphorus away from his beloved :

> ' Here the dark earth in summer's embrace warm
> Sees the young leaves unfold their verdant charm.
> The birds beneath the cypress shade sing sweet
> And tender nestlings their soft notes repeat.
> The goldfinch trills his lay, the turtle dove
> Moans from her thicket in the holly grove.
> But what delight is mine ?   I more desire
> Your voice than all the notes of Phœbus' lyre.
> Two loves beset me, friend ; to see your face
> And once again my darling to embrace,
> That young gazelle whose image burns my heart
> Though lawyers' parchments keep us still apart.'

Those who have ever lived near those blue waters,
where cypresses and laurels, fig-trees and roses, grow
together close beside the sea, will recognize the beauty
of Agathias' description ; and they will smile perhaps
to notice that the young lawyer professes to regard
Paul as a greater attraction even than his daughter.
That Agathias was never a very ardent suitor may be
reasonably inferred from his *Advice to young lovers*,[1]
and Paul in his jesting reply [2] suggests that a little of
Leander's fervour would soon bring the absent one
across the narrow strait.   In any case, whether by
swimming or by the less romantic ferry-boat which
Paul advises, Agathias soon afterwards returned.   The
next episode—considering Agathias' views on courtship
only to be expected—was a rather violent lovers'
quarrel, in which the stronger sex was, as usual, vic-
torious, and Agathias tumbled heavily off his high
horse.   Paul, in his capacity of well-wisher to both
parties, thought it prudent to intercede with his
daughter on his friend's behalf,[3] and as his intervention
was backed up by an apology from the miserable
offender,[4] Agathias was received again into favour.

[1] *A. P.* v. 216.   [2] *A. P.* v. 293.   [3] *A. P.* v. 300.   [4] *A. P.* v. 299.

After this things went smoothly with the young couple and the marriage took place. Paul presented his daughter with a gold cup as his wedding gift, and for it invented a posy.[1] Agathias for his part gave his wife her bridal veil, with the inevitable set of verses ;[2] and then, for all we know, they lived happy ever after.

By his marriage Agathias had at least secured his social position, and he soon became a 'scholasticus,' one of the high legal functionaries of the imperial court, and wrote the history of his own times which we still possess. Its five books form a continuation of Procopius, beginning where he leaves off in the spring of 552 and then narrating the events of each year until 558. The campaigns of Narses in Italy form his main subject and here he is at a disadvantage compared with Procopius, for he has no practical knowledge of warfare and depends for his information on the accounts of other men. Still, his narrative is clear and accurate, and when possible it is enlivened by picturesque details, such as appear in the account of Narses' stratagem against the people of Lucca, whose hostages he pretended to kill although really their necks were protected by blocks of wood, and in the description of the Byzantine soldiers after their victory, who, 'if they had the chance, would sell their shields and helmets for a lyre or a jug of wine.'

But with Agathias neither his legal nor his historical studies interfered with a constant flow of verse, and we have a very large number of epigrams from his hand. Of his twenty-three love poems several are marred by grossness of language, several are somewhat unpleasant because of a certain self-satisfaction which was plainly in Agathias' character. But there are a full dozen of outstanding merit, and the three poems to Rhodanthë are beautiful both in thought and expression. The

[1] *A. P.* ix. 770.   [2] *A. P.* v. 276.

first is a vivid picture of the autumn vintage where Rhodanthë's loveliness forces the revellers about the pressing vat to forget the pleasures of the wine god. Then comes the pretty fancy of his lady's girdle, kissed by each lover in turn and so made into a ferry plying from lip to lip.

The third is the well-known *Swallows* :[1]

> ' All the night long I grieve ; and when I fall
> In that uneasy sleep that morning brings
> I start awakened : faint I hear the call
> Of swallows twittering ere the day begins.
> Again I feel the smart of tears, again
> Rhodanthë's image burns my fevered breast.
> I close my weary eyes : 'tis all in vain :
>   I know no more of rest.
>
> O cruel swallows, cease to vex me still ;
> I did not rob fair Philomel of song.
> Go to the hoopoe's nest upon the hill
> And there your plaint for Itylus prolong.
> But let me sleep, that I to dream may try,
> And fancy in Rhodanthë's arms I lie.'

Here the trick of literary allusion which Agathias loves is used with some success, and there is a curiously modern air about the phrasing of the verse. But usually with Agathias there is too little passion and too much literature : indeed many of his epigrams seem to be based on scenes in the novelists and dramatists who preceded him. The poems on the lucky fisherman who married an heiress, for example, on the guilty lovers killed together by a falling roof, and on the chaste wives of Mytilene, are doubtless all taken from the love stories then so popular. And sometimes —for Agathias is a Christian in spite of all his invocations to the Paphian goddess—the book from which he quotes is our own Bible, as in this little epigram on Lot's wife :[2]

[1] *A. P.* v. 236.   [2] *A. P.* vii. 311.

'No corpse doth lie within this stone,
No tomb without this corpse doth own ;
For corpse and tomb here both are one.'

This habit of literary reference combined with an immense prolixity—counting by lines we have more of Agathias in the *Anthology* than any other author— renders him often very tedious. The many poems he contributes to the satirical section can hardly be described as mirth provoking, for in the brevity that is the soul of wit and in any true sense of humour he is lamentably deficient. Nor does he avoid a subject because it is trivial or even offensive. The two epigrams, followed by a version from a pupil's hand, that tell us of a domestic calamity, how his pet partridge was unfortunately killed by a greedy and voracious cat, are comparatively amusing. We may excuse the very indifferent verse he composes on hot and cold baths, on houses, and gardens, and bridges, as being partly due to the difficulty of their subject. But to write three epigrams on a draught-board is to try the reader's patience : to write four on a latrine is to pass the limit.

However, his weaknesses as a poet do not affect the merits of Agathias as an editor ; it is to him we owe the poets whom we have next to mention, and it is he, rather than Meleager, who is responsible for the form in which the *Anthology* is now arranged. The preface to the *Cycle*, a rather tiresome production complicated with a panegyric of Justinian, tells us that he arranged his selections in seven books according to subjects— dedicatory, descriptive, sepulchral, hortatory, humorous, amatory, convivial—and it is this system rather than Meleager's alphabetical arrangement that since his time has been generally followed.

394

The Poets of ' The Cycle '

Justinian's courtiers were as fond of writing epigrams as the Roman senators of the early Empire were of writing epics. Consequently, when Agathias conceived the idea of publishing a volume of contemporary verse to be called *The Cycle* his project was sure of success from the start. He himself and Paul were the chief contributors, but there are many others, most of whom seem to have been men of high official rank, such as Julian, Macedonius, and Leontius.

Julian, who had been governor of one of the districts of Egypt, is still represented in the *Anthology* by some seventy epigrams. Many of them are tedious to modern taste but there are some pretty pieces; prettiest of all perhaps the little Anacreontic which is the one amatory poem that Planudes alone preserves (*A. P.* xvi. 388). Most of his epigrams are in the Seventh and Ninth Books, literary epitaphs and literary descriptions—no less than six on Myron's celebrated heifer statue—and they all incline to the artificial. The Omar metre suits the best of them well enough, this for example :

> ' Come fill the Cup with Wine : all Mortals must
> Themselves assume the Mantle of this Dust.
> " Drink "—from my Grave beneath I still will cry,
> As oft I chanted ere my Voice was hushed.'
>
> *A. P.* vii. 32.

Macedonius the Consul also has nearly fifty epigrams to his credit in our collection. Like most of the Byzantines he is at his best in his love poems, and of the fourteen pieces in the Fifth Book scarcely one is without merit. *Love's Vintage* may be taken as a specimen :[1]

> ' This is love's vintage hour : within my arms
> I hold imprisoned all thy rosy charms,
> The crown of my desire, nor can see
> In spring or summer aught so fair as thee.

---

[1] *A. P.* v. 228.

Thy autumn beauties every treasure hold :
O may they bloom for aye, nor e'er grow old.
And yet what care I ! When the grapes lie piled,
Men do not heed the curling tendrils wild.
And so my love will constant last, I trow
E'en when the tendril wrinkles line thy brow.'

Leontius, a high legal functionary, is a poet of less distinction. Of his twenty-six epigrams many are very trifling examples of occasional verse, written in praise of a fashionable inn, a popular jockey, or a favourite singer. The most successful is one of several which extol the attractions of Byzantine baths : [1]

' The Graces came one day
    To use this water cool,
When Love in sportive play
    Was hiding near the pool.
He stole their clothes away
    And left them naked quite ;
So here they now must stay
    Ashamed to face the light.'

These three Byzantines come next after Agathias and Paul in the number of their contributions to the *Cycle*. Of others less generously represented there is Irenæus, judge of the high court, with his verses to Chrysilla : [2]

' Come, my Chrysilla, come,
    And make my arms your home.
Why, sweet, with downcast eyelids stand ?
Why pluck your gown with trembling hand ?
    Love leaves no room for shame.
And if your lips refuse me " Yes,"
    One gentle nod will still confess
    The power of Venus' name.'

Eratosthenes, another legal light, shows a pretty wit in such epigrams as this : [3]

' To thee, dear Bacchus, Xenophon doth proffer
    This empty cask : naught else hath he to offer.'

---

[1] *A. P.* ix. 616.   [2] *A. P.* v. 253.   [3] *A. P.* vi. 77.

Marianus has a special interest for English readers. The last two of Shakespeare's Sonnets are plainly suggested, probably through the medium of a French or Italian translation, by the following piece, written in praise of a certain hot spring called 'the bath of Love':

> ' The little Love god lay asleep,
> Giving the nymphs his torch to keep,
>   Beneath the plane tree's shade.
> Then said they : " Come, let's quench the fire,
> And with it quench love's fierce desire
>   That makes poor nymphs afraid."
>
> No sooner said than done : the brand
> Was taken in a maiden's hand
>   And plunged beneath the wave.
> But lo, it blazed and blazed anew
> And soon the stream all burning grew
>   Wherein their limbs they lave.
>
> So all the nymphs who gathered there
> As Cupid's servants listed were,
>   And yielded to his might.
> And 'tis from thence the waters come
> That in this bath now make their home
>   And give to men delight.'

A. P. ix. 627.

Paul the Silentiary (fl. A.D. 540)

It may perhaps be said that Agathias and his friends are chiefly attractive because they write in Greek, and that after all they are only minor poets. But there was one official in Justinian's court who cannot be placed in that category. Paul the Silentiary is a very remarkable genius, one of the most delightful of love poets and one of the most brilliant writers of description in verse that the world has seen. His three long poems all belong to this second type, and two of them are on the same subject, being descriptions of the great church of Santa Sophia. The shorter of the two, a piece of some three hundred hexameter lines, is an

elaborate account of the Ambo or pulpit which stood
in the centre of the church :

> ' E'en as some island rises from the main
> With vineyards set and fields of golden grain,
> And sailors as they pass it on the sea
> Forget awhile their toils and misery ;
> So, in the middle of our temple grand,
> The pulpit towered in stone doth upright stand.'

The other poem is much longer, and begins with
one hundred and thirty-four iambics, compliments to
the five hundred clergy attached to the temple, and
congratulations to Justinian on the universal peace that
he has given the world. Then, in nearly a thousand
lines of hexameter verse, Paul describes the several parts
of the church, and achieves with wonderful success the
difficult task of combining exact detail with poetic
imagination. One passage enumerating the marbles
used in the building may serve as a specimen of his
manner :

> ' But who, full-mouthed, in Homer's thunderous measures shall
> sing of the fields of marble collected on the lofty walls and about the
> spreading pavement of the mighty church ? The iron with its
> searching tooth has quarried for us green slabs from Carystus and
> gathered in a harvest of many-coloured marbles from the Phrygian
> hills, some rosy to see mingled with misty white, others gleaming
> softly with flowers of purple and of silver. There is a wealth of
> porphyry too, uplifted, that once filled a river-boat on the broad
> Nile, and now shines bespangled with bright stars. You may see
> the flashing emerald of the Laconian rock and the dazzling marble
> with mazy veins which the deep gullies of the Iassian heights have
> sent, showing slanting streaks of livid white and red. From the cliffs
> of Lydia comes the stone whose pallid flowers mingle, intertwined
> with scarlet, and near by is gleaming jasper shining with yellow gold
> which the Libyan sun has nurtured in the steep clefts of Moorish
> hills and warmed with golden light.'

The *Santa Sophia* was written by Paul at the
Emperor's command, and was recited as an opening
Ode on December 24, A.D. 563, when the new church

was consecrated. Paul's third long poem, the description of the Pythian Baths, was also probably a commission, given this time not by Justinian, but by the Empress Theodora. With her beauty and her talent as her only instruments Theodora rose from the lowest depths of venal vice to become the most important personage in the world of her time. Her health, however, in her later days was always weak, and she probably never recovered completely from the effects of her youthful licentiousness. Though her married life was beyond reproach, she bore her husband no children, and finally she was directed by her physicians to try the Pythian warm baths among the hills of Bithynia, which then enjoyed a reputation only second to the waters of Prusa. Among the four thousand attendants who escorted the Empress on her journey Paul was certainly one, for he was the chief of the eighty silentiaries whose function it was to act as masters of the ceremonies and to secure silence around the imperial chamber. As a record of his sojourn we still have the poem, about two hundred lines in dimeter iambics, in which he celebrates the wonders of the hot springs :

'Come and listen to my song
    If you wish to know, Sir,
How the baths will make you strong,
    Streams that freely flow, Sir ;
Where there nothing is to pay—
Just enjoy your holiday.

Pray attend and I will tell
    All that knowledge teaches ;
Hearken to the sermon well,
    Which dame Nature preaches.
You will find there's no expense,—
Test it by experience.'

So Paul, in the most lightly tripping verses, and with inexhaustible verve and gaiety, catalogues all the

399

wonders of the springs; how one makes men drunk, another gives them an aversion for strong liquor; how one runs with milk, another with pitch; how one, small and circular, is always brimful with water and will supply fifty baths at one time—'but if you bring to it more than fifty bathers it at once overflows and spills the inconsiderate pleasure seekers.'

Still, though Paul's three long poems are wonderful pieces of workmanship, modern readers will probably prefer the madrigals which Agathias preserved for us. Paul is the perfect amorist, and of these forty love poems there is scarcely one that does not invite translation. Many of them, indeed, have already appeared in English with rather scant acknowledgment, for our minor Jacobean and Caroline poets were well acquainted with Paul, and do not hesitate to insert his choicest things, almost word for word, in their own compositions. *The Lovers*, for example, is constantly imitated :

> ' I saw the lovers. Held in passion's chain
> They kissed and clipped, then clipped and kissed again,
> If thus they might their endless thirst abate
> And dull the torment of their parted state.
> Fain were they in each other's heart to hide
> And so at last a change of raiment tried.
>
> He, as Achilles once on Scyros shore,
> A maiden's smock upon his body wore ;
> She, like Diana kilted to the knee,
> Strode boldly forth in manly tunic free.
> But soon their lips, once more together pressed,
> Unquenched the craving of their love confessed.
>
> E'en as two stems unite to make one vine
> And tendrils none can part together twine,
> So close their bodies did they interlace
> With limbs entangled in a soft embrace.
> Thrice happy they on whom such fetters lie,
> Who never know our parting's agony.' [1]

---

[1] *A. P.* v. 257.

It must be granted that love poems in all ages and in all countries tend to run in one groove and to enlarge on the same theme. The chief difference is in the amount of frankness in details allowed by convention ; and Paul is very frank. He is not so tenderly passionate as Asclepiades or Catullus, he is not so dexterous as Philodemus or Ovid ; but there is a warmth and richness, both of language and of sentiment, in his love poems that give such pieces as *Beauty Unadorned* a special charm : [1]

> ' The rose no garland needs, nor you, my queen,
> Proud silken robes and veils of jewelled sheen.
> Pearls cannot match your bosom lying bare
> Nor gold the glory of your tangled hair.
> The burning sapphires of the Indian mine
> Before you pale ; your eyes more brilliant shine.
> Your close-joined breasts Love's magic girdle make
> And bees their honey from your wet lips take.
> Nay, I would never dare before your throne to come
> Save that in those bright eyes soft Hope still makes his home.'

If Paul is to be compared with any of his predecessors, it should be with Meleager. In the poem where he laments the absence of his faithless mistress we have the very accent of the Syrian singer, and the *Prayer to Venus* is a perfect example of the influence of a dead poet not overshadowing, but rather strengthening, the genius of his successor. But Paul is usually himself and himself alone, and many of his poems are plainly the records of personal experience. Here is one typical example : [2]

> ' Out upon it, lack-a-day,
> Foolishly I swore,
> Vowed that I would keep away
> For a week or more—
> Now each day it seems a year,
> I must break my oath, I fear,
> And to-morrow see my dear,
> If I don't before.

---

[1] *A. P.* v. 272. [2] *A. P.* v. 256.

Prithee, Venus, blot my word
  On the mindful scroll ;
Say my vow you never heard,
  Wipe it from the roll.
Sure it would too cruel be,
Angry gods as well as she,
If they both should take from me
  Punishment for toll.'

This is in Paul's usual vein, and he gives us some realistic details as to his personal appearance ; for, although he was an elderly lover, he does not take himself too seriously. He was prematurely grey, but was careful with manicure and hair-dressing to enhance his attractions. On one unfortunate occasion, when he had taken such pains to curl his hair that it would have lasted for three days, an unappreciative mistress poured over him a jug of cold water and ruined his toilet. At another time, he laments his efforts at adornment—sea-green tunic, well-brushed hair, manicured nails—wasted by his lady's sudden and unexpected departure. In the same spirit he compares love to the effects of a mad dog's bite ; and taking his love poems generally an unkind critic might say that they are always either wanton or frivolous. This is scarcely true, but certainly Paul offers an interesting problem in psychology—a character as curious as that of Theodora herself. Lord High Chamberlain, a married man, and a Christian, he shows in his poems few of the qualities that we now generally associate with those three states of life. He does not perhaps, except in the Menecratis epigram, offend very grievously against our standards of propriety, but he is quite lacking in official gravity, in marital constancy, and in Christian chastity. The obligation of his religion and of his marriage vows can scarcely be said to have any weight with him, and the only reference he makes to either is one casual line at the end of a love poem addressed to a passing mistress. He died in A.D. 575, ten years after Justinian, just before the fifty years of plague began which ravaged the western world ; and as he was happy apparently in his life, so he certainly was happy in the hour of his departure.

Aristænetus (fl. A.D. 560)

The amatory adventures of which Paul tells us in his verse are also the staple subject of the *Love Letters* of Aristænetus. Love stories, such as those which Heliodorus and Achilles wrote in the third century A.D. were, as we know, immensely popular with the Byzantine public, and it was at Constantinople in the eleventh century that the novel once more revived ; but in Justinian's time the novelette seems for the moment to have been more in vogue than the romance. Aristænetus uses the epistolary form, but the super-scription is the only point of resemblance with a real letter, and his book is actually a collection of fifty short stories, some humorous and some coarse, taken mostly from the new comedy or from those books of anecdotes, which, as we have seen, were so widely read throughout the Hellenistic world.

Aristænetus follows Lucian and Alciphron as closely as he can, but he is far inferior to both of his masters, and perhaps his best letter is that in which he makes the one address the other : [1]

' *Alciphron to Lucian*

'As a public festival was being held just outside the town, and everyone was busy eating, Charidemus too invited his friends to a banquet. A certain woman was there—I need not mention her name—whom Charidemus himself—you know how amorous our young friend is—had seen walking before him in the market-place and had looked at once and persuaded to come to his dinner. His

---

[1] Aristænetus I. v.

guests were all assembled when our pretty fellow of an host came in with an old gentleman on his arm, whom he had invited to meet us. As soon as the lady saw grandpa approaching she slipped away like lightning, and in a flash was off next-door.

'When she was safe there she sent for Charidemus and said : "You do not know what a lot of mischief you have done. That old friend of yours is my husband, and he plainly recognized my shawl which I slipped off in your house. He is probably brimming over with suspicions already, but still, if you will give me the shawl and some of the sweets on the quiet, I will deceive him completely and divert the course of his nasty jealousy." She got what she asked for and hurried back home, and by all the luck in the world arrived before her lord and master, so that she had time to arrange with her neighbour how to gull the old fellow.

'It was not long before he came rushing in, panting with fury and bawling in rage,—"You wanton," he shouted, "you shall not insult my bed with impunity"—and then on the evidence of the shawl he had seen he began to accuse her of adultery, and in his mad passion to look about for a knife.

'Just at that moment—it was not too soon—the neighbour popped in her head, and—"Thank you very much, my dear, for your shawl," says she, "I am very much obliged to you. I have gratified my wish to go to that dinner, and it was not much to boast about after all. Here is your share of the sweets they served us." All this of course sobered the old fellow's temper ; his anger disappeared, and he so repented of his fury that he became now as mild as he had been savage. He actually apologized to his wife. "Pardon me, my dear. I confess that I was out of my senses. This is a reward for your virtue : some kind angel mercifully sent our friend here to preserve us, and by her intervention she has saved us both." '

Musæus (fl. A.D. 550)

We have now come to our last name. When and where Musæus lived are questions which cannot be answered with certainty, but we have some reason to think that he should be placed about the middle of the sixth century and that he lived in Constantinople. At any rate Agathias knew him and alludes to his poem twice, once in the *History*[1] and once in an epigram,[2]

---

[1] *History*, v. 2.   [2] *A. P.* v. 263.

and the description which he gives of the Straits suggests, at least, that he was well acquainted with the district. But whoever he was and wherever he lived, Musæus was a great poet, and taking a subject which had already been touched upon by several Romans he gave it the form in which it has won immortality.

The first mention of the legend of Hero and Leander comes in Virgil : [1]

> ' Quid iuvenis, magnum cui versat in ossibus ignem
> durus amor ?   Nempe abruptis turbata procellis
> nocte natat cæca serus freta ;   quem super ingens
> porta tonat cæli, et scopulis illisa reclamant
> æquora ;   nec miseri possunt revocare parentes
> nec moritura super crudeli funere virgo.'

' What of the youth, within whose frame stern Love plies his fierce fire ?   Over seas roughened by bursting storms he swims late in the blinding darkness ;   above his head heaven's huge gate thunders, and the waves that dash upon the rocks call out upon him. But neither can his hapless parents bring him back nor the maiden doomed to a cruel death upon his corpse.' Then Ovid made Hero one of the ladies to whom he ascribes his imaginary epistles ;   and finally Statius in the *Thebaid* repeats the chief incidents of the story as forming part of the design woven upon the purple cloak which Adrastus gave to Admetus.

The tale was familiar, but Musæus by his treatment made it his own, and his poem, an epic idyll in three hundred and forty hexameters, deserves a full description. The poet first invokes his Muse in fifteen lines and then begins his story. Hero and Leander, ' the fairest stars of their two cities, lived, the one in a tower at Sestos, the other at Abydos, across the Straits. One day, the feast of Adonis, Hero came into the

---

[1] *Georgics*, 3, 258.

town to pay homage to the Cyprian, whose maiden votary she was, and there Leander saw her for the first time—'And upon him came bewilderment, boldness, trembling, shame : but manfully by love's guidance he took boldness to himself, and gently stepped forward and stood face to face with the maiden.'

Upon the next scene, the lovers' interview in the temple where evening twilight is falling, Musæus spends all the resources of his art. Leander pleads and Hero reluctantly listens—'Softly he pressed the maiden's rose-like fingers, and from the depths he heaved a great sigh ; but she in silence, as though angered, drew her rosy hand away.' Then little by little his beauty and his fervent words win her over, and at last—'She too now received within her the bitter-sweet goad of love, and the heart of maiden Hero was warmed with delicious fire, fluttered like a bird by the beauty of Leander the desired.' She tells him her name and where she lives, in a tower 'beset with noises of the sea, and high as heaven, with ocean as my only neighbour ; and ever by night and day the roaring of the wind-swept waves assails my ears.' At that Leander has a sudden inspiration ; he vows that on the next night he will swim across the Straits, if Hero will light a lamp in her tower to guide him on his way ; and so the pair separate.

After this the story moves more quickly. We see Leander the next day at Abydos as night begins to fall waiting anxiously for the glimmer of the beacon. At length the lamp shines out, and after praying to Love for help, 'he drew his mantle with both hands from his lovely limbs, and bound it about his head, and leaped from the beach, and cast his body into the sea.' His arrival at Sestos is embroidered by Marlowe in his own manner :

' By this Leander being nere the land,
Cast down his wearie feet, and felt the sand.
Breathlesse albeit he were, he rested not,
Till to the solitarie tower he got,
And knoct and cald, at which celestiall noise
The longing heart of Hero much more ioies
Then nymphs and sheapheards, when the timbrell rings,
Or crooked Dolphin when the sailor sings ;
She stayd not for her robes, but straight arose,
And drunke with gladnesse, to the dore she goes,
Where seeing a naked man, she scriecht for feare,
Such sights as this to tender maids are rare,
And ran into the darke herselfe to hide,
Rich jewels in the darke are soonest spide.
Unto her was he led, or rather drawne,
By those white limmes, which sparckled through the lawne.
The neerer that he came, the more she fled,
And seeking refuge slipt into her bed.'

Musæus is less romantic and more direct than this. In the Greek Hero is waiting for her lover on the beach, and after washing off the brine and anointing him with perfumed oil she leads him to their nuptial couch, where, without marriage songs or bridal feast, their union is consummated.

So that night passed and many a summer night afterwards. Even when winter had come Hero would still light her lamp and Leander would still swim across to the haven of her arms. At last the hour of fate arrived ; the waves grew fiercer as the storm rose high ; the lamp was blown out by the wind ; and Leander struggling in vain against the tempest perished in the waves—' the cruel blast quenched the faithless lamp, and with it poor Leander's life and love.' The next morning Hero saw his dead body on the shore as she looked out from her turret window, and flung herself face downward from the height. She fell upon the corpse, and as Musæus says—' even in death they had enjoyment one of the other' : or as Chapman puts it :

407

'She fell on her love's bosome, hugg'd it fast.
And with Leander's name she breathed her last.'

The *Hero and Leander* has been the delight of poets in all ages. At the Renaissance its author was confused with the mythological bard of the same name who was supposed to have been contemporary with Orpheus, and when Aldus Manutius started his printing-press at Venice, it was one of the first Greek books which he issued ; for, as he says, he wished ' Musæus, the most ancient of poets, to form a prelude to Aristotle and the other sages who will shortly be imprinted at my hands.'

In Elizabethan England it was well known, and Christopher Marlowe and George Chapman, the prince of English translators, showed their appreciation by enlarging it in a paraphrase to about five times its original length, producing in the process one of the most charming things in our language. Its popularity in the eighteenth century is proved by the fact that between 1715 and 1760 Theobald, Catcott, Sterling, Luck, Bally, Eusden, and Fawkes all published translations, and that the last of these seven was reprinted over and over again. But no English version, however good, can quite reproduce the grace and the pensive beauty of the Greek. The *Hero and Leander* is the swan song of Greek poetry, and as Homer is its morning sun rising from the sea in golden light and filling all the world with gladness, so Musæus is the last pink glow of sunset, which lingers faintly in the western sky until night's darkness falls.

SELECT BIBLIOGRAPHY

Note.—Where authors are included in the Loeb Library (L.L.) no further reference is given, for full bibliographies are usually furnished in that excellent series.

GENERAL HISTORIES

Histoire de la Littérature Grecque. Vol. 5. A. and M. Croisset. Paris, 1901.
Geschichte der griechischen Litteratur. Vol. 2. Christ and Schmid. Munich, 1920.

PART I

Geschichte der griechischen Litteratur in der Alexandrinerzeit. 2 Vols. F. Susemihl. Leipzig, 1891.
Cambridge Ancient History. Vol. 7. Cambridge, 1928.

Droysen, J. G. *Geschichte des Hellenismus.* Gotha, 1876.
Ferguson, W. S. *Hellenistic Athens.* London, 1911.
Holm, A. *Greek History.* Vol 4 (Eng. trans.) London, 1906.
Tarn, W. W. *Hellenistic Civilization.* London, 1927.
Sandys, J. E. *History of Classical Scholarship.* Vol. 1. Cambridge, 1906.
Couat, A. *La poésie Alexandrine.* Paris, 1882.
Hicks, R. D. *Stoics and Epicureans.* London, 1910.
Zeller, E. *Stoics, Epicureans, and Sceptics.* (Eng. trans.) London, 1880.
Wright, F. A. *Poets of Greek Anthology.* London, 1926.
Swete, H. B. *Introduction to the Old Testament in Greek.* Cambridge, 1900.
Wilamowitz-Moellendorff, U. von. *Hellenische Dichtung in der Zeit des Kallimachos.* Berlin, 1924.
Kock, T. *Comicorum Atticorum Fragmenta.* 3 Vols. Leipzig, 1880.
Muller, C. *Fragmenta historicorum græcorum.* 5 Vols. Paris, 1841–70.
Powell, J. U. *Collectanea Alexandrina.* Oxford, 1925.
Powell, J. U., and Barber, E. A. *New Chapters in Greek Literature.* 1st and 2nd series. Oxford, 1921–29.
Bury, J. B. *The Ancient Greek Historians.* London, 1909.

SELECT BIBLIOGRAPHY

Bury, J. B. (Editor). *The Hellenistic Age.* Cambridge, 1923.
Grenfell, B. P., and Hunt, A. *Oxyrhynchus Papyri.* 1–17. London, 1898–1927.
Edgar, C. C. *Zenon Papyri.* 1, 2. Cairo, 1925.
Jacoby, F. *Fragmente der griechischen Historiker.* Berlin, 1923.
Mahaffy, J. P. *Greek Life and Thought.* London, 1896.
Heath, T. L. *History of Greek Mathematics.* Oxford, 1921.
Theophrastus. *Characters.* J. M. Edmonds. L.L.
Theophrastus. *Plants.* A. Hort. L.L.
Menander. F. G. Allinson. L.L.
The New Comedy. Legrand. (Eng. trans. J. Loeb.) London, 1917.
Aristoxenus. (Ed.) H. S. Macran. Oxford, 1902.
Euclid. T. L. Heath. Cambridge, 1926.
Aristarchus of Samos. T. L. Heath. Oxford, 1913.
Heron. (Ed.) Schmidt, Schœne and Heiberg. Leipzig, 1919.
Lycophron. A. W. Mair. L.L.
Aratus of Soli. G. W. Mair. L.L.
Archimedes. T. L. Heath. Cambridge, 1927.
Callimachus. A. W. Mair. L.L.
Apollonius Rhodius. R. C. Seaton. L.L.
Theocritus. J. M. Edmonds. L.L.
Herodes. A. D. Knox. L.L.
Cercidas. A. D. Knox. L.L.
Polybius. W. R. Paton. L.L.
Moschus and Bion. J. M. Edmonds L.L.
Parthenius. S. Gaselee. L.L.

PART II

Decline and Fall of the Roman Empire. Vol. 1. Gibbon. London, 1912.
Histoire de la Littérature Grecque Chrétienne. Vols. 1 and 2. A. Puech. Paris, 1928.
The Silver Age of the Greek World. J. P. Mahaffy. London, 1902.
The Mission of Greece. R. W. Livingstone. Oxford, 1928.
Diodorus Siculus. (Ed.) C. Müller. Paris, 1842.
Nicolaus of Damascus. (Ed.) G. Dindorf. Leipzig, 1860.
Strabo. H. L. Jones. L.L.
Dionysius of Halicarnassus. *De Compositione verborum.* (Ed.) W. Rhys Roberts. London, 1900.
—— *The Literary Letters.* (Ed.) W. Rhys Roberts. Cambridge, 1901.

SELECT BIBLIOGRAPHY

On the Sublime. W. H. Fyfe. L.L.
On Style. W. Rhys Roberts. L.L.
CEBES. *The Tablet.* (Ed.) C. S. Jerram. Oxford, 1878.
APOLLODORUS. Sir J. G. Frazer. L.L.
PHILO. Colson and Whitaker. L.L.
JOSEPHUS. H. St J. Thackeray. L.L.
EPICTETUS. W. A. Oldfather. L.L.
PLUTARCH. *Lives.* B. Perrin. L.L.
—— *Moralia.* F. C. Babbitt. L.L.
DION OF PRUSA. *Opera.* (Ed.) von Arnim. Berlin, 1896.
POLEMON. *Declamations.* (Ed.) H. Hinck. Leipzig, 1873.
ARISTIDES. (Ed.) B. Keil. Berlin, 1898.
MAXIMUS OF TYRE. (Ed.) F. Dübner. Paris, 1840.
POLLUX. *Onomasticon.* (Ed.) Bekker. Berlin, 1846.
LUCIAN. H. W. Fowler and F. G. Fowler. Oxford, 1910.
ALCIPHRON. F. A. Wright. London, 1926.
THE APOSTOLIC FATHERS. K. Lake. L.L.
JUSTIN. (Ed.) K. Rauschen. Bonn, 1904.
MARCUS AURELIUS. C. R. Haines. L.L.
ARRIAN. (Ed.) A. G. Roos. Leipzig, 1921.
APPIAN. H. White. L.L.
PAUSANIAS. Sir J. G. Frazer. London, 1913.
ARTEMIDORUS. (Ed.) R. Hercher. Leipzig, 1864.
GALEN. *Opera.* (Ed.) Kuhn. Leipzig, 1830.
—— *On the natural faculties.* A. J. Brock. L.L.
THE PHILOSTRATI. *Opera.* (Ed.) Olearius. Leipzig, 1709.
—— *Lives of the Sophists.* W. C. Wright. L.L.
—— *Life of Apollonius.* F. C. Conybeare. L.L.
AELIAN. (Ed.) Hercher. Leipzig, 1864.
DIOGENES LAERTIUS. R. D. Hicks. L.L.
ATHENÆUS. C. W. Gulick. L.L.
BABRIUS. (Ed.) W. G. Rutherford. London, 1883.
OPPIAN. A. W. Mair. L.L.
THE GREEK NOVELISTS. *Scriptores erotici.* Paris, 1856.
HELIODORUS. Tr. Underdowne and Wright. London, 1925.
ACHILLES TATIUS. S. Gaselee. L.L.
CASSIUS DIO. E. Cary. L.L.
HERODIAN. (Ed.) Mendelssohn. Leipzig, 1883.
CLEMENT OF ALEXANDRIA. R. G. Butterworth. L.L.
ORIGEN. Migne, *Patrologia Græca*, 11–17. Paris, 1860.
PLOTINUS. (Ed.) Creuzer. Oxford, 1835.
—— Tr. S. M'Kenna. London, 1927.

411

SELECT BIBLIOGRAPHY

PART III

Decline and Fall of the Roman Empire. Gibbon. Vols. 2–4. London, 1912.
Histoire de la Littérature Grecque Chrétienne. A. Puech. Vol. 3. Paris, 1928.
Cambridge Medieval History. Vol. 1. Cambridge, 1911.
MIGNE. *Patrologia Græca.* (*P. G.*) Paris, 1860 *sq.*
Life and Letters in the Fourth Century. T. R. Glover. Cambridge, 1901.
EUSEBIUS. K. Lake. L.L.
SOCRATES and SOZOMEN. Migne. *P. G.* 67.
—— Tr. Zenos and Hartranft. Oxford, 1891.
ATHANASIUS. Migne. *P. G.* 25–28.
—— Tr. A. Robertson. Oxford, 1892.
BASIL. Migne. *P. G.* 29–32. *Letters.* R. J. Deferrari. L.L.
GREGORY OF NYSSA. Migne. *P. G.* 46.
—— Tr. Moore and Wilson. Oxford, 1893.
GREGORY OF NAZIANZUS. Migne. *P. G.* 35–38.
—— Tr. Browne and Swallow. Oxford, 1894.
JOHN CHRYSOSTOM. Migne. *P. G.* 47–64.
SYNESIUS. Migne. *P. G.* 66.
NONNUS. *Dionysiaca.* (Ed.) Koechly. Leipzig, 1857.
HIMERIUS. (Ed.) F. Dübner. Paris, 1849.
THEMISTIUS. (Ed.) G. Dindorf. Leipzig, 1832.
LIBANIUS. (Ed.) R. Foerster. Leipzig, 1903.
JULIAN. W. C. Wright. L.L.
EUNAPIUS. W. C. Wright. L.L.
QUINTUS SMYRNÆUS. A. S. Way. L.L.
COLUTHUS and TRYPHIODORUS. A. W. Mair. L.L.
PALLADAS. *Greek Anthology.* W. R. Paton. L.L.
ZOSIMUS. (Ed.) Heyne. Bonn.
PROCLUS. (Ed.) V. Cousin. Paris, 1864.
PROCOPIUS. *History of the Wars.* H. B. Dewing. L.L.
—— *Buildings of Justinian.* Tr. A. Stewart. London, 1887.
—— *Secret History.* Tr. Athenian Society. London, 1896.
AGATHIAS. *Histories.* (Ed.) Niebuhr. Bonn, 1828.
—— *Epigrams. Greek Anthology.* W. R. Paton. L.L.
PAUL THE SILENTIARY. *St Sophia.* (Ed.) Græfe. Leipzig, 1822.
—— *Epigrams. Greek Anthology.* W. R. Paton. L.L.
ARISTÆNETUS in *Epistolographi Græci.* (Ed.) Hercher. Paris, 1873.
MUSÆUS. (Ed.) Dilthey. Bonn, 1874.
—— Tr. E. E. Sikes. London, 1920.

412

INDEX

Achilles Tatius, 304–306
Aelian, sophist, 278–281
,, tactician, 260
Aeschrion, 49
Aëthlius, 49
Africanus (Julius), 328
Agathias, 388–394
Alcaeus of Messene, 122
Alexander the Aetolian, 55
,, Polyhistor, 161
Alciphron, 243–247
Ammaeus, 185
Ammianus, 169
Anacreontica, 150
Antagoras, 66
Anthology, 160, 394
Antigonus of Carystus, 76–77
Antipater of Sidon, 148–151
Anyte, 39–40
Apion, 197
Apocrypha, 84–85
Apollodorus, grammarian, 143
,, comedian, 30
,, mythologist, 190–191
Apollonius, grammarian, 233
,, of Perga, 80
,, of Rhodes, 95–100
of Tyana, 191–192
Apollonius of Tyre, 293
Appian, 257–259
Aratus of Sicyon, 75
,, of Soli, 73–75
Arcesilasu, 128
Archias, 149
Archimedes, 80–81
Aristarchus, astronomer, 80
,, philologist, 118–119
Aristaenetus, 403–404
Aristides (Aelius), 228–231
,, (Quintilianus), 141
Aristobulus, 58
Aristophanes of Byzantium, 118
Aristoxenus, 19–21
Arrian, 207, 255–257

Artemidorus of Ephesus, 265
,, of Daldis, 265–267
Asclepiades, 52–54
Asclepiodotus, 260
Athanasius, 331–333
Athenaeus, 283–288
Atthides, 60
Atticus (Herodes), 226–227

Babrius, 288–289
Barnabas, 247
Basil, 334–337
Berosus, 60
Besantinus, 169
Beyond Thule, 293
Bion of Smyrna, 140–141
,, the Borysthenite, 67–68

Callimachus, 85–94
Callisthenes, 58
Callixenus, 119–120
Carneades, 128–129
Cassius Dio, 308–311
Cebes, 190
Celsus, 254–255
Cercidas, 114–115
Chamaeleon, 75
Chariton, 307–308
Chriae, 124–125
Chrysippus, 129–130
Chrysostom (John), 342–346
Claudian, 374
Cleanthes, 36
Cleitarchus, 123
Clement of Alexandria, 312–317
,, of Rome, 247
Coluthus, 373
Conon, 80
Crantor, 128
Crates of Mallos, 130
,, of Thebes, 37–38
Crinagoras, 166–167
The Cycle, 394
Cyril of Alexandria, 347

413

INDEX

INDEX

PRINTED IN GREAT BRITAIN
BY THE EDINBURGH PRESS